Developing Teaching Skills
in Physical Education

Developing Teaching Skills in Physical Education

FOURTH EDITION

Daryl Siedentop
Ohio State University

Deborah Tannehill
Pacific Lutheran University

Mayfield Publishing Company

Mountain View, California
London • Toronto

Library of Congress Cataloging-in-Publication Data
Siedentop, Daryl.
    Developing teaching skills in physical education / Daryl
Siedentop, Deborah Tannehill. — 4th ed.
        p.   cm.
    Includes bibliographical references (p.   ) and index.
    ISBN 0-7674-1023-8
    1. Physical education teachers—Training of—United States.
2. Physical education and training—United States—Curricula.
I. Tannehill, Deborah.   II. Title.
GV363.S5   1999
613.7'071'073—dc21   99-30614
                                                               CIP

Manufactured in the United States of America
10   9   8   7   6   5   4   3   2

Mayfield Publishing Company
1280 Villa Street
Mountain View, California 94041

Sponsoring editor, Michele Sordi; production, Publishing Support Services; manuscript editor, Sylvia Stein Wright; design manager, Glenda King; text designer, Richard Kharibian; cover designer, Laurie Anderson; illustrations, Lotus Art; manufacturing manager, Randy Hurst. The text was set in 10/12 Sabon by TBH Typecast, Inc., and printed on 50# Finch Opaque by R. R. Donnelley & Sons Company.

. . . For Bobbie

. . . and for Betty-Lee Tannehill

CONTENTS

PREFACE

What does it take to deliver an effective, meaningful physical education in the context of today's schools? This book is about answers to that question. We contend that the ability of teachers to deliver an effective, meaningful physical education to diverse students and help them sustain it requires (a) the knowledge to conceive and plan meaningful curricula, (b) the managerial and instructional skills to implement those curricula, (c) the administrative skill to produce an organizational structure within school time that optimizes the impact of the program, and (d) the creative energy to link the school program to opportunities for children and youths outside of school. Effective physical education, therefore, lies at the point where curriculum, instruction, organization, and program extension come together.

It is not easy to plan and deliver an effective physical education. If it were, there would be many exemplary programs. Fortunately, we are now in a better position to achieve an effective physical education than ever before. We have several widely replicated curriculum models that have been well received by students, school administrators, and parents. We have learned more about effective class management and effective instruction in the past 25 years than we learned in the previous 100 years. We are beginning to see signs that different school and class organizational structures can improve the achievement of important outcomes. We have many examples of how school physical education programs link to community efforts to positively impact the physical activity habits of children and youths.

We have brought all those ingredients together in this fourth edition. The text is significantly different from the third edition—and, we trust, significantly better. While the first three editions were dominated by managerial and teaching skills information, the fourth edition includes substantial information about curriculum: both how to develop curricula that meet NASPE standards and how to adopt and adapt what we refer to as "theme curricula" that have proved successful in today's schools.

In addition to the increased focus on curriculum, the fourth edition includes three new chapters on important topics related to today's physical education. First, an entire chapter is devoted to new methods of assessing outcomes in physical education. In keeping with the text's main theme of a successful, meaningful physical education, the assessment protocols are heavily oriented toward authentic assessment. Second, a new chapter treats teaching and curriculum strategies for full-inclusion classes, where teachers must provide an equitable physical education for students with disabling conditions while simultaneously meeting the needs of the other students. Third, we have included a chapter with multiple examples of how the physical education program can be extended beyond class time so that its impact is greatly increased.

Many of the key features that have made the book successful in previous editions have been retained. We have made every effort to present not only knowledge about issues but also the skills necessary to put the knowledge to work. We continue to emphasize how skills can be practiced, how they can be observed, and what kinds of feedback are necessary to improve them. We continue to base our suggestions on what research tells us, and we have relied primarily on research conducted in schools under typical conditions. We take positions, but we do not advocate a singular approach to teaching or curriculum. With respect to teaching skills, our position is that the characteristics of effective teaching can be found in many different teaching styles. With respect to curriculum, our position is that many different approaches can be successful if they are well planned and appropriately implemented but that successful curricula typically focus on meaningful outcomes and allow time to achieve those outcomes.

We believe that effective teachers are consistently reflective, although we also recognize the daily demands on teachers are such that reflection often comes in small spurts and stolen moments. We suggest throughout the text that reflection can be aided substantially by data gathered through observation—and we provide many ways to accomplish that task.

ORGANIZATION

This edition is divided into four parts. Part One (Chapters 1–3) presents the knowledge base for becoming an effective physical education teacher. It examines what we know in general about effective teaching and what physical education research tells us about effective teaching; further, it presents a model through which you can grasp the daily dynamics that shape the particular characteristics of classes.

Part Two (Chapters 4–7) focuses on class management and instruction. The concepts of preventive management and development of cooperative behavior form the foundation of successful teaching. Discipline strategies evolve from these concepts, along with specific approaches that provide teachers with options for dealing with disruptive behavior. This all moves toward the final goal of creating a community of learners within which a caring pedagogy prevails. Finally, these concepts are extended to deal with classes that include students with disabling conditions.

Part Three (Chapters 8–12) focuses on curriculum, assessment, and planning for effective instruction. The curriculum emphasis is divided between basic concepts and planning principles and presentations of main-theme curricular models that have proved successful. Meaningful assessment for significant learning outcomes is tied directly to the chapters on curriculum through examples that emphasize the model curricula. Finally, two "design" chapters focus on building task progressions and planning units and lessons.

Part Four (Chapters 13–16) focuses on skills and strategies for delivering an effective physical education. This section starts with general instructional skills and strategies and then moves to specific instructional formats that are popular within physical education, ranging from whole-group formats to small-group formats to models based on tutorial instruction. A new chapter focuses on extending the impact of the physical education program, with many examples of within-school and outside-of-school extensions. The final chapter includes multiple formats for assessing the effectiveness of the instructional program.

ACKNOWLEDGMENTS

Systematic, field-based research in schools is not done in isolation—it requires a team effort. We have been fortunate to work with an extraordinary team of faculty, graduate students, and practitioner colleagues. Mary O'Sullivan, Sandy Stroot, and Sam Hodge form our most immediate faculty support group. We have had the privilege of working closely with a number of talented doctoral students, the most recent of which have been Mensah Kutame, Jan-Erik Romar, Phil Ward, Judy Oslin, Connie Collier, Nancy Knop, Clive Pope, and Becky Berkowitz. Our practitioner partners have been constant sources of information and inspiration: most notably Chris Bell, Carol Jones, Gary Moore, Kelly Marshall, Pat Price, Bob Price, Kelly Robbins, and Danielle Dayton. Deborah would especially like to thank Zak for her professional and personal support. Daryl would like to acknowledge, again, the significant role that Bobbie has played in helping him to understand the extraordinary perseverance of reflective practitioners that enables them to continue to be effective. Our many preservice teachers have provided invaluable critique of and reactions to our curriculum and instruction ideas.

We also thank the following individuals for their thoughtful reviews: Lynne Fitzgerald, Morehead State University; John Helion, Westchester University; Kevin Hussey, East Tennessee State University; Steve Klesius, University of South Florida; Thomas L. McKenzie, San Diego State University; and Jerry Polacek, Illinois State University, Normal.

PART ONE

The Knowledge Base for Becoming an Effective Teacher

Teachers are effective when students achieve important learning outcomes in a way that enhances their development as productive human beings and citizens. Nothing is more important to the improvement of schools than an effective, high-quality teaching force. Teachers and teacher organizations have worked hard to make teaching a full-fledged profession. To be a professional, however, requires that your chosen vocation have a distinct body of knowledge related to performing effectively. Part One of this book is designed to provide you with the most important knowledge for becoming an effective physical education teacher.

When you master the content of these chapters, you will be able to discuss the concept of teaching effectiveness, cite and utilize the results of research in those discussions, and understand the teaching skills and strategies you must learn and perfect in order to become a highly effective, professional physical educator.

CHAPTER 1

The Active Teacher—
The Learning Student

We propose an audacious goal. . . . By the year 2006, America will provide every student with what should be his or her educational birthright: access to competent, caring and qualified teaching.

—NATIONAL COMMISSION ON TEACHING
AND AMERICA'S FUTURE (1996)

OVERALL CHAPTER OUTCOME

To explain to a lay audience, using the concepts and terms introduced in this chapter, the main features of effective teaching and how it promotes student learning

CHAPTER OBJECTIVES

- To value the role of motivation and practice in learning to teach effectively
- To describe the purpose and procedures of the NBPTS
- To enunciate the characteristics of the learning student
- To outline the NASPE attributes of a physically educated person
- To describe the characteristics of the active teacher
- To explain how novices can become effective teachers
- To clarify why learning in physical education is important
- To describe how teaching and learning can be assessed
- To explain the nature of expertise as it relates to teaching

Of all the factors that influence how children learn and grow in schools, the quality of their teachers is most important. What teachers know and can do affects all the experiences their students have in schools. The National Commission on Teaching and America's Future (NCTAF) has presented convincing evidence to support these assertions—and, in so doing, has underscored the importance of ensuring that *all* children and youths have the opportunity to learn from competent, caring, and qualified teachers. The other side of these assertions suggests that weak teaching is a pervasive problem in America's schools. This would include teachers without proper certification and licensure, those who are teaching in areas where they had inadequate subject-matter preparation (for example, lacking even a minor in the subject they are teaching), and those who have both the certification and the subject-matter preparation but are not working hard and effectively for the betterment of their students. Teachers in America's schools are either "part of the cure" or "part of the problem." We must make sure that all newly certified teachers are very much a part of the cure—that is what this book is about.

2

PHYSICAL EDUCATION TEACHERS AS ENGAGED PROFESSIONALS

Our three goals in writing this book are (a) to help you better understand how to be an effective teacher in physical activity settings, (b) to help you improve your teaching skills, and (c) to motivate you to want to become an effective, engaged, professional physical educator. Of these three goals, the desire to become an effective teacher and to stay engaged with continuing professional development is the foundation upon which your future success is built. It isn't *bad* teaching that plagues physical education so much as it is *non*teaching (Locke, 1975). You may have seen or even participated in physical education classes that could best be described as "supervised recreation." The teacher may have had the skills to be effective, but wasn't motivated to use them. You have observed teaching from a student's view most of your life. Sometimes teaching looks simple, but that is an illusion. Effective teaching is very complex. To teach several classes well each day, five days a week, for the length of a school year is difficult and requires both skills and the motivation to persevere in using and improving them.

Learning to teach effectively is like learning to be good at a sport. If you want to get better, you have to know a lot about the skills and strategies of the sport, practice frequently under good conditions, and get help in the form of instruction, supervision, and feedback from those who know more than you do. Once you gain skills in doing a sport, you must have sufficient motivation to continually maintain and improve those skills, especially when the techniques and strategies of the sport evolve. So it is with becoming an effective, engaged teacher, that is, a *professional physical educator.*

Effective physical educators *intend* the students in their classes to learn and to enjoy doing the activities they are learning. To accomplish this, effective teachers manage students well to decrease disruptions and increase time for learning. Effective physical educators then organize learning time with activities matched to student abilities so that an optimal amount of learning takes place. The assumption here is clear: Effectiveness in teaching physical education should be judged by the quality and quantity of student learning. This starts with the *intention* to have students be different in a positive way as a result of being in your class.

This book is written with the assumption that you want to be that kind of teacher—competent, qualified, and caring. If you have the motivation to become an effective teacher and persevere in that quest during your first several years of teaching, you can achieve a level of effectiveness that will mark you as a competent, professional physical educator. Effective teachers orchestrate a repertoire of teaching skills to meet the ever-changing demands of the learning situation. Few things are more enjoyable than watching a motivated, skilled physical educator working with a group of students who are obviously learning and obviously enjoying the learning. You can be that kind of teacher.

THE NATIONAL BOARD
FOR PROFESSIONAL TEACHING STANDARDS

In the United States, initial teacher certification is done at the state level. Thus, you will earn or have already earned a certificate or license to teach in that state and in others that offer reciprocity. That certificate is your beginning license to teach, but for America's schools to fulfill their promise, teachers need to go beyond their beginning preparation. One important initiative that speaks directly to the NCTAF goal of ensuring by 2006 that all students have access to competent, qualified, and caring teachers is the National Board for Professional Teaching Standards (NBPTS). In 1987, the NBPTS was created as a nonprofit organization to establish rigorous standards for what effective teachers should know and be able to do. The NBPTS operates a national voluntary system to assess and certify experienced teachers who meet the rigorous standards, thus achieving the highest honor the teaching profession can bestow. In Ohio, teachers who achieve NBPTS certification are rewarded by having $2,500 added to their base salary. Teachers who are NBPTS certified are often called upon to mentor new teachers in their districts, to advise experienced teachers seeking NBPTS certification, and to use their high standing in the physical education profession to inform and influence education policy related to teaching and physical education. Box 1.1 shows the five areas in which teachers are assessed for NBPTS certification.

Look closely at those five propositions. Although nobody expects newly certified teachers to be able to meet these standards, they do present the "yardstick" by which teachers can measure themselves and continue their professional development. How ready are you to teach the range of activities typically found in a physical education curriculum? Would you be able to take students beyond the basic skills of a sport? How confident are you that you can teach lower-skilled or noninterested students as well as the eager, skilled students? Do you have the skills and teaching tactics to ensure that girls and boys in your classes are treated equitably and treat each other well? What skills do you have to manage large groups of diverse learners, some of whom may be uncooperative? If you watched a videotape of your own teaching, do you know enough to be able to learn from the viewing and improve? If you are reading this text as part of a university class, do you view your teacher and classmates as a community of learners devoted to teaching and committed to helping students? Are you a "student of teaching"? How do you think a physical education teacher who essentially "throws out the ball" would fare in relation to those propositions? Our nation needs more skilled, committed teachers. You can choose to become one of those, or you can succumb to the stereotype of the ineffective physical educator that is held by so many—become part of the "problem" or part of the "cure."

The assessment format for certification consists of two parts. Teachers first develop a portfolio that includes examples of student work products, videotapes and other evidences of teaching, commentaries on the goals of instruction and the effectiveness of efforts to achieve those goals, and reflections on

BOX 1.1   NBPTS Core Propositions Related to Certification

1. *Teachers are committed to students and their learning.* Board-certified teachers are dedicated to making knowledge accessible to all students. They act on the belief that all students can learn. They treat students equitably, recognizing individual differences and taking account of those differences in their practice.
2. *Teachers know the subjects they teach and how to teach them to students.* Board-certified teachers have a rich understanding of the subject they teach and appreciate how knowledge in their subject is created, organized, and linked to other disciplines and applied to real-world settings. Accomplished teachers have specialized knowledge of how to convey and reveal subject matter to students.
3. *Teachers are responsible for managing and monitoring student learning.* Board-certified teachers create, enrich, maintain, and alter instructional settings to capture and sustain the interest of their students and to make the most effective use of time. Accomplished teachers command a range of instructional techniques, know when each is appropriate, and can implement them as needed.
4. *Teachers think systematically about their practice and learn from experience.* Board-certified teachers are models of educated persons, exemplifying the virtues they seek to inspire in students—curiosity, tolerance, honesty, fairness, respect for diversity, and appreciation of cultural differences. Accomplished teachers use their knowledge of human development, subject matter, and instruction and their understanding of students to make principled judgments about sound practice.
5. *Teachers are members of learning communities.* Board-certified teachers contribute to the effectiveness of the school by working collaboratively with other professionals on instructional policy, curriculum development, and staff development. Accomplished teachers find ways to work collaboratively with parents and community professionals to engage them productively in the work of the school.

Source: National Board for Professional Teaching Standards, 1989. Reprinted with permission.

the process. Teachers then complete a series of exercises developed at the NBPTS assessment center. These exercises and the portfolios are scored by practicing teachers from all over the United States who have been specifically trained to follow a uniform NBPTS procedure. Only practicing teachers can act as assessors.

The Physical Education Standards Committee of the National Association for Sport and Physical Education (NASPE) is now working on standards and assessment protocols for physical education teachers to be able to achieve NBPTS certification. When this project is completed, physical education teachers will be able to work toward national recognition as an NBPTS-certified teacher, a mark of excellence.

Teaching becomes more enjoyable when students are enthusiastically engaged in learning. We start this chapter with a focus on the learning student, and then we will turn to our explanation of the active teacher. We do that because we want to emphasize that it is *what students do* that is at the heart of understanding effective teaching. The quickest and surest way to assess the degree to which a physical education teacher is effective is by watching closely what students do in class. You cannot assess teacher effectiveness by focusing on what the teacher is doing. Indeed, a casual observer can get fooled by focusing solely on the actions of a teacher and ignoring the more important focus on the actions of students. In physical education, the learning student has these characteristics:

- is cooperative
- is eager to learn and enthusiastic about the opportunity to learn more
- is responsible for his or her own behavior
- enjoys learning and practices purposefully to improve
- is helpful to peers who are similarly engaged in learning

Students who exhibit these characteristics are a joy to work with, and they also continually "stretch" a teacher because they want to know and do more. But how do girls and boys become "learning students"? Students can acquire these characteristics over time through the influence of effective teachers. Assuredly, home backgrounds and community expectations play a role here. The bulk of the evidence, however, suggests that the influence of teachers, over time, is crucial in helping boys and girls become "learners" in the sense we have used the term here.

Students learn most of what they know and can do through repeated practice—through "plenty of perfect practice," as Box 1.2 suggests. Repeated practice is necessary for achieving the mastery students need to use skills, tactics, and knowledge in applied settings. This is true for learning fractions in mathematics, and it is true for learning the forearm pass in volleyball, mastering weak-side help defense in basketball, or making decisions about what exercise equipment is truly helpful. Repeated, successful, relevant practice leads to accuracy and speed, the two necessary components of skilled performance and decision making. To be useful in applied settings, such as games, skills and tactical knowledge need to reach the level of "automaticity" (Bloom, 1986), where they can be used quickly and accurately in response to the changing demands of the setting. If we want students to build lifelong habits of participation, this is the level of performance that physical education needs to achieve for it to be successful as a school subject.

The learning student is increasingly able to take responsibility for his or her own learning. The goal is to help students become *independent* learners. "One of the prominent, recurring themes in the history of school reform is that 'effective' schooling enables every student to become an *active* learner; one

---

BOX 1.2 Plenty of Perfect Practice

A physical education teacher education program in Adelaide, South Australia, once used the phrase "plenty of perfect practice" as its main guideline for effective teaching. Plenty of perfect practice is realized when student learning experiences can be described as follows:

Pertinent: Lessons are appropriate for the abilities, interests, and experiences of students.

Purposeful: Learners are kept on task in a climate that is both safe and challenging.

Progressive: Skills and strategies are organized in ways that lead to sequential, significant learning.

Paced: Activities are difficult enough to be challenging yet allow successful practice, and the sequence of activities is smooth and has brisk momentum.

Participatory: Students are constantly active and learning is equitable for all students.

The notion of plenty of perfect practice is thoroughly consistent with both teacher effectiveness research and learning theory. It provides a simple, convenient reminder of what is important in planning for and implementing effective learning in physical education.

---

who assumes responsibility for acquiring knowledge and skills and sustains a pattern of self-directed, lifelong learning," (Wang & Palinscar, 1989, p. 71). We don't know as much as we need to about how to produce such learners. There are many suggestions for self-directed learning, but little research to validate the suggestions. Perhaps the most successful is student cooperative practice (Slavin, 1980), where students are taught to help each other during independent work and sometimes are even judged on a common product. Cooperative practice seems to develop the kinds of skills and predispositions that are common among self-directed learners. What is most obvious is that boys and girls cannot become independent learners unless they are gradually required to work cooperatively and make decisions, are given good feedback on their efforts, and are held accountable. Here, too, plenty of perfect practice is the key.

The learning student in physical education learns the knowledge, skills, and strategies that will enable him or her to achieve a physically active, healthy lifestyle. Box 1.3 describes in detail what NASPE suggests are the attributes of a physically educated person. These attributes are stated as *outcomes,* which means they represent what students should know and be able to do as a result of their experiences in physical education. As you review the suggested NASPE outcomes, you will understand just how difficult effective teaching in physical education is and that to contribute to some important degree to the achievement of those outcomes, your students must take on the characteristics of the learning student. What does it mean for a student to be

BOX 1.3   NASPE Outcomes for the Physically Educated Person

The physically educated person

Has **learned the skills necessary to perform a variety of physical activities**

1. Moves using concepts of body awareness, space awareness, effort, and relationships
2. Demonstrates competence in a variety of manipulative, locomotor, and nonlocomotor skills
3. Demonstrates competence in combinations of manipulative, locomotor, and nonlocomotor skills performed individually and with others
4. Demonstrates competence in many different forms of physical activity
5. Demonstrates proficiency in at least a few forms of physical activity
6. Has learned how to learn new skills

Is **physically fit**

7. Assesses, achieves, and maintains physical fitness
8. Designs safe personal fitness programs in accordance with principles of training and conditioning

Does **participate regularly in physical activity**

9. Participates in health-enhancing physical activity at least three times a week
10. Selects and regularly participates in lifetime physical activities

Knows **the implications of and the benefits from involvement in physical activities**

11. Identifies the benefits, costs, and obligations associated with regular participation in physical activity
12. Recognizes the risk and safety factors associated with regular participation in physical activity
13. Applies concepts and principles to the development of motor skills
14. Understands that wellness involves more than being physically fit
15. Knows the rules, strategies, and appropriate behaviors for selected physical activities
16. Recognizes that participation in physical activity can lead to multicultural and international understanding
17. Understands that physical activity provides the opportunity for enjoyment, self-expression, and communication

Values **physical activity and its contributions to a healthy lifestyle**

18. Appreciates the relationships with others that result from participation in physical activity
19. Respects the role that regular physical activity plays in the pursuit of lifelong health and well-being
20. Cherishes the feelings that result from regular participation in physical activity

Source: Reprinted from *Moving into the Future: National Standards for Physical Education* (1995) with permission from the National Association for Sport and Physical Education (NASPE), 1900 Association Drive, Reston, VA 20191-1599.

"competent" in many different forms of activity, such as volleyball, tennis, aerobic dance, and field hockey? Moving beyond competence, what does it mean for students to become proficient in a few activities? How much time will that take? How much will you have to know about the activity to help a typical class of students become proficient at archery or golf? What will students need to know and be able to do to achieve the outcomes related to physical activity, fitness, and health? And what will you do as a teacher so that your students come to value physical activity and a healthy lifestyle?

Just as important, learning students, through the process of becoming physically educated, will learn important lessons about themselves. They will learn to see themselves as capable learners. They will learn to see themselves as physically competent and active. They will learn that school and educational experiences in general are helpful and supportive. They will learn that, to get better at something, it is useful to find an effective teacher. These lessons help to shape a lifetime learner.

How does a teacher develop and sustain a learning environment that moves girls and boys toward becoming "learning students"? It is in answering that question that the complexity of teaching effectiveness is revealed. It is not easy to achieve these results with students today. Yet it can be done, and the place to start is to believe that it can be done, that is, to believe that an effective teacher can achieve such a result and then expect to acquire the skills to be that kind of teacher. There is a true "pot of gold" waiting for those who have such expectations and work hard to achieve their goals, namely, the joy of working with groups of excited, cooperative, appreciative learning students.

THE ACTIVE TEACHER

The general picture that emerges from 35 years of teacher effectiveness research is that of a teacher who believes that he or she can make a difference with students, develops a management system that helps students stay on task, plans and implements an instructional program that is action oriented, motivates students and holds them accountable for performance, and does so within a class climate that is supportive and respectful (Brophy & Good, 1986). This is what we call the "active teacher." We choose this label to emphasize the difference between the effective physical educator and the stereotype of the teacher who just "throws out the ball," who doesn't seem to care much about students other than keeping them from being too disruptive.

Active teachers keep students consistently engaged and help them become better learners. Active teachers frequently use whole-group instruction and well-organized small-group instruction. When students are assigned tasks to work on themselves, the teacher supervises the work carefully. In the classes of active teachers, students are seldom passive. They respond frequently. The pace of instruction and practice is brisk, yet within the students' abilities and developmental levels. Eventually, students receive the "message" of this approach to teaching, and they learn to work independently and cooperatively with a sense of purpose. What follows are brief summaries of the major findings from teacher effectiveness research (Brophy & Good, 1986; Doyle, 1986; Evertson, 1989; Rosenshine & Stevens, 1986; Smith, 1983), which describe the important strategies used by active teachers.

1. *Belief in their own efficacy.* Active teachers believe that students can learn and that they have the skills to help them learn.

2. *Time, opportunity to learn, and content covered.* Active teachers allocate as much time as possible to content coverage and provide all students with sufficient opportunities to learn. Conversely, they seriously limit time devoted to things other than subject-matter objectives.

3. *Expectations and roles.* Active teachers communicate high, realistic expectations to their students and develop a clear, work-oriented class climate. Teacher and student roles are carefully defined, with students being given adequate instruction and practice time to learn their roles.

4. *Class management and student engagement.* Active teachers establish class routines early in the school year, and manage by using these well-established structures. Rules are clear and consistently related to equally clear consequences. Management is predominantly positive. The purpose of effective management is to create maximum time for learning the subject matter.

5. *Meaningful tasks and high success.* Active teachers design instructional tasks that are meaningful to students and lead to authentic outcomes. Tasks are challenging but also allow students to experience success.

6. *Pacing and momentum.* Active teachers create and sustain a brisk pace for class activities and prevent events from disrupting the momentum of this pace. The result is a climate of energy and purposefulness.

7. *Appropriate guidance.* Active teachers communicate content with clear, brief demonstrations and explanations, followed by sufficient guided practice, with frequent feedback and checking for understanding, to allow students to be able to benefit from independent practice.

8. *Active supervision.* When guided practice shows that students understand the tasks and have eliminated major technical errors, they are shifted to independent practice, which is actively supervised by the teacher, who monitors progress and maintains a task-oriented practice session.

9. *Accountability.* Active teachers hold students accountable for appropriate participation in practice, for task completion, and for performance outcomes.

10. *Clarity, enthusiasm, and equitable support.* Active teachers communicate clearly, are enthusiastic about their subject matter and their students' achievements, and are supportive of all students in their efforts to learn and improve.

11. *Building from student understanding.* Active teachers begin by assessing what their students understand about the activities and their meanings, then use this information in planning and implementing lessons. They frequently solicit student input, with the result that students feel they have a say in class life.

Research has shown that these characteristics of active teachers are particularly useful and relevant to teaching (a) children, (b) less-skilled students,

(c) students from educationally disadvantaged backgrounds, (d) beginners at any age level, and (e) well-structured activities in which learning tends to build sequentially. What most physical educators do in their daily work falls into one or more of those categories. Highly skilled, eager, bright students can also learn from teachers who have these characteristics, but, of course, they tend to learn no matter what methods teachers use.

ACTIVE TEACHING: A FRAMEWORK, NOT A METHOD

Active teaching is not a recipe that has to be followed exactly. Rather, it is a framework for understanding the major skills that effective teachers show in their work. There is substantial room within this framework for the individual styles of teachers to develop. Nor does active teaching mean that there is only one way to design lessons or present content. As you will see in Part Four, this framework is equally applicable to whole-group and small-group teaching and to curricular approaches as diverse as Sport Education and Adventure Education.

Active teaching is related to what in other places has been called explicit instruction, systematic teaching, direct instruction, or effective teaching (Rosenshine, 1979; Rosenshine & Stevens, 1986). The active teaching framework, however, also contains the skills and strategies that are suggested for teaching approaches for small-group instruction (Cohen, 1994a), cooperative learning (Slavin, 1983), and reciprocal teaching (Rosenshine & Meister, 1994). What all these approaches share is the development and sustaining of learning students through their various formats. The active teaching framework provides an understanding of the skills and strategies that are most likely to develop learning students. Again, the real evidence of effective teaching is seen in the activities of learning students; that is, the purpose of effective teaching is to help students learn. Effective teachers accomplish this by creating and sustaining a total learning environment for their students (Rink, 1996).

BECOMING AN EFFECTIVE TEACHER

Can you become an effective teacher? Can you develop the skills and implement the strategies that are likely to develop and sustain classes of learning students? Yes! Evidence from research on teacher improvement shows that teachers can begin to acquire these skills during their preservice preparation programs and continue to develop them during their initial years of teaching, through both specific staff development programs and reflection on their own teaching (Birdwell, 1980; Randall & Imwold, 1989; Siedentop, 1981, 1986; Stroot, 1996).

What does it take to become an effective teacher? First, you must want to do it. Then you need to get plenty of perfect practice. You need to practice the relevant teaching skills, such as developing class routines, implementing guided practice sessions, supervising independent practice sessions, and keeping class momentum moving forward briskly. When you have the opportunity to practice these skills, you will also benefit from supervision that provides sufficiently specific feedback for you to improve. Just as when a teacher says "nice job" to a student practicing, but doesn't give any technical feedback about the skill being practiced, it is not enough to have a supervisor say "good class" when you have finished teaching, but not provide any details. The supportive comment will probably make you feel good momentarily, but without specific feedback, it is unlikely to help you improve.

How to be an effective teacher is no mystery. Much is known about the skills and strategies used by effective teachers. We know that skills and strategies need to be practiced under conditions that are increasingly "real" and that specific feedback on performance is necessary for improvement. We also know that, as teaching skills improve, measures of student engagement improve (Birdwell, 1980; Randall & Imwold, 1989). We know that teacher candidates can learn to discriminate the critical elements and common errors in the sport skill performances of children and youth (Matanin, 1993; O'Sullivan, 1996; Wilkinson, 1991) and use that information to give more relevant feedback to students (Oslin, Stroot, & Siedentop, 1997). Even a seemingly "natural" quality such as enthusiasm can be practiced and improved, and when enthusiasm is improved, students recognize it (Rolider, Siedentop, & Van Houten, 1984). And the evidence is abundant that teacher candidates can learn to effectively manage and teach with a positive interaction style (Siedentop, 1981).

To become an effective teacher, you must also have sufficient knowledge in the subject matter you teach. This remains one of the most perplexing problems in teacher preparation in physical education (O'Sullivan, 1996). Most school district physical education curriculums include a wide variety of activities. In many schools, teachers might do as many as 12–18 different activity units during a school year in what is typically called a multi-activity curriculum. Most physical educators probably lack sufficient knowledge and experience in that many activities to effectively plan and teach even short units. This is particularly true if the activity includes tactical knowledge in addition to skill development. Learning to play volleyball, for example, requires knowledge and practice in tactics as well as the skills of serving, passing, setting, blocking, and spiking. To play the game in a way that leads to enjoyment, students must learn to execute offensive and defensive tactics as well as the skills. The tactics and skills, along with the rules and conventions of the activity, form a significant portion of what is called "content knowledge" for teaching physical education. To be effective, teachers must have a depth of content knowledge in the activities they teach.

The NASPE goals for a physically educated person cannot be easily achieved through a multi-activity curriculum. To become competent in an activity requires time and a more in-depth approach to the curriculum. Certainly, to become proficient, in the sense conveyed by the use of that term in the NASPE outcomes, requires much more time than is available through a multi-activity format. We explain this point of view and our alternative to the multi-activity model in Part Three.

THE IMPORTANCE OF LEARNING IN PHYSICAL EDUCATION

With all this talk about learning students and active teachers, you might be thinking: "What's the big deal here? Isn't it enough for kids to have some fun in PE and blow off a little steam?" Let's begin to answer that question by posing two more questions: Why should taxpayers continue to pay for having physical education in the school curriculum? Why should those expensive facilities and teachers' salaries be supported? There are many good ways to answer this "support" question because, when physical education is well planned and effectively taught, students benefit in many ways.

From a state or national perspective, however, there is one overarching contribution that physical education can make to the national welfare—the development of citizens who voluntarily seek to sustain healthy, physically active lifestyles. Persons who are physically active and lead reasonably healthy lives not only gain many *personal* benefits, but also contribute to important national goals. The promotion of physically active, healthy lifestyles has become a major public-health issue because of the enormous costs associated with health care and health insurance. In recent years, three important public policy documents have appeared that, taken together, have moved the importance of physical activity directly onto the center stage of national concerns:

- The 1991 publication of the U.S. Public Health Service's *Healthy People 2000*. This document deals with broad issues of developing and sustaining a healthy citizenry and proposes a set of national objectives to be achieved by the year 2000. Several of these objectives deal with physical education and its relationship to educating a physically active citizenry.

- The 1996 publication of the U.S. Department of Health and Human Service's *Physical Activity and Health: A Report of the Surgeon General*. Known widely now as the surgeon general's report, this document makes it clear that physical inactivity is a major risk factor in a number of serious national health problems and that physically active lifestyles are important to prevent and remediate them.

- The 1997 publication of the U.S. Public Health Service Center for Disease Control and Prevention's *Guidelines for School and Community Programs to Promote Lifelong Physical Activity Among Adolescents*. This document, more than any other, lays out a series of policy suggestions that establish the joint responsibility among physical educators and health educators and among schools, communities, and parents for developing physically active lifestyles among children and youth.

All this attention to physically active lifestyles has begun to put the spotlight on school physical education programs and what they do or do not accomplish. Policy makers expect physical education to contribute to achieving these national goals. Does this mean that promoting a physically active lifestyle is the *only* goal for physical education? The NASPE outcomes shown in Box 1.3 clearly indicate that, for us to say we have helped children and youth become physically educated, we must achieve the broad range of goals—including outcomes related to knowledge, participation skills, and valuing. This will not happen without effective teachers. This is why becoming an active teacher should be your goal and why helping your students become learning students is the important intermediate goal to achieving the NASPE outcomes.

ASSESSMENT FOR ACTIVE TEACHING AND LEARNING STUDENTS

To become an active teacher with learning students, you need good information about your own teaching skills and strategies and also information about what your students are doing and how they are responding to your teaching. This is best done through a program of regular assessment. We take *assessment* to mean the collection of reliable, useful information in order to improve performance. Assessment differs from *evaluation,* which refers to making a judgment about the worth of a performance. An assessment is reliable when the information generated closely corresponds to what actually happened. An assessment is useful when the information generated is strongly related to teaching effectiveness.

Assessment of teachers and their students should take place during actual teaching episodes. What you are able to write about effective teaching on a quiz or paper may be important for some purposes, but it is not an assessment of actual teaching. It is equally clear that no single assessment of teaching gives a complete picture, just as no individual statistic from a basketball game is sufficient to assess player or team performance. Several indicators of effectiveness are needed before a complete picture begins to emerge. Likewise, multiple assessments over time are necessary to provide a fair and accurate assessment of the educational effectiveness of a class.

Three assessment categories are suggested here. The first consists of *teacher process variables*. These include measures of teaching skills such as providing verbal explanations, demonstrating skills to be learned, providing feedback to learners, desisting misbehaviors, and reinforcing appropriate behaviors. Teacher process variables also include strategies such as organizing for class, managing transitions within class, dealing with intrusions, and maintaining the momentum and pace of class activities. Teacher process variables are assessed through direct observation of the teacher while he or she is teaching.

A second assessment category consists of *student process variables*. These relate to students' actions that potentially contribute to or detract from learning. Examples include the amount of time it takes students to relocate from one place to another during class, the level of off-task behavior during a lesson, the amount of time a student is engaged in successful practice during a lesson, and the number of appropriate skill responses made by a squad during a volleyball practice task. Student process variables are assessed through direct observation of students during classes.

A third assessment category consists of *student outcome variables,* sometimes referred to as *product* variables. These reflect student achievement and changes in knowledge, skill, or attitude that are related to program goals. Examples of outcome variables might be to correctly perform a folk dance to appropriate music, to complete a planned floor exercise routine, to be able to run a mile under 7 minutes, and to reach goals in a weight-lifting class. Authentic outcomes would also include individual and team statistics from a round-robin basketball tournament, as well as the successful completion of a hill climb in an Adventure Education program. Assessments of outcomes might also include interviews or other reflective evidence from students that their attitudes toward physical education or their valuing of physical activity have changed positively, as well as more complex kinds of outcomes such as appropriate strategic participation in a well-played field hockey game.

Assessment should always be related to goals set for student learning, particularly assessments of outcome variables. A concept that will be used throughout this book is "alignment." When a teacher's goals, activities, and assessments are aligned, desired outcomes are more likely to be achieved. Different physical educators often have quite different student learning goals for classes or units. One might focus on creativity, confidence in participation, and learners' sense of themselves as skilled movers. Another teacher might have personal and social responsibility of students as the main goal of his or her teaching. Still another might be committed to the Sport Education curriculum model with ninth graders and a personal fitness curriculum with tenth graders. In each of these situations, assessment of teacher process and student process variables would be similar, but assessment of student outcomes would be quite different. Regardless of what outcomes teachers are trying to achieve with their students, they still have to manage transitions effectively, provide clear, concise instructions, and ensure that students get adequate amounts of successful practice.

Educators are also interested in achieving long-term goals. The most important long-term goal for physical education at the moment, from a national policy perspective, is to have a larger proportion of adult citizens lead healthier lives in general and be more physically active. Physical educators have to aim at goals that show the influence of physical education beyond immediate class goals, yet bridge the gap between what students do now and what they will do years later when they are adults. Some of these goals might be voluntary participation in intramural sport programs or in out-of-school physical activity programs, watching less television, maintaining a personal fitness program, and being a more intelligent sport spectator and a more knowledgeable consumer of sport and fitness products. The assumption is that achieving these goals makes more likely the development of healthy lifestyle habits and a lifelong commitment to regular physical activity.

ASSESSING TEACHING AND LEARNING AS THEY HAPPEN

Although we are certainly interested in long-term goals and we should work diligently to achieve them, practicing teachers, and those preparing to become teachers, can't wait for outcome measures to provide information for the improvement of teaching. When you teach a lesson or a unit, you want—and need—to know now how you did and how you can get better. Thus, on-site measures of teaching are necessary for you to improve on a day-to-day basis.

Three levels of on-site assessment are useful for the improvement of teaching: (a) assessment of discrete teacher and student behaviors, (b) assessment of teaching units, and (c) assessment of criterion process variables. Each of these foci provides different information used to assess and improve aspects of teaching.

Level 1: Assessment of Discrete Teacher and Student Behaviors

A *discrete behavior* is a single behavior with an identifiable beginning and end. Examples are skill feedback statements, student skill responses, teacher questions, and student disruptions. Assessment of discrete behaviors is particularly useful at the beginning stages of skill development. Discrete behaviors can be counted or timed. Counting produces a record of the frequency of the behavior, which becomes even more useful when converted to a rate measure by dividing the frequency by the length of the observation, typically producing a rate per minute measure that can be used for comparative purposes regardless of the length of observations. For example, if you provide 24 skill feedback interactions during a 12-minute practice episode during one lesson, the rate would be 2 per minute, which could then be easily compared to your skill feedback interaction rates during other practice episodes that differ in length.

Some discrete behaviors are more meaningful when timed rather than counted; for example, it would be important to know how much time students were nonengaged during a 20-minute practice episode. Here, too, however, you can convert the time data, for example, 5 minutes of the 20-minute episode, into a percentage figure (25 percent) in order to compare it to nonengagement data from practice episodes of different lengths.

Qualitative measurement, rather than or in addition to quantitative assessment, is sometimes useful. For example, you might want to get information about the appropriateness or accuracy of the feedback interactions, in addition to or in place of the simple measures of frequency and rate. To do this, the observer would have to watch the student performance, listen to the feedback, and judge its accuracy and/or appropriateness. Here, too, however, one could eventually convert such information to a quantitative measure of percentage of feedback interactions that contained accurate information.

Level 2: Assessment of Teaching Units

A *teaching unit* is a combination of teacher and learner variables that provides information about important class processes related to teacher effectiveness.

An example of a teaching unit that has been useful in improving managerial skills is the *transition episode*. A transition begins when a signal is provided (by the teacher typically) so that students begin to accomplish some task that helps move a lesson forward but does not directly involve them in the subject matter. The transition ends when students begin to engage in the next task. Examples of transition episodes would be when four volleyball teams have ended two games and the teacher wants to change opponents for the next game, children putting away hoops they have used for one task and getting balls they will use for the next task, classes relocating from a gathered formation in which they have watched a demonstration to dispersed locations where they will begin to practice the skill demonstrated, and students who were practicing with partners seeking another partner group to form quads for a subsequent practice task. Assessments of transition episodes might include the length of the episode, the number of episodes per lesson, the average length of episodes, and the number of teacher prompts and interactions per episode.

A teaching unit important to instruction rather than management is the cycle of teacher prompt, student response, and teacher feedback that occurs so frequently in lessons whose focus is skill or tactical improvement. The teacher provides a brief prompt ("Keep your shoulders level while swinging."). The student attempts a response. The teacher assesses the response and provides feedback ("Much better. They were nearly level.").

Another instructional teaching unit is the sequence of events when the teacher describes an instructional task to a class or group of students, then the students begin to practice, and the teacher supervises the practice. Was the task described clearly? Were students' initial attempts congruent with the task description? If students modified the task, how did the teacher respond? These are all useful questions because students learn what they practice, and if they are not practicing tasks appropriately, they will not learn what the teacher intended them to learn.

Level 3: Assessment of Criterion Process Variables

A *criterion process variable* is a student process variable that provides direct information about student learning. Assessing criterion process variables allows you to obtain immediate and regular information related to student learning without having to wait for outcome measures. There are two criterion process variables for which there is evidence of a direct link to student achievement. One is Active Learning Time (ALT), which is a time-based variable, and the other is Opportunity to Respond (OTR), which is a response-based variable.

ALT is an estimate of the amount of time students are successfully practicing tasks related to content goals. Key features here are that the student has to be actively engaged, the engagement has to be in a task related to content goals, and the engagement has to be successful. In Chapter 2, you will see that ALT rates in physical education are often very low.

OTR is a measure of the number and/or rate of appropriate, successful responses made by students. A response is "appropriate" if its major critical elements were done well. It is successful if it conforms to the expectations for the task as described by the teacher in the context of the practice activity. It is important both to assess the number of OTRs and then to calculate a ratio of the number of appropriate/successful OTRs to the total OTRs.

Both ALT and OTR assessments provide teachers with information about the degree of learning that is likely taking place in their classes. We call them "criterion" process variables because we believe they provide a "bottom line" for understanding effectiveness. In that sense, the improvement of teaching skills through assessment of discrete teaching behaviors and teaching units should have a "payoff" in terms of higher rates of ALT and/or OTR.

EXAMPLES OF ASSESSMENT IN ACTION

Bill is a student teacher in physical education. His classes seem disorganized and he seldom gets to finish all the activities he planned. His cooperating teacher and he decide he should get reliable information on the managerial time spent in class, particularly information related to transitions within the class. This is a useful teaching-unit assessment because research has shown that effective teachers typically have low management time and efficient transitions. The cooperating teacher creates a simple form on which to record each managerial episode and transition in the class. The start and end times are noted, as well as Bill's interactions within each episode. The goal is to reduce the length of episodes and for Bill to prompt students to be quick and to reinforce them when they do respond appropriately. This is done for four consecutive lessons so a baseline of information can be established. Bill is pleased to note that each day the length of the transitions is less and he has become more effective in his interactions. And the time he gains in effective management allows him to finish all the instructional activities he has planned.

Chris is an experienced elementary physical education specialist. She recently read an article in the *Journal of Physical Education, Recreation & Dance (JOPERD)*, the national magazine for professional physical educators, about the importance of teachers distributing their attention equally among boys and girls and more- and less-skilled students. The article suggested that research shows teachers typically interact more with boys than girls and more with more-skilled than with less-skilled students. The article made Chris curious about how she distributes her attention in her classes, an assessment of a discrete teaching behavior. For the next several days, Chris carried a small clipboard with her as she taught her classes, recording in columns the number of interactions she had with boys and girls and among children of various skill levels. These data became her baseline. She was pleased to see that her attention was equitably distributed by skill levels, but surprised and not pleased to see that she interacted more frequently with boys than girls. She decided to try to produce a 50/50 distribution for gender-related interactions. She monitored her performance for several days and achieved the goal quite easily.

Mark has been teaching for many years. This term he has a student teacher, Jennifer, with him. At the start of the term, Jennifer talks with him about what she has recently learned about the importance of students getting a lot of successful practice opportunities, an assessment of a criterion process variable. Mark honestly reports that he has no idea how many OTRs his students get. They decide to help each other. At the beginning of the term, Jennifer observes Mark teaching several classes. Together they select two more-skilled and two less-skilled students for Jennifer to observe. She does this for three lessons to produce a baseline of information. Mark is quite surprised to see that students are not getting many OTRs and that the less-skilled students are hardly ever successful. He and Jennifer talk about what they might do to change the situation. When Jennifer begins to teach, Mark codes her students in the same way. Jennifer has planned activities that allow time for students to get sufficient numbers of OTRs, but finds that she too has less-skilled students who are too infrequently successful. They plan together to improve the situation. They have both become "students of teaching."

Most of the skills of effective teachers can be assessed in similar ways, and when they are, improvement can usually be made with some focused effort. Chapter 16 presents information on how to observe reliably and build observation systems and also presents several well-tested systems.

TOWARD THE EXPERT PHYSICAL EDUCATION TEACHER

Physical education will prosper as a subject matter to the degree that those who teach it are effective and even expert. The more effective and expert teachers become, the more likely they will be to engender the respect of parents and the community. This will make the teaching profession more esteemed—and better paid, too!

The study of teacher expertise is a relatively new research enterprise (Berliner, 1986). Once it was discovered that effective teaching has discernible characteristics, it was natural that researchers would try to distinguish between effectiveness and expertise. If effective teachers promote student learning and growth, expert teachers do so to a greater degree; that is, the difference is one of degree rather than kind. Expert teachers are able to design content, deliver it, and motivate learners in ways that go beyond effectiveness. And, although experts might know more about their students and the context for learning, it's absolutely clear that experts know their subject matter more completely than do effective teachers.

Siedentop and Eldar (1989) used the expertise research literature to examine seven effective elementary physical education specialists. Their conclusions about expertise included the following:

1. *Expertise is highly specific to context and subject matter.* It is useful to talk about an expert volleyball teacher at the middle school level or an

expert gymnastics teacher with young children. However, the expertise shown in one subject and at one level may not generalize to other subjects and levels.

2. *Expertise is performance oriented.* Expert teachers often may not be able to explain their own expertise. The expertise is in the *doing* rather than the explaining of it.

3. *Experience is a necessary condition for expertise, but not a sufficient condition.* Expertise probably develops over long periods of time in ways that are not clearly understood. Thus, it is unlikely that expertise can be taught in the same way as effective teaching skills.

4. *Expertise lies at the nexus of highly skilled teaching and mastery of a particular subject matter* (that is, gymnastics or pole vaulting or basketball). Thorough mastery of a subject is a necessary condition for teaching expertise. You can teach effectively with a limited knowledge of a subject, but to teach expertly, you have to have expertise in the subject.

5. *Teaching effectiveness is within reach of most first-year teachers.* The skills are identifiable and can be improved through practice. Expertise takes longer and the paths toward its achievement are less clear.

SUMMARY

1. If teachers are properly motivated, they can learn to be effective with good practice.

2. Effective teaching is intentional—it is achieved when students reach goals.

3. The NBPTS offers national recognition and certification through a rigorous examination of teaching accomplishments in five core areas.

4. The surest way to assess the effectiveness of teaching is by analyzing what students do.

5. The learning student is cooperative, enthusiastic, responsible, engaged, and helpful.

6. Repeated practice at the appropriate level of challenge and interest is the key to successful learning.

7. The NASPE definition of a physically educated person describes the outcomes that learning students should achieve in physical education.

8. The active teacher organizes an efficient, effective, and inclusive learning environment.

9. The concept of active teaching accommodates a range of instructional approaches—there is no one best way to be effective.

10. To become an effective teacher, you must know the skills and tactics of effective teaching, have ample opportunity to practice the skills, and receive helpful feedback based on observations of your practice.

11. Learning in physical education is important from a number of perspectives, including public-health goals, personal benefits, and leisure benefits—all of which derive from a physically active lifestyle.

12. Assessment of teaching requires good information, which must be reliable and valid.

13. Teacher process variables describe teaching behaviors, student process variables describe student behaviors, and student outcome variables describe achievement.

14. Assessment should always be related to goals set for student learning.

15. Assessment can be at the levels of the discrete teacher and student behaviors, teaching units, or criterion process variables.

16. ALT and OTR are both good criterion process variables, one based on time and the other on frequency counts.

17. Teaching expertise combines highly effective teaching with mastery of a subject field and the ability to relate to students in a particular context.

CHAPTER 2

Teaching Effectiveness in Physical Education

Teacher expertise—what teachers know and can do—affects all the core tasks of teaching. . . . No other intervention can make the difference that a knowledgeable, skillful teacher can make in the earning process. . . . That is, teachers who know a lot about teaching and learning and who work in environments that allow them to know students well are the critical elements of successful learning.

—National Commission on Teaching and America's Future (1996)

OVERALL CHAPTER OUTCOME

To describe what research reveals as the "typical" physical education class from a teacher and student perspective and to compare this evidence to what is known about effective teaching

CHAPTER OBJECTIVES

- To describe the development of RTPE
- To outline the main benefits derived from RTPE
- To explain what research says about how students spend their time in physical education classes
- To illustrate the concept of ALT-PE and what RTPE says about it
- To clarify the concept of OTR and what RTPE says about it
- To describe the important kinds of teacher knowledge and what RTPE says about them
- To delineate what RTPE reveals about student alienation and gender issues
- To explain research related to teacher improvement in PE
- To compare and contrast what is known about RTPE with the characteristics of effective teaching

We ended Chapter 1 with the assertion that teaching effectiveness is within the reach of most first-year teachers. Our descriptions of the learning student and the active teacher in Chapter 1 provided a general view of what we have learned from school-based research on teaching effectiveness in various subjects across the K–12 spectrum. The focus in Chapter 2 is on research done specifically in the context of physical education. In both cases, however, we are presenting research that was done *in schools with regular students*. This is not theory or speculation about teaching effectively. These are not results from laboratory simulations of teaching. The research results we describe and the implications we draw from them form a fundamental knowledge base for professional preparation for teaching physical education. If we want teaching to be more highly valued by other professionals and the public, then we must continue to build a strong research base on teaching effectiveness, and we must use the research base already developed.

BACKGROUND

The research on teaching physical education (RTPE) reviewed in this chapter is primarily from studies in which the data were obtained through direct observation of physical education classes in regular schools. We consider this to be the most relevant database for understanding teaching effectiveness in physical education. We have included other research that helps us understand the context for teaching in today's schools, particularly research related to how students feel about and interpret their experiences in gym class.

RTPE is a fairly young research field, slightly more than a quarter-century. It began with simple observational studies describing the activities of teachers and students. The prototype for these early studies was a group of research projects undertaken at Teachers College at Columbia University under the leadership of Dr. William Anderson. The Anderson and Barrette (1978) monograph entitled *What's Going on in the Gym?* exerted substantial influence on a generation of RTPE researchers. In the late 1970s and early 1980s, a host of observation instruments was created for observing physical education classes. (An observation instrument is a category system for recording class activities, typically the number of behaviors, the amount of time, or both, that show what teachers and students are doing.)

Most of the early studies were descriptive, using different category systems to provide lenses that yielded research pictures of what teachers and students were doing and what their interactions were like. Descriptive studies attempt to provide valid information about classes, which can then be analyzed in a number of ways to estimate relationships among events. Programs at Boston University (Dr. John Cheffers and his students using the Cheffers Adaptation of the Flanders Interaction Analysis System—CAFIAS), Ithaca College (Dr. Vic Mancini and his students also using CAFIAS), and Ohio State University (Dr. Daryl Siedentop and his students using a variety of behavioral category systems) formed an early descriptive database in the United States. Similar programs at the University of Laval in Canada and the University of Liège in Belgium produced similar databases for physical education internationally.

Not all the studies were descriptive. A series of experimental studies at Ohio State University (Siedentop, 1981), in which the purpose was not only to describe events, but also to intentionally change them through an intervention, focused on how teacher and student behaviors could be changed during teaching field experiences, particularly in student teaching. The same types of category observation systems were used along with a supervisory intervention that systematically used feedback from those observations to help teachers change their own behaviors and interactions. The feedback was also used to help student teachers change certain student behaviors and to improve how time was spent in class.

In the 1980s, research was conducted using the Active Learning Time–Physical Education system (ALT-PE) (Siedentop, Birdwell, & Metzler,

BOX 2.1 The Funnel Effect in Student Engaged Time

Teachers often plan a certain amount of time for students to be engaged in lesson activities. They also no doubt expect that most of that engaged time will be functional for their learning. But time planned by the teacher does not always translate well into functional learning time for the student. This can be seen in the three kinds of time described below and how time is lost in what Metzler (1980) called the "funneling effect."

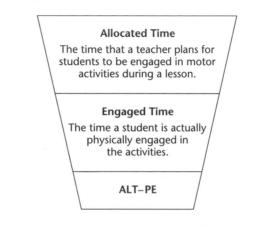

Allocated Time
The time that a teacher plans for students to be engaged in motor activities during a lesson.

Engaged Time
The time a student is actually physically engaged in the activities.

ALT–PE

What is important for student learning is the amount of time at the bottom of this funnel. When engaged time is far less than allocated time, the teacher usually has a problem managing and organizing students. When ALT-PE is far less than engaged time, the teacher has problems with designing activities in which students can experience success.

Source: Adapted from Metzler, 1980.

1979; Siedentop, Tousignant, & Parker, 1982). ALT-PE is the amount of time a student spends engaged successfully in activities related to lesson objectives. (The ALT-PE instrument is shown in Chapter 16.) This research program was based on solid evidence from classroom research that student learning was strongly correlated with the amount of accumulated ALT. The manner in which valuable learning time is lost in many classes is shown in Box 2.1. Both descriptive and intervention research was completed using the ALT-PE as the main data collection instrument. So much ALT-PE research was completed during the 1980s that two major reviews were presented, the first by Dodds and Rife (1983) and the second by Metzler (1989), one of the originators of the instrument.

A powerful form of classroom research was process-product studies—in which data from systematic observations of students and teachers (process variables) were correlated with learning outcomes (product variables) in order to distinguish the higher achieving classes from lower achieving classes. Researchers in physical education conducted fewer of these studies because of the lack of reliable and valid outcome measures. Dr. Steve Silverman (1996) and his students have completed a series of programmatic process-product studies in physical education that has produced results very similar to those from classroom research.

Early descriptive and intervention research relied almost exclusively on quantitative methods, but in the 1980s, qualitative methods began to be used and by the end of the decade had become the dominant form of RTPE. Quantitative methods rely on numbers, statistics, and graphic pictures of what teachers and students do—rates of feedback, percentages of comments to boys and girls, amounts of time in management, and the like. Qualitative research uses long-term narrative descriptions of what teachers and students do, especially trying to capture the perspectives of those in the learning environment. Qualitative researchers present their findings and analyses in words and stories rather than with tables and graphs. The early lead in qualitative research was provided by Dr. Larry Locke and Dr. Pat Griffin at the University of Massachusetts. In the 1990s, qualitative research became the favored methodology for many physical education investigators. More recently, researchers have utilized both quantitative and qualitative methods in the same study (Ennis, 1994; Kutame, 1997; Romar, 1995; Siedentop, Doutis, Tsangaridou, Ward, & Rauschenbach, 1994). Some have suggested that the two approaches, when used carefully together, can add to our growing understanding of teaching and learning in physical education by utilizing the best features of each methodology.

In the 1990s, RTPE expanded greatly. Lee (1996) and her students took their lead from cognitive psychology to focus on student thinking as a mediating variable between instruction and outcomes. Griffey and Housner (1991) conducted studies of teacher expertise in physical education. Rovegno (1993) and her students utilized constructivist learning theory to focus on how teachers and students actively construct knowledge based on their interpretations of events as compared to the base of knowledge and understanding they bring to the learning context. Hastie and Siedentop (1999) and their students continued the work started by Siedentop in the 1980s using the ecological paradigm to understand how teachers and their students negotiate the processes of learning across time. (The results of the ecological research program are described in detail in Chapter 3.) Graham (1995) and his students have recently focused on bringing the "student voice" into physical education research, examining the meanings and reactions children have to their physical education experiences. Several researchers have done studies that coalesce around the problem of student alienation within physical education. Ennis (1994a) and her students focused on value orientations of teachers and more recently on problems of physical education in urban school settings. All in all, the field of RTPE is rich and varied, providing physical educators with an expanding knowledge base about the context of physical education and how we all can become more effective in what we do.

BENEFITS OF RTPE

Even though RTPE is a relatively young field, benefits have clearly been derived from its increasing productivity. A brief list of some of those benefits follows:

- Teachers and researchers have a technical language that reflects their understanding of effective teaching practices. Terms such as transitions, ALT-PE, desisting, management time, and the competent bystander have specific meanings that are understood by researchers and, increasingly, by teachers.

- Extensive RTPE in class management and discipline (Jansma & French, 1994; Luke, 1989) has resulted in techniques that have proven effectiveness. Strategies such as time-out, contracting, positive practice, effective desisting, and a host of primary prevention techniques are now widely available. (These are described in Chapters 4 and 5.)

- Results from RTPE have been markedly similar to those from classroom research, thus giving teachers confidence that what works in classrooms also works in the gym and on the playing fields.

- RTPE has verified that the most fundamental ingredient in student learning is the quality and quantity of student practice—effective teachers design interesting, authentic learning tasks and motivate students to stay engaged with them.

- The number and quality of observation instruments have greatly expanded, and these instruments are readily available to both researchers and teachers (Darst, Zakrajsek, & Mancini, 1989). Chapter 16 discusses a variety of observation instruments useful for teacher preparation and development.

- The *Journal of Teaching Physical Education* is devoted primarily to RTPE, and the *Research Quarterly for Exercise and Sport* has a major section devoted to pedagogy research. Professional journals such as the *Journal of Physical Education, Recreation and Dance* have sections in which research results are interpreted for practitioners.

- The knowledge and skills presented in teaching methods textbooks have become increasingly research based (Gallahue, 1998; Graham, Holt/ Hale, & Parker, 1998; Rink, 1993b; Siedentop, 1991).

- Other books and materials have focused more specifically on special topics in teaching effectiveness such as gender equity (Griffin & Placek, 1983) and classroom management (Jansma & French, 1994).

- Teacher educators in physical education have become more knowledgeable about the research base for their field and ways of applying it to teacher education programs. As a result, newly certified teachers are much more likely to know about and have skills in class management, discipline, supervision of practice, unit planning, and instructional strategies than they were 25 years ago.

- Through RTPE, teacher education programs have become much more sensitive to issues of equity, and their students are more likely to be aware of and able to do something about ensuring equal treatment regardless of race, gender, skillfulness, or handicapping condition.

If there is as much progress over the next 25 years as there has been over the past 25 years, we can look forward enthusiastically and optimistically, expecting that our understanding of the complexities of teaching physical education will continue to grow. If this knowledge and the skills required to use it in schools are taken seriously by women and men studying to become licensed physical education teachers, we can also expect that these new teachers will enter the profession as effective first-year teachers. If they use that knowledge and those skills with their students, we can expect that physical education in schools will improve dramatically.

WHAT STUDENTS DO IN PHYSICAL EDUCATION

We start our review of RTPE by looking at what students do in physical education classes because *if you want to learn about or evaluate the effectiveness of a physical education teacher, you have to watch the students, not the teacher*. Effective teaching is seen in purposeful learning among students. To see the degree of purposeful learning in a class, you have to observe what the students are doing. In each of the areas discussed, there is evidence of very effective teaching in physical education, and there is evidence of very ineffective teaching. Although it is important to find out where the "norm" is (that is, what appears to be the most typical features of physical education classes), it will also become clear throughout this chapter that teachers can learn to do better (that is, we can improve on the norm).

Quantitative research evidence about student behavior in physical education is of two primary varieties: time based and response based. We attend to the time-based data first. Students often spend less than 30 percent of class time engaged in motor activities—a startling finding. Naturally, students cannot be in motor activity all the time—there are managerial chores to accomplish, transitions, equipment changes, and instruction. Rates of successful engagement in activities are much lower. What are they doing if they aren't engaged in some sport or fitness activity? They are most likely in managerial or transition time—or they are waiting.

The term *waiting* refers to time prior to, between, and after instructional, managerial, and practice activities—time when students are not involved in anything related to the managerial or instructional objectives of the lesson. Waiting time often accounts for 25 percent of class time—and, far too often, students use waiting time to engage in off-task or disruptive behavior. High amounts of waiting time are clear signals that a teacher is not organizing and managing class activities to keep students productively engaged.

Students also spend large chunks of time in managerial tasks—taking roll, organizing for practice, choosing teams, transitioning from place to place, and changing equipment within a lesson. Management and transitions often account for 20–25 percent of class time. Managing effectively in physical education is not easy because there are large spaces, often large classes, and a subject matter in which students move around a lot. In many classes, students spend as much as 50–70 percent of class time in management, transition, and waiting. However, in more effective classes, physical education teachers organize and manage so that management time is less than 10 percent and waiting time, in many cases, is less than 5 percent.

The third large chunk of class time for students is spent receiving information—directions, organizational information, descriptions of skills, plans for drills, lectures about safety, or descriptions of a game. Students typically spend 15–30 percent of class time listening to the teacher in a whole-class format. A certain amount of effective instruction is important, even crucial. Students need to know what to do and need good instruction and demonstrations. Effective teachers find ways to convey the *right amount* of information effectively and efficiently and then get students quickly into practice. However, many students in physical education are overinstructed and underpracticed.

The fourth chunk of student time is spent in motor engagement—practicing skills, playing games, performing fitness activities. This important kind of time has been described with several related terms—engaged time, motor engaged time, physically active time, active learning time, functional time, and ALT-PE. Regardless of what term is used, it is important to recognize the difference between two kinds of motor engaged time. The first kind would be counted whenever a student was physically active in lesson content, whatever the nature of the involvement. This kind of time is important for the health-related goals of physical education. National goals in *Healthy People 2000* call for students to be physically active at least 50 percent of all PE class time. The second kind of time—ALT-PE or functional time (Metzler, 1989)—is counted when a student is *successfully* engaged in activities related to lesson content. This second kind of time is related to learning and achievement. All functional time is also engaged time and contributes to health goals, but not all engaged time contributes to achievement goals. Therefore, teachers should strive to have their students' engagement be as successful as possible and related directly to class goals. To the extent that practice time is functional, both the health goals and motor performance goals of physical education can be achieved.

Effective teachers plan, organize, manage, and instruct so as to help students accumulate as much ALT-PE as possible across a unit of activity—in some cases, as much as 50–80 percent of class time can be spent in ALT-PE (Birdwell, 1980; Siedentop et al., 1994). Box 2.1 shows the relationships among how teachers plan to use time, time students are engaged, and functional time in PE classes. The following generalizations are warranted from the research examining how time is used in physical education classes:

1. The focus of activity in a unit greatly affects the amount of ALT-PE accumulated by students, with fitness and dance highest, individual sports next, and team sports and gymnastics lowest.

2. Elementary students get more ALT-PE than do middle or high school students.

3. Lower-skilled students get substantially less ALT-PE than do middle- or higher-skilled students.

4. Students get more ALT-PE toward the end of a unit than in the beginning of units.

5. Girls in elementary classes get about the same amount of ALT-PE as boys. Evidence from middle and high school classes is less clear.

6. Students with disabling conditions who are included in regular classes get less ALT-PE than do other students (Aufderheide, 1983).

7. If there is a substantial gap between time teachers allocate for actual practice and the amount of engaged time, the problem is likely to be poor management.

8. If there is a substantial gap between engaged time and ALT-PE, the problem is more likely related to poor instructional design, with practice activities too difficult for the skill levels of the students.

9. ALT-PE can be substantially increased through improving managerial effectiveness.

10. The amount of successful practice is related to improved outcome measures (Silverman, 1985).

The second method for focusing on what students do in physical education is to observe the responses they make, producing a response-based record rather than a time-based record. This research has come to be known as "Opportunity to Respond" (OTR) research. OTR research has been particularly helpful in shedding light on the instructional practices of teachers. There has been a substantial amount of OTR research in physical education, with results that are similar to those produced by the time-based research. Most OTR research not only records the number of responses students make in practice and games, but also evaluates the quality of those responses. Quality of response can be evaluated in two ways: (a) rating the technical appropriateness of the response and (b) rating the success of the response in the context of the activity. The best response is both technically appropriate and successful. To be judged "technically appropriate" most often means that the major critical elements of the skill are performed correctly, given the developmental level of the student. OTR research tends to report data in two ways—the rate of responses (responses per minute of practice time) and the ratio of successful and/or appropriate responses to total responses. The evidence suggests the following generalizations:

1. Lower-skilled students generally have lower OTR rates and a lower percentage of successful responses.

2. In game settings, lower-skilled students very seldom make responses that are either appropriate in form or successful in the context of the game (Brown, 1986; Parker, 1984).

3. OTR rates and ratios are substantially higher when specific accountability measures for performance are applied (Alexander, 1982; Lund, 1990; Ward, 1993).

4. Students often modify practice tasks to make them easier or more challenging (Tousignant & Siedentop, 1983).

5. Students learn best when they get more opportunity to practice tasks they will be tested on (Pieron, 1983; Silverman, 1985).

6. Without specific attention by the teacher and specific expectations for practice, many lower- and medium-skilled students participate in repeated practice trials using techniques that are inappropriate for future success (Lund, 1990; Siedentop et al., 1994).

7. In the early stages of learning, students profit more from practice than from explanations and demonstrations. Effective teachers tend to devote 50 percent less time to instruction during these early stages (Behets, 1997).

8. When teachers structure learning tasks to control the quality and quantity of OTRs, students often get as many as 15 times more OTRs than when learning tasks are less well designed and structured (Silverman, Subramaniam, & Woods, 1998).

9. With "inclusion" styles of teaching (see Chapter 14), students choose alternative levels of task difficulty with decisions made on the basis of perceived success, thus creating better conditions for their own successful practice (Byra & Jenkins, 1998).

10. When specific accountability measures are tied to successful practice goals, students achieve not only higher rates of OTRs, but also higher percentages of successful OTRs (Lund, 1990; Ward, 1993).

11. Curricular models such as Sport Education (see Chapter 9) allow for longer units of instruction and instructional formats within which students make important improvements—both lower- and higher-skilled students (Hastie, 1998).

The time- and response-based RTPE provides significant evidence about the practices of more- and less-effective teachers in physical education. Preventive managerial systems (see Chapter 4) provide the foundation for teaching effectiveness because they produce the optimal amount of time teachers can use for instruction and practice. Effective teachers, however, then have to organize instructional and practice time effectively by designing appropriate practice tasks and developing effective motivational and accountability systems. Unfortunately, too many physical education teachers manage poorly and do not provide effective, equitable learning environments for their students. Appropriate and successful physical activity seems to be the "right stuff" for a meaningful physical education, but RTPE suggests that the right stuff is missing in far too many physical education classes.

RESEARCH ON TEACHER
SUBJECT-MATTER KNOWLEDGE

The work of Shulman (1987) has brought the issue of teacher knowledge to the forefront of research on teacher effectiveness. Teachers, of course, have to have various kinds of knowledge to be successful—general knowledge of students, general pedagogical knowledge, local knowledge about the students they teach, knowledge of the content included in the curriculum, and the ability to transform their content knowledge and deliver it to students in ways that help them learn. This last form of knowledge, called *pedagogical content knowledge* (PCK), is particularly relevant to effective teaching.

How much does a PE teacher have to know about basketball or folk dancing or gymnastics to plan and deliver an effective unit of instruction to diverse groups of learners? The most practical answer is: "That depends on how long the unit is, who the students are, and how serious the teacher is about students actually gaining important knowledge and skill as a result of experiencing the unit." If you are teaching short units in the typical multi-activity format used in American physical education, you probably don't have to have a great deal of PCK beyond very beginning skills and tactics. Subsequently, that is all you can expect students to achieve, even when units such as these are planned and delivered effectively. But what if you wanted students to really become immersed in an activity and accomplish some important learning goals over a longer period of time? Then you would have to know not only more about the activity, but also more about how to transform that knowledge and use it to help your students reach those goals. You would need more PCK, that is, how to take your knowledge of gymnastics and relate it to *these* students under *these* conditions so that optimal learning occurs. RTPE on teacher knowledge is still a young field, but the following points can be made from the current knowledge base:

1. Teachers who have richer content knowledge and more PCK are better able to (a) accommodate diverse learners, (b) sequence activities, (c) detect common performance errors and correct them, and (d) plan for remedial activities (Dodds, 1994; Harari & Siedentop, 1990; O'Sullivan, 1996; Schempp, Manross, Tan, & Fincher, 1998).

2. Many teachers do not have adequate knowledge of the critical elements of the skills they are teaching or the capacity to recognize common performance errors and correct them (Gangstead & Beveridge, 1984; O'Sullivan, 1996; Wilkinson, 1991).

3. Preservice teachers can improve their PCK through being taught observational skills (Barrett, Allison, & Bell, 1987; Matanin, 1993).

4. Preservice teachers can improve their PCK through teaching experiences in which the focus is learning about the activity by carefully watching the attempts of children to learn it (Barrett & Collie, 1996).

5. Teachers with competitive backgrounds in a sport and teaching experience have substantially higher levels of PCK than do teachers without

sport-specific backgrounds and/or experience (Harari & Siedentop, 1990).

6. Lack of content knowledge and PCK sometimes results in a misalignment between the goals a teacher has for a unit of instruction and the activities planned to reach those goals. For example, a teacher might want students to learn to play a game well, but have little knowledge about the tactical aspects of the game and use only isolated skill tasks in a unit (Romar, 1995).

7. PCK is crucial for the way a teacher develops tasks and progressions. Decisions about what to teach and how to teach it develop from content knowledge and PCK (Doutis, 1997).

8. Content knowledge and PCK make an immediate and detectable difference in what teachers do and what students experience when teaching beginning skills to novice students (Kutame, 1997).

9. Some teachers who adopt curricular innovations, such as Sport Education, that require longer units of instruction find that their content knowledge and PCK are inadequate to answer questions students ask as they try to improve their performance (Grant, 1992).

Tinning (1992) underscores the importance of a certain kind of teacher knowledge by distinguishing between content knowledge and PCK in a simple and instructive manner. He describes knowing about and being able to perform an activity (content knowledge) as "weak" practical knowledge—there is no guarantee that this knowledge can be usefully presented to students in ways that help them learn. Teachers who can transform their knowledge about an activity and articulate it to specific groups of learners in language and concepts they understand have "strong" practical knowledge. A significant issue in teacher education and the continuing professional development of teachers is the degree to which programs help them acquire and refine strong practical knowledge.

DO NO HARM:
ALIENATION IN PHYSICAL EDUCATION

A fundamental tenet of the oath physicians take is to "do no harm." Teachers might well take a similar oath—with an even more important addition: "Make sure students do no harm to each other." One of the saddest results of RTPE is the degree to which it reveals that in some places students experience substantial harm in physical education classes. Although many physical education researchers who spent numerous hours observing classes have long thought this to be true, it wasn't until researchers began to focus on the "student voice" that the evidence became clearer. Using surveys, focus groups, and individual interviews, researchers have investigated the experiences students have in physical education and their views about those experiences. Locke

(1999), reviewing a recent doctoral dissertation examining the experiences of high school students in physical education, summarized the too often sad picture that emerges:

> Certainly, many of the findings will not surprise readers who have followed the growing research literature that attends to the voices of students. The domination of class by pupils with greater skill, the inequitable distribution of teacher attention, the isolation and verbal abuse of low-skilled students, the general lack of adequate instruction in playing strategy, the near universal devaluing of physical education as subject matter, the progressive alienation of females from both physical activity and (ultimately) their bodies, and the persistent unwillingness or inability of some teachers to confront such problems do not represent startling insights. (p. 370)

Such results are surely startling for many who have not followed the research literature carefully, but we all should be startled by them!

A small but growing amount of research coalesces around themes of student alienation and gender. The harm students experience in physical education classes is not always immediately evident. There is no evidence in RTPE that teachers intentionally try to harm students or allow them to harm one another. To the contrary, the evidence on teacher value orientations (Ennis, 1996) suggests that most teachers want students to learn and say that they highly value student personal growth and development. There is no evidence in RTPE to suggest that teacher verbal abuse of students is common in physical education. To the contrary, the evidence suggests that teachers tend to be neutral or primarily supportive in their interactions with students. How, then, can one explain this emerging body of research that suggests students experience harm within physical education classes and become alienated from the subject matter? Research does not yet allow us to answer that question, but some beginning estimates can be made.

Subtle forms and patterns of interaction may disadvantage some students. Differential attention based on gender and ability appears to be the most prevalent form of discriminatory behavior, much of which may be unintentional but nonetheless damaging to students. The frequency and content of teacher interactions with boys and girls are often different beginning as early as kindergarten (Colvin, 1995). A more widespread problem is that too many students are bored, embarrassed, and marginalized within their physical education classes and eventually become alienated from physical education (Carlson, 1995). Too many students find physical education to be meaningless. The repetitive use of boring activities leads them to stand around, fake participation, and generally become disengaged from the instructional system. To the extent that this happens, physical education has become miseducative. In an instructional setting that is so casual that it can be described as "no sweat" for both teachers and their students (Siedentop et al., 1994), many students inevitably get bored, and others behave in ways that are harmful to some of their classmates. That is, the absence of a meaningful curriculum and a pedagogy that draws students into serious engagement with activities creates conditions under which harmful things take place. The Sport Education model (described in Chapter 9) uses a small-group (teams) format in which players have individual responsibilities that contribute directly to the success or failure of the class. A growing body of evidence from examinations of the model suggests that lower-skilled students and girls are less marginalized and that relationships among members of teams become positive and supportive.

An even larger problem appears to be that too many teachers are not aware that students abuse and disadvantage other students during the course of lessons or allow it to happen. Students tease and embarrass one another. Girls and lower-skilled students are prevented from fairly participating—they become effectively isolated within their classes. Higher-skilled students (most often boys) hog space and dominate play. Little wonder then that some students become alienated from physical education and do everything in their power to minimize their participation. Most students who experience harm feel powerless to do anything about it, so they find ways to tune out and disengage. Again, however, there is evidence that it doesn't have to be this way. Studies examining specific teaching strategies that emphasize social behavior with classes, where teachers hold students accountable for prosocial behavior, show consistently positive results (Giebink & McKenzie, 1985; Patrick, Ward, & Crouch, 1998; Sharpe, Brown, & Crider, 1995). Physical educators also have ample access to a thoroughly tested pedagogical format in which personal and social responsibility are the foci of curricular choices and pedagogical strategies (Hellison, 1995). This model is described in detail in Chapter 5.

Research on gender issues has yielded somewhat similar findings. Teachers (both male and female) interact somewhat differently with boys and girls as early as kindergarten (Colvin, 1995). Boys and girls learn early what are "appropriate" activities and "appropriate" ways of participating, mostly to the disadvantage of girls. Gender-differentiated roles exist in the wider cultures of schools and communities, but physical activity and sport have been areas in which role differentiation based on gender has been particularly rigid to the disadvantage of females (Williamson, 1996). Even in the post–Title IX era, discriminatory practices in physical education based on gender are too prevalent. Curricular choices too often reflect traditional male sporting interests. Girls are intimidated by boys during activity. Girls sometimes have less opportunity to participate, and when they do participate, their roles are marginalized. Stereotypical gender-appropriate behavior—passivity, dependence, cooperation, intuition, and nurturance for girls, as opposed to independence, activity, competition, rationality, and aggression for boys—is too often reinforced (Chepyator-Thomson & Ennis, 1997). Because these stereotypes are still prevalent in the wider culture, it is to be expected that, unless confronted, they will find their way into physical education.

Are physical education teachers aware of these problems? Do they see them as they are teaching? If they do look for them or see them, do they confront them? Little specific research has sought to answer those questions. However, increasing amounts of evidence indicate that, for too many students, the physical education experience is characterized by a host of negative outcomes, ranging from boredom to severe alienation. The evidence also suggests that, unless teachers make clear their expectations for how students should treat each other, monitor student activity for indications of inequitable treatment, and hold students accountable when they behave in ways that result in harm to other students, these problems are likely to continue.

There is now some evidence that designing interesting curriculums and providing students with authentic units of instruction that engage them in meaningful activity, using instructional practices that require some group involvement and cooperative practice, tend to reduce marginalization of lower-skilled students and girls and build a climate of mutual respect and tolerance (Hastie, 1998; Pope & Grant, 1996). Teacher educators need to incorporate these issues into their preparation programs and ensure that preservice teachers are helped during their field experiences to learn to plan and instruct in ways that not only reduce the incidences of such events, but begin to make physical education an experience in which such outcomes are contested, where respect, cooperation, and equal opportunity become the norm.

EVIDENCE ABOUT TEACHER IMPROVEMENT AND ITS EFFECTS

Although the evidence from descriptive research on teachers and students in physical education does not present a consistently optimistic picture, the evidence on teacher improvement and its effects is more hopeful. There is substantial evidence that teachers can develop effective teaching skills during their preservice preparation (Siedentop, 1986). There is also evidence that physical education teachers on the job can improve their teaching skills and that, when they do, their students get substantially more ALT-PE (Birdwell, 1980). Finally, there is also evidence that student teachers can improve markedly with appropriate supervision and that, when they do, their students experience more ALT-PE (Cramer, 1977; Hutslar, 1977; Randall & Imwold, 1989; Siedentop, 1981).

The bulk of this evidence suggests the following conclusions about teacher improvement and its effects:

1. Teachers in training can develop effective teaching skills if they get adequate practice and supervision.

2. Teachers on the job can improve their teaching skills, and, when they do, their students get more ALT-PE.

3. Student teachers can improve their interactive teaching skills and the behavior of their students (less management time, more ALT-PE, fewer disruptions) if they get adequate supervision.

4. Both preservice and in-service teachers can learn positive interaction styles.

5. Both preservice and in-service teachers can learn to provide more specific skill feedback.

6. Preservice teachers can learn to discriminate critical elements and common errors in a variety of sport skills.

7. Both preservice and in-service teachers can reduce management time significantly.

8. Both preservice and in-service teachers can learn to become more enthusiastic in their teaching (Rolider, Siedentop, & Van Houten, 1984).

9. Direct intervention on improving ALT-PE with preservice teachers can result in marked increases in student ALT-PE (Randall & Imwold, 1989).

Women and men preparing to become physical education teachers can develop effective teaching skills if they are provided knowledge about those skills, the opportunity to practice them, and systematic feedback about their progress. The evidence about improvement of in-service teachers suggests that developing of effective skills can begin during teacher education and continue throughout a professional career in teaching. Of all the research that has been completed, this certainly has to be the most encouraging.

These rather optimistic statements need to be tempered with other research that has investigated the problems teachers encounter in their first several years of teaching, what is typically referred to as the "induction period." The strength of a preservice program is a major determinant of how well prepared a teacher is to be successful in the first several years of teaching. Nonetheless, the problems encountered in schools are substantial because there is a great risk of "washout" (Stroot, 1996), during which the impact of a good teacher education program diminishes. Teachers are seldom prepared for the lack of support they get or the degree to which physical education is a marginalized subject matter in many schools (O'Sullivan, 1989; O'Sullivan, Siedentop, & Tannehill, 1994). Too many school administrators (and other teachers) believe that physical education is not an important school subject and have few expectations that it be taught seriously or achieve important outcomes. The physical education teacher is often physically isolated from other teachers in the school (Stroot, 1996)—and too often isolated even in places like the teacher's lounge or lunchroom.

Effective physical education teachers can overcome this and become highly valued colleagues (Siedentop, 1989), and their programs can come to be seen as making important contributions to the education of children. (There is more evidence that this can be true for elementary PE specialists than for high school physical educators.) Still, it is just as likely that PE teachers can become valued as people and no longer isolated from the faculty of a school, but *still have the subject they teach be devalued.*

THE EFFECTIVENESS OF PHYSICAL EDUCATION TEACHING

One way to assess the general level of teaching effectiveness in physical education is to take the profile of the effective teacher described in Chapter 1 (what we called the "active teacher") and compare it to the general findings of RTPE. These comparisons require judgments. We present ours and invite you to make your own analysis and disagree with us where you think appropriate. It would also be interesting for you, as you read our analysis, to contrast the profile of the active teacher with your physical education teachers in elementary and secondary schools.

1. *Belief in their own efficacy.* Evidence for this variable is thin. Some evidence suggests that teachers judge their efficacy by self-evaluation of their own teaching skills (how they demonstrate, give feedback, and the like) rather than by the progress of their students. This allows them to think they are teaching fairly well when their students are making little progress.

2. *Time, opportunity to learn, and content covered.* Our estimate is that too much content is covered in multi-activity programs and that students generally do not get sufficient opportunity to practice skills, especially in a success-oriented fashion.

3. *Expectations and roles.* RTPE is thin on this point, but the general picture that emerges does not support a conclusion that there are high expectations for learning. Student roles are too often defined minimally as appropriate behavior and minimal effort in participation.

4. *Class management and student engagement.* Classes have too much management and transition time. Students spend too much time waiting. Subsequently, there is too little time for productive student engagement.

5. *Meaningful tasks and high success.* Tasks are too often decontextualized from how they will be applied. Students get too few OTRs. Lower-skilled students are seldom successful.

6. *Pacing and momentum.* Long student waiting times destroy pacing and momentum. Classes too often have gaps that become boring and tend to produce off-task behavior.

7. *Appropriate guidance.* Too much time is spent in instruction. Guided practice with correction of common errors is infrequent. Students are too quickly dispersed to independent practice, where they tend to be unsuccessful.

8. *Active supervision.* Supervision is uneven. The primary goal appears to be to keep students on task, which is often achieved. But if they are not being successful in their practice, being on task doesn't result in improvement.

9. *Accountability.* Accountability for outcomes (skills, tactical play, fitness, and the like) is far too infrequent. The major accountability focus is often on attendance, dress, nondisruptive behavior, and minimal participation.

10. *Clarity, enthusiasm, and equitable support.* Results differ here. One is most likely to see clarity in the managerial system of the class. Instructional systems are more typically casual and lack clarity and enthusiasm. One is more likely to see enthusiasm and expectations for equity in the classes of elementary PE specialists.

11. *Building from student understanding.* Because many instructional systems are so casual, with few serious expectations for performance, teachers are unlikely to take the time and make the effort to build from student understanding.

This pessimistic review does not mean that *all* physical education teachers teach ineffectively. Many physical education teachers work under conditions that are less than favorable for effective teaching. However, we cannot ignore what the descriptive evidence implies about the general level of teaching in our subject field. Fortunately, there is also evidence from research specifically intended to evaluate and assess effective teaching in physical education—and that evidence is more optimistic.

The evidence about effective teaching in physical education comes from four sources: the teacher improvement research cited previously, descriptive studies aimed at assessing effectiveness as it exists in schools (McLeish, 1981; Phillips & Carlisle, 1983), small-scale studies aimed at assessing effectiveness experimentally (DeKnop, 1986; Pieron, 1983; Silverman, 1985), and studies aimed at examining the work of teachers who had been identified as effective (Siedentop, 1989). Although this is not a large body of research, the studies completed tend to show that an effective physical education teacher performs in ways that are remarkably similar to his or her classroom counterpart.

McLeish and his colleagues' analysis (Howe & Jackson, 1981) categorized 104 physical education lessons into best ($n = 18$), average ($n = 48$), and poor ($n = 38$). It indicated that the major determining factors distinguishing the best from the poor were higher rates of appropriate learning time and lower rates of waiting time. Time spent in a knowledge focus did not discriminate among the three groups. McLeish reached the following conclusion:

> The theoretical basis of the ALT-PE system is what is now conventionally referred to as *learning theory.* By this we mean that we accept as established fact certain basic principles: (1) that learning is maximized in direct proportion to the number and type of opportunities to learn; (2) we learn best by concentrating on practicing the motor, cognitive, or psychomotor skill by actually doing; or (3) by observing others performing the skill. There is (4) no advantage to be gained in practicing the skill at a difficulty level which results in a level of failure rate greater than 10 percent. Effective teaching means structuring the lesson to maximize the amount of time in direct practice by each individual at a level which at once ensures a continuing development of the skill compatible with the minimal number of mistakes. (McLeish, 1981, p. 29)

The notion that successful practice is related to outcomes is thoroughly demonstrated in classroom research and similarly in RTPE. Phillips and Carlisle (1983) studied 18 teachers and their students, concluding that learning outcomes were most dramatically related to the specific motor engagement rates of the students. Engaged skill learning time and success time were three times as great in the more effective classes. Silverman and his students (Silverman, 1985; Silverman, Devillier, & Ramirez, 1991; Silverman, Kulinna, & Crull, 1995) have repeatedly shown that successful skill practice is directly related to improved outcomes. Silverman (1985) concluded that the number of practice trials students got and the difficulty level of those trials were most strongly related to learning, more so than the amount of time students were engaged in skill practice.

A group of faculty and students from Ohio State studied seven effective elementary physical education specialists for an entire school year (Siedentop, 1991). They found that the teaching practices of these seven looked remarkably similar to the active teacher–learning student characteristics described in Chapter 1. These seven teachers clearly intended that their students learn and made those intentions clear, particularly through the way they managed students and provided substantial amounts of ALT-PE for them. The average ALT-PE in their classes was more than 45 percent, about three times higher than the average shown in descriptive research (Eldar, Siedentop, & Jones, 1989). These teachers also spent a great deal of time developing gymnasium routines at the start of the school year and then used those routines to keep classes running smoothly and efficiently, another common strategy of effective classroom teachers (Fink & Siedentop, 1989). Student practice was always supervised carefully, and students were held accountable, mostly through informal mechanisms, for learning the skills and strategies they were being taught.

In summary, the research on effective physical education teaching confirms that the strategies that produce differentially higher learning outcomes in the classroom are those that do so in the gymnasium, too. It would be very useful to us all if this kind of research were to expand in the future, giving us more detail about how effective physical education teachers cope with the many problems that confront them daily in their work.

SUMMARY

1. RTPE is only a quarter-century old, but it has produced a substantial body of knowledge from descriptive, interventionist, and qualitative research.

2. Benefits from RTPE include a technical language, well-tested class management and discipline strategies, a large number of observation instruments, journals and research-based methods textbooks, and improved initial teacher preparation.

3. Students spend the largest amount of time waiting, with the next largest amount of time in managerial tasks, and the smallest amount of time engaged in content-related activity.

4. ALT-PE is typically low for less-skilled students and lower still for students with disabling conditions.

5. ALT-PE can be improved, and greater amounts of successful practice are related to improved outcome measures.

6. Students often get too few OTRs, and too low a percentage of those is either technically incorrect or unsuccessful.

7. Subject-matter knowledge and PCK have been associated with more effective teaching.

8. PCK can be improved through specific training and careful observation of students as they learn.

9. Many students become alienated by their physical education experiences, particularly less-skilled students and girls.

10. Evidence suggests that teachers too often do not watch out for and correct instances of students dominating, embarrassing, and marginalizing one another.

11. Evidence also suggests that prosocial behavior among students can be increased with specific attention and strategies by the teacher.

12. The gender-stereotyped roles attached to females are frequently reproduced and strengthened in physical education classes.

13. Teachers preparing to teach and in-service teachers can improve their practice. When they do, their students get more and better opportunities to learn.

14. RTPE shows a profile that is substantially at odds with the characteristics of effective teaching.

CHAPTER 3

The Ecology of Teaching and Learning in Physical Education

What, then, is the practical utility of an ecological approach to research on teaching? It would seem that the ecological model can best be viewed as an analytic framework for understanding how classrooms work. Such an understanding would appear to be especially useful to teachers for interpreting problems and generating solutions to meet the practical contingencies of specific classrooms.

—WALTER DOYLE (1979)

OVERALL CHAPTER OUTCOME

To explain to a group of fellow physical education teachers the dynamic interrelationships among the systems that form the ecology of a PE class

CHAPTER OBJECTIVES

- To explain teaching as work and the dual-directional influence between teachers and their students
- To distinguish among managerial, instructional, and student-social task systems
- To distinguish among stated, actual, and contingency-developed tasks
- To describe how accountability, ambiguity, clarity, and risk affect task accomplishments
- To delineate the role of negotiations in achieving a particular balance in a class ecology
- To explain how and why supervision and accountability drive task systems
- To describe results of ecological research in PE
- To show the role of content knowledge in a learning ecology

This book is about teaching skills. We are most interested in how effective teachers use their skills in response to the changing demands of class dynamics. Skills cannot be applied mechanically, without reference to the particular context of how a group of students (a class) and a particular activity (the subject matter) interact with other factors such as weather, equipment, time of day, how the class session fits in a unit, and where you are in a school year. This chapter provides a framework for understanding the dynamics of classes—what we refer to as the *ecological model*.

Two factors are fundamentally important to understanding the ecology of class life. These factors are among the most often misunderstood by laypersons who criticize teachers. First is the understanding that subject-matter work in school classes occurs in groups over long periods of time (Doyle, 1983). To understand teaching, one has to understand it as work. Although there are clear performance aspects to teaching and skills and strategies to be learned and perfected, it is a mistake to view teaching primarily from a performance perspective. Teachers meet many classes each day, every day of the week, for an entire school year. This is not like a sport, music, or drama performance, where there is lots of practice and then a performance. When one has to perform every class, every day, all year, it becomes work. Teachers and students have to live together peacefully for all those classes throughout the school year. The ecological model will help you understand the dynamics of that work setting.

The second mistake that laypersons make when they think about teaching is to assume that the direction of influence in classes is solely from teacher to student. We understand that teachers are meant to influence students, both in learning gains and in social growth. It is also clear, however, that, in the dynamics of class life over time, students exert strong influence on their teachers—and sometimes the influence of students is stronger than that of the teacher. The ecological model will help you understand the dynamic *dual-directional* influences among teachers and their students.

The purpose of this chapter is to provide an overall view of teaching physical education, a total framework in which the skills and strategies of effective teaching can be interpreted and understood. It is sometimes said that people "can't see the forest because of looking only at the trees." This chapter provides a view of the "forest," and the chapters that follow tend to focus on the many different kinds of "trees" that inhabit it.

This chapter is about the ecology of physical education. In its generic sense, *ecology* refers to the study of the habitat of living objects, the relationships between organisms and their environment. An ecology is typically made up of a number of systems that interact with each other so that a change in one system influences what happens in the other systems. Ecologies often exist in a delicate balance that can be upset when one or more of the systems is disrupted or altered. Just as the natural environment we live in can be understood as an ecological system, so too can teaching/learning in physical education.

The ecological framework described in this chapter developed from research on real teachers in real classrooms. The ecological model was originally described by Doyle (1979) and first applied to physical education by Tousignant and Siedentop (1983). Our understanding of the ecology of physical education has since been informed through a series of research studies at Ohio State University (Alexander, 1982; Jones, 1989; Kutame, 1997; Lund, 1990; Marks, 1988; Romar, 1995; Siedentop et al., 1994; Son, 1989; Tinning & Siedentop, 1985). The information in this chapter derives from the ecological model defined by Doyle and the study of that model in the context of physical education.

THE TASK SYSTEMS THAT COMPRISE
THE ECOLOGY OF PHYSICAL EDUCATION

Teaching/learning in physical education can be viewed as an ecology with three primary systems, each of which is developed around a series of tasks to be accomplished. These systems are the *managerial task system,* the *instructional task system,* and the *student-social system.* The interactive influence among these three systems forms the ecology of physical education.

A *task* is defined by a goal and a set of operations to achieve it. Tasks are communicated through "a set of implicit or explicit instructions about what a person is expected to do to cope successfully with a situation" (Doyle, 1981, p. 3). A *managerial task* relates to the organizational and behavioral aspects of physical education—all the non-subject-matter functions necessary for students and teachers to exist together over a period of time. For example, a single managerial task occurs when a teacher says, "Form into four groups for volleyball teams by counting off in fours." An *instructional task* relates to the subject-matter activity of physical education, the intended learnings students are to acquire by participating in the instructional activities. For example, a single instructional task occurs when a teacher says, "Work in pairs, 6 feet apart, and keep the volleyball in play by forearm passing to one another." The *student-social task system* is different in that it is typically arranged and directed by students rather than the teacher. Nonetheless, it is clear that students have a social agenda when they come to physical education, and that agenda can be interpreted as a task system. A *student-social task* relates to the intentions for social interaction that students seek in physical education. Examples of student-social tasks range from having fun with a friend during the appropriate completion of the instructional volleyball task just described to going completely off task with fellow students to engage in some behavior that is social in nature but viewed as disruptive by the teacher. Student-social tasks are not "announced" publicly and then pursued, as are the managerial and instructional tasks. These tasks are often communicated among students in clever, subtle, and often surreptitious ways. The pursuit of these tasks often interacts with the other task systems in ways that produce problems for the teacher.

Effective teachers find ways to blend the student-social system into the instructional system. This is typically accomplished through an exciting curriculum in which students have fun participating and through strategies such as small-group work (see Chapter 12), which require student interaction that is task related within a created social grouping.

A *task system* is a regularized pattern for accomplishing tasks. It is composed mostly of the tasks that tend to recur frequently within physical education. Thus, there is a managerial task system composed of all the many different managerial tasks that recur frequently, such as entering the gym, taking roll, transitioning, organizing for instruction, regrouping, getting equipment out and away, staying on task, obeying rules for behavior, and class closure. The instructional task system is composed of all the learning tasks that teachers ask students to engage in, such as taking part in drills, playing in games, doing fitness activities, writing tests, and taking part in activities designed for social or affective outcomes. The student-social system is much more difficult than the others to define because it is less predictable and less

Teacher states task
   Student responds (congruent or modified)
   Teacher supervises
     Teacher responds to student task-efforts
     Actual task develops

FIGURE 3.1   *A contingency-developed task
(Source: Adapted from Alexander,
1982)*

easily observed. It is composed of all the individual and group social intentions of the students in a class. In any class of 28 students, there might be a number of different social tasks being pursued by different individuals and groups. One group of students may find ways to socialize within the boundaries of the instructional task system. Another group, however, may find their fun in disrupting the instructional task system. This tends to make the student-social task system more variable than either the managerial or instructional task systems, and thus more difficult to analyze. Make no mistake, however. The student-social task system does operate and does affect what happens in the other two systems.

TASKS AND THEIR DEVELOPMENT

To understand the ecology of physical education, you must be able to see how tasks develop—how the actual task systems develop over time and interact with one another. Managerial and instructional tasks begin as *stated tasks* that the teacher usually describes verbally. However, the *actual* managerial and instructional tasks that students develop over time are primarily a result of how teachers respond to student task-efforts, rather than how the tasks were described originally. An "actual" managerial or instructional task tends to develop through the following sequence. The teacher states a task. Students respond to that task. Their responses may or may not be congruent with the task described by the teacher; that is, they may do the task as stated or modify it in some way. The teacher then supervises the students and, on occasion, responds to their task-efforts. It is this cycle of stated task–student response–teacher supervision–teacher response that eventually defines the actual task: what Alexander (1982) described as the *contingency developed task system*. The cycle that determines the actual task is shown graphically in Figure 3.1. The key variable in how tasks develop is the teacher's reaction to students' task-efforts. Teacher reaction is typically also a key variable in how the student socializing develops in class. Although student-social tasks do not begin with a task statement, the development pattern of socializing is often determined by how the teacher reacts to student efforts to engage in social interactions. The better and more completely teachers can organize and define tasks (managerial or instructional) and the better and more completely they can plan lessons and units that incorporate appropriate student socializing in fun ways through the subject matter, the less will the entire system be determined by teacher reactions.

Once you understand the cycle through which the actual tasks in a class get defined, a number of questions immediately arise. How clearly do teachers state tasks? How different are the actual tasks from those stated originally? How often and in what ways do students modify tasks? How often and how well do teachers supervise beginning task responses? How do teachers respond to modified tasks? How do students learn what is acceptable and unacceptable in any of the three task systems? These are exactly the questions we have asked in our research program. The answers to these questions form the basis for the remainder of this chapter.

IMPORTANT CONCEPTS
IN THE ECOLOGICAL FRAMEWORK

Four related concepts help to further our understanding of how tasks develop: accountability, clarity/ambiguity, risk, and task boundaries. *Accountability* refers to the practices teachers use to establish and maintain student responsibility for appropriate conduct, task involvement, and outcomes. In his original formulation of the ecological framework, Doyle recognized that accountability drove the instructional task system. Without accountability, he found, task systems become very loose and sometimes are even suspended. "Moreover, if accountability is not present; i.e., if answers are not required or if any answer is acceptable, then the task system itself is suspended" (Doyle, 1980, p. 103).

Accountability comes in many different forms. Among them are tests that students perform for grades, teacher feedback, teacher praise and reprimands, active teacher supervision, challenges and competitions, public recognition of performance, and keeping records of performance. Eventually, task systems are defined by what teachers hold students accountable for, both in the managerial and instructional systems. In the student-social system, teacher accountability is also a key variable. However, the accountability is typically only for keeping socializing within boundaries defined by the managerial and instructional systems. When socializing begins to threaten the stability of those boundaries, then teachers typically intervene to control and redirect it.

Clarity and *ambiguity* are related concepts that refer to the degree of explicitness and consistency in defining tasks. These concepts are relevant both in the original description of a task (the stated task) and in how the task eventually develops (the actual task). A fully explicit task defines the conditions students are to perform under, the performance expected, some standard by which to judge the performance, and the consequences for performance (Alexander, 1982). An example of an explicit managerial task would be "I want squad 4 to play squad 1 on court A and squad 2 to play squad 3 on court B. I want you to be in your six-person game formation to begin the game, with the odd-numbered team serving within 15 seconds after I blow my whistle." A task that is less than fully explicit becomes ambiguous; that is, there are gaps in information about performance expectations. Students may not know exactly what to do, under what conditions to do it, how well it needs to be done, or the consequences of doing it well or poorly.

Clarity and ambiguity also affect the cycle through which tasks develop. Here, however, the concepts refer to consistency of the teacher's responses to student task-efforts. If one kind of response is accepted by a teacher on one occasion but not on another, then the task becomes ambiguous, and student responses are likely to become more varied.

Risk refers to the interaction among the ambiguity of the task, its difficulty, and the degree of accountability applied to it. Ambiguous tasks always produce risk for students until it becomes clear to them that the tasks are either not difficult or are tasks they will not be held accountable for. A difficult task with strong accountability results in a high degree of risk for the student. Easy tasks and loose or weak accountability measures result in less risk for the students. Risk and ambiguity are related, especially when accountability is strong. If a task is ambiguous, it becomes very risky for the student, who will not know what the performance expectations are for completing the task. Effective teachers find ways to organize their content and present it to students as a series of exciting, unambiguous challenges that are reasonably free of risk.

Task boundaries refer to how tightly or loosely accountability is applied to task completion and how clear and unambiguous are the requirements for task compliance and completion. Task systems can have narrow and consistent boundaries. This typically occurs when tasks are explicit and accountability is strong and consistent. Task systems can also have very loose boundaries, which occurs when tasks are ambiguous and accountability is loose, inconsistent, or both. Again, however, accountability drives the task systems. Weak or inconsistent accountability tends to eliminate risk and makes ambiguity irrelevant; that is, when students know that they will not be held accountable, then trying to cope with an ambiguous task is less of a problem and provides little risk.

The student-social system is seldom as well defined as the managerial and instructional task systems, thus making it more ambiguous and often riskier. Still, students often persist in trying to see what the boundaries of the student-social system might be in any given class. Chapter 9 presents a series of curricular models that tend to accommodate the student-social system within the pursuit of learning goals—models such as Adventure Education and Sport Education, which engage students in meaningful tasks, require student cooperation in the achievement of those tasks, and create a social system within the context of the activities.

NEGOTIATION WITHIN TASK SYSTEMS

Students learn about the boundaries of task systems in several ways. Some teachers explain the boundaries very carefully and hold students accountable quickly and consistently. These accountability strategies can focus on compliance or cooperation (see Box 4.1). Other teachers explain boundaries clearly, but their students learn gradually that the *actual* boundaries are different than those explained; that is, the actual boundaries develop contingently through the process described earlier for task development. Still other teachers simply do not explain boundaries clearly and leave students to learn through daily experience what they have to do to stay within the boundaries and what behaviors are considered to be crossing the boundaries and thus unacceptable. Students also bring their own social agendas with them when they come to physical education. Thus, they must learn what kinds of student-social interactions are allowable and under what conditions.

One of Doyle's initial findings was that students attempt to negotiate tasks to fix the "ecological balance" of the task systems at a level they can handle and enjoy. *Negotiation* can be defined as any attempt by students to change tasks, to change the conditions under which tasks are performed, or to change the performance standards by which task completion is judged. How teachers respond to student attempts to negotiate the demands of task systems tends to be the primary factor in determining the ecological balance among the three task systems—management, instruction, and student-social—within a class.

In classrooms, negotiation tends to be verbal, particularly within the instructional task system. A teacher assigns an instructional task, and students attempt to reduce its ambiguity and risk by verbally negotiating with the teacher. How long does the theme have to be? Can it be on this topic rather than the one you assigned? Can it be turned in Tuesday instead of Monday? How much will this count toward our grade? Will you take off for spelling errors? Does it have to be typed? All of these questions serve to negotiate the demands of this particular task. How the teacher responds to the questions, and later to the themes that are turned in, will determine the actual task.

In physical education, students negotiate task demands by modifying the task during practice rather than by asking questions. When a teacher describes an instructional task, the students go about doing the task, but often they modify it so that it is somewhat different than the one the teacher described. They can modify the task upward to make it more challenging than the task described by the teacher, or they can modify it downward to make it easier to do successfully. When the teacher supervises this practice and responds to the modified tasks, the actual nature of the task gets defined by what the teacher accepts. Over time, students learn how much they can modify an assigned task and still stay within the boundaries of the instructional task system.

For example, a teacher asks her students to organize in pairs with partners 8 feet apart. The task is to forearm pass the volleyball back and forth between partners so that the ball goes over head height with each pass, but not more than 3–4 feet over the head. Some of the students in class are on the school volleyball team. For them, this is an easy task, so they modify it by moving farther apart and passing the ball higher. For others, the task is too difficult, so they move a bit closer together and don't pay much attention to the height of the pass. A few other students use sets instead of forearm passes when the ball comes to them at or above shoulder level. The teacher is now supervising this practice. How she responds to each of these modifications will determine the *actual* task in this case, and it will also provide students with knowledge about the degree to which they can modify assigned tasks and still stay within the boundaries of the instructional task system (e.g., they will know how much they can change the assigned task without being considered off task).

Students often negotiate in their social task system by trying to pair up with friends or get certain students together on a team. These negotiations are often hidden as instructional negotiations, but they have a clear social emphasis and purpose.

NEGOTIATION BETWEEN TASK SYSTEMS

Negotiations also occur among the three task systems that form the ecology of the gymnasium. For most teachers, the initial and fundamental goal of teaching a class is to gain and maintain student cooperation (Doyle, 1981). Teachers are responsible for many classes each day. Administrators expect them to have control of their classes. For these reasons, it is understandable and should be expected that a teacher's primary concern is to establish and maintain an orderly class in which students cooperate with good behavior rather than disrupt constantly. Research also has revealed that teachers tend to establish the boundaries of the managerial system first, often in the first few days of the school year (Brophy & Good, 1986).

The issue here is clear. It is understandable that the managerial task system is established quickly and that students need to cooperate with the demands of that system to produce a peaceful class throughout the school year. How do teachers negotiate with students to produce consistent compliance with the demands of the managerial task system? Remember, teachers also have an instructional task system to develop, and students have their own social agendas they want to attend to during class. Clearly, several kinds of negotiations might occur among these three systems that form the ecology of the class. Teachers might reduce the demands of the instructional system to gain cooperation with the managerial system. Teachers might allow for certain kinds of student social interaction to gain the necessary cooperation. In some cases, for some students, teachers might simply suspend the instructional task system and allow those students to engage in nondisruptive socializing rather than instructional tasks, as long as they cooperate with the demands of the managerial task system. Each of these negotiations produces a different ecology. Each has been identified in research studies. The degree to which teachers need to negotiate with their students to produce the necessary cooperation is determined by the difficulty of the context in which the teaching takes place, the intentions and expectations the teacher has for learning and achievement, and the degree to which the teacher possesses effective teaching skills.

The way that the managerial, instructional, and student-social task systems interact and influence one another determines the ecology of the gymnasium.

The sensitive, effective teacher will understand how these systems interact and work to develop an ecology that students not only cooperate and behave well within, but one that is also learning oriented and accommodates student-social needs. To develop and maintain this kind of ecology in a typical class in today's schools is not easy. It requires that teachers have strong intentions to build this kind of educational environment and the managerial and instructional skills to make it happen.

An imaginative curriculum with authentic outcomes is the best way to engage students in a learning-focused ecology, but one that is lots of fun for students. When students have lots of fun *within* the class activities, part of which involves social interactions with classmates, there is no need to develop and sustain a student-social system *outside* the instructional system.

SUPERVISION AND ACCOUNTABILITY

Early in his studies of classroom ecologies, Doyle (1979) indicated that accountability drives task systems. Without accountability, the task system is suspended, and what happens is attributable solely to student interests and enthusiasms. This is most true for the instructional task system.

All the evidence suggests that accountability is as powerful a force in the ecology of physical education as it is in the classroom. However, the ecologies of the classroom and the gymnasium operate differently. In the classroom, what Doyle (1979) called the "performance-grade exchange system" tends to be the primary accountability mechanism. Students in classrooms often are required to perform for grades—quizzes, homework, themes, and so forth. The classroom is smaller than the gymnasium or playing field, and the placement of students within the classroom makes supervising their work easier, whether they are working in a whole-group format or independently at their seats. Negotiations in the classroom are often verbal, with students asking teachers questions or making requests that tend to reduce the risk and ambiguity associated with an assignment.

In physical education classes, it is less common to have students perform for grades in specific assignments on a regular basis. Many physical education teachers test for skill and knowledge at the end of units, but seldom involve students in performance-grade exchange assignments on a daily basis throughout a unit. Gymnasia and playing fields are often quite large, and students move about them in ways that make supervision difficult. Negotiations in physical education more often occur through students' modifying tasks than asking questions or making requests, which makes negotiations difficult for the teacher to see and respond to. Thus, as regards supervision and accountability, the physical education setting is considerably more complex and difficult than the classroom.

Supervision and accountability may be the two most important teaching skills in the repertoire of the effective physical educator. *Supervision* refers to the practices teachers use to establish and maintain student responsibility for appropriate conduct, task involvement, and outcomes. Teachers use many different forms of accountability—public recognition, verbal interaction, keeping records, challenges, and performance-grade exchanges. They must also actively supervise students to ensure that these accountability mechanisms work. The most important aspect of supervision is monitoring student work. *Monitoring* means to "watch, observe, or check, especially for a special purpose" (Webster's *New Collegiate Dictionary*, 1979, p. 737). The special purpose in this case would be for the teacher to see if student performance was congruent with the tasks described and assigned in the managerial and instructional task systems.

Here is a typical example. Joe is teaching basketball to ninth graders. He is focusing on the two-person "pick and roll" strategy that is fundamental to many different basketball offenses. He has the class together as a whole. He describes and demonstrates the main technical points of the pick and roll with the help of several students. The explanation is clear and to the point. The demonstrations are well set up. Joe has the demonstrators show both the correct technical aspects of the pick and roll and the most common errors. Joe then has the students "walk through" the strategy so that he can be sure they all understand the critical elements—what we later refer to as "guided practice." He provides feedback and answers student questions.

Joe then describes clearly how he wants the pick and roll practiced at the several basket areas in the gym. He uses four students to demonstrate how the practice drill should be done, what to emphasize, and what to avoid. Again, he provides feedback and answers questions. He then disperses the students to the basket areas and signals the beginning of the drill—what we later refer to as "independent practice." Up to now, what has been described appears to be a terrific lesson. But here, at the critical point where students will *practice* the pick and roll, the crucial teaching skills of supervision and accountability are lacking. As students begin practicing independently, Joe makes some notes on a clipboard. He then stays at one end of the gym and watches one of the groups, but makes no comments. He sits down to chat with a student who has been ill and did not bring gym clothes for today's lesson. Eight minutes have passed since he dispersed the students. One of the groups has been playing a two-versus-two game with no effort to practice the pick and roll in the drill described. Another group is performing the drill incorrectly. A third group is practicing the drill appropriately, but making critical errors in technique each time they do it. Another group, at the far end of the gym, did the drill for a few minutes, but has now started a shooting game.

How would you describe the ecology of this class? Joe knows basketball. He demonstrates and explains well. The drill he designed appeared to be a good drill, appropriate to the skill level of the class. At 8 minutes into the practice phase, however, almost nothing is happening that one would consider to be good in terms of the assigned practice task. At this rate, few of the students will learn to be good at the pick and roll maneuver. However, none of the students is being disruptive. All of them are physically involved in something related to basketball, even though a very small percentage is actually doing the assigned practice task, and an even smaller percentage is doing it successfully. In some parts of the gymnasium, the student-social system appears to have taken over completely, even though it is "masked" by active involvement in basketball. Joe obviously does not supervise actively. He does not monitor student performance. There appears to be no accountability for performance except what comes with his direct physical presence near a practice group.

The instructional task system in Joe's class has been almost completely suspended. Students apparently understand that they will not be supervised carefully. There is little evidence of accountability for performance. Students are not disruptive, so one might assume that there is accountability in the managerial task system. Some students have modified tasks to have more fun, thus accommodating their social agenda within a modified instructional task rather than going off task. All the students are physically active, so one might assume that Joe holds them accountable if they are not physically involved in some task related to the activity. A visitor who walked into this gym would see active students who seem to be enjoying themselves. The groups at the various baskets are all doing something somewhat different, but nonetheless doing some kind of basketball. There would be no signs of disruptive behavior. What would the visitor conclude about this class and this teacher? Looking at the same class from the ecological perspective, what would you conclude?

Issues of supervision and accountability appear to be related mainly to teaching skills, but, in fact, are also strongly related to curriculum. "Content-embedded accountability" can be a very important factor leading to a learning-focused ecology. When teams are competing in a round-robin league format over an extended period of time, all working to finish as high in the standings as they can, there is accountability *embedded* in the content. When small groups are planning a half-day bicycle field trip and then actually taking the trip to reach a destination successfully, there is accountability embedded in the content. When a health-fitness class has established collective goals to achieve by the end of a semester, there are regular weekly progress checks toward those goals, and some rewards and celebrations are planned when and if they are achieved, there is accountability embedded in the content. The more accountability that is naturally embedded in how content is organized and presented and how students are organized to pursue the content goals, the less teachers will need to supervise for cooperation, and the less they will have to be the major accountability mechanism in the system.

SOME RESULTS FROM TASK SYSTEM RESEARCH IN PHYSICAL EDUCATION

If you look carefully at the quote that introduces this chapter, you will see that the primary usefulness of the ecological model is that it provides a framework within which teachers can interpret what goes on in their classes and generate solutions to problems that arise. It helps teachers to be able to understand the ongoing events in their classes within a framework that takes into account the two-way influence between them and their students. The major purpose of this chapter so far has been to explain an ecological framework through which physical education teachers can interpret the managerial, instructional, and social dimensions of their classes.

What follows are some results from research in school physical education that has utilized the ecological framework (Alexander, 1982; Fink & Siedentop, 1989; Jones, 1989; Kutame, 1997; Lund, 1990; Marks, 1988; Romar, 1995; Siedentop et al., 1994; Son, 1989; Tousignant & Siedentop, 1983). Remember, the results described represent a summary of research studies done in schools. Although what is described is typical of the results of those studies, there is no doubt variation from teacher to teacher, and we do not intend to suggest that these results are typical of all physical education teachers.

1. The managerial task system tends to be more explicitly described and more carefully supervised than the instructional task system. Accountability for compliance in the managerial system is more quickly and consistently applied; thus, its boundaries are more narrow and consistent than those of the instructional system.

2. Actual instructional tasks tend to develop contingently and often differ from stated tasks. Students modify tasks to make them more or less difficult or to make them more fun. How teachers react to these modified tasks sets the boundaries of the instructional task system, which is typically less consistent and broader than the managerial system.

3. Teacher supervision is prerequisite to reacting to student task-responses. When teachers do not supervise actively and monitor student task-responses, the instructional task system becomes very loose, allowing students to modify the tasks at will and, on occasion, to cease engaging in them completely.

4. Instructional tasks are seldom described in fully explicit terms. The conditions tasks are to be practiced under are often not described fully, nor are the criteria for judging their completion. Students learn these aspects of the task, if they learn them at all, through the way the teacher reacts to their responses.

5. Some students don't pay much attention to teacher descriptions of instructional tasks. They learn what is required by asking fellow students during the transition from instruction to practice or by watching students begin the practice task. Students learn quickly how much or how little attention they have to pay to task descriptions.

6. Managerial tasks are typically a set of routines. They become established structures and require less teacher attention, especially in the classes of effective teachers. Students are held accountable for compliance with these routines. Rules are typically made clear and enforced. Teachers who need to interact frequently to keep students well behaved

are typically less effective managers because they have failed to establish a routine managerial task system.

7. In a well-supervised instructional task system, students will modify tasks to make them either more challenging (modify them up) or easier (modify them down). Teachers tend to set the limits to these modifications through their reactions to student task-responses. Some teachers sanction these modifications in the way they initially describe tasks to students.

8. In a poorly supervised instructional task system, students modify tasks both for the previous reasons and also to engage in social interactions with their peers.

9. Cooperation with the demands of the managerial task system appears to be the most important and most immediate goal of the teacher (just as in classrooms). Teachers sometimes appear to accomplish this goal by trading cooperation within the managerial system for demands in the instructional system; for example, if students attend class, wear the appropriate uniform, and behave well, they can earn a high grade in the class. Thus, the first goal of the teacher—and sometimes the only goal—is for the student to be what Tousignant (1981) called a "member in good standing" of the class.

10. Other teachers require that students be both members in good standing and make a visible effort to engage in the assigned instructional tasks. Accountability in this kind of system is directed at effort, so students who are perceived to be consistently engaged in tasks get high grades, no matter how well or poorly they perform.

11. In fewer instances, we have seen accountability systems that require some skill or knowledge performance to earn high grades, but these occur less frequently than do the systems described in points 9 and 10.

12. On a few occasions, we have seen teachers describe an accountability system that involves performance, but, in fact, students have only to be a member in good standing and make a consistent effort to earn the highest grade. We have called these systems examples of "pseudo-accountability."

13. Some clever students hide within the instructional task system. Those students who appear to take part in the instructional tasks but actually avoid most involvement have been called "competent bystanders" (see Box 3.1). Some students engage in the instructional system appropriately for a while and then shift their engagement so that it is more social even though it appears to be on task (see Box 3.2).

14. Instructional task systems that seem to be highly on task and intended to produce skill outcomes are characterized by consistent accountability measures, although few of these can be characterized as performance-grade exchanges. Effective teachers hold students accountable through

---

BOX 3.1   The Competent Bystander

In her analysis of task systems in middle and high school physical education, Tousignant (1981) observed student strategies for hiding nonparticipation in the instructional task system, but doing so in such a clever way that the teacher did not notice. She called students who used these strategies *competent bystanders*.

The competent bystander always behaves well in terms of the managerial task system. This is what teachers would call a well-behaved student. Yet the same student cleverly avoids participation in the instructional task system and does so in such a way that the teacher does not notice. The competent bystander is always in line, moving from fourth to third to second place, but then reinserting himself so that he avoids being first and having to take a turn. In game play, the competent bystander attaches herself to a good player, knowing that the good player will perform the necessary action when the ball comes in their sector. Or in basketball, for example, the competent bystander cruises up and down the floor, but manages to stay away from all the action involving the ball.

Remember, this is a *competent* bystander. The teacher, when asked about this student's skill involvement, typically responds that the student is fairly well skilled and actively involved. By always being within the boundaries of the managerial task system, the student is seen to be "good."

When you next observe a physical education lesson in a school, try to see if there are any competent bystanders in the class.

---

challenges, public performance, frequent task-related feedback, frequent prompting for on-task behavior, and recording performances. Elementary physical education teachers also use many informal accountability mechanisms, such as point systems, posters, and challenge systems.

15. Most physical education classes appear to be highly social. The differences among them seem to lie in whether the student socialization takes place in ways that disrupt or suspend the instructional task system or whether teachers find ways for students to socialize while still taking part appropriately in the instructional task system.

16. Management systems in which students participate in developing rules, routines, and consequences (sometimes in the form of a class contract) typically achieve a student buy-in that helps to achieve the goals of the managerial system and engages students as helpers in sustaining the system.

17. Some curricular models, such as Sport Education, have strong content-embedded accountability that engages students and results in highly task oriented behavior that is, at the same time, a strong social system. Teachers who have used this model, and others such as Adventure Education, notice quickly that they no longer have to act primarily as a traf-

---

BOX 3.2   Hiding Social Engagement Within Instructional Tasks

In a recent study of task systems in Korean high school physical education, Son (1989) found a particularly interesting kind of engagement pattern in some highly skilled students. A teacher would describe an instructional task. The highly skilled student would very successfully perform the task exactly as described. The student would proceed to do four to six repetitions of the task. Then, however, a curious change would occur. The highly skilled student would modify the task to make it easier and then engage in it, but in an unsuccessful manner. What could explain this task modification and unsuccessful engagement with a highly skilled student?

   Clearly, the student knew that he could do the task and, indeed, did it successfully several times. Then it was time to do a little socializing, but to do so in a way that was hidden within the instructional task system. This was accomplished by modifying the task to make it easier and then to engage in that task, but with little thought to success. Instead, the student's attention was diverted from task success to socializing with a fellow student. If the teacher saw the students, he would see task engagement, albeit it on a slightly modified task and without high success. Although this might result in some feedback from the teacher, it would no doubt be related to the instructional task performance rather than to the socializing. Typically, however, because the students are on task, the teacher would not intervene, and the students would have successfully hidden their pursuit of their own social goals within the instructional task system.

---

fic director or cop and, instead, are more likely to interact with students about the activities and how to get better at doing them.

THE ROLE OF CONTENT KNOWLEDGE IN A LEARNING ECOLOGY

One factor contributing to the success of an instructional system is the teacher's knowledge of the content being learned by students. Knowing a lot about a particular content—gymnastics or basketball, for example—doesn't in any way guarantee an effective learning ecology, but it is hard to imagine how students can learn much about some activity that their teacher doesn't know much about. In one study (Romar, 1995), the teacher's primary goal for a middle school basketball unit was for the students to participate in a well-played game. This goal, which we think is very appropriate, stresses tactical knowledge and student abilities to execute offensive and defensive strategies under game conditions. The analysis of instructional tasks for the unit, however, revealed that all the practice tasks had a skill focus and none had a tactical focus. At the end of the unit, the games were sloppy, were dominated by better players, and showed few signs of offensive or defensive strategies. The teacher was disappointed!

When teachers know about the content they are teaching and have a strong commitment to its value, the likelihood of a learning-focused ecology increases. Of course, teachers still have to be effective managers. They still have to develop and maintain the cooperation of students in the learning endeavors. They still have skills to plan and implement effective lessons and units in that content. If teachers do all this, however, *and* have both strong knowledge in and a strong commitment to the value of the content, the chances for an effective learning ecology are multiplied.

TOWARD A LEARNING-FOCUSED ECOLOGY

Teachers and students need to cooperate to make daily life in physical education pleasant for all concerned. Students come to physical education expecting to have fun and to have it be a social experience. This suggests that you must understand the dynamics of the managerial and student-social systems and how they interact with the instructional system to form a class ecology. Physical education cannot become a valued school subject if the main goals of teachers are for students to behave well and have fun—there have to be important learning gains as well. The managerial system should serve primarily to establish and sustain cooperation in ways that save time that you can then devote to the instructional system. The chapters on curriculum and instruction will help you understand the dynamic interaction between how you conceptualize and plan to deliver content and how you actually implement those plans during classes. The ecological model provides you with a framework both to predict what might happen in classes and to interpret events when they do occur, all of which will help you understand what it means to be an effective teacher.

SUMMARY

1. Teaching needs to be understood as work in which there is a two-way influence between teachers and students.
2. An ecology is an interrelated set of systems in which changes in one system affect the other systems.
3. The managerial, instructional, and student-oriented systems comprise the ecology of PE.
4. Tasks begin as stated tasks, but the tasks students actually perform are typically contingency developed.
5. Accountability refers to practices teachers use to establish and maintain student responsibility for appropriate conduct, task involvement, and outcomes.

6. Clarity, risk, and ambiguity of tasks interact to affect the degree to which students negotiate or avoid task involvement.

7. Task boundaries can be tight or loose, depending on task clarity and accountability.

8. Students in PE typically negotiate tasks by modifying them and seeing how teachers respond to the modifications.

9. Some teachers trade lowered demands in the instructional system for compliance with the managerial system. The first goal of teachers is to gain and maintain the cooperation of students.

10. Supervision and accountability drive task systems.

11. Research has revealed many features of PE ecologies, including information about task explicitness, contingency-developed systems, task routinization, patterns of involvement, tactics of noninvolvement, accountability formats, and curricular attractiveness.

12. Teachers with strong content knowledge and a commitment to the value of that content tend to produce more learning-focused ecologies.

PART TWO

Developing Cooperation and Community Among Learners

Most women and men who enter the teaching profession do so because they enjoy teaching and want to help children or youth learn and grow. Most want to learn about teaching skills and strategies to apply them. Most teachers who fail do so because they lack class management skills, which makes it difficult for them to build and maintain a productive learning environment. They tend to have too many discipline problems. In some cases, in order to gain student cooperation, they reduce demands in their instructional system; that is, they make "treaties" that prevent them from sustaining a productive learning environment. If you believe that you simply have to teach well and then all the management and discipline problems will take care of themselves, you are simply wrong!

The chapters in Part Two describe the relationships among class management, discipline, and instruction. They also identify skills and strategies you can use to develop a cooperative class and to eventually work toward building a learning community in which students are fully invested in achieving the learning goals of the class. You will learn about the importance of preventive strategies and how these, combined with clear and consistent discipline strategies, can form the foundation from which you can work toward developing a community of learners, including learners with disabling conditions who are included in your classes.

59

CHAPTER 4

Preventive Class Management

Effective classroom management is the key to student success in the classroom. According to both research and practice, the inability to establish an orderly learning environment through effective classroom management clearly contributes to misbehavior and disruptions.

—H. JEROME FREIBERG (1996)

OVERALL CHAPTER OUTCOME

To observe a physical education class and accurately assess the degree to which a preventive management system is in place and how effective it is

CHAPTER OBJECTIVES

- To explain the nature and purpose of preventive class management
- To show why a preventive management system is important
- To differentiate among systems that are based on compliance, cooperation, and community
- To enunciate myths about teaching
- To characterize the nature and role of rules and routines
- To describe the important routines and how they develop
- To illustrate options for kinds of rules and how they develop
- To explain managerial time and how it can be reduced
- To describe the skills and strategies important to a preventive class management system
- To clarify how the effectiveness of a managerial system can be assessed

Effective class management in physical education doesn't just happen. Classes that run smoothly, are free from disruptive behavior, and optimize the amount of time for instruction and practice are the result of teachers who understand class management and have the skills to develop and sustain a successful managerial task system. Research over the past 30 years has shown conclusively that effective teachers are, first of all, good class managers. Being a good class manager doesn't make you an effective teacher, but it will provide the opportunity for you to be effective if you have the teaching skills and motivation to put them to use consistently. Effective class management, therefore, is a *necessary* precondition for effective teaching and learning.

There is an old adage that "an ounce of prevention is worth a pound of cure." Nowhere is this truer than in the manner in which teachers manage classes. As the lead quote to this chapter indicates, many of the discipline problems that teachers encounter occur because of poor management; that is, in poorly managed classes, students are likely to become disruptive. As Chapter 3 showed, an effective managerial system is necessary to produce the time for students to learn and practice. Inadequate or unskilled class management, therefore, has two negative outcomes. First, it tends to increase discipline problems, and, second, it reduces time that can be used for learning and practice.

Preventive class management refers to the proactive (rather than reactive) strategies teachers use to develop and maintain a positive, predictable, task-oriented class climate in which minimal time is devoted to managerial tasks and optimal time is therefore available for instructional tasks. Routines for accomplishing managerial tasks are taught, and students are given sufficient opportunities to practice them. Appropriate ways of behaving during managerial and instructional tasks are also part of the instruction and practice. Students are encouraged to perform managerial tasks well and to behave appropriately, and their efforts to do so are recognized and rewarded. When you visit a class taught by an effective class manager, you see the managerial tasks done smoothly, quickly, and with little attention from the teacher. Unless you were there at the outset of the year or semester, however, you wouldn't have seen how the teacher taught the organizational and behavioral skills necessary for the system to run so smoothly.

The *managerial task system* establishes the structures through which physical education class becomes a predictable, smoothly operating system. The managerial task system establishes the limits for behavior and the positive expectations for students; students know what the managerial tasks are and how and when to perform them. As you will see throughout this chapter and the next two chapters, teachers can decide what the specific elements of the managerial system will be and teach the system directly to students, or they can work with the students to develop the system jointly (see Box 4.1).

Teachers and students work together for long periods of time. The elementary physical education specialist might have six to eight classes per day, and not only do these classes meet for the entire year, but in many schools, the teacher will have many of the same children for several years. The middle school or secondary school teacher might have five to six classes a day, at least for one semester and often for a full school year. It is important to both the teacher and students that their "life together" be reasonably peaceful and cooperative. No teacher can withstand a "state of war" with students on a daily basis throughout the school year. A level of cooperation that allows both teacher and students to function effectively and without high levels of tension or anxiety must be achieved.

The best preventive class management systems are developed as "social contracts" between teachers and their students. When students are actively brought into the development of the system and understand why the rules, procedures, and routines are important for their class experiences to be successful, they tend to develop an ownership of the system—they buy in to the system and what it is meant to accomplish. Time spent with students establishing rules and procedures and consequences for breaking rules is time well spent. Teachers should view this as an important learning experience for their students, one in which the student voice is heard and respected. The development of a social contract between teachers and their students is fundamental

---

BOX 4.1   The Three C's: Compliance, Cooperation, and Community

Effective class management and discipline can be achieved in three ways. First, teachers can organize rules and consequences so that students *comply* with the managerial system and behavior rules. Thus, teachers who are sufficiently skilled can establish an effective management system and bring students into compliance with the demands of the system. Second, teachers can solicit the *cooperation* of students by (a) making them understand how the managerial system benefits them and (b) bringing them into the decision-making process about how the system is developed and maintained. Third, teachers can attempt to build a learning *community*, a shared decision-making community that enables teachers and students to develop and sustain relationships in which self-discipline, responsibility, helping others, and the larger good of the group are emphasized.

There may be some students and some classes for which compliance is the best a teacher can achieve. There may be some students and some classes for which cooperation is the best a teacher can achieve, and there may be some teachers who think cooperation is the most appropriate goal to work toward. Other teachers may work with students over an extended period of time and want to try to develop a learning community. The point here is not to suggest that learning communities can always be achieved given the conditions and time constraints under which many PE teachers work. The point is for you to recognize the differences among the three approaches and to understand the various strategies necessary to achieve them. Part Two should enable you to gain that understanding.

---

to what we later describe as learning communities and a caring pedagogy (see Chapter 6).

An effective management system is also important because it is necessary to create the time teachers and their students can devote to learning. For teachers for whom student learning is important, time is the most precious commodity. Time spent managing students and responding to disruptive behavior takes away from time for instruction and practice. Teaching is fun! Watching students improve through practice is satisfying. Constantly having to manage groups of students and discipline misbehaving students is neither fun nor satisfying.

MYTHS AND TRUTHS ABOUT MANAGEMENT AND TEACHING

The first myth is that good management and discipline are inherent in good teaching; that is, if you teach well, you will have no management or discipline problems. Choose a good activity and teach it well, as this myth goes, and your students will be well managed and behaved. This is at best simplistic and at worst simply wrong. The truth is that the foundation for good teaching is effective management and discipline. Being a skilled manager doesn't automatically make you a good teacher, but it creates the time and opportunity for you to be a good teacher. The skills and strategies to become an effective class manager are well known and can be learned and perfected by any teacher who understands their importance.

The second myth is that students will come to physical education with the necessary behaviors to be cooperative learners. There are two reasons why assuming this to be true is dangerous for teachers. Some teachers have traditionally relied on parents to raise their children in such a way that the children come to school with certain behaviors well developed and other behavioral predispositions pretty much in place. Teachers assume that children have learned to pay attention, to respond to instructions, to respect an adult authority figure, and to try to learn in school classes. Teachers assume youths will respect each other, will not be openly hostile toward teachers, and will make some effort to learn. In some schools, for some children and youths, these assumptions may still hold, but in many schools and for many children and youths, they do not. The truth is that many elementary teachers spend far more time than they want helping children learn basic behaviors to be successful in school. The truth is that many middle and secondary school teachers spend far more time than they want managing and disciplining unruly, sometimes hostile, youths. This is one reason class management and discipline skills have been at or near the top of teacher concerns for several decades.

The third myth is that, because children and youth typically enjoy physical activity, they will be enthusiastic about learning in physical education. The fact is that many students come to physical education anxious about being there or determined to do as little as possible. Let's face it: Some students hate PE! The saddest comment we can make about our profession is that some students have *learned* to hate PE by *being in poorly managed and poorly taught PE classes.* You should assume that the motivations students bring with them to your classes are very different, running the gamut from those who want to avoid PE as much as they can to those who love it and want as much of it as they can get. Your task is to make PE work for both of these kinds of students and for all those in between the extremes. Effective class management is foundational to effective teaching no matter what instructional approach is taken. This is true for direct, teacher-controlled instruction, and it is true for wholly learner-centered and learner-controlled instruction. It is true in a classroom in which students are organized in neat rows of desks, and it is also true for the gymnasium and playing fields.

ROUTINES AND RULES: THE FOUNDATION OF THE MANAGERIAL TASK SYSTEM

An effective managerial task system begins with the development of routines and the establishment of class rules for appropriate behavior. *Routines* specify procedures for performing tasks within the class. Any task that is repeated frequently should be made into a routine. A set of routines provides the structure that allows classes to run smoothly, free of delays and disruptions. Routines also relieve the teacher of the need to be a constant "traffic director."

Rules identify appropriate and inappropriate behaviors and the situations within which certain behaviors are acceptable or unacceptable (e.g., talking to a classmate is often acceptable and even encouraged, but not when the teacher is trying to explain something to the class). Some rules identify a range of behaviors (e.g., be cooperative) that are situational and can have a range of meanings (e.g., being cooperative in helping put away equipment differs from cooperating with teammates in a game). Other rules are behavior specific (e.g., always have permission before using gymnastics apparatus). Both routines and rules need to be taught, and students need opportunities to practice them with clear, consistent feedback and clear, consistently applied consequences.

Evidence from the study of effective teachers shows that their major teaching focus in the first few days of a school year (or a new semester with new students) is the establishment of class routines and rules (Brophy & Good, 1986; Fink & Siedentop, 1989; Siedentop et al., 1994). Elementary physical education specialists typically teach routines and rules along with content, creating activities that emphasize certain organizational and behavioral situations that allow them to teach the routines or rules, allow students ample opportunity to practice the routines or the behavior specified by the rules, which also provides teachers frequent opportunity to provide feedback, correct errors, and reinforce children who perform the routines well and those who behave in ways specified by the rules. Middle and secondary school teachers typically specify the rules and explain them, along with the consequences of breaking the rules. Often these class rules and procedures are passed out to students as part of class materials, and, in some cases, students are asked to take them home and have their parents sign them as an indication that students and parents understand the procedures, rules, and consequences of violations. In the first days of the first unit, the teacher explains each new class routine when it first is appropriate to use (see Box 4.2).

ROUTINES AND THEIR DEVELOPMENT

Routines should be taught for all procedural aspects of lessons that recur frequently, such as what students should do when they enter the gymnasium and when the teacher gives a signal for attention or the appropriate way to get out and put away equipment. Routines that are used commonly in physical education are shown in Table 4.1.

Routines need to be taught as specifically as one might teach how to dribble or pass. This means explanations, demonstrations, student practice with feedback, and all other elements related to learning are used for teaching routines in much the same way they are for teaching sport skills. For example, most elementary PE specialists specify an attention/quiet routine because they

---

BOX 4.2 Getting Started on the Right Foot

Research has indicated clearly that teachers who spend time in the early part of the school year—the first several weeks—teaching specific classroom and gymnasium routines not only have an easier time managing and disciplining throughout the school year, but also have students who learn more. Teachers who take time to specifically teach routines such as how to contact the teacher, use equipment, and move around the available space have fewer problems. Gymnasium routines become part of the content that is taught, which has a high payoff.

Hayman and Moskowitz (1975) found that what junior high school teachers did on the very first day went a long way toward determining their overall effectiveness for the year. Before patterns of inappropriate behavior can develop, the teachers taught specific patterns of appropriate behavior—laid down the ground rules for getting along together in the class. According to Emmer and Evertson (1981, p. 342), "All classroom management systems, good, poor, or in-between, have a beginning. The way in which teachers structure the first part of the year has consequences for their classroom management throughout the year."

---

frequently have to stop class activity to provide instructions or feedback or to change the activity. This routine involves a specific teacher signal for gaining the attention of students (a whistle, hand clap, the word "freeze") and the students quieting quickly and facing the teacher. Teachers frequently choose for the first few lessons of the school year activities that allow for many stops and starts, just so they can teach these routines. The seven teachers in the Fink and Siedentop (1989) study used this routine 346 times in the first several days of teaching first and fifth grade classes. Many teachers at all levels teach an entry routine, that is, what students are expected to do when they enter the teaching space. Some teachers teach a fitness-related warm-up for this routine; others teach a series of stretching activities specific to the physical activity focus of the unit; still others teach a skill warm-up, taking a skill or combination of skills that are fundamental to the unit being studied so that students begin to practice these skills immediately upon entering the teaching space.

The keys to teaching routines successfully are no different from the keys for teaching sport skills or strategies. The following teaching strategies will prove helpful:

- *Explain and show.* Explain the procedure in language that is age specific, and show students what it looks like.

- *Show nonexamples.* Show students the wrong way to do something at the same time you are showing the right way.

- *Rehearse.* Provide opportunity to practice the procedure. Have a goal for each rehearsal and give immediate feedback (for example, "On the 'go' signal, you have 15 seconds to organize into partners and find a free space in the gym—go!").

TABLE 4.1   Routines Typically Used in Physical Education

Routine	Purpose
Entry	What to do when entering the gym, often includes an initial practice activity or warm-up and a specific space to go to
Attention/quiet	A teacher signal for attention and the expected student response
Home base	A specific place (spot, number, team home) for a student or group of students to go to when instructed
Gather	A way to move from a dispersed situation to a central location and how to organize at that central location (can be a place or wherever the teacher is)
Disperse	A way to move, on cue, from a gathered format to any dispersed format
Gain attention	The appropriate way for a student or group of students to gain the attention of the teacher
Retrieve	The appropriate procedure for retrieving a ball when it has invaded the space of classmates during a game or drill
Partners	A procedure for students who have been unsuccessful getting into an assigned format (also holds for triads, quads, etc.)
Finish	A procedure for ending a lesson that typically includes a cooldown and a closure
Leave	A procedure for leaving the space and returning to the classroom or locker room
Boundaries	Procedures for staying within defined boundaries, including the concepts of self-space and general space
Housekeeping	All specific procedures for dealing with dressing, changing shoes and jewelry, using the bathroom, getting drinks, or leaving the space during a lesson

- *Expect perfection, reward direction.* Routines can be learned easily and performed consistently, but you must expect perfection and support students as they gradually get better and better. A "that's good, but we can do better" attitude should prevail.

- *Use positive models.* When individuals or groups perform the procedure appropriately, point it out to the rest of the class. This both provides support for cooperative students and shows the rest of the students how the procedure looks when it is well done.

- *Provide frequent feedback.* Praise success. Praise improvement. Give behavior-specific feedback rather than general feedback.

- *Use activities to practice routines.* Create activities that allow for practice of routines. For example, use an activity in which students have to change partners frequently to practice the attention/quiet routine and the partner routine.

- *Check for student understanding.* Ask students to describe the procedure and why it is important to do it well.

You may need to add routines for specific activity units, particularly safety routines for activities such as apparatus work in gymnastics or wearing protective goggles in floor hockey. If you use small-group teaching, squad leaders or team captains can be given responsibility for routines being performed well.

RULES AND THEIR DEVELOPMENT

Rules specify behaviors students need to avoid or exhibit to make classes appropriate environments for all students to learn and grow as persons. Rules teach; they help students learn the behaviors and attitudes needed to live cooperatively with others over extended periods of time (Wynne & Ryan, 1997). Rules can specify both behaviors students should learn and the situations in which they are appropriate or inappropriate (e.g., talking to a classmate is sometimes acceptable, sometimes expected and encouraged, and sometimes inappropriate). The behaviors specified in rules need to be learned and practiced, just as do content skills. Class rules should be related to consequences. Consequences should be explained to students. Many elementary PE specialists post them, along with class rules, conspicuously in the gymnasium. Rules, to be effective, need to be made clear and then enforced fairly and consistently. Physical education rules should cover behavior in the following categories:

1. *Safety.* This involves behavior appropriate to certain kinds of equipment as well as behavior relative to classmates—using gymnastics equipment only with permission, walking a safe distance behind a student swinging a golf club, always wearing protective glasses when playing floor hockey.

2. *Respect others.* This involves behavior related to the teacher and classmates—encourage others, don't insult, don't talk back.

3. *Respect the learning environment.* This involves behavior related to equipment and the physical space—don't sit on balls, keep the gym clean, put away all the equipment you used.

4. *Support the learning of others.* This involves behavior related to sharing, supporting, and helping the group—share equipment and space, don't tease, encourage classmates.

5. *Try hard.* This involves behavior such as using time well, staying on task, and making an effort to learn—be on time, be on task, always try hard.

Rules tend to differ from routines in that they often specify general categories of behavior that occur in different situations. Rules such as "respect your classmates," "play fairly," and "be cooperative" refer to groups of behaviors that differ from situation to situation but tend to have the same effect. When you are developing and teaching rules, the following guidelines will be helpful:

- Rules should be as short and direct as possible.
- Rules should be communicated in language and symbols that are age appropriate.
- No more than four to seven rules should be used because too many rules cannot be effectively written by teachers or remembered by students.
- When possible, state rules positively, but make sure that both positive and negative examples are provided.
- Make sure class rules are consistent with school rules.
- Develop a hierarchy of consequences (least to most severe), and clearly specify their relationship to rule violations.
- Early in the year (or semester), prompt rules often, give frequent, specific feedback, and consistently acknowledge students who follow rules.

Rules sometimes need to be taught differently than routines. The behaviors that fulfill a class rule such as "respect others" will differ from situation to situation; therefore, the range of behaviors that comply with the rule—and those that violate it—needs to be taught. Consider the following four rules developed for elementary or middle school PE (Sander, 1989):

Traffic rule: Stop, look, and listen when the teacher speaks or signals.

Friendship rule: Be polite. Cooperate with classmates.

Golden rule: Do not use rude language, fight, or argue.

Safety rule: Handle all equipment safely and carefully.

Teachers should prompt compliance with the friendship rule often, by pointing out opportunities to behave in ways that fulfill the rule and by publicly acknowledging instances of good examples of friendship as well as instances of student behavior that is not friendly. Students need to be reminded of rules at times other than when a rule violation occurs, for instance, referring to the golden rule at times other than when there is an argument or inappropriate language. Asking students about behaviors related to rules is a good way to judge the degree to which they are beginning to understand the rules (for example, asking children about safe and unsafe ways of using floor hockey sticks).

To move beyond compliance toward cooperation and, eventually, a learning community (see Box 4.1), students must understand why rules are chosen or jointly developed and why positive or negative consequences are related to following or violating rules. Reasons for rules and consequences, and the relationships among them, do not have to be conveyed through lectures—indeed, that would be ineffective. However, students need to understand why safety is important and why cooperation among learners is essential both for their own development and for the good of the class as a whole. This is best accomplished through giving concrete examples, recognizing positive instances of rule following, and providing lots of specific feedback. Helping them understand why rules are important begins to move the students' perceptions that they are the teacher's rules to a sense that they are *their* rules.

Almost all teachers develop class rules. Not all, however, teach them effectively; nor do all enforce them consistently. "A code without enforcement, or with uneven enforcement, is worse than nothing" (Wynne & Ryan, 1997, p. 93). Student perceptions of the fairness of the rules and the consistency and fairness of the application of consequences are fundamentally important to their buying in to the managerial system. Teachers should never develop rules they can't consistently enforce, nor should they specify consequences they cannot consistently deliver (see Chapter 5 for a full discussion of consequences).

MANAGERIAL TIME: WHAT IT IS AND WHY REDUCE IT

Managerial time refers to the cumulative amount of time students spend in managerial tasks, that is, all the organizational, transitional, and non-subject-matter tasks in a lesson. It is time when no instruction is given, no demonstrations are made, and no practice is done; therefore, it contains no opportunities for students to accomplish instructional goals. Roll taking, getting equipment out, waiting for an activity to begin, organizing teams, moving from one place to another, and handing out parental consent forms for a field trip are all examples of managerial tasks that contribute to managerial time. We are not suggesting that these tasks are not necessary. But less-effective teachers spent too much time accomplishing the managerial tasks (see Chapter 2). Research also supports the commonsense notion that disruptive student behavior is more likely to occur during managerial tasks than during instruction or practice tasks. Effectively implementing managerial tasks, therefore, not only reduces managerial time and increases chances for instruction and practice, but also reduces the likelihood of disruptive behavior.

An important concept in understanding and reducing managerial time is the *managerial task* or, as it is sometimes referred to, the *managerial episode*. Each managerial task constitutes an episode of time and behavior. Managerial tasks begin with some event (most frequently a signal or instruction from the teacher), and they end when the next instructional event or activity begins. The total time in all episodes is the managerial time for that lesson. Focusing on managerial tasks allows a specific analysis of where in a lesson and for what purposes managerial time is being accumulated. The following are examples of managerial tasks:

- Students come from the locker room and await the first signal from the teacher to begin the class (time from the official beginning of the period to the moment when the first instruction is given).

- A teacher blows her whistle and tells the class to assemble on one side of the gym (time from the whistle until the class is assembled and another instruction is given).

- A teacher, having explained a drill, signals students to go to their proper places to begin the drill (time from the dispersion signal to the moment the activity actually begins).

- Inside a gym, a teacher finishes instructions for an activity and sends the class outside to begin the activity (time from signal to leave until the outside activity begins).

- A teacher takes roll (time from the signal for beginning roll taking until the next instruction or activity begins).

Often it is not any one managerial task that wastes a major portion of class time, but rather the accumulation of individual episodes that are each a little too long. Many teachers are surprised at the number of managerial tasks in a typical lesson, but are pleased to learn that managerial time can be reduced substantially—and often easily.

A particularly important managerial task is the *transitional task*. In any PE lesson, there are often several instructional tasks, requiring teachers to change from one task to another or from one variation of a task to another (for example, teams changing courts, making substitutions in games, changing the demands of a partner volleying practice task). In elementary school PE lessons, it is not uncommon to have 15–20 transitional tasks per lesson. In middle and secondary school PE lessons, there are typically fewer transitions, but the spaces are larger and the class size is greater, so loss of time is often more dramatic. Transitions, therefore, account for a large portion of accumulated managerial time. Effective teachers establish routines for all recurring managerial and transitional tasks.

When a managerial task system is well established, it not only reduces managerial time and the opportunities for disruptive behavior, but also quickens the pace of a lesson and maintains the momentum of that pace throughout the lesson. A quick pace that is maintained throughout the lesson is important to convey to students that they are in a learning environment. A quickly paced, upbeat lesson in which the pace is maintained through a well-established managerial task system probably does more than any other factor to impress upon learners the teacher's intent that they learn and improve. Research (Kounin, 1970) has shown that slowing the pace of the lesson or breaking its momentum with interruptions or other "slow-down" events tends to increase disruptive behavior and lessen the learning time students acquire.

THE SKILLS AND STRATEGIES MOST IMPORTANT TO PREVENTIVE CLASS MANAGEMENT

An effective managerial task system is developed and maintained by using key strategies and some important teaching skills. The primary goal is to develop a *system* that enables students to do a great deal of self-management, that makes them want to be responsible members of the class, and that allows teachers time to attend to learning-related issues rather than managerial issues.

Starting Lessons

What you do at the start of a lesson frequently sets the tone for the entire lesson. Younger students often come to the gym ready for activity and eager to become involved. Some older students straggle in and are already trying to avoid participation. For both groups, and for all those in between, the start of lessons is important. Here are some tips for getting started:

- *Control the initial activity.* When students enter the gym, they should have something to do that contributes to lesson outcomes.
- *Make the beginning activity an entry routine.* Whether it is a fitness warm-up, stretching, or a practice drill related to unit outcomes, the beginning activity should be familiar and fun. The start-of-class routine also allows the teacher to cover last-minute equipment or lesson needs and attend to specific requirements of individual students. If multiple routines have been taught, the routine for the day can simply be posted at the entry to the teaching space.
- *Start the class on time.* Promptness in beginning establishes the pace and momentum of a class and underscores the importance of what is done in physical education.
- *Use a time-saving method for taking roll.* If you are required to report attendance, you need a strategy that allows you to fulfill that obligation but does not create student waiting time. Roll should be taken during the initial activity routine. For example, if you use a home bases format, students go to their home base as they enter the gym and do a prescribed warm-up or skill routine, and attendance can be taken simply by noticing vacant home bases. Student captains or coaches can also be used to take attendance.

Managing Transitions

Effective management of transitions is the best place to save overall management time and also likely to be the best way to decrease chances for disruptive behavior that occurs during "dead times" in class. Well-managed transitions also send a clear message to students that what happens in physical education is important and requires their attention, cooperation, and enthusiasm. Effectively managing transitions is the surest way to produce what teaching research has described as a "task-oriented climate," so often associated with high learning gains. Here are some suggestions for managing transitions:

- *Develop clear attention, gathering, and dispersal routines.* Make sure the students begin the routine on a "go" signal, which is also taught. These are the important keys to moving students around spaces efficiently.

- *Always have something for students to do when the transition is completed.* This can be either the start of the next activity or specific directions explaining what to do in the new space. Nothing is more detrimental to management and discipline than waiting time at the end of transitions.
- *Consider having children practice a locomotor skill (skipping, hopping, etc.) as they do the transition.* This will give them some skill practice during the transition and provide some focus for their movement from place to place.
- *Establish a time goal.* When establishing expectations for quick transitions, say, for example, "Let's do this in less than 20 seconds," count the time as the transition is being made, and compliment the group when the goal is met. Next time the goal can be reduced slightly until students get the idea of how quickly transitions can be accomplished.

Managing Equipment Transitions

Equipment transitions not only take time; they also often create dead time for students not involved in them. Dead time creates opportunities for off-task behavior that can spread and disrupt the smoothness and momentum of the class. There are several ways to avoid this:

- *Have an equipment manager.* If you use teams/squads, consider having this primary team/squad role in each group. That person would organize team/squad members to manage the equipment appropriately.
- *Find different systems for children to exchange equipment.* This could be, for example, month of birth or color of clothing. The point is to keep a smooth flow of students exchanging items. If you use a home base routine that involves numbers or colors, you can use this system for managing equipment exchanges.
- *Organize your equipment storage.* Find ways that facilitate exchange according to whatever system you develop.

Managing Formations for Practice

Effective teachers provide for many practice opportunities for their students to learn the skills and strategies that are the focus for a lesson. Practice often requires grouping students (scattered, pairs, triads, quads, and the like). Much of the lost management time in lessons can be attributed to students not organizing efficiently for practice formations. The following practices can facilitate efficient organization:

- *Teach commonly used formations as routines.* A teacher who uses pairs, triads, and quads frequently should teach them as routines. A teacher should be able to say, "Form yourselves in practice triangles with players

10 feet apart and each triangle at least 15 feet from the next. Go!" This routine combines a form of a partner routine and the disperse routine.

- *Structure the space for a lesson.* Use cones, hot spots, floor lines, or chalk both inside and outside to delineate practice groupings.

- *Mark the gym floor in a grid format.* For elementary school PE, consider working with your school principal and maintenance personnel to permanently create these marks that facilitate groupings for various activities. Paved outdoor spaces can also be painted in a grid format. A grid system is simply a grid of 8- to 10-foot squares. Each square can become a home base. Corners can be used to quickly organize into pairs, triads, or quads. Adjacent squares can be used to organize into larger spaces with more students. When game lines are needed, the grid lines can be used for that purpose also.

Managing the Momentum and Pace of the Lesson

Momentum refers to the *smoothness* with which the various segments of a lesson flow together. A lesson with momentum has no breaks, no times when activities or transitions slow down. *Pace* refers to the degree to which the lessons move forward quickly. Quickly paced lessons that are smooth have been clearly associated with more effective teaching and learning. The following techniques contribute to the smoothness of lessons:

- *Start class on time and with a well-paced activity.*
- *Manage transitions so that dead time is eliminated.*
- *Have a procedure for dealing with intrusions.* The procedure for dealing with notes from the principal, a public address announcement, a slightly injured student, or a child who begins to cry should allow you to deal with the intrusive event and still keep the class activity going. Some elementary school teachers have had success with teaching children a simple cue that tells them the teacher is going to be busy for a few moments and they are to continue their activity and behave responsibly.

- *Make your expectations for a smooth, well-paced class clear to your students.* Recognize and praise students who try hard and move quickly. Students will soon learn what the norm for the class is to be.

- *Show enthusiasm for the lesson, activity, and students.* An important teacher behavior for showing enthusiasm is what we call "hustles." Hustles are verbal and nonverbal behaviors that energize students. Interjections such as "let's go," "quickly, quickly," and "hustle!" are cues for students to pick up the pace.

Important Teacher Interaction Skills for Management Success

Good management doesn't just happen. It is the result of a clear, proactive strategy. It is accomplished through instruction and practice; that is, it is taught and learned. During the teaching and learning phase, the teacher's interactive behavior is crucial to success. Here are some suggestions:

- *Give explicit instructions, frequent prompts, and regular feedback when establishing the managerial task system.*

- *Give feedback to individuals and to the class as a whole.* Specific feedback, including information on time spent and time saved, is more important than general feedback (such as "good job").

- *Have high expectations and communicate them frequently at the outset.* An *expectation* is shown through teacher interaction that describes a process or outcome that is to be achieved. Expectations can describe process ("I expect you to move quickly when you change stations.") or outcomes ("I want you to complete the equipment exchange within 30 seconds.").

- *Communicate feedback and expectations.* One good way to do this is to post records of managerial performance by students. You can wear a simple wrist chronograph that allows easy measurement and record the times of various managerial episodes. At the outset of the year or semester, this approach can help you set goals and post performance improvements related to those goals.

- *Gradually reduce interactions as students become more proficient at management routines.* The idea is to have students eventually manage themselves and to have most of the managerial tasks of a lesson become routine. Intermittently, however, continue to praise and recognize students' good behavior and performance.

ASSESSING THE EFFECTIVENESS OF THE MANAGERIAL TASK SYSTEM

The managerial task system should be assessed periodically to make sure it is running as smoothly and efficiently as possible and to identify possible weak components (for example, a particular transition that regularly takes too much time). Monitoring managerial task performance is not difficult and does not need to be time-consuming for the teacher. Cumulative time is a major mark of effectiveness. Managerial task lengths can be easily recorded with a wrist chronograph. You could also tally the number of prompts and interactions you have with students during managerial tasks (the more prompts and interactions, the less students are engaged in self-management). You might also occasionally observe selected students to see how often they have to wait for the next lesson segment to begin or the frequency with which they are off task during managerial tasks. Not all these observations have to be made in the same lesson—you still have to teach. When you find that managerial tasks are performed quickly, that the next activities begin without student waiting, and that all this gets done without many prompts, desists, or feedback to students, then you will *know* that you have developed and are maintaining an effective managerial task system.

SUMMARY

1. Preventive management refers to the proactive strategies used by teachers to develop and maintain a positive, on-task climate.

2. An effective management system produces cooperation between teacher and students and among students and saves time that can be used for learning.

3. Routines are procedures for performing specific tasks within a class, particularly those that recur frequently.

4. Routines need to be taught early in the school year and taught well so they become habit.

5. Rules identify general expectations for behavior that cover a variety of situations.

6. Rules need to be taught specifically, pointing out positive and negative examples and helping students learn why each rule is important.

7. Rules need to be enforced consistently and fairly.

8. Managerial time is the cumulative amount of time students spend in organizational, transitional, and noncontent tasks.

9. Managerial episodes are single units of managerial time.

10. Transitions are managerial episodes between one class focus (instruction, practice, and so forth) and the next class focus.

11. Several skills and strategies have been identified for developing and maintaining an effective managerial task system, including initial activity control, start times, and effective routines.

12. Teachers should pay specific attention to managing transitions, equipment, formations for practice, and the pace and momentum of the class.

13. Interaction skills in preventive management include explicit instructions, frequent feedback, high expectations, and records of performance.

14. Monitoring how time is spent and checking how often students are on and off task are ways to assess the managerial task system.

CHAPTER 5

Discipline Techniques and Strategies

Discipline problems are a major concern for most teachers. They are particularly vexing for beginning teachers. Poor discipline in our schools not only interferes with student learning but erodes teachers' morale and undercuts the public's confidence in our schools. In addition, poor school and classroom discipline subvert the proper moral growth and development of students.

—EDWARD WYNNE AND KEVIN RYAN (1997)

OVERALL CHAPTER OUTCOME

To develop a comprehensive, proactive discipline strategy for a particular developmental level of students that incorporates a specific effort to develop personal and social responsibility

CHAPTER OBJECTIVES

- To define discipline
- To develop a reasoned perspective on the use of punishment as a disciplinary strategy
- To explain why discipline is important
- To explicate the concept of primary prevention
- To describe the Hellison model for teaching personal and social responsibility
- To explain and apply strategies for changing behavior
- To describe effective praise and interaction strategies
- To designate and apply strategies for decreasing misbehavior and increasing appropriate behavior
- To offer constructive alternatives to punishment
- To delineate methods of formalizing behavior change strategies
- To explain the ultimate goal of a discipline system

Discipline must be considered in the context of the skills and strategies associated with developing a preventive managerial task system as described in Chapter 4. Discipline problems are much less likely to occur when an effective managerial task system is in place. The material in this chapter must also be considered in the context of the material presented in Chapter 6 because effective discipline is fundamental to becoming a caring teacher and developing a successful learning community.

We have no illusions about the difficulty of developing and maintaining discipline in today's classes. Some students try to be fully disengaged from physical education. Others seem to enjoy disrupting classes and being rude to teachers. Immature students often make fun of and exclude those who don't "fit in." A few students can become physically abusive of others, especially in physical activity settings, where confrontations can occur. To further complicate things, the trend toward the full inclusion of students with disabling conditions has required teachers to further develop and refine their discipline skills to deal effectively with students' disabling behavioral problems (see Chapter 7).

Discipline is about developing and maintaining appropriate behavior between teachers and their students and, just as important, among students. This includes, as a basic goal of a discipline program, the absence of certain behaviors that threaten the peaceful, cooperative, productive nature of a class. We define *appropriate behavior* for students as that which enables the achievement of educational and personal growth goals in an educational setting. Different settings might require other definitions of appropriate behavior; thus, we will not attempt to define in any specific way what any teacher ought to teach and enforce regarding discipline. But to be productive, all educational settings need high rates of appropriate behavior, no matter how it has been defined. It is insufficient to define appropriate behavior solely by the absence of inappropriate behavior.

The term *discipline* has always been important in a teacher's vocabulary. Teachers are often evaluated, at least partially and sometimes wholly, on their ability to maintain good discipline in classes. We believe that discipline has to be viewed from a positive perspective as well as from the more restricted meaning that focuses on the absence of misbehavior. Too many define discipline solely by the absence of inappropriate behavior; to them, discipline means "keeping the troops in line," and the military analogy is not used without reason. For some teachers, maintaining discipline amounts to developing and sustaining a rigid atmosphere in which students avoid misbehavior because of the fear of serious consequences. In some rare instances, in certain school contexts, such an approach may be necessary at the outset as a means of gaining control in out-of-control situations. But discipline has to include not only the absence of disruptive and inappropriate behavior, but also the development of prosocial behavior. Think about how we use the term when we talk about a good sports team; that is, players are *disciplined* in their preparation and performance. It certainly means more than just the absence of mistakes.

When the term *discipline* is used in its verb form, it often implies and focuses on punishment: "I had to discipline the student" almost always means that a punishment was meted out. Punishment is a useful and sometimes necessary behavior change technique. It has a technical meaning we describe later in this chapter and a number of school-based applications that teachers should be familiar with and know how to use effectively. Punishment is, therefore, a set of valuable techniques in a total class management and discipline skill repertoire. We use the term *skills* purposefully because punishment techniques have to be used skillfully. The purpose is to stop and redirect inappropriate behavior into more useful and productive forms of prosocial behavior. As Box 5.1 indicates, punishment should not be used in retribution, to "flex your muscles," or to otherwise demonstrate your power.

If punishment is the sole or main weapon in the teacher's arsenal of discipline skills, then chances for success are severely limited. There is too much punishment in schools simply because too few teachers have the skills to develop and maintain prosocial behavior through more positive strategies.

BOX 5.1   Punishment: The Two-Edged Sword

Classes need rules and standards of conduct. To enforce them, a system of consequences is necessary, and some consequences will be punishments. Punishment is a two-edged sword in that it is a weapon that can be used to protect as well as to commit terrible acts against the weak. Punishment is misused by some teachers, and many others do not use appropriate punishment techniques with sufficient skill. Teachers also sometimes use punishment to retaliate personally against a student who has bothered them in some way or when they become frustrated with their ability to get a class to do its work. Punishments controlled by teachers are all about power.

> Power is a basic fact of human life, and some people have more of it than others. Much power is legitimate, such as the power a parent has over a child. Some power, such as the power of a bully in the playground, is illegitimate. The classroom is a prime setting for learning about power. Teachers have it and legitimately need it. The issue, though, is how they use it. The great potential for misuse of power does not mean that it should be extinguished or surrendered to students. It means, however, that power should be exercised with fairness. (Wynne & Ryan, 1997, p. 101)

And, we would add, used skillfully.

Remember, the basic purpose of a discipline program is not just to reduce instances of inappropriate behavior, but also to build a solid base of prosocial behavior that contributes both to personal growth objectives and to a more productive learning environment.

WHY DISCIPLINE IS IMPORTANT

Discipline is important for many reasons. First, parents and administrators expect classes to be well managed and well disciplined. Although parents and administrators understand that disruptions sometimes occur and that occasionally some students will become difficult discipline problems, they *expect* that a certified teacher can handle the disruptions and problems and still teach effectively. For many years, teachers have ranked discipline problems as one of the most important topics for continuing professional development. Many more teachers get poor evaluations based on their ability to maintain discipline in their classes than they do for ineffective instructional skills. Nothing produces teacher fatigue and burnout more than having to deal constantly with discipline problems. For your own sanity and well-being, learn as much as you can about both preventive class management and discipline strategies and practice the skills associated with their effective use.

79

Developing
Prosocial
Behavior:
Practicing
Primary
Prevention

Evidence from teaching research has shown conclusively that effective teachers are good class managers. One of the strongest predictors of *ineffectiveness* is the degree of off-task and disruptive behavior in classes. But don't assume that well-managed and effectively disciplined classes *necessarily* are classes where students learn more. There is a difference between creating the conditions for learning to take place and actually facilitating that learning. Unfortunately, there are physical education classes throughout this country in which there is an adequate level of class management and students are well disciplined, but very few skill, strategy, or fitness goals are achieved by learners. Effective management and discipline creates the opportunity for learning to take place, but the teacher must seize that opportunity and fill it with good instruction and learning experiences if the learning goals are to be realized. Effective management and discipline are *necessary* preconditions for learning to take place, but they are not *sufficient* in and of themselves to guarantee learning.

DEVELOPING PROSOCIAL BEHAVIOR: PRACTICING PRIMARY PREVENTION

Effective discipline is best achieved through a set of proactive strategies, the goal of which is the development and maintenance of appropriate student behavior. All teachers must come to grips with what they believe to be appropriate behavior in physical education classes. This will include behavior in three major categories: (a) interactions between the teacher and students, (b) interactions among students, and (c) interactions with the physical environment (e.g., equipment, facilities, lockers, etc.). Because context and personal beliefs are important in this area, we do not suggest specific behaviors within these categories. What is important, however, is that teachers build a consensus among their students that the behaviors that are necessary within each category are the right ones for building and maintaining a productive class environment. Only through consensus building can students come to view the behavior norms within a class as "our" norms rather than "her" or "his" norms. When this is done right, students and teachers establish what amounts to a "social contract" that students believe in and help sustain. Teachers have a much easier time promoting appropriate behavior in their classes if there is a schoolwide set of norms for behavior. The likelihood of students feeling that behavior norms are "ours" is very much enhanced by adoption of schoolwide behavior norms that all teachers expect and support.

Finnicum (1997) argues that physical education teachers should practice "primary prevention," a concept borrowed from medicine. Primary prevention refers to altering the environment to reduce the likelihood that diseases will develop (for example, creating a safe supply of drinking water in a neighborhood or ensuring that all infants are vaccinated). Secondary prevention refers to detecting the early signs of disease and initiating treatment. Much of what follows in later sections of this chapter is, in this sense, about secondary prevention. The most important kind of primary prevention for physical education teachers is helping children and youth learn how to be responsible for their own behavior and then to act responsibly and helpfully toward their classmates.

Fortunately, physical education has a well-tested model for achieving the goals of primary prevention—the Teaching Personal and Social Responsibility (TPSR) model developed by Don Hellison (1978, 1983, 1985, 1995, 1996). The model provides a progression of goals through which students move toward becoming fully responsible citizens of the physical education class and extend those behaviors and values outside of class. The goals of TPSR are as follows (Hellison, 1996):

Goal 1: Respect for the rights and feelings of others

Maintaining self-control

Respecting everyone's right to be included

Respecting everyone's right to a peaceful resolution of conflicts

Goal 2: Participation and effort

Learning what effort means in different situations

Being willing to try new things

Developing an optimistic yet realistic sense of personal success

Goal 3: Self-direction

Staying on task independent of teacher supervision

Developing a sound knowledge base

Developing, implementing, and evaluating personal plans

Learning to work for deferred consequences

Goal 4: Caring: sensitivity and responsiveness to the well-being of others

Learning appropriate interpersonal skills

Helping others without prompting or external rewards

Contributing to the good of the group

Being sensitive about other students and expressing that appropriately

Goal 5: Generalizing outcomes: responsibility outside of physical education

Working on these goals in the classroom, on the playground, and at home

Hellison (1996) suggests that respect is the first issue in the learning progression because the class is a community in which the rights of all classmates must be protected (see Chapter 6 for more on the class as a community). Understanding TPSR as a progression does not mean that you teach respect first, then participation, as if learning about and practicing being respectful is now completed. To the contrary, you must revisit each goal in the progression again and again as you move toward the higher goals.

Many teachers who use the Hellison model rely on turning these goals into a set of levels that provide a simple vocabulary and set of concepts that allow teachers and their students to understand, think about, prompt, and evaluate the level of their personal and social responsibility (Hellison, 1985, 1996).

Level 0: Irresponsibility. Students make excuses, blame others, and often deny personal responsibility for what they do and what they fail to do.

Level 1: Respect. Students may not participate well in class activities or show improvement, but they are in sufficient control that they don't interfere with classmates or the teacher; and they maintain this self-control without constant teacher supervision.

Level 2: Participation. Students not only show respect, but participate fully in class activities.

Level 3: Self-direction. Students not only participate and show respect, but are able to work without direct supervision and can begin to plan, implement, and evaluate some of their own physical education.

Level 4: Caring. Students not only show respect, participate, and engage in self-directed activities, but also support and show concern for classmates and are willing to help others.

The levels allow teachers a shorthand method of communicating with students and an easy system for students to evaluate their own progress. Questions like "What level are you at now, Billy?" or "What do you need to do to move to level 3?" are common. The levels also provide students and teachers a way to learn about what behaviors are examples of each level.

The degree to which any teacher has to rely on TPSR as a primary prevention strategy will differ from school to school and often among classes within the same school. For some teachers, who are confronted with many children or youths who exhibit level 0 or level 1 behavior frequently, TPSR should become the main goal of the curriculum until most students are at level 3. For teachers in these situations, Hellison (1996) has suggested a range of instructional strategies to teach personal and social responsibility. The two fundamental strategies are "awareness talks" and "experiencing the levels" because the success of this model depends upon all students being fully aware of the levels and learning what the behaviors at the various levels look and feel like. Teachers who utilize TPSR most often display the levels on large posters so students can see them and refer to them when needed and as constant reminders of the importance of personal and social responsibility.

Awareness talks are brief episodes during which teacher and students discuss levels and various behaviors that are positive and negative examples of a level. These talks can occur at the start of class, at any "teachable moment" (when an event in class provides opportunity for learning about the levels), or as a closure during which students reflect on and evaluate their own behavior. One teacher developed a large "target poster" with level 4 as the bullseye and the other levels as outer rings of the circle target. When children leave the gymnasium, this teacher has them file past the target and touch the level at which they feel they operated during that class, which is a form of reflection and self-evaluation (Hellison, 1996).

Teachers use various ways to help students experience the levels. Partner tasks require both respect between partners and participation. Self-paced challenges allow for beginning experiences in self-direction. Children learning the concept of personal space and how to maintain it while moving among classmates who are also in motion can learn that doing so is an important form of respect. Cooperative learning tasks can help teach respect (Parker, 1997), as can involvement as a team member in a sport season (Siedentop, 1994). Helping spot classmates in a tumbling activity, acting as a retriever for a classmate practicing tennis serves, or fulfilling the role of coach or squad leader can help students experience caring behaviors that are examples of level 4. It is also important that students be taught a specific form of conflict resolution. Children can be taught to use "odds and evens" or "paper, scissors, rock" techniques; older students might benefit from a "talking bench" where they go to talk out their conflict with the contingency that settling the issue is necessary for them to return to activity.

For other teachers, who work with students who have had basic opportunities to learn respect and participate with at least some measure of effort, the TPSR model can be used as a primary prevention strategy along with teaching a specific curriculum such as Adventure Education, or Sport Education (see Chapter 9). If posters that indicate specific behavioral expectations associated with the levels are deemed unnecessary and specific strategies, such as awareness talks, do not appear to be instructionally necessary, but teachers still want students to be aware of personal and social responsibility and grow in their understanding of and commitment to becoming a caring classmate, they may substitute word prompts such as respect, effort, self-direction, and caring to represent the levels (Hellison, 1996). With their own interactive behavior, teachers can prompt such behavior, provide feedback about positive and negative examples of those levels, and generally make students aware of the need to grow toward being a socially responsible citizen of the class.

Teaching personal and social responsibility may become a significant part of the physical education curriculum for certain classes. Alternatively, it might become an initial unit in the school year for students with whom a teacher has not worked previously. Or it may become embedded in activity units as part of a general classroom management system, thus accounting for only a small part of the overall lesson planning and implementation. However, children and youth don't always grow in personal and social responsibility as an automatic outcome of being involved in sport or fitness activities. To the contrary, such activities have the potential to teach students to be followers or self-directed, to be selfish or caring, to be respectful or abusive of their classmates. The activities themselves tend to be neutral, but they provide the opportunity for students to learn to be one kind of person or another. If you want your students to be personally and socially responsible in the sense described, make sure these values and the behaviors that reflect them are taught effectively and

**BOX 5.2 Shouldn't Students Behave Well
Without Having To Be Rewarded?**

There is no good answer to this question. When teachers use behavior change techniques, they are often criticized by people who assume that students should always behave well just because that is "expected" and the "right thing." That may be good enough for mature adults who behave properly because they have been taught to do so and value the acceptance that society provides for these ways of behaving. It is seldom enough for students who are not very far along to adulthood. No teacher should feel that using specific behavior change techniques is inappropriate. However, teachers need to use the techniques skillfully and wisely. Far too often, teachers use large consequences (rewards or punishments) where small ones would do nicely. An important principle of behavior change programs is referred to as the "principle of least intervention." What it means, quite simply, is that you do as little as possible to get the job done. If you can teach young children to behave appropriately by using social praise and positive feedback, then special privileges or material rewards would be unnecessary. But in some situations, privileges and rewards are much more useful because systematic social praise is ineffective or not powerful enough. Eventually, students should behave well without always being rewarded.

the learning environment is conducive to students understanding, practicing, and improving them.

CHANGING BEHAVIOR

School discipline is about changing behavior—changing disruptive behavior to helping behavior or changing rude, abusive interactions to polite, supportive interactions. Good discipline is not just about eliminating unwanted behavior, but also about building and sustaining appropriate behavior. Situations involving misbehavior sometimes need punishment, but they always also need *treatment*. Every time a teacher desists or punishes an inappropriate behavior, the opportunity arises to replace it with a more appropriate behavior. Effective teachers do just that: They work on a replacement strategy rather than an elimination strategy.

Behavior is most quickly and surely changed through the careful, consistent application of contingencies. A *contingency* is the relationship between a situation or context, a behavior, and a consequence. The consequences provide the "reasons" for behaving that students need so they can learn new and appropriate forms of behavior. Once students begin to learn and get better at behaving appropriately, the consequences can be greatly reduced. Students eventually will behave well because it is expected, because others do it, because it's the right thing to do, or because of self-pride (Box 5.2). In the beginning, however, they need more immediate, concrete reasons for behaving in some ways rather than others.

Certain basic strategies apply to every behavior change situation, whether it is learning how to stay on task, respect classmates, follow rules, or use equipment properly. Understanding these strategies and learning how to implement them form the basic foundation of a teacher's discipline skills.

1. *Be specific.* Make sure students know exactly what you want them to stop doing and exactly what you want them to do instead. Specificity helps students learn more quickly, and it also avoids having students believe you don't like them. Particularly when you are using punishment, the goal should be to eliminate the behavior, not make the student feel that he or she is a bad person.

2. *Define the change contingency carefully.* The contingency should specify the situation, the behavior, and the consequence. "If you do X in *this* situation, then Y will happen." "If you are not in class at 3 minutes past the hour, then you will receive a detention mark." "Class, if you all stay on task during our practice drills for the next 10 minutes, then you can pick an activity to end the class for the last 10 minutes."

3. *Think small and move gradually.* Behaving better is *learning.* Students learn in small increments. Get them behaving better tomorrow than today, and quite quickly they will be behaving very well. "Reward direction, not perfection" is the best guideline. Don't try to change too much at one time. Start with one significant behavior problem, define it and its replacement specifically, provide a consequence, observe the degree of change, and then move on.

4. *Start where the student is.* Don't expect miracles of good citizenship from a student who has been constant trouble for years. First, get to know your students and what they bring to your class in terms of appropriate and inappropriate behaviors. Start with respect and participation; then build gradually on behavior change successes. Continued success at small improvements will allow more ambitious behavior change expectations.

5. *Be consistent.* State a fair contingency and follow through on it. Nothing confuses students more, or makes them more distrustful, than teachers who say one thing and do another or who are not consistent in their expectations and treatment of students from one class to the next.

These five strategies underlie all behavior change, from decreasing inappropriate behavior to increasing prosocial behavior, to building new forms of behavior among students who simply have not yet learned how to behave in certain situations. Small, specific improvements are achieved by applying contingencies consistently, by using effective consequences, and by gradually moving to larger chunks of behavior. As the behaviors become habit, the immediate contingencies that supported their growth gradually fade.

Students always behave for a reason. They show off, are rude, or stay off task because doing so results in some consequence they want to achieve (perhaps they get peer attention, avoid embarrassment for participation, or even get some inadvertent recognition from the teacher). The task facing teachers is to develop more appropriate forms of behavior by providing more appropriate reasons for behaving well.

EFFECTIVE INTERACTIONS FOR DEVELOPING AND SUSTAINING DISCIPLINE

The number of interactions teachers have with their students during a single lesson number in the hundreds. An interaction occurs whenever a teacher behavior conveys information to a student—a one-word prompt ("careful"), feedback ("keep that line straighter"), a nonverbal act (a smile or frown), praise ("thanks for helping with the equipment"), instruction ("I want all partners to watch each other perform and give feedback"), or an expectation ("I expect you all to play this game without arguing"). Few things distinguish the more effective teacher from the less-effective teacher better than the skillfulness of their interactions. This section is about identifying interactive skills that are particularly important for effective classroom management and discipline.

Teachers tend to be far too stingy in their support of appropriate student behavior. That assertion is well grounded in teaching research and is certainly borne out by our observations of physical education in schools. Typically, teachers react negatively or correctively to students when they misbehave. Physical education classes are too full of "be quiet," "pay attention," "listen-up," "sh-h," and "that's enough, over there." There is far too little "Thank you, Jack, you are being very good today," "That's the way to get started quickly, well done," or "Tomeka, you are really being a good helper."

Don't expect to build good behavior and have a warm, nurturant, caring physical education climate without focusing frequently on good behavior and finding multiple ways to recognize and reinforce it. Box 5.3 shows examples of various types of positive interactions teachers can use to motivate and support appropriate behavior. Let's be very clear about what research says and what we advocate. The hard-liner and stern taskmaster will find little comfort in these pages—not, at least, if those terms mean someone who creates a harsh and punitive class climate and sustains it through an overreliance on punishment and threats of punishment. Thirty years of research on effective teaching show that the foremost predictor of classes in which students achieve less is a harsh, punitive climate and teachers who too often shame and ridicule students to get them to conform. You don't have to make physical education a warm, fuzzy place in order for students to achieve, but you must at least make it a place in which students are safe from harm, either from yourself as a teacher or from their classmates.

The interaction techniques that follow are essential for helping students learn and grow in physical education—and for developing and sustaining a management and discipline system. Each technique can be practiced and improved. The skillfulness that comes from experience in using them is not only in refining the techniques themselves, but also in knowing the right technique to use in terms of the situation, such as the kin of students, the setting, and the type of behavior.

**BOX 5.3   Motivating Appropriate Behavior
Through Positive Interactions**

General positive interactions (no specific information content):

Yes	Good	Nice job	Excellent
Beautiful	Terrific	Way to go	Nice going
Thanks	That's the way	You're doing better	Everybody did well
Great	Outstanding	Nicely done	Fantastic

Nonverbal positive interactions:

Smiling	Nodding	Clapping hands	Thumbs-up
O.K. sign	High fives	Winking	Applauding

Specific positive interactions (can be combined with nonverbal acts):
    Squad 2 did a great job of organizing quickly that time!
    Thanks for paying attention, Jack!
    Did you all see the way William helped Deborah?
    The entire class worked hard at that drill!
    This group [pointing] was quiet right at the signal!
    Great job of getting ready—you took only 12 seconds!
    I appreciate your cooperation with the equipment, Mary!

Positive interactions with value content (value content describes why the behavior is important):
    That's the way to get quiet. Now we can begin the game more quickly!
    Thanks, Bill. When you make an effort, the other guys seem to also!
    Ann, you did a great job this week, and I'm sure you had more fun!
    Squad 3 did a great job with the equipment. Now we can start earlier!
    Nice going! When you work that hard in drills, you play the game better!

---

1. *Clear, specific prompts.* A prompt is a teacher interaction that reminds students what is expected of them. When the teacher is developing behavior (or, indeed, a managerial task system), students should be prompted often. Some teachers tend to prompt students only after a misbehavior has occurred. This is an error in technique because it ties reminders only to misbehaviors. Prompts should also be specific; that is, they should contain specific information about a behavior or the situation in which it should or should not occur. As students grow in their capacity to behave well, prompts can gradually decrease in number.

2. *Conveying high, yet realistic, expectations.* Students deserve to be told what is expected of them. Most discipline-expectation interactions will be directed toward process behaviors—behaving safely, courteously, and helpfully and staying on task, for example. These should be realistic for the setting and students, yet they should also be optimistic about what students can accomplish.

3. *Frequent and appropriate praise.* Teachers can praise students individually, in groups, or as a class. Providing effective praise is a *skill*. It can be

BOX 5.4   **Guidelines for Delivering Effective Praise**

Effective praise:
- Is delivered immediately and contingently, yet does not intrude on task-related behavior
- Identifies specific aspects of behavior that were done well
- Provides information about why the behavior is important
- Is matched well to the behavior being reinforced
- Is related to standard criteria or previous performance rather than compared to other students
- Properly attributes success to effort and ability
- Includes expectations for continued success and improvement
- Shows variety, sincerity, and enthusiasm

Major technique errors in delivering praise are:
- Providing only nonspecific, global reactions
- Not providing specific information about the performance
- Comparing too often against peers
- Over- or underexaggerating relative to the performance
- Intruding on task-related behavior
- Being insincere, unenthusiastic, bland

Source: Adapted from Brophy, 1981.

done well or poorly. The most common technique error is what Hughley (1973) calls "the global good"—high rates of simple, repetitive statements, such as "good job" or "way to go." Praise is effective when it reinforces appropriate student behavior; that is, the appropriate behavior increases as a result of praise. Ineffective praise is not reinforcement; that is, it doesn't result in improved behavior. Box 5.4 shows guidelines for delivering effective praise.

4. *Effective nonverbal interactions.* Many have suggested that nonverbal interactions are at least as powerful as what is said to students. The idea is that students perceive nonverbal interactions as reflecting the actual feelings and thoughts of the teacher. When verbal and nonverbal acts are contradictory, students accept the latter as more valid (Galloway, 1971). Nonverbal actions can be used as negative consequences, as expressions of disapproval—a finger to the lips, standing with hands on hips staring at students, frowns, and so forth. They can also be positive—a sincere smile, thumbs-up sign, muted clapping of the hands, and so forth. The skillful use of nonverbal interaction starts with ensuring that nonverbal and verbal acts are in synch and not contradictory. The next step is to try to use more positive than negative nonverbal acts.

One study suggested strongly that student perceptions of their teacher's enthusiasm were directly related to the number of times the teacher actually smiled during class (Rolider, Siedentop, & Van Houten, 1984).

5. *Public and private interactions.* Effective teachers know when to communicate approval or disapproval privately to students—a whisper in the ear, a private pat on the back, a little talk after class. They also understand the power of "conspicuous praise" (Wynne & Ryan, 1997): the public recognition of the good behavior of one student to the entire class, the names of daily fair players on the bulletin board, and so forth. Asking students who behaved well to write their names on a good behavior poster is another example. Teachers of youths must avoid assuming that public praise and private interactions are only for children. A sincere comment of appreciation to a 16-year-old after class, accompanied by a pat on the back, is still a powerful motivator of good behavior.

6. *Effective use of verbal desists.* The most common strategy for dealing with misbehavior or disruptions in class is the verbal reprimand—what we refer to as a *desist*. Verbally desisting a misbehavior is a useful strategy when it is done skillfully. Research has shown that there are specific methods and skills for using desists effectively (Kounin, 1970).

Desists must be *clear,* that is, contain specific information about what the student did wrong. Instead of "stop that," it should be "stop sitting on the basketball; it ruins its shape." Desists should also have *firmness;* that is, teachers should follow through on the delivery of the desist so the student knows that what is said is meant. Maintaining eye contact or moving closer to the offender are examples of firm follow-through. Effective desists are also *timed* appropriately and accurately *targeted.* A well-timed desist stops the misbehavior immediately after it starts and before it can spread to other students. An accurately targeted desist is directed toward the original offender, not a secondary offender. Effective teachers seldom make timing or targeting errors. When students learn that you time and target your desists appropriately, they know that *you know* what is going on in the class—what in research is called "withitness" (Kounin, 1970). It will seem to your students that you have eyes in the back of your head. Desists should not be punitive or harsh. Angry desists simply make students uncomfortable and don't improve behavior.

STRATEGIES FOR DECREASING MISBEHAVIOR AND INCREASING APPROPRIATE BEHAVIOR

Disruptive behavior should be stopped quickly, before it can spread and interfere with the lesson. Even when a good managerial task system is in place, disruptive behavior will sometimes occur. When it does, you need effective alternatives for dealing with the misbehavior—and then clear and effective strategies for redirecting the student or students into more productive patterns of behavior. Behavior reduction strategies always need to be accompanied by efforts to replace the inappropriate behavior with prosocial, productive behavior. The following strategies have been shown to be effective in a wide variety of school settings:

1. *Consistency in ignoring tolerable behavior.* Although disruptive behavior needs to be stopped immediately, there are levels of behavior that might not be wholly appropriate but are *tolerable* to the teacher. These are typically minor infractions or minor off-task behavior that does not interfere with the flow of the lesson or the teacher's capacity to teach the class (Wurzer & McKenzie, 1987). All teachers will have different levels of behavior they are willing to tolerate. What is important is to be consistent from day to day and from student to student about what you will and will not tolerate. Tolerable infractions do not warrant verbal desists or punishments. Instead, teachers should deal with tolerable infractions by gradually reinforcing more appropriate behavior. Table 5.1 shows positive ways to deal with minor misbehaviors.

2. *Omission training.* When teachers reward or praise students for *not* behaving inappropriately, they are using omission training. Thanking students for not talking during an explanation or having a typically misbehaving child earn a point for each gym period during which she does not argue with classmates and granting her a privilege for every five points earned are examples.

3. *Positive practice.* With this strategy, the teacher requires a student to engage in an appropriate behavior a specified number of times as a consequence of misbehaving. The appropriate behavior is always the replacement for what was being done wrong. For example, if a student doesn't put equipment away properly, you might have him or her do it appropriately five consecutive times.

4. *Time-out.* One of the most widely used and successful punishment strategies in schools is time-out, when a student is required to sit out from the ongoing lesson for a short period of time as a consequence of misbehaving or breaking a rule. A time-out strategy is analogous to the penalty box in hockey, especially in the sense that teachers have a specific place where the offending student goes to spend a specified amount of time. It is helpful if you have the student verbalize to you what he or she did wrong after the time-out period before returning to lesson participation. A time-out should be of short duration, seldom longer than 2 minutes. A timer (such as an egg timer or clock) should be used for the student to time his or her own time-out suspension.

5. *Reward cost.* An effective punishment strategy is for a student to lose points or privileges as a consequence of misbehaving. Reward cost is the most common form of punishment in society; that is, many rule violations result in loss of money. To use reward cost, the teacher would have to have an ongoing system of points and/or privileges that students earn by behaving appropriately.

TABLE 5.1   Constructive Alternatives to Punishment

Examples of Inappropriate Behavior	Reinforcing Alternate Behavior	Reinforcing Fewer Infractions	Reinforcing Absence or Nonoccurrence
Being out of squad	Reinforce in-squad behavior: *"Thanks, Dana, for staying in line!"*	Reinforce reduced occurrences of out-of-squad behavior: *"Dana, I appreciate that you've stayed with your group more."*	Reinforce the non-occurrence: *"You weren't out of squad once today, Dana. You earn two points."*
Blurting for attention	Reinforce hand raising: *"Yes, Chris, you had your hand up?"*	Reinforce reduced rates of blurting out: *"Well done, Chris, you reached your target today."*	Reinforce not blurting out for increasingly longer time periods: *"You didn't blurt out once, Chris, during that discussion. Well done!"*
Tardiness to class	Reinforce promptness: *"I'm glad to see you before the bell, Pat."*	Reinforce reduced tardiness: *"You were late only once this week, Pat. That's much better."*	Reinforce lack of tardiness for extended periods: *"You've been on time every day for a week, Pat! I'm really pleased."*
Skill errors	Reinforce proper execution of skill/play: *"That's the right way to follow through, Robin."*	Reinforce reduced skill/play errors: *"You're getting better, Robin. You followed through on all but two of your shots."*	Reinforce the absence of errors over a time period: *"Great, Robin, you didn't forget to follow through on any of your shots during the game."*
Incomplete tasks	Reinforce task completion: *"Thanks, Jamie, for putting all those racquets away."*	Reinforce reduced numbers of incompleted tasks: *"You did better putting away racquets today than yesterday, Jamie."*	Reinforce the nonoccurrence of incompleted tasks: *"You haven't failed to put racquets away once all week, Jamie. That's great."*

(Adapted from Wurzer & McKenzie, 1987. This table is reprinted with permission from *Strategies*, 1987, 1(1), 7–9. *Strategies* is a publication of the American Alliance for Health, Physical Education, Recreation and Dance, 1900 Association Drive, Reston, VA, 22091.)

6. *Reinforcement of fewer infractions and/or alternative behaviors.* There are positive strategies to reduce inappropriate behaviors (Wurzer & McKenzie, 1987) that allow teachers to develop more appropriate behavior without undue reliance on punishment. Omission training is one such approach, as are reinforcing few infractions and reinforcing alternative behaviors (see Table 5.1). Teachers can praise or reward students for doing less of what they have been doing, eventually eliminating the problem behavior. They can also praise or reward behavior that is incompatible with the problem behavior. The two approaches, when used in combination, are particularly effective in changing student behavior without having to use punishment.

Regardless of which of these strategies is used, teachers should pay particular attention to the guidelines suggested earlier; that is, start where the student is, move gradually in small steps, and use interactions consistently.

FORMALIZING THE BEHAVIOR CHANGE STRATEGY

Teachers can do much to build and maintain good behavior simply by using their own teaching behavior skillfully and systematically. Establishing class rules, prompting students frequently, using hustles, using higher rates of positive interactions for good behavior, ignoring pesty behavior that is not disruptive to the class, and desisting skillfully can improve and maintain good behavior and a warm, nurturant gymnasium climate. More drastic strategies are called for when things are so seriously out of control that they need special and immediate attention. In such cases, consider making the basic behavior change strategy more formal in order to give it even greater power and specificity with one offending student, a small group of students, or even an entire class. What follows are some ways in which behavior change strategies have been formalized in school settings and resulted in important behavior changes among students.

Behavior Proclamations

A *behavior proclamation* is a formal statement of contingencies that might apply to an individual student, a group of students, or even an entire class. The proclamation states the behavior to be performed (and perhaps the behavior to be avoided) and the rewards that can be earned for fulfilling the contingency. The teacher decides both the level of behavior necessary and the amount of reward to be earned. The behavior is monitored frequently, and the reward is earned when the specified amount or length of behavior has been achieved. An example of a behavior proclamation is found in Figure 5.1. Naturally, the behavior proclamation must specify, clearly and understandably, what the students are to do or not do. Also, the reward specified must be sufficiently desirable to motivate the good behavior.

```
┌─────────────────────────────────────────────────────────────┐
│                                                             │
│                      Good Behavior                          │
│                                                             │
│   Betsy Smith            will  (1) take part in all games   │
│                                (2) not argue with           │
│                                classmates for four (4)      │
│                                weeks in Phys. Ed.           │
│                                                             │
│   For this good behavior    Betsy        will get to        │
│   help Mrs. Jones after school 15 minutes a day for         │
│   two (2) weeks                                             │
│                                                             │
│                              Mrs. Jones                     │
│                              Physical Education Teacher      │
│                                                             │
└─────────────────────────────────────────────────────────────┘
```

FIGURE 5.1 *Example of a behavior proclamation*

Behavior Contracts

A *behavior contract* differs from a behavior proclamation in that the student (or students) has a role in defining the behaviors, deciding on a reward, and establishing the precise contingencies (how much, for how long, and so forth). Teachers should not use behavior contracts unless they are willing to negotiate with students on these matters. From a learning and development point of view, the behavior contract is an important step forward from the behavior proclamation and starts students on the road to self-control. The elements of the contract are the same as for the proclamation. It is important that all parties sign the contract. Many teachers who use contracts successfully also have a third party sign the contract, thus underlining the importance and seriousness of having each party fulfill his or her side of the bargain. An example of a behavior contract for an individual student is shown in Figure 5.2. Contracts can also be written for groups of students.

Good Behavior Games

One of the quickest ways to turn around a group of students who are misbehaving too frequently is to use a *good behavior game*. Behavior games have been used successfully in many different kinds of elementary physical education settings (Huber, 1973; McKenzie, 1976; Siedentop, Rife, & Boehm, 1974; Young, 1973). Many different kinds of behavior games can be developed. What follows is a description of the most common game formats used to reduce inappropriate behavior quickly.

Behavior Contract

Sarah Caldwell and Mr. Roman agree that the following plan will be in effect for the next four weeks.

Starting date ___January 6___ Ending date ___February 3___

Sarah will

1. Remember to bring her gym clothes for each PE day

2. Not disturb the class by talking or fooling around with Melanie

3. Participate in all activities and try hard to improve skill

Mr. Roman will

1. Give Sarah individual help on the balance beam

2. Count one point for each day Sarah meets the three points stated above

3. Let Sarah help with the 4th grade class for two weeks if Sarah earns seven (7) points during this contract

Signed ___Sarah Caldwell___

___Mr. Roman___

___Mrs. Sylvia, Principal___

FIGURE 5.2 *Example of a behavior contract*

1. The class is divided into four groups. Groups are allowed to choose a name for their team.

2. It is emphasized that each team can win and that teams are competing against a behavior criterion rather than against each other.

3. Four to six behavior rules are explained thoroughly.

4. Rewards are discussed and decided on by the group.

5. The game is explained. Points will be awarded each time a signal goes off (the students won't know when the signal will occur). The teacher will check each group when the signal occurs. If all team members are behaving according to the rules, the team gets one point. If any team member is breaking any of the rules, the team gets no point.

6. A cassette audiotape is preprogrammed with a loud noise to occur periodically (a bell or a buzzer works well). Eight signals are programmed. The intervals between the signals vary. Several tapes are preprogrammed. When class begins, the teacher simply turns on the tape recorder with the volume up (often he or she doesn't know when the signals will occur).

7. When the signal occurs, the teacher quickly glances at each team and makes a judgment on its members' behaviors. Teams that win a point are praised and told about their point. Teams that do not win a point are told why. (After doing this for a few days, the teacher can usually manage this kind of behavior game easily, not taking more than 15 or 30 seconds at each signal to record and announce points.)

8. At the end of the period, the teacher totals the points and posts the scores for the day.

9. At the end of a specified period (ranging from 1 day to as long as 8 weeks), the rewards are earned by each team that has met the criterion.

10. If one player on a team loses more than two points for his or her team 2 days in a row, the team meets and decides whether this player should sit out from gym class for a day (this "doomsday" contingency very seldom needs to be used).

11. With each consecutive game played, it is possible to reduce the number of signals per class and increase the length of the game. As good behavior becomes the norm for the class, the game can gradually be phased out.

THE ULTIMATE GOAL OF A DISCIPLINE SYSTEM

Discipline systems should have the short-term capacity to reduce inappropriate and disruptive behavior quickly and effectively and then to begin to develop and support appropriate behavior to achieve the goals of a lesson or unit. Discipline systems also need to be focused on longer-term goals such as student self-control and self-direction. In the longer term, it is important that schools help students grow as independent decision makers who can weigh the consequences of their own actions and behave responsibly toward adults and toward their own peers. Students also need to learn to accept the consequences of their actions and not to make excuses or blame others for what was clearly their own misbehavior. Eventually, they need to learn to behave well without supervision and to persevere in appropriate behavior even though there may be some motivation from peers to do otherwise.

Students tend to learn these things to the extent they are effectively taught them and to the extent that school is a place in which there are clear expectations for good behavior and they get treated fairly and consistently regarding those expectations. If you can develop in your physical education classes a system that is consistent with the school system, yet is specific to a physical activ-

BOX 5.5   A Fair Player System for Effective Discipline

Fair Player	Unfair Player	Nonplayer
Follows class rules	Finds ways to cheat	Avoids management system
Compliments peers	Puts peers down	Avoids peers
Gives others a chance	Hogs ball or space	Hides out during activity
Perseveres	Gets frustrated and quits	Doesn't even try
Tries to be helpful	Teases and pouts	Gives "get lost" messages
Tries to involve classmates	Is insensitive to others	Lurks on outside of activity
Is appropriately assertive	Is too aggressive	Is nonassertive
Wins and loses graciously	Taunts when winning and pouts when losing	Fears failure
		Is bored or anxious

ity setting, you will have a better chance to succeed in this important endeavor. One such approach is shown in Box 5.5. The benefit of this kind of system is that it helps students learn the behaviors that differentiate between a fair player, an unfair player, and a nonplayer. When there are consistent consequences for students who operate in each of those three categories, then chances of developing classes full of fair players increase.

It is important for teachers to have students who conform to rules and expectations, but too often in physical education a system is put in place so that students do conform but are left in a pattern of conformance rather than being helped to grow into more mature, self-directed persons. To become truly self directed, students must be weaned gradually and carefully from the normal kinds of behavioral supports that school provides for them as they are learning how to become responsible persons.

SUMMARY

1. Discipline should be viewed as a means for developing and sustaining appropriate behavior between teachers and students and among students.

2. Discipline is more than punishment; indeed, if punishment is the main strategy, then the discipline system is inadequate.

3. Discipline is important because administrators and parents expect orderly learning environments, and teachers find them more enjoyable.

4. Well-disciplined classes create conditions in which learning may take place, but the time must be filled with good learning activities.

5. The Hellison model is a sound approach to helping students learn personal and social responsibility within classes and outside them.

6. Basic strategies for changing behavior include being specific, defining contingencies, starting with small chunks of behavior, making gradual changes, being consistent, and starting where the student is.

7. Strategies for increasing appropriate behavior include clear, specific prompts and rules, high yet realistic expectations, frequent reinforcement, effective nonverbal interaction, and effective public and private communication.

8. Effective praise requires following known guidelines and avoiding major technique errors, as well as using a variety of techniques.

9. Specific strategies to reduce misbehavior and increase appropriate behavior include appropriate ignoring, omission training, positive practice, time-out, reward cost, and reinforcing alternative behaviors.

10. Formal behavior change strategies include behavior proclamations, behavior contracts, and good behavior games.

11. The ultimate goal of a discipline system is to bring students into responsible, mature relationships with their peers, the subject matter, and the school society—and to generalize those behavioral predispositions outside the school in the community and the home.

CHAPTER 6

Developing a Community of Learners

What is a sense of community? It is a student's experience of being a valued, influential, contributing participant in a group whose members are committed to each other's learning, growth, and welfare.

—E. SCHAPS AND C. LEWIS (1998)

OVERALL CHAPTER OUTCOME

To explain to a group of parents the differences between traditional school and class organization and that of a learning community model, including a caring pedagogy and antibias teaching

CHAPTER OBJECTIVES

- To describe the characteristics of learning communities
- To demonstrate how fairness and caring can be established within learning communities
- To explain how the learning community in the story shows the characteristics described earlier
- To outline the dimensions of a caring pedagogy
- To provide negative and positive examples of a caring pedagogy
- To characterize the concepts of equity pedagogy and culturally relevant teaching
- To describe the types of discrimination and stereotyping that occur in physical education classes
- To differentiate between acceptable and unacceptable practices in an equity pedagogy
- To enunciate the purpose and strategies of an antibias pedagogy

In Chapter 4, we suggested that the climate of your classes and your relationships with the students you teach can be characterized by compliance, cooperation, or community. For schools to be effective in meeting their goals, students must comply with rules and procedures; but when students comply primarily in order to avoid punishments, the climate of classes is typically not positive, and learning goals are more difficult to achieve. When students actively cooperate in following rules and implementing class procedures, the climate of classes improves markedly, and student performance is likely to improve. The next step would be to build and sustain a learning community within your classes. If you were to successfully develop a learning community, you would likely have students who do the following (Garcia & Krouscas, 1995; Schaps & Lewis, 1998):

- are supportive of each other
- take responsibility for their own actions
- hold themselves accountable for class success
- cooperate with one another
- trust each other
- feel empowered to make decisions

- feel positive about the class identity
- are committed to core values of fairness and caring

Doesn't that sound like the kind of class that would optimize the learning potential of all the students? Doesn't that describe the kind of class you would enjoy teaching? The problem, of course, is that this idyllic state of affairs doesn't just happen: Learning communities have to be developed and then sustained. Many schools are now trying to put in place some of the organizational features that contribute to community building. The challenge to build learning communities has grown out of the belief among an increasing number of educators that children and youth will not only experience positive social growth and develop the values that will help them become productive citizens, but will also improve their academic performance and more likely become self-directed learners.

CHARACTERISTICS OF LEARNING COMMUNITIES

A learning community exists when students feel valued, feel they are supported by their teacher and classmates, are connected to one another, and are committed to each other's learning, growth, and welfare (Lewis, Schaps, & Watson, 1995; Schaps & Lewis, 1998). Learning communities are not gimmicks, nor are they an educational fad. You can't just decide one day that learning communities sound like a good thing and expect to develop one the next week. Learning communities have specific characteristics that take time and effort to develop. Learning communities are bounded environments that persist over time. Members share important common goals, and they cooperate to achieve those goals. They share allegiance to significant symbols and take part together in rituals that emphasize their community. Public schools that serve diverse, heterogeneous groups of learners are not easy places within which to develop learning communities, but when they do develop, they can be powerful in their impact on academic and social outcomes.

Boundaries

Communities have boundaries that set them apart. Boundaries can be physical, symbolic, or conceptual. When schools are situated in unsafe neighborhoods, it is crucial that school and class boundaries be secure. Creating smaller school organizations within larger schools (schools within schools or "house systems") is an attempt to create boundaries within which communities can develop. A curriculum that has a clear focus creates a boundary (taken to a larger scale, this is one of the features of magnet schools). Indeed, a *focused curriculum* is a primary feature of school learning communities. When students wear uniforms, a boundary is created; that is, the uniform differentiates between the members and nonmembers. Teams that have names and colors create boundaries. Teams within a physical education class, as in the Sport Education curriculum model (see Chapter 9), can become microcommunities if they persist over time.

Persistence

Whatever group is meant to develop into a community must persist over time, simply because it takes time to develop shared values, pursue common goals, and develop mutual respect and caring. Some elementary schools are experimenting with having one teacher stay with the same class for several years. Elementary physical education specialists have a unique opportunity to work with children from kindergarten through the fifth grade, even though the composition of classes changes from year to year. High schools are experimenting with keeping the same teacher in the same subject with the same students for several years, a practice that is common in some European educational systems and in Japan. These are organizational changes that could be accomplished at very little cost and reap many potential benefits.

Common Goals

Students sharing common goals is different from students sharing similar goals. Common goals exist when success is defined collectively. This is opposite to situations in which some students can succeed only to the extent that others fail. In most schools, academic work is defined individually. In learning communities, educators seek ways to increase the collective pride in and benefit from individual successes. Class goals become important. Students applaud and celebrate the successes of classmates because they contribute to the larger, collective goals—to the common good of the community.

Cooperation

There are numerous ways students can learn about and eventually engage in cooperative practices. Striving to achieve group goals, participating as peer teachers, successfully filling leadership roles as managers or coaches, and helping with class chores are among the most obvious. In learning communities, teachers express strong expectations of cooperation, take time to show students what cooperation means in specific situations, and celebrate it when it occurs. A cooperative class environment is a building block toward a *caring* class environment. In learning communities, students eventually grow to care about each other's successes and failures. This goal is more likely to be achieved if students and teachers come to know about each other in ways that extend beyond the curricular focus.

Symbols and Rituals

All communities develop significant symbols and rituals as a means of building and sustaining identity. This is true of ethnic, religious, and sport communities, and it also is true of learning communities within schools. At the school level, educators have always focused on this feature through what is typically called "school spirit." In physical education, classes might adopt a class name and a class uniform. They might also develop a series of ritual celebrations, for example, public performances of what they have learned, within-class tournaments, or special field trips. One middle school class in New Zealand, using the Sport Education model, adopted an olympic focus for its program. Each class team represented a country. Rather than use existing countries, they created countries, then created national flags, anthems, and uniforms for their fictional countries. Students and their teacher then developed a series of new sport activities that comprised the olympic competition for the year. They did all the olympic rituals—flag ceremonies, singing the olympic hymn, the pledge of the athletes, the pledge of the officials, medal ceremonies, and the like. The focused curriculum, along with the activities and rituals, created a situation in which all students in the class were invested in the success of the program and cooperated to have their "olympic year" be a success.

Fairness and Caring

Learning communities are built and sustained on qualities of fairness and caring. How many times have you heard a child or youth say, "That's just not fair!" Of all the growing sensibilities that youngsters have, fairness is among the most important. These elements are also at the heart of educational movements toward breeding good citizenship among students in schools (Schaps & Lewis, 1998). To be a good class citizen, students have to be committed to a prevailing system of justice within the class. A main focus of the system is learning to care about the rights of classmates as well as their own rights. Here are some strategies for creating a sense of fairness and caring within learning communities (Schaps & Lewis, 1998):

- A collaboratively developed system of discipline and procedures
- Regular class meetings to solve problems and develop class norms
- Challenging learning activities that emphasize respectful treatment of classmates
- Opportunities for teachers and students to get to know one another as persons
- Dealing with issues of curricular values, such as fair play or gender bias in sports

101

Learning
Communities
in Physical
Education:
A Story

BOX 6.1   A Middle School Learning Community

Schools throughout the world are adopting the learning communities model to increase their effectiveness. The JIS Middle School is organized into nine learning community teams that have the following attributes:

• Student-centered approach

• Commitment to outcomes by members of the team valuing achievement and showing a commitment to success for all students

• Recognition and reward of worthy achievements

• Spirit of advocacy with regard to students

• Collaborative team policies for behavioral expectations and climate

• Community building among teachers, students, and parents

• Proactive posture in which teams attempt innovations and initiate projects

• Healthy give-and-take that recognizes and celebrates differences

The nine JIS Middle School teams (55–80 students each) are further divided into "houses" of approximately 18 students, with each house having a teacher leader who acts as a guide, advocate, and friend for the students under his or her care. Within their houses, students express concerns, have their progress monitored, and discuss events related to the learning teams and the larger issues of citizenship and civility. Although the school has a common core curriculum, learning community teams differentiate their curricular foci. Each team has its own name, logo, T-shirt, color, and other features that set it apart. The teams plan a series of specialized activities to build and nurture the sense of community (assemblies, field trips, special dinners, team meetings). Students also represent their houses and learning community teams in clubs and intramurals.

Source: Adapted from http://www.jisedu.org.ms.msinfo/attributes.html.

Eventually, such practices create a framework and set of expectations for interactions within the class, whether those interactions are social in nature or related to learning tasks. The learning community model is quickly becoming a favored approach to school reform, particularly at the middle school and high school levels. Box 6.1 shows how one middle school is implementing the model.

LEARNING COMMUNITIES IN PHYSICAL EDUCATION: A STORY

Many talented elementary school physical education specialists are probably already developing and sustaining something like what we describe here as a learning community. In schools with a fairly stable student population, a PE specialist might have the same children in classes two to three times per week for 6 years. Many of these specialists are skilled at creating learning conditions under which children are good citizens in the manner described earlier. Certainly, the students learn together across time, although not always in the same class from year to year, unless the school is quite small. Less frequently, special attention is paid to creating symbolic and conceptual boundaries that define groups within the school or common goals that emphasize the collective achievements of classes are pursued. Nonetheless, the success of elementary school PE in many places may well be due to the degree to which some of the conditions of learning communities are sustained over time.

Unfortunately, we cannot describe a learning community at the middle or high school level based on evidence from the physical education literature or from our own knowledge of such programs. Instead, we tell a story of what a physical education learning community might look like.

Brad and Chandra are members of the Health Posse, the name their physical education class chose for its yearlong participation in a health-fitness focus in the physical education curriculum. Ms. Cardio is their teacher. Brad and Chandra chose the health-fitness focus for their ninth grade physical education, but some of their friends chose the Sport Education focus, and a few others chose the dance focus. All the students will be pursuing their chosen focus for the entire school year. The Health Posse meets daily, but other classes meet in 2-hour blocks twice a week, and one of the classes is scheduled to meet for 4 hours once per week.

The Health Posse is midway through the school year and has become a highly focused and united group. The class started the school year with a series of discussions and assessments to see where they were in regards to health fitness and where they thought they wanted to be at the end of the school year. Those early discussions also led to a class social contract and a system of rules and procedures that had some individual and collective consequences attached to them. A class board of directors was elected. The board meets regularly with Ms. Cardio to discuss class problems and collaboratively design future activities.

After 15 class sessions, the Health Posse decided to divide into four teams based on activity interests—aerobics, strength training, walking, and running/cycling. The teams quickly became the Steppers, Pumpers, Strollers, and Roadies. Twice each week the teams pursue activities specific to their interests, and when the whole class focuses on one of those activities, the members of that team play the leadership role in instruction and practice. Thus, on days when the Health Posse does strength training, the Pumpers provide the instructional leadership.

Early in the school year, it became clear that the class did not have sufficient equipment, so, in conjunction with another health-fitness focus class (the Junkies), students began a series of fund-raising activities that included car washes, autumn leaf raking, and soliciting local fitness clubs for used equipment. Each group plans, at the end of the school year, to leave a class gift to the physical education program to improve the equipment for students in the health-fitness focus.

103

Learning
Communities
in Physical
Education:
A Story

By the fifth week of the first term, the Health Posse had developed a series of collective goals in a number of areas, including total distances run or walked, a collective bench press goal, an average recovery heart rate goal, and an average daily caloric intake goal. They discussed how to monitor their performances relative to these goals and began a series of discussions about the help they could provide each other in reaching the goals. The initial goals covered a 6-week period, after which they assessed their progress, celebrated their successes, and used the information to set goals for the remainder of the year.

Ms. Cardio worked with the board of directors to plan a series of out-of-class activities, some designed as homework related to the focus and others designed as social opportunities to spend time together having fun. The first homework activity was for each of the teams to arrange a field trip to visit a venue in the community in which their activity was performed by adults; thus, the Steppers participated in an aerobics session at a local family fitness center, the Strollers joined a local senior walking group for an early morning mall walk, the Pumpers spent an evening in a local weight-lifting facility, and the Roadies joined a local cycling club for a Sunday excursion. After the field trips, brief reports were made, and the class discussed issues such as what kinds of adults were present, how much it cost, and what the climate of the facility and activity seemed to be. The first social activity was a barbeque, which followed their first car wash fund-raiser.

It's toward the end of first semester now, and Brad, who is a Roadie, and Chandra, who is a Pumper, feel bonded to their teammates and classmates. Brad is an avid cyclist—Ms. Cardio has asked him to teach a class session early in the second semester identifying the advantages and disadvantages of mountain and road bikes and also the care of bicycles. Chandra sustained a muscle injury early in the first term, and her Pumper teammates took over the responsibility for her rehabilitation and provided all kinds of emotional support for her during her recovery.

The weekly class discussions have become more lively as the students have come to understand that they each have a say in what happens in class and have begun to feel a measure of responsibility for its overall success. There were many bumps in the road—personality conflicts, disagreements about class activities, and occasional violations of the class social contract. When problems occurred, they got worked out, rather than ignored. Ms. Cardio explained that problems are opportunities for learning and growth and that resolving conflicts amicably and respectfully is essential for both individual and group success. Both Brad and Chandra feel that their teacher and classmates are very supportive of what they do and who they are. Each has also come to enjoy being able to help classmates. Just before the end of the first term, the board of directors, with Ms. Cardio's approval, decided to spend a small portion of the accumulated funds raised to purchase class T-shirts, and there is now a brightly decorated and highly informative Health Posse bulletin board in the gym.

The plans for the second semester are very exciting. The Strollers have decided to try to form an all-school walking club. The Roadies have identified one road race and one cycling event that they will train for and compete in as a team. The Pumpers have organized a series of whole-class weight-lifting competitions for the second semester, with students competing toward collective goals for their respective teams. The Steppers have decided to create an aerobic dance production and have gained permission to perform it at a school assembly at the end of the year. After a suggestion by the board of directors, the entire class decided to offer a friendly challenge to the Junkies to compete on several of the collective goals that had been developed, and the challenge had been accepted. The two health-focus classes have also decided to jointly host a family night midway through the second term to show their families and friends what they have been doing and share their successes with them through a health-fitness-carnival. The joint committee that will do the preliminary planning for the family night has already been assured of some local TV coverage for the event.

The Health Posse appreciates Ms. Cardio. She listens to them and respects their points of view, and it quickly became clear that she expected respect in turn. She demands a lot from them, but in a way that is encouraging and supportive—and she always makes time to provide constructive feedback. She encourages them, but also is quick to remind them of the provisions of the social contract they agreed to. Most class members believe that Ms. Cardio sees them as individuals and respects the differences among them. They have also come to respect her knowledge of health fitness—and it doesn't hurt that she is quite fit herself. She seems to be willing to go the extra mile for the class. She shows up at the out-of-school events and has tried to get to know the class members personally. Brad and Chandra really believe that she wants them to succeed—and she wants the Health Posse to know about and value a lifestyle that is healthy and active.

This story was about a learning community in physical education. The community has boundaries, persists over time, has common goals, cooperates toward achievement of those common goals, has symbols and rituals to build and sustain its identity, and has developed a climate of fairness and caring. These students not only are learning a great deal about health fitness and engaging in a substantial amount of weekly moderate to vigorous physical activity, but are also learning about respect, helping, supporting, working toward common goals, and being responsible members of a group. Is there any reason why this story or similar stories that focus on Adventure Education, Sport Education, or dance couldn't be true for programs in physical education?

PHYSICAL EDUCATION TEACHERS WHO CARE

One of the most important educational movements of recent times has been the focus on a caring pedagogy (Noddings, 1992). Caring is an umbrella concept that is revealed in many ways as teachers and students interact and as students interact with each other. A caring school and a caring pedagogy protect children and youth and invest in their ongoing development (Chaskin &

BOX 6.2   Caring in Physical Education

Gubacs (1997) studied one male and one female teacher and their 47 students to investigate teacher and student definitions and perceptions of caring in the teaching/learning process. Using several methods, she found that teachers and students agreed that caring is an essential element in an effective educational environment. Students had clear views about caring and noncaring behavior among teachers and were able to distinguish easily between them. Terms like "respect" and "being nice" were most commonly used to describe caring. Students believed that caring means a teacher would help them solve their academic and social problems. Both students and their teachers agreed, however, that there are limits or lines in student-teacher relationships that neither should cross. One teacher said, "Caring is to be one with the students, not one of the students" (p. A-80).

Source: Gubacs, 1997.

Mendley-Rauner, 1995). A caring pedagogy also creates the conditions within which children and youths protect the rights and interests of classmates and behave in ways toward their peers that show caring and respect. Caring is not so much a set of specific tools to achieve specific goals as a way to develop the context within which many good things can happen, in terms of both personal growth and academic achievement.

The dimensions of caring shown by teachers are remarkably consistent with many of the characteristics of effective teachers (see Chapter 1). Bosworth (1995) described the following teaching practices that show caring: helping students with class assignments, valuing students as individuals, treating students respectfully, being tolerant, explaining class tasks and checking for understanding, encouraging and supporting students, and planning class activities that are fun as well as challenging. Teachers who care also show personal attributes such as being nice, liking to help students, being success oriented, and being involved in students' lives, both within and outside of class. These suggestions are strongly congruent with what Wentzel (1997) found when she investigated the differences between teachers whom students described as caring and not caring. Teachers who were perceived not to care were described as teaching boring classes, ignoring students, embarrassing students, forgetting names, not answering questions, not correcting work, and the like. However, caring does not mean that teachers become buddies with students—teachers are adults and have professional and legal responsibilities for the students under their care (see Box 6.2).

When we advocate a caring pedagogy, we are not suggesting that social and personal growth—students feeling good about themselves—be substitutes for a strong focus on learning and performance. We agree with Lipsitz (1995, p. 666), who argued that "the issue is not whether we uphold expectations for our children, but what those expectations will be, how they will be expressed and implemented, and whose shared responsibility it will be to make sure that they are achieved." Teachers don't truly care about students when they fail to offer a challenging and interesting curriculum or fail to translate that curriculum into meaningful class activities. A caring pedagogy certainly is about personal and social growth, but it is also about achievement. Indeed, some evidence (Goodman, Sutton, & Harkavy, 1995) suggests that a learning climate characterized by caring and respect promotes learning and performance no matter what instructional method is used. We must try to create a synergy between the learning goals and social goals of physical education. To achieve this, teachers must truly care that their students learn and improve. If the students feel respected and accepted by their teacher and classmates, they are more likely to apply themselves during learning tasks. A caring pedagogy doesn't avoid challenge, constructive criticism, or mistakes, but rather creates a climate in which such features are expected and respected.

Believing that all students can learn, and trying to act on that belief, does not mean all students learn in the same way or should achieve the same outcomes. Children and youth are different in their talents, previous experiences, interests, and expectations. To the extent possible, within the demands of class size, facilities, and equipment, caring teachers make every effort to accommodate these differences. Specific strategies and techniques for differentiating instruction and practice can be found in Chapters 13 and 14.

EQUITY PEDAGOGY
FOR A CULTURALLY RELEVANT EDUCATION

Women and men preparing to become teachers need to acquire the knowledge and skills to work effectively with all students—and they need to strengthen their predisposition to use their knowledge and skill to provide an equitable, culturally relevant education for all their students. We started this book with a similar statement, arguing that the knowledge and skills can be acquired, but that the motivation to use them was most important for becoming effective. What is absolutely clear is that (a) students in public schools are increasingly diverse, (b) our society has historic inequities that prevent us from achieving the ideal of a democratic, humane, and just society, and (c) the global community is increasingly interconnected (Zeichner, 1998).

Not all students attend schools that are culturally diverse, but those who attend essentially monocultural schools will have to work and live in a culturally diverse society. Their education will be incomplete if they are not prepared to do this. The goal described at the start of this section—to give teachers the knowledge, skills, and predispositions to provide an equitable, culturally relevant education—is not easy to achieve for teachers or teachers in training who expect to teach students who are much like themselves and have little experience with students who are different (Young, 1998). We are not suggesting that teachers are intentionally biased or mean-spirited toward persons differ-

BOX 6.3   Am I Ready To Be Effective in a Diverse Class?

- Am I knowledgeable about the cultural, linguistic, and socioeconomic backgrounds of the students I teach and the community from which they come?

- In my own behavior, do I model respect for, and inclusion of, persons who are different?

- Do students perceive me to be sincerely interested in and respectful of contributions made by ethnic and racial minorities, women, poor persons, and persons with disabling conditions?

- Have I used, or do I know where to find, resources to help me combat and confront bias based on gender, race, religion, or socioeconomic status?

- Am I able and willing to recognize and constructively address conflicts that arise based on gender, race, religion, or socioeconomic status?

Source: Adapted from Eisenhower National Clearinghouse for Mathematics and Science Education, n.d.

ent from themselves. However, the evidence suggests that knowledge of and attitudes toward students of color and poor students are typically based on stereotypical images held by families and communities and strongly fostered by the media (Zimpher & Asburn, 1992). This is what one might expect when persons have not had the opportunity to learn from close, personal relationships with poor or minority children and youth. It is thus no wonder that many beginning teachers are frightened at the prospect of teaching in diverse schools and their expectations for student performance and behavior are often stereotypical and inadequate. Box 6.3 poses a series of questions you can ask yourself to judge your current capacity to work effectively in a diverse school. A final problem is that some teachers and teachers-to-be find it difficult to believe that others are treated unfairly in schools simply because they have never experienced unfair treatment. This is most typical of middle-class male students from monocultural backgrounds, especially those who have been good students and are physically skillful.

In Chapter 2, we reviewed research that shows that students are often disadvantaged in physical education—because of gender, skillfulness, physical appearance, and race. Some of this disadvantage comes from teacher insensitivity or lack of skillfulness: unequal expectations, differential interaction patterns, biased selection of activities, and the like. Much of it, however, comes from teachers being unaware of or ignoring how students treat each other. Everybody who has spent time in physical education classes or on playgrounds observing children and youth in activity understands that students can and do disadvantage and abuse one another and that groups of students are stereotyped and often ostracized from a fair opportunity to participate. The predictable result is student alienation from physical education as a school subject and, subsequently, from a physically active lifestyle.

This chapter is about developing learning communities in physical education and the role of a caring pedagogy within that framework. A major characteristic of learning communities is the common commitment to fairness and caring about one another. A caring pedagogy is meant to establish and sustain a fair learning environment, within which members care about and respect one another. This section extends that concept to its logical conclusion, developing and sustaining an equitable learning environment that is culturally relevant and prepares students for participation in larger, culturally diverse communities.

WHAT TO DO—TOWARD AN EQUITY PEDAGOGY

We propose three profiles related to issues of diversity and bias in teaching: a profile of unacceptable characteristics that result in inequitable, biased learning environments, a profile of acceptable strategies that result in an equitable pedagogy of caring, and a profile of preferred strategies that move beyond a pedagogy of caring to antibias teaching that confronts issues of bias and helps students resolve them within the learning community. An equity pedagogy is defined as "teaching strategies and classroom environments that help students from diverse racial, ethnic, and cultural groups attain the knowledge, skills, and attitudes needed to function effectively within, and help create and perpetuate, a just, humane, and democratic society" (McGee-Banks & Banks, 1995, p. 152).

Given this definition, identifying the unacceptable teaching profile is fairly easy. In physical education, we find it unacceptable for teachers to create and sustain learning evironments within which teachers do the following:

- Interact differentially with students based on race, gender, socioeconomic status, or motor skillfulness
- Communicate differential expectations based on those features
- Provide more academic feedback to boys than girls
- Make gender- or race-stereotyped statements
- Let boys or skilled students dominate practice and games
- Use sexist language in teaching (see Box 6.4)
- Ignore student gender and cultural differences in choice of activities
- Ignore and do not intervene in biased interactions among students
- Ignore and do not intervene when students harass, intimidate, and/or embarrass one another

All the characteristics of this profile have been documented from observation of classes in physical education (Evans, 1986; Felshin & Oglesby, 1986; Griffin, 1981, 1984; Turvey & Laws, 1988). It is not difficult to change this profile. The teaching skills that need to be changed are fairly straightforward—sensitive, equitable interaction patterns; thoughtful curricular planning; ap-

---

BOX 6.4   Avoiding Sexist Language in Teaching and Coaching

Sport has traditionally been male oriented. Many of the common terms in sport are, therefore, male-oriented terms. There are alternatives—and they should be used.

Sexist Terms	*Nonsexist Equivalents*
Guard your man closely	Guard your opponent closely
We don't have the manpower to win	We don't have the depth to win
Second baseman	Second base player
The defenseman	The defense
Three-man teams	Three-person teams
Third man (lacrosse)	Third player
Boys' and girls' push-ups	Extended and knee push-ups
Man-to-man defense	Player-to-player defense
Sportsmanship	Fair play

   Can you think of other examples? And good alternatives for them? When you teach or coach, do you make some of these communication errors? How can you correct them?

Source: Adapted from Griffin & Placek, 1983.

---

propriate modeling; careful, sensitive monitoring of student behavior; and intervention strategies to remediate and develop equitable, prosocial behavior and interactions among students. What is more difficult is to understand that this profile is unacceptable and then make the commitment to see that it gets changed.

   To move from the unacceptable profile to the acceptable profile requires that an equitable pedagogy of caring be developed and sustained. We have already provided the basic description of a caring pedagogy. In this section, we add the application of a caring pedagogy to learning environments of diverse learners. In an important sense, *all* physical education classes are diverse learning environments because they have boys and girls and they have students at markedly different skill levels—and bias based on gender and skillfulness have been two of the historic inequities of the minisocieties of physical education.

   A caring pedagogy in a diverse learning environment requires more than good intentions. It requires skills and knowledge that relate diversity issues to pedagogy and subject-matter knowledge (McGee-Banks & Banks, 1995). This would include knowledge about racism, sexism, stereotypes, prejudice, and institutional bias (see Box 6.5). It also suggests that teachers understand the histories, characteristics, and intragroup differences among major racial and ethnic groups. It is, for example, nearly impossible for teachers to truly respect cultural differences among students and to communicate that respect to their students if they do not have accurate knowledge of those differences and are, instead, dealing primarily from media stereotypes.

BOX 6.5   Individual and Institutional Inequities

Inequity exists at both the individual and institutional levels. Prejudice at either level is unfortunate. Because much power is vested in institutions, inequitable treatment at that level is particularly disabling. Shown below are some examples of race and gender inequities at each level.

Individual	*Institutional*
Using a racial slur to refer to someone from another race	The school providing twice the support for the boys' team as it does for the girls' team
Parents allowing their son, but not their daughter, to play on teams	An organization denying membership to blacks and Hispanics
Calling a young girl who enjoys sports a tomboy	A school newspaper devoting more space to boys' sports than girls' sports
Laughing at a racist or sexist joke	All sports administrators being white males

Can you provide other examples of inequitable treatment at the individual and institutional levels? How much of it do you believe is intentional?

Source: Adapted from Griffin & Placek, 1983.

The teaching skill profile for an equity pedagogy would begin by reversing all of the negative characteristics of the profile previously described. Interactions would be equitable. Expectations would be positive and equitably challenging for all students. Curricular decisions would take differences into account. Modeling, prompting, and feedback would be equitable and appropriate. All students would have equal opportunity to participate, to provide leadership, and to have their voices heard. Skilled students and boys would not dominate participation. Harassment or embarrassment of students by students would be proactively prevented and remediated immediately when it did occur. This is probably the easy part of this shift from unacceptable to acceptable and can be accomplished by observing and providing feedback about teaching practices and behavior and then monitoring student activity.

A learning community of diverse learners cannot be built or sustained, however, without the learners themselves coming to grips with their cultural differences and learning to understand and respect classmates who come from backgrounds different from theirs. Students have to feel safe to share their concerns, to disagree with classmates, and to participate in discourse and activities that are intended to build respect and community. A learning community has to be open and challenging, yet also highly supportive, if it is to be a *safe learning space* (Young, 1998). Most students would have had little expe-

---

BOX 6.6   To What Degree Am I Engaged in Antibias Teaching?

- Do my students see me as actively confronting instances of stereotyping, bias, and discrimination when they occur?

- Do I teach and encourage students to understand and respect the feelings and points of view of others who are different than them?

- Do my students understand that I do not judge student performance based on race, gender, or socioeconomic differences?

- Do I plan activities that help students to identify prejudice and discriminatory practices in physical activity and sport?

- Do I help students to develop skills and predispositions to respond appropriately to instances of bias, discrimination, and harassment?

- Do I plan activities which help students to examine and analyze how class, race, and gender in physical activity and sport are represented in the media, school, and local community?

Source: Eisenhower National Clearinghouse for Science and Mathematics Education, n.d.

---

rience expressing deep concerns about gender, race, ethnicity, and socioeconomic status. Their initial efforts might be halting and clumsy. They might well fear being ridiculed by their classmates. The learning space needs to be "hospitable not to make learning painless but to make the painful things possible" (Palmer, 1993, p. 74).

To move from the acceptable profile to what we believe to be a preferred profile, teachers must be willing to plan for and implement activities that confront inequities and help students develop the knowledge and predispositions to become advocates for equity and fairness throughout their lives. This is not to suggest, however, that within this preferred profile, teachers do not focus on helping students become competent in the subject matter of physical education—the issue is that *all* students should achieve success, and that can't happen if the learning environment is inequitable and not culturally relevant to students from different backgrounds. What is added to this main agenda is making the confrontation of bias, particularly as it relates to physical activity and sport, a part of the content that students master, in terms of both knowledge and skills. In the preferred profile, a strong element of antibias teaching is added within the learning community. Box 6.6 asks another series of questions that will allow you to assess the degree to which you engage in antibias teaching.

We are not suggesting that antibias teaching should take the form of an "in your face" confrontation. Such an approach would effectively eliminate the notion of a safe learning place described earlier. In diverse learning communities, students will understand that they bring differences to the setting. What they are unlikely to understand are the perspectives of their classmates who were socialized differently and whose attitudes and behaviors reflect other cultural norms. The goal should be to address these disparities in ways that allow for a growing tolerance, respect, and appreciation of diverse perspectives.

Students will exhibit biases in nearly all physical education classes. Evidence (Chepyator-Thomson & Ennis, 1997; Nilges, 1995; Williamson, 1996) indicates that gender bias is nearly always present in physical education, beginning in kindergarten and continuing through high school. Both boys and girls tend to reproduce in class the gender-appropriate roles they have learned in the wider community and from the media. Failure on the part of teachers to address the limitations of these roles serves inadvertently to reinforce them. Teachers who work to provide an equitable learning environment will ensure that girls at least get equal attention and opportunity to participate and to have their voices heard. Although this would be a vast improvement over many current conditions, it still falls short of an antibias pedagogy that brings gender stereotypes in sport and physical activity to the attention of all students and creates the conditions within which these stereotypes can be broken down, thus empowering girls to take full advantage of their physical capabilities and to broaden their horizons about what is possible for them in physical activity and sport. The same scenario could be repeated for issues of race, ethnic heritage, and skillfulness.

Antibias teaching does not require any new or remarkable teaching skills or strategies. It does require the motivation to attempt it and the perseverance to see it through. How do teachers address these issues? First, they make them part of the content of physical education and willingly give time to address the issues. This, in one sense, is analogous to our argument about the time taken to establish class routines and procedures at the start of the school year (see Chapter 4). The time taken away from activity practice is more than made up for through increased effectiveness throughout the school year. The difference here is that issues of bias in physical activity and sport are legitimate content issues for physical educators to pursue. Students need time to be made aware of these issues and to process them through discussion and activity.

Teachers also use the many teaching skills described in this book to make their antibias teaching effective. They *develop and enforce class rules and routines* that make it clear that biased behavior is inappropriate. They *prompt students* in situations where inequities might arise. They *utilize antistereotyping comments* ("Ron, Glenda is the best setter on your team. You should get the ball to her as often as possible."). They *avoid sexist language* (see Box 6.4). They *use corrective feedback* to correct stereotyped or biased comments or actions ("Jake, don't say Tom throws like a girl. Girls can learn to throw as well as boys can. I want you to think about how Tom and the girls feel when that is said."). They *use girls as demonstrators as often as boys* and not just for activities too often labeled "girls'" activities. They *utilize antistereotyping role models* (bulletin boards with female basketball players, male dancers, and the like). They *invite antistereotyping guests* to class (girls from the school who have gone on to athletic success). They *utilize universal representation* in class

> **BOX 6.7   Ground Rules for Discussions**
>
> If there are any special teaching skills related to antibias teaching, they are most likely to be in conducting class and small-group discussions, simply because discussions are not as commonly used in teaching physical education as they are in classroom subjects. Students will need clear ground rules, practice, and feedback to learn to participate in ways that are consistent with the tenets of a learning community.
>
> They are likely to talk over one another, blame one another, and take disagreements personally. Below is one set of ground rules developed for a South Carolina curriculum to fight bigotry.
>
> - Listen patiently and carefully to each student who speaks.
> - Express yourself honestly and openly.
> - Search for truth from each person's perspective.
> - Avoid shaming, belittling, or blaming.
> - Maintain each person's confidentiality.
>
> Students need to learn that offensive remarks hurt—they hurt the target of the remark, they eventually hurt the person who makes the remark, and they certainly negatively affect the spirit of the community.
>
> *Source:* Adapted from Roefs, 1998.

examples, choices of leaders, and representations on bulletin boards (in fitness units, they do not always use slim, ultrafit, highly attractive persons with certain body types, but rather show that fit persons come in all sizes, shapes, and looks). They consistently reinforce with their students the notion that *sustained effort rather than innate ability, is the key to achievement.* They *assign antistereotyping tasks* within class and as homework (review how girls are shown in advertisements related to sport products, assess the amount of space or time given to women's sports in the local newspaper or TV station, analyze the kinds of sports that African Americans are associated with in TV advertisements, analyze the access and costs of recreational opportunities in various socioeconomic areas of a community). They *promote equity* through celebrations that emphasize multicultural awareness or the accomplishments of persons who have experienced bias. They *shape class discussions* around incidents of bias outside of class and gradually help students discuss their feelings about bias in their own lives and within their own class. They develop agreements with students about how class and small-group discussions are conducted (see Box 6.7). They *use "why are" questions* for discussions that reveal institutional bias (Why are most of the school administrators in the district male? Why are most head coaches white? Why are girls less active during

---

BOX 6.8 How District Policy Can Support Antibias Teaching

The Durham school district approved an antiracism and ethnocultural equity implementation policy in 1995. The policy set in motion a series of districtwide programs, the major focus of which is the area of curriculum. Among the initiatives are the following:

- Students participate in a 5-day Students Together Against Racism (STAR) Program to build student leadership skills and develop plans to combat discrimination and create an environment of social harmony in schools.
- Staff participates in antiracism training and forms antiracism resource teams in schools.
- Antidiscrimination curriculum units are developed at all levels.
- All curriculums are reviewed to detect bias and stereotyping.
- An Ethnocultural Equity and Race Relations Department is created to provide in-service education and consult with the antiracism resource teams.
- Antibias employment practices are instituted.
- New teachers are oriented to the program and receive mentoring.

A teacher's efforts to develop and sustain an antibias teaching agenda would be very much enhanced by district policies similar to these. What policies exist in districts in your area?

Source: http://www.durham.edu.on.ca/Anti-Racism.html.

---

school recess? Why do boys tend to "hog the ball" in games?). They *select culturally sensitive activities* and help extend the student's understanding of activity biases and stereotypes in the wider culture. They *group students* and *assign leadership roles* in ways that both ensure equity and allow for advances in the general antibias agenda of their teaching.

And, of course, they do this using the skills associated with a caring pedagogy, so that students are not threatened, but rather feel safe and secure to express themselves both to the teacher and to their classmates, understanding that they will be respected and supported in their efforts to grow and contribute to the learning community. In other words, antibias teaching is forwarded by the application of effective, caring teaching skills.

Finally, the goals of antibias teaching are much easier to reach if the school or, better still, the school district has policies and programs that support such efforts. We have known for some time that schools that have common, consistent behavioral expectations and discipline codes are more effective. We have known for some time that elementary schools in which approaches to teaching reading are similar from class to class produce more effective readers. The lesson to be learned from this is that consistency throughout schools and districts results in much stronger outcomes. Box 6.8 shows how one school district has supported antibias teaching.

1. Students in successful learning communities are supportive, responsible, accountable, cooperative, trusting, empowered, identified with the class, and committed to fairness and caring.

2. Learning communities have boundaries, persist over time, share common goals, value cooperative practices, identify with community symbols and rituals, and are committed to fairness and caring.

3. Strategies for sustaining fairness and caring include collaboratively developed class procedures and discipline codes, class meetings to solve problems and develop class norms, challenging learning activities emphasizing respect, opportunities to know one another, and willingness to deal with values in the curriculum.

4. A caring pedagogy invests in the development of students and sustains conditions within which students protect the rights and interests of classmates.

5. Teacher practices such as helping, valuing students, treating students respectfully, being tolerant, encouraging, and supporting are viewed by students as caring.

6. Caring teachers plan challenging and significant activities and help students achieve important outcomes.

7. Students are often disadvantaged in physical education because of irrelevant attributes such as gender, skillfulness, race, and physical appearance.

8. An equity pedagogy builds class environments that help students from diverse backgrounds achieve outcomes to function well in society and create and sustain a more just and humane society.

9. Unacceptable practices include stereotyping or discriminatory teacher actions and an unwillingness by the teacher to prevent the behavior and/or intervene when students behave in discriminatory ways toward classmates.

10. To become a caring teacher requires skills and knowledge that relate to diversity issues in pedagogy and in the content being taught.

11. Antibias teaching purposefully confronts issues of stereotyping and discrimination and works specifically with students to help them become more tolerant and more willing to be advocates for antibias practices in schools and in the larger community.

12. Students will need to be taught specific communication skills to be able to take part usefully and fairly in antibias discussions within class.

13. District policies that support antibias teaching provide an important support infrastructure for teachers, who can then pursue such agendas vigorously in their classes.

CHAPTER 7

Strategies for Inclusion: Teaching Students with Disabilities

The existence of individual differences . . . mandates what teachers readily realize in the typical classroom or gymnasium situation; all children have varying styles and rates of performance and learning. The inclusion of those persons labeled as handicapped, disabled, delayed, or just plain different is a simple extension of the educational realization of individual differences. The presence of persons in a group with more apparent differences doesn't alter the basic fact that differences were there all along. It simply forces the teacher and learners to better face those differences.

—LANGENDORFER (1986)

OVERALL CHAPTER OUTCOME

To design a lesson that will promote learning for students with disabilities

CHAPTER OBJECTIVES

- To describe the different ways students with disabilities experience physical education
- To identify the six categories of disabilities that are integrated into general physical education
- To describe the school district's responsibility to students with disabilities
- To define *least restrictive environment*
- To explain the purpose and process of developing an Individualized Education Plan
- To explain the six suggestions critical to the planning of learning outcomes for students with disabilities
- To identify the four criteria to guide evaluation of any proposed modifications to accommodate students with disabilities
- To describe the two most frequently used support systems for students with disabilities, buddy system and peer tutoring
- To explain a variety of methods for accommodating students with disabilities
- To explain how and when to use a variety of instructional strategies for facilitating learning for students with disabilities

Students with disabilities experience physical education in various ways, from participating in separate adapted physical education classes to being placed in what for them is the "least restrictive environment." In other instances, students with disabilities are included in general physical education and appropriate support personnel are provided. Basically, the issue has been one of *where* students with disabilities are taught rather than *how* they are taught. There is no one way for students with disabilities to be taught and nothing in the law that suggests where they must receive instruction. As a result, school districts have interpreted these terms differently; thus, there is no standard or typical program to guide practice. It is not our intent to walk you through the multiple meanings of these terms or all of the nuances that frame them.

More and more frequently we are seeing school districts educating all students, including those with disabilities, in general physical education. In practice, this does not mean that all students are striving toward the same goals and experiencing the same instructional methods. Rather, it means that all students are provided with educational experiences that are designed to meet their own individual needs while receiving the level of support appropriate for them to achieve success. In this chapter, we provide a set of strategies and tactics that promote learning for students with disabilities. The intent is to describe a variety of methods shown to be effective in facilitating learning for students with disabilities and to allow each of you to select those that best meet the needs of the children and youth you teach and the setting within which that teaching occurs.

Regardless of *where* your district places students with disabilities, many physical educators have students with diverse needs, strengths, abilities, and skills in their classes on a daily basis. These children may fall into one of six categories: (a) visually impaired, (b) physically and other health impaired, (c) mentally challenged, (d) behaviorally challenged, (e) hearing impaired, and (f) multiple handicapped. In each instance, several physical education goals are the focus of instruction and, ultimately, student learning. Too frequently we see social interaction being the focus of instruction so that children and youth leave physical education with improved social skills and the ability to integrate into the general population, yet lack the curricular content to achieve success in physical activity. Both aspects of learning must be attended to equally because each plays an integral role in the development of the student with disabilities. It is the school district's responsibility to identify and evaluate any student who might qualify, because of a handicap, for special accommodations in the classroom. In addition, the district is required to have a multidisciplinary team determine the appropriate placement for any qualified children. Any student who meets the qualifications for specially designed instruction or services must have these documented in an Individualized Education Plan (IEP) that is designed collaboratively with the multidisciplinary team (see Box 7.1).

I learned perhaps one of the greatest lessons about teaching toward individual differences from one of my athletes who happened to be a single leg amputee. As I struggled to design workouts for her to meet what I viewed as her needs and presumed abilities, or disabilities, I observed her getting frustrated with my attempts to modify training. Finally, Karen came to me and said, "Coach, I am not different from any one of your other athletes who has a weakness. Marilyn has weak upper body strength, Sherri has no cardiovascular endurance, and I have a weak left leg. Think of it like that, and design my throwing workouts to fit any athlete with weak leg strength." She allowed me to look at her from a new perspective and one that made her different, but different and able. She basically told me that the best way to help her improve performance is the same as it is for any other athlete: providing challenging, well-designed training with feedback and encouragement while allowing her a voice in her own training. Not all disabilities are the same and should not be considered in the same realm; each student is unique, different, has her or his own needs, and must become the focus of our planning.

PLANNING FOR LEARNING

Part Three focuses on planning for meaningful learning outcomes, determining how to teach and assess those outcomes, and designing lesson and unit plans to reflect these planning endeavors. Deciding what you are going to

118

Strategies for
Inclusion:
Teaching
Students with
Disabilities

BOX 7.1   IEP Evaluation

The IEP is written by a multifaceted evaluation (MFE) team consisting of the parent(s)/guardian, the student's teacher, a school district representative, the student, where appropriate, and other individuals at the parent's or school district's request.

Other personnel providing services to the student are encouraged to be part of the IEP team.

The document should contain an identification of the student's disability, a statement of the student's present levels of performance, long- and short-term instructional objectives that relate to present levels of performance, evaluation procedures, and a statement of what is determined to be the least restrictive environment for the student.

Least restrictive environment can range from placement in the regular classroom to attending school in a learning center located at the public school building to home instruction.

Teachers and related service providers who will be implementing the IEP must be informed about the student's IEP and should be given a copy.

The IEP may be reviewed at any time during the school year at the request of the parent(s) or school district, but must be reviewed annually.

The student's instructional needs are re-evaluated by an MFE team every three years.

The IEP is a legally binding document which means that parents can sue if they believe the school is not carrying out the plan that has been agreed to for educating their child.

Source: Ohio Schools, 1996.

---

teach and then teaching and assessing exactly that is termed *instructional alignment*. We know that students learn more in settings where there is alignment between intended outcomes, learning process, and assessment. Increasing the alignment of instruction for students with disabilities is even more critical (Koczor, 1984) and can increase achievement substantially. This suggests that the outcomes selected for these students and the strategies and tactics employed are thoroughly developed and their implementation, well planned. Although the important outcomes you develop may indeed be appropriate for the majority of learners, there may be a small group of students for whom they are not realistic or who do not have the appropriate prerequisite skills and knowledge to master them. With this in mind, and as you design learning outcomes, and instruction to meet those outcomes, the following suggestions will be useful (Pratt, 1994):

1. *Don't give up too easily.* Try any means possible to facilitate mastery of important outcomes by every student before deciding that they can't be achieved by a few and lowering the expectations. This might be achieved through grouping of learners, innovative learning tasks, peer

or buddy systems to facilitate learning, or any number of options you will read about later in this chapter.

2. *Find each student's strengths.* Cultivate the interests of all students, and utilize their strengths to build the learning environment. Perhaps most important is not to underestimate students or assume that, if a child has a disability in one area, he or she must be disabled in others. Frequently, student performance will match your expectations, and if you expect too little, that is what you will get. Planning instruction with success in mind and carefully designing learning experiences in which each child can attain some measure of success and feel like an important part of the lesson are critical.

3. *Provide all learners, especially those with disabilities, time to learn and to demonstrate that learning. That* students learn is more important than *when* they learn. This suggests allowing multiple performance attempts, providing ongoing and frequent feedback, and ensuring that practice is realistic and applied. If the intent of learning is for the student to demonstrate some type of skill, then be sure that the assessment in fact measures that performance.

4. *Emphasize progress, achievement, and performance quality.* Use performance as a learning tool, rather than just as a means of evaluation. As you will see in Chapter 10, assessment should be ongoing and provide learners with knowledge of their progress. Learners must also have the opportunity to compare their current performance to their own previous performance, rather than to that of their peers.

5. *Focus on learning.* If you design realistic learning opportunities, students can achieve success while building self-esteem about movement and physical activity. Too often, students with disabilities are faced with goals that they cannot realistically achieve or learning experiences that might lead to success, yet are beyond their capabilities.

6. *Focus on meaningful learning outcomes.* Be certain that the outcomes identified for all learners represent critical knowledge and skills for them in life outside of school. This should be a question you ask of all learners, not just those with disabilities. However, students with disabilities must acquire functional skills and knowledge that they will be able to apply to daily life.

The Council on Physical Education for Children (1992) defines "developmentally appropriate" as activities geared toward a student's developmental status, previous movement experience, fitness and skill levels, body size, and age. By the time preservice teachers complete a certification program in physical education, most are able to design instruction that is appropriate for students across the K–12 spectrum. However, they generally have difficulty knowing what is appropriate for students with disabilities and tend to base their planning on a student's chronological rather than developmental age. These children then leave physical education with sets of skills that bear no

120

Strategies for
Inclusion:
Teaching
Students with
Disabilities

relationship to one another, with no knowledge of how to apply them to any form of physical activity, and therefore unable to participate in an enjoyable way in any leisure pursuit.

ACCOMMODATING STUDENTS WITH DISABILITIES

Our objective has to be that *all* students in our classes learn and grow. It is not acceptable that we consider ourselves successful with the mere *presence* of students with disabling conditions in our classes. If we maintain a focus on individual needs, this educational objective can be achieved. Individualized instruction is not always equal, means different things to each student, and varies by the setting and environment in which it is practiced. Physical educators may not be able to design learning experiences that provide equitable opportunities for all students, in all instances, and in all classes. However, from our perspective, partial participation is better than no participation, especially when designed with individual learners in mind. Participation with assistance, using adapted equipment, or through game and activity modifications allows opportunities for all students to learn and achieve.

Most students with disabilities can be included in general physical education in ways that are safe yet challenging and provide opportunities for success without drastically changing the physical education that students without disabilities experience. Some changes that do impact the entire class might have positive benefits for all students. For example, modifying equipment to slow a game down (raising net height in volleyball or using a lighter, larger ball in tennis) will allow all students to move into position, emphasize specific skills and tactics, concentrate on skill performance, and thus improve game play. However, this is not always the case and is not easily done. A recent study of effective teachers (LaMaster, Gall, Kinchin, & Siedentop, 1998) examining their views on inclusion practices and perceived outcomes reported that, although these teachers worked hard to find new means of instructing and organizing students with disabilities that resulted in learning gains, they were frustrated and discouraged in doing so. They were frustrated that there were few resources to provide support for their efforts and in their own feelings of inadequacy on how to deal with the challenges of inclusion.

A teacher first must decide what is important to teach in physical education and then determine whether a student with disabilities has the necessary prerequisite skills or identify the discrepancies between what the student has and what is needed. Once this is completed and the teacher has set goals for this learner to achieve, what modifications are necessary to allow this learner to achieve success can be determined. Modifications can be made to classroom organization, instructional strategies, or the games, activities, and sports used to reach physical education goals.

Whatever modifications are being contemplated, we must consider their impact on all students as well as the teacher. Block (1994) suggests four criteria to guide evaluation of any proposed modifications:

1. Does the change allow the student with disabilities to participate yet still be challenged?
2. Does the modification make the setting unsafe for the student with a disability as well as for students without disabilities?
3. Does the change affect students without disabilities?
4. Does the change place an undue burden on the regular physical education teacher?

If, when analyzing a modification, you find that it has a detrimental impact on any one of these individuals, you should reassess and revise it (Block, 1994).

CLASSROOM ORGANIZATION ISSUES

How the learning environment is arranged and how students are organized to receive instruction and interact with the environment are classroom organization issues. Numerous formats (see Chapter 13) can be adapted for the classroom that will facilitate learning for students with disabilities: one-on-one instruction, buddy systems, peer teaching or tutoring, small and large groups, teaching stations, self-paced independent work (personal goals facilitated by task cards or the teacher), cooperative learning (shared goals guided by peer support and collaboration), and reverse mainstreaming (students without disabilities integrated into a class of students with disabilities to participate and serve as role models). Choice of organizational format will depend upon the situation, the number of students with and without disabilities, and the attitudes of those students. A combination of these formats that integrates a number of these within one class session might most effectively meet the needs and abilities of all students.

Regardless of which organizational format is selected, you must determine what support is needed for students with disabilities and who will provide it. Sometimes a student with a disability can be supported through a buddy system, peer tutoring, or the entire class. Many students with disabilities will not need additional support. There are, however, students who may need instructional support or who have a medical condition or behavior problems that may pose a risk to themselves or others. In these cases, you must determine who will provide support. Selecting and training personnel to provide adequate, appropriate, and safe support to the student with disabilities is ultimately the responsibility of the regular physical education teacher. Table 7.1 provides a continuum of support to assist in this decision-making process.

Two of the most successful and frequently used support systems for students with disabilities are the buddy system and peer tutoring. The buddy system is an informal way to provide assistance to students with disabilities in a regular physical education class. This assistance might be a student who is assigned as a buddy for a unit, a semester, or the year. "The buddy is not only a friend, model, and mentor, but also a storyteller, writer, and reader: a listener, playmate, and tutor" (Pratt, 1994, p. 251). Having a buddy makes the

TABLE 7.1   A Continuum of Support to Regular Physical Education

LEVEL 1: NO SUPPORT

    1.1 Student makes necessary modifications on his or her own.

    1.2 RPE* teacher makes necessary modifications for student.

LEVEL 2: APE** CONSULTATION

    2.1 No extra assistance is needed.

    2.2 Peer tutor "watches out" for student.

    2.3 Peer tutor assists student.

    2.4 Paraprofessional assists student.

LEVEL 3: APE DIRECT SERVICE IN RPE 1× per week

    3.1 Peer tutor "watches out" for student.

    3.2 Peer tutor assists student.

    3.3 Paraprofessional assists student.

LEVEL 4: PART-TIME APE and PART-TIME RPE

    4.1 Flexible schedule with reverse mainstreaming

    4.2 Fixed schedule with reverse mainstreaming

LEVEL 5: REVERSE MAINSTREAMING IN SPECIAL SCHOOL

    5.1 Students from special school go to regular physical education at regular school 1–2× per week.

    5.2 Nondisabled students come to special school 2–3× per week for reverse mainstreaming.

    5.3 Students with and without disabilities meet at community-based recreation facility and work out together.

* Regular physical education
** Adapted physical education

Source: Reprinted by permission from M. E. Block and P. L. Krebs, 1992, "An alternative to least restrictive environments: A continuum of support to regular physical education," *Adapted Physical Activity Quarterly,* 9(2):104.

environment a safe place for the student with a disability to learn, grow, and develop in physical activity while having someone to monitor his or her performance and provide feedback. A buddy needs to be provided with at least minimal training on what this role is and how to provide helpful and safe assistance.

A more formal system of providing assistance is peer tutoring, which can take the form of either classwide peer tutoring (CWPT) or one-on-one tutoring. In CWPT, two students of approximately equal skills take turns serving as the tutee (practicing specific skills/behaviors) and the tutor (providing feedback/cue/prompts). One-on-one tutoring generally involves one student who is older or more skilled serving as the tutor to a younger, less-skilled tutee (or student with a disability). In either case, the roles are more formal than in the buddy system and require that the tutor be knowledgeable, understand the specifics of the task to be achieved, and be able to provide feedback and maintain a record of performance progress.

Other organizational considerations useful in managing a physical education classroom that has students with and without disabilities are included in Box 7.2.

INSTRUCTIONAL STRATEGIES

These instructional strategies can be incorporated into the design of learning experiences for students with disabilities. Many of these same strategies will resurface in the planning section of this book because they are also appropriate when designing instruction for all students. Here we highlight how and when to use these strategies for students with disabilities; we refocus them toward students without disabilities later as a prompt to you that all learning must be designed with individual differences in mind.

Physical positioning. Some children will be more attentive and better able to grasp content and what they are expected to do if they are positioned in close proximity to you or to the content being presented. This might be especially true for students who are hearing impaired or have difficulty maintaining their attention span.

Modeling. Demonstrating a behavior or skill is critical for most students when learning a motor skill. Additional demonstrations can be provided to an entire group or one-on-one for students who need an additional model. These follow-up demonstrations might focus on one specific aspect of a skill or a sequence of steps to model or highlight difficult concepts to grasp.

Structure. Behavior disabilities require structure; more is better. For these learners, signals and routines that remain constant provide the most consistent environment. Structured teaching strategies such as using behavior cards for timed feedback will also facilitate learning.

Input. Asking the learners what else you might do to help them learn is always a useful strategy. Too often, we fail to gain the student's voice.

Prompting aids. Cards to signify number of laps, floor markings to guide movement, laminated cards with pictorial directions to guide practice or routines, and picture icons on posted notices are all examples of tools to aid learning.

Expanded student opportunities. Use modifications of equipment, facilities, rules, and number of students as a means to extend opportunities for participation.

BOX 7.2   Organizational Issues in Accommodating Students with Disabilities

Time & Duration

Consideration must be given to the time of day, length of time (duration) of an activity, and season of the year and how it relates to individual students. Specific disabilities, how an individual student tires, and types of medications and their side effects all factor into the issue of time.

- A student medicated in the afternoon might be more successful taking physical education in the morning.
- One child might be able to handle 10 minutes in activity before a rest; another might be able to negotiate only 2 minutes without resting.
- A student with sinus allergies that affect him or her in the morning might feel better taking physical education in the afternoon.

Signals

Teachers typically use signals to initiate a specific managerial behavior (start, stop, gather, quiet, leave). Because students need to learn a signal and what it means, we typically see teachers using a consistent signal for a desired behavior. When a student with a disability is in class, signals must be chosen carefully or an additional signal taught to this student.

- Hand signals might accompany a verbal cue.
- Teachers may seek the assistance of students to let a disabled peer know a signal has been given.
- Some students may require physical assistance to respond to a signal.

Routines

Routines are intended to control behaviors that occur frequently and could be disruptive. They supply structure and order in the classroom and are useful in providing students with knowledge of expected and appropriate behavior. Routines are especially helpful for students who have difficulty with change or whose disability makes them less able to adjust to occasional inconsistency in class. Having routines for all students is helpful for keeping the class running smoothly, but they are essential for students with disabilities.

- Entry routines with designated home bases are helpful in creating a consistent setting.
- Maintaining the same routines from one unit/season to the next is important for students with some types of disabilities.

Grouping

Grouping of students may vary, depending upon the nature of the instructional goal and intended learning. In some instances, like abilities are appropriate, and in others, mixed abilities may be more effective. Decisions about numbers of students in groups may impact learning experiences.

- A less-skilled student might be placed on a team with more players so that the team is not disadvantaged.
- Players of similar ability might be paired up against one another in games.
- Methods of selecting teams should always reflect sensitivity to all students.

Source: Adapted from Block, 1994.

Linking new and old. Help students connect new information and what they previously learned. This allows them to transfer skills and concepts to "real" situations and apply their knowledge across settings and situations. This might begin by specifically providing students with the connections between old and new knowledge and progress to allowing them to make those connections themselves. This will increase their ability to apply learning to new situations.

Practice in real settings. Providing opportunities for students to practice skills, concepts, and knowledge in realistic situations will make them more meaningful to them and also improve their ultimate performance. Too frequently, we see children and youth practicing skills in isolation, removed from the authentic ways they are intended to be performed. If you want a child to learn to participate in a physical activity such as being able to play a game, why would you emphasize practicing skills and tactics in ways that don't reflect the game itself? A child with a disability could end up leaving a physical education program able to demonstrate a set of disjointed skills and movements, yet have no idea how to combine them into functional and enjoyable activity.

Not all children are the same, even if they have the same disability. This suggests that teachers observe their students interacting with the content and attempting the tasks that have been designed. In order to provide children and youth with opportunities to succeed, you can modify activities to meet their individual needs. These modifications can be made to equipment, playing fields/boundaries, time, motor patterns, and rules, as the following examples suggest:

- Decrease/reduce the playing area.
- Shorten the playing time and provide frequent rests.
- Modify the rules governing play.
- Use larger, lighter equipment.
- Simplify the activity; slow the pace; modify the play patterns.

As you design learning experiences, ask yourself what modifications you can make for individual students that won't impact the nature of the activity for other students. Is it necessary for all students to serve from behind the end line in volleyball, or could some serve from half court? Generally, all students will have more opportunities for success if there are fewer players on the field/court, and numbers need not change the purpose of the game. Is there a way to modify the size of the playing field to accommodate students with physical restrictions or limited mobility? There may be students for whom two serve attempts rather than one might allow them a chance to succeed. Throughout your planning, examine all aspects of participation that might allow accommodation without impacting the nature of the activity, its purpose, the number of players, the size of playing field, starting and restarting play, expectations for performance, and the playing implements.

126

Strategies for
Inclusion:
Teaching
Students with
Disabilities

The PE-Central Web site provides an extended list of adaptations, modifications, and changes to activities that will allow all students to be successful. In addition, it provides sport/activity-specific modifications to guide planning. Bowling, for example, could be modified as follows:

- Simplify/reduce the number of steps.
- Use two hands instead of one.
- Remain in a stationary position.
- Use a ramp.
- Use a partner.
- Give continuous verbal cues.

As you progress through the PE-Central Web site, you will find links to numerous informative Web sites specific to adapted physical education, such as Cyber-Active, Special Olympics, and national standards for adapted physical education.

As you modify instructional content and activities, consider specific disabilities of students. Guidelines to assist with planning and implementing physical education for specific categories of disabilities can be a useful resource for the general physical education teacher (Box 7.3).

SUMMARY

1. There is a variety of ways students with disabilities experience physical education, and this can vary greatly between school districts.

2. Students with diverse needs, strengths, abilities, and skills are more frequently being included in general physical education with the expectation that each is provided with educational experiences designed to meet his or her own individual needs.

3. Children with disabilities fall into six categories: visually impaired, physically or other health impaired, mentally challenged, behaviorally challenged, hearing impaired, or multiple handicapped.

4. School districts must identify, evaluate, and develop an IEP for any student who might qualify for special accommodations in the classroom.

5. The least restrictive environment ranges from the regular classroom to the learning center at the public school to home instruction.

6. When designing learning experiences for students with disabilities, don't give up too easily; find each learner's strength; provide all learners time to learn and grow; emphasize progress, achievement, and quality of performance; and focus on learning and meaningful learning outcomes.

7. When you are modifying instruction to accommodate students with disabilities, the four criteria that must be met are focus on the student with the disability, safety, students without disabilities, and the physical education teacher.

BOX 7.3 Possible Needs of Children with Various Disabilities

Autism

- Consistent and structured motor routines
- Support for slow progress
- Physical assistance, demonstration, and verbal input
- Basic and fundamental skill instruction
- Small-group or one-on-one activities
- Low-organization games with few rules
- Play skill instruction

Cognitive Disabilities

- A consistent routine
- Simplicity in plans, directions, and expectations
- Basic or fundamental skill progression
- Physically assisted demonstrations
- Frequent changes in activity (if frustration is evident)
- Small-group activities
- Social and self-help skills built into gross motor time
- Basic motor and sensory motor instruction

Physical Impairments

- Input from occupational or physical therapist regarding how best to facilitate movement, as well as contraindications for certain types of movements
- Sensory motor (tactile and balance) activities
- Perceptual motor activities (e.g., balance and spatial relationships)
- Rhythm and music activities
- Emphasis on fun aspects, not skill or accuracy
- Activities that provide rest and relaxation
- Adapted equipment for certain activities
- Games that require cooperation

(continued)

8. Determining and using appropriate support for students with disabilities are critical and can include a buddy system, peer tutoring, or involvement of the entire class.

9. Organizational considerations that have implications for accommodating students with disabilities include time and duration of activity, signals, routines, and grouping.

128

Strategies for
Inclusion:
Teaching
Students with
Disabilities

BOX 7.3 Possible Needs of Children with Various Disabilities (*continued*)

Visual Impairments

- Orientation to the equipment and space
- Clearly marked boundaries and equipment with bright or sharp contrast of colors or raised edges
- Consistent motor routines
- Auditory cues (e.g., whistle, clap, beep) to signal changes
- Buddy systems during games
- Movement experienced in a variety of ways (e.g., slow, fast, on all fours, on one foot)
- Beeper and bell balls to help locate objects
- Rhythmic activities
- Goals with an auditory component (e.g., use of a metronome behind a basket on a basketball court)

Hearing Impairments

- A specialized communication system
- A consistent motor routine
- Games that (initially) require little or no auditory input
- Balance activities
- Rhythmic activities
- Simple stunts and trampoline activities

Severe Mental or Physical Impairments

Children with more severe impairments—mental, physical, or both—should also be included in gross motor time. Another person may be needed to facilitate the movements or actions needed to participate in the activities. The assistance of other adults such as teaching assistants, therapists, older students, or classroom teachers is invaluable. Some children may be able to participate only if they are guided through an activity. It is important that they are physically assisted in the company of their peers and given the opportunities to play and socialize in games, songs, and circle activities while in the gym or multipurpose room.

Source: Reprinted by permission from K. Davis, 1998, "Integrating children with disabilities into gross motor activities," *Teaching Elementary Physical Education,* 9(4):10–12.

10. To facilitate learning for students with disabilities, the teacher should know how and when to use physical positioning, modeling, structure, student input, prompting aids, expanding student opportunities to respond, linking new to old, and practicing in real settings.

PART THREE

Planning for Meaningful and Effective Learning

One of the saddest situations in physical education is to see a well-managed class, led by a teacher with good teaching skills, working on content that is boring, insignificant, or developmentally inappropriate for the particular group of students. Designing a meaningful, challenging curriculum is a key element in building a successful physical education program. Translating the intent of that curriculum into units of instruction, then a series of lessons, each of which has an appropriate progression of well-designed learning tasks, is the basic stuff of good planning.

The chapters in Part Three will help you understand how to align your goals for physical education with the activities designed to meet those goals and the assessments to show how well students have achieved the outcomes that define the goals. Part Three starts with curriculum concepts and principles, then introduces you to exemplary main-theme curriculums, then discusses assessing learning outcomes and designing task progressions to achieve them, then helps you see how goals get translated into units of instruction and daily lessons. This will help you understand how to make the content of physical education come alive for diverse learners.

CHAPTER 8

Curriculum Concepts and Planning Principles

A discussion of curriculum is not complete without reiterating why . . . why is curriculum important? As a teacher, a curriculum is not a discussion of abstractions or a handing down of the traditional. Curriculum is at the heart of what we do as teachers and what we have as our legacy to the next generation.

—SUSAN KOVALIK (1994)

OVERALL CHAPTER OUTCOME

To produce a curriculum outline that reflects the suggested planning principles and is based on the NASPE framework

CHAPTER OBJECTIVES

- To differentiate between curriculum and program
- To describe the attributes of a successful physical education
- To define important terms used in the curriculum process
- To delineate how curriculum is typically developed in schools
- To specify the six curriculum principles
- To explain the different "goods" to which physical education curriculums are devoted
- To describe the six-step model for curriculum planning
- To explicate the NASPE definition of a physically educated person
- To clarify the role of the NASPE content standards
- To explain the various ways in which a K–12 articulated curriculum might be organized
- To elucidate the equity issues important for curriculum planning

A curriculum is a set of objectives and outcomes that describes what students are to achieve in a particular subject matter and the activities planned to achieve those outcomes. All the experiences that students have in physical education while they attend a particular school represent that school's *program*. Those experiences in physical education ought to add up to something significant in the lives of students. Physical education should excite students, engage them enthusiastically in activities they find meaningful, and eventually help them develop lifelong commitments to physically active lifestyles.

Sadly, physical education curriculums do not always achieve those goals. Too many children and youth move through their physical education experiences bored, uninterested, and even eventually alienated from the physically active lifestyle that most curriculums aim to develop. Too many students wonder where all the excitement is that they see and experience in school sport, in community activity programs, on television, and in fitness centers. In too many school districts, elementary school, middle school, and high school physical education is planned and delivered with no serious effort to articulate the programs at the three levels to achieve significant K–12 curriculum goals.

131

The Role of
Curriculum in
a Successful
Physical
Education

One major culprit is the continued widespread use of the short-unit, multi-activity curriculum model—what many refer to as a "smorgasbord" curriculum. Because physical education has many goals, teachers plan the curriculum as a series of short activity units, with a few lessons of isolated, basic skill practice and then a few class periods of a tournament or series of games. Perhaps most alarming is that these same "introductory" units tend to be taught over and over again throughout the curriculum, so that students' physical education experiences are repetitive, boring, and unchallenging. Thus, a ninth grade student in high school physical education might well experience a short volleyball unit in which the first several lessons introduce the serve, forearm pass, set, and spike. These skills are then practiced in drills that often isolate the skills from the context in which they might be used in games—even so, students seldom get sufficient practice opportunities to become confident about their skills. Then, for several lessons, teams are assigned and games are played. Game play is typically of low quality because students don't have sufficient skills to enjoy the game, having had little opportunity to learn the tactical and strategic elements of volleyball. Many of those students might have had nearly identical volleyball units in middle school and in the upper elementary grades, so they leave school with little appreciation for what a great sport volleyball can be and ill equipped to pursue volleyball as a recreational sport in their adult years. Their curriculum has failed them.

THE ROLE OF CURRICULUM IN A SUCCESSFUL PHYSICAL EDUCATION

A successful physical education, one in which most students achieve a large proportion of the goals, is the result of curriculum and instruction coming together in appropriate ways and is greatly enhanced when facilitative structural arrangements can be put in place. A successful physical education requires the following:

- A meaningful, relevant curriculum that is articulated across grade levels
- Effective teaching that helps students become enthused, self-reliant learners
- Organizational arrangements that allow for meaningful engagement and provide sufficient time and support to achieve meaningful outcomes

A dull curriculum, perceived by students as boring and irrelevant, will fail, *even when it is taught very effectively.* An exciting and relevant curriculum can also fail *if it is taught ineffectively.* A meaningful curriculum that is delivered effectively through appropriate instructional strategies will succeed. Organizational arrangements such as block scheduling, persisting groups, learning communities, use of nonattached school time for extra programming, and links to community programs can all strengthen and invigorate the curriculum.

This chapter introduces the concepts and language of curriculum and the fundamental principles that guide its development. The chapter also introduces the curriculum suggestions made by our national professional leaders that should form the basis of the curriculum design suggestions made here. You have already been introduced, in Chapters 1 and 6, to basic information on teaching effectiveness and structural issues such as persisting groups and learning communities. This chapter will be most relevant to those who are required to or want to develop their own curriculum or, more appropriately, work with other physical education teachers in a district to develop a district curriculum, utilizing the guidelines developed by the National Association for Sport and Physical Education (NASPE). The concepts and principles in this chapter will be necessary if you have to "start from scratch" to build a curriculum. Chapter 9 introduces you to well-tested "exemplary" curriculum models, describing the alternative of building a district curriculum by utilizing those already well developed models in combinations at various grade levels. Chapters 10 and 11 will equip you with the knowledge and understanding to take a curriculum plan and build meaningful units and lessons so that the curriculum is delivered as effectively as possible. Part Four will then help you understand the teaching skills necessary to make all that planning come alive and be effective with your students.

IMPORTANT CURRICULUM TERMS

To become knowledgeable and skilled in the area of curriculum, you must be able to use the common technical terms. These terms and concepts are employed by teachers and administrators in their everyday work in schools, and a mastery of them is necessary for you to read the professional literature.

Most school districts and many states have and require a *curriculum guide,* which is a formal district document explaining the objectives to be achieved in a subject and the activities thought to contribute to those objectives. A curriculum guide is also often referred to as a *curriculum syllabus* or a *graded course of study.* Curriculum guides have become very detailed in some districts that have moved toward an *outcomes-based curriculum,* in which specific outcomes rather than general goals form the basis of the curriculum and thus require more detail in terms of what activities and experiences contribute to the outcomes.

An *objective* is a statement of instructional intent that specifies what knowledges, attitudes, and behaviors are meant to be learned. Physical educators have traditionally designed objectives in four domains: fitness, motor skill, cognitive, and social. Not only do curriculums have general objectives in those domains, but unit objectives become more specific, and traditional lesson planning suggests that each lesson should have identified objectives.

An *outcome* is a description of what a student will know and be able to do as the result of participating in the activities in a program. Outcomes should be defined in ways that show immediately how the outcome would be assessed; that is, the very statement of the outcome suggests when it can be known that the outcome has been achieved. Outcomes can be viewed as "ends," and curriculum objectives can be viewed as "means" (Lambert, 1996). Outcomes must guide the development of objectives because, if they do not, objectives might be achieved, but the desired outcome will not be reached.

One reform agenda in education has been to stress the importance of *authentic* outcomes (Wiggins, 1993b). An outcome is authentic if it requires a performance in a context similar to the one in which the knowledge, skills, and strategies will eventually be used (Siedentop, 1996). Authentic outcomes are evaluated through measures of *authentic assessment* (see Chapter 10), in which the assessment allows students to demonstrate the necessary performance qualities in the appropriate context; for example, authentic outcomes in sport activities would relate to actually performing the sport in a competitive setting, such as a basketball game. Authentic assessment would require information on points scored, shooting percentages, turnovers, rebounds, and the like, as well as measures of how successfully the strategy was implemented.

In most subjects, primary attention is paid to *content outcomes,* strategically appropriate skills and knowledge that represent what is essential for successful performance in a particular activity. Educators, however, have always believed in the importance of *process outcomes,* those skills and attitudes that manifest themselves in areas such as problem solving, effective communication, teamwork, and fair play.

When final outcomes are established for a curriculum, it then becomes necessary to define how the outcomes will be translated to various grade levels for purposes of planning units and lessons. The final outcomes of a curriculum are defined in terms of *exit standards.* The next important step in curriculum planning is identifying *content standards,* which define what students should know and be able to do at a particular level (National Association for Sport and Physical Education, 1995). The use of content standards as a planning device should be accompanied by the definition of *performance standards,* which tell teachers and students how well the student has to perform to meet the content standards, that is, how good is "good enough" for that level. Behaviors that indicate progress toward a performance standard are called *performance benchmarks.* Identifying performance standards and benchmarks related to those standards leads quickly and easily to *standards-based assessment.*

THE PLAIN TRUTH ABOUT CURRICULUM DESIGN

How does a district graded course of study for physical education get developed? We wish we could report that curriculum development in schools is always an important enterprise and that the document produced truly guides the physical education program toward significant achievement of important outcomes. Sadly, such is not the case in many places.

Typically, a committee is appointed to do all the preliminary work, including development of an overall district philosophy and a set of goals and discussion of which activities best meet the goals. The committee will be comprised mostly (sometimes exclusively) of physical education teachers, but might also include a school administrator, a district curriculum director, and a parent. Very seldom does curriculum building in schools involve students, although an assessment of student needs is often part of the process. The graded course of study is often broad in scope because it has to allow for sometimes quite divergent points of view of various physical educators within the district. Curriculum goals are defined quite broadly, and there is often a large number of them. The committee then identifies activities "appropriate" for meeting the goals, which usually results in the inclusion of nearly every physical activity known to humankind, simply because teachers are at risk for liability if they teach an activity that is not on the approved list in the graded course of study. Very seldom is there serious effort to truly develop a sequenced K–12 curriculum that adds up to something significant; thus, in many districts, the elementary school physical education curriculum often differs in goals and substance from the middle school curriculum, which in turn is still different from the high school curriculum. The graded course of study is developed with sufficient breadth that it accommodates these different approaches at various school levels. The curriculum goals and objectives are sufficiently numerous and broad to allow individual teachers to do just about whatever they want in their own planning and classes. Once completed, the graded course of study often finds a place on the shelf and is not truly used until the next time the district requires that all curriculums be revised and updated. One national curriculum consultant has called such curriculum guides well-intentioned, fictional documents (ASCD, 1998b).

One of the main problems with curriculum design undertaken in the manner described is that teachers set out each year to "cover the curriculum." The curriculum is so broad, with so many objectives, that teachers move quickly through short units in their attempts to cover the full curriculum plan for the school year. The result is often that the curriculum has indeed been "covered," but very little learning has taken place because there is insufficient time for students to develop mastery in any of the activities. Physical education has suffered from this approach to curriculum planning. Approaches to thinking about curriculum have to change for physical education to become a more exciting subject in which students learn and grow.

PRINCIPLES OF CURRICULUM DESIGN

There are places where curriculum is taken seriously. Good curriculum planning can truly guide the instructional activities of physical education. In a most real sense, what you design for in curriculum planning is what you get (ASCD, 1998a). If you design for important achievement of significant outcomes, then that is what you will get. There are six principles that need to be utilized when planning curriculums:

1. *Develop a clear statement of a limited set of "goods" that physical education should achieve.* Curriculum building in physical education inevitably begins with value decisions about what outcomes are most important to achieve, that is, the "good" that a particular curriculum represents. However, there are very different points of view about what constitutes the primary good of physical education. We advocate a *limited* set of goods. Successful curriculum efforts are the result of a focused vision of a manageable set of goods that leads to a clear, limited focus for outcomes. There are legitimately different visions in our profession about the most important values that physical education should achieve, but it is a mistake to start the curriculum-building process by including so many different visions of the good that designing a focused curriculum becomes impossible.

2. *Less is more.* A clear, limited vision for a physical education curriculum will inevitably lead to reducing the number of outcomes to be achieved, thus allowing more time within the curriculum to achieve them. This, in turn, will lead to longer units of instruction. The curriculum concept of "less is more" has been particularly associated with reform of the high school curriculum (Sizer, 1992), but it can apply throughout the K–12 spectrum.

3. *Use authentic outcomes to improve motivation and learning* Authentic outcomes are contextualized performance capabilities, most often assessed through a final performance or an "exhibition" (Wiggins, 1987). The public performance of a folk dance or a jump rope routine, the performance of a free exercise routine in a gymnastics competition, the individual and collective performances of a floor hockey team in a round-robin tournament, or the achievement of the goals of a semester-long nutrition and exercise program are all examples of authentic outcomes. Authentic outcomes provide goals for students. Working toward a final exhibition of their skills helps motivate them to engage in serious learning. And it is more fun!

4. *Design down.* Good curriculum design begins with the exit outcomes and proceeds backwards to ensure that all components are directly related to achieving the outcome. If, for example, curriculum designers decide they want students to become competent in at least one sport from each of four categories (invasion, court-divided, target, and form sports), that would represent a good, and they could then begin to define what "competent" means for high school students, then start there and design down to see where they would have to start with beginning learners to reach the desired outcomes. The design-down principle requires that curriculum developers always ask how a proposed curriculum element would contribute to the exit outcome.

5. *Plan for and check alignment.* Alignment exists when the goals, activities, instruction, and assessment of a physical education program are matched and compatible. If you have skilled, tactical play in volleyball as an outcome, but lessons consist mostly of isolated skill drills and the assessments are a serving test and a wall-volley test, then you have a serious mismatch—a nonaligned unit. If, however, the goal of skilled, tactical play is achieved through a series of sequenced activities that contextualize skills as they will be used in game play, learning tasks are also organized around important strategic principles for volleyball, and performance is evaluated by various analyses of actual game play, then you have a match—an aligned unit. If your curriculum suggests that developing independent learners is a good, but there is no evidence that students have increasing responsibility and choice, then the curriculum is far from aligned.

6. *Carefully consider the distribution of sequenced experiences.* Many curriculums are developed with the assumption that experiences should be sequenced across the K–12 spectrum, that nearly every unit of instruction should include some activities related to the major goals of the curriculum. Thus, teachers commonly assume that every unit should contribute to fitness, motor skill, cognitive, social, and other goals. They also assume that the best way to help students learn activities such as volleyball, folk dance, or track and field is to provide several units of instruction that are distributed across grade levels (for example, volleyball units repeated in 5th, 8th, and 10th grades). But this approach to distribution seldom achieves its intention. Rather than three 6- to 8-day units at those three levels, a 24-day unit at one level would result in better learning and more enjoyment for the students. Chapter 9 describes more distribution possibilities.

THE GOOD IN PHYSICAL EDUCATION

What goods do students acquire from a physical education program? Is it a lifetime commitment to physical fitness? Is it the ability and desire to participate in recreational sports? Is it the capacity to cooperate with others toward group goals and the ability to provide leadership in groups when and where necessary? Is it a sense of comfort with and ownership of their own body and confidence in their ability to control it to perform various physical activities? Is it an aesthetic experience, the appreciation and valuing of the beauty of physical movement activities? Is physical education mostly about learning to be responsible for oneself and helpful to others? All these things, and others, have been suggested by various scholars and professionals as representing the primary goods of physical education.

Building a curriculum begins with making value decisions about what is most important. Value decisions should always be contextualized—that is, the good in physical education is always about a particular group of students, who live in particular circumstances, and at a particular time, when society values some goals more than others (as in the several historic periods when society has become very concerned about the fitness levels of children and youths). This is not to suggest that local needs or societal concerns are the primary driving force for curriculum design. Rather, it suggests that value decisions about the vision of a curriculum should not be made without considering these issues.

Developing a guiding vision for a curriculum is not about the technical planning of a graded course of study—this is about the "stuff" of physical education. Values will guide answers to questions such as "What am I trying to contribute to the lives of these students?" and "How do I want their lives to be enriched by having had these experiences?" Values arise when parents tell a teacher what characteristic or quality they would most like their son or daughter to gain from physical education.

Different visions of the good, of course, would lead to diversified curriculum choices and eventually to various programs of experiences, especially when the curriculum design principles described in the previous section are utilized. To achieve the goals of a curriculum, you must align the outcomes and content standards with the vision. There has been a growing consensus nationally that not all goods can be achieved in any one program—and that trying to achieve too many goals results in too little achievement.

> The generally accepted goals of physical education are to promote physical fitness, self-esteem, and cognitive and social development. However, the practice—the proliferation of and emphasis on teaching too many activities in too short a time—has made these goals more difficult to attain. The smorgasbord approach of requiring team sports, individual sports, dance, physical fitness activities, all within the space of one school year lessens those students' opportunities to master any one activity through which they can meet the stated goals. (Taylor & Chiogioji, 1987, p. 22)

There is a point at which students should have an increasing role in helping define the good. In high school programs, this is most often achieved through an elective curriculum, in which student needs and interests drive both the range of activities offered and student selection from within that range of activities. Teachers also have some obligation to help educate younger students to see the difference between an immediate felt need or preference for certain goals and activities (for example, when many male students just want to play basketball in every class throughout the school year) to a more educated sense of what the possibilities are and what their own preferred future might be like in physical education (when students have a better sense of the health and leisure needs and possibilities for their lives).

Our first curriculum planning principle suggests that a limited, focused set of goods be defined. Too many physical education curriculums adopt all of the many goods. In trying to be all things to all students, they frequently fail to achieve anything of substance. The result is often the fragmented program, with a series of short-term experiences that leave students bored and uninterested. Given the amount of time allotted to physical education in a school program, choices must be made about which goods are more important than others—for these students, in this place, at this time. If we had 2 hours per day, 5 days per week, for the length of a school year, for all the K–12 years, we would have a wider vision for the curriculum and could develop more expansive programs that deliver a broader range of significant outcomes. To pretend, however, that multiple major goals can be achieved in the limited time available to most physical education programs is to risk fooling yourself and the public. In Chapter 9, we introduce and develop the concept of "main-theme" programs. Main-theme programs develop because the physical educator responsible for them had a vision about what was the primary good to be achieved and then developed content to achieve that vision and allowed enough time for students to reach significant outcomes.

A MODEL FOR CURRICULUM PLANNING

The following six-step process for curriculum planning (ASCD, 1998b), when combined with the design principles described in the previous section, allow physical educators to create and deliver curriculums that achieve significant outcomes and capture the enthusiasm of students, school administrators, and parents.

1. *Know the territory.* A good curriculum plan is specific rather than generic (ASCD, 1998a). A curriculum should always serve a specific group of learners. Physical educators should understand the current performance capabilities of students, the characteristics of the students and the community in which they live, the facilities and administrative characteristics of the school, and the perspectives of the students in the school and the parents and caregivers of those students.

2. *Develop a clear program vision.* The "vision thing" is about deciding what limited set of goods the physical education curriculum will achieve. Having completed step 1, the vision will now be for *these* students, in *this* place, and in *this* time.

3. *Define the outcomes that fulfill the vision.* We say "outcomes" rather than "goals" because there should be a high degree of specificity about what students will know and be able to do when they complete their physical education.

4. *Assess how instructional practices and organizational conditions can help or hinder achievement of the outcomes.* As Chapters 13 and 14 show, there is a variety of instructional practices available to physical education teachers, and their use must be aligned with goals and assessment practices (for example, the use of small groups to help develop collaborative learning or the utilization of persisting groups to develop teamwork and leadership qualities). Organizational structures such as block scheduling (see Box 8.1), the linking of school programs and community opportunities, and longer units of instruction also will affect the potential to achieve outcomes.

BOX 8.1   Block Scheduling as a Structural Aid to Curriculum Success

We have emphasized that organizational arrangements can enhance the possibility that a curriculum will be successful in achieving its goals. One such arrangement is block scheduling, which is increasingly used in middle and high schools. Two configurations are most common. One is the A-B, alternating day model. Classes meet every other day for 90 minutes for an entire school year. The other is the 4 × 4 model. Classes meet every day for 90 minutes for one semester. Although 90 minutes appears to be the norm in block scheduling, class length can range from 80 to 120 minutes.

One study (Shortt & Thayer, 1998–99) found that schools with block-scheduled classes showed marked improvement over those with traditionally organized school days. Academic performance was better. There was increased attention to staff development and instructional programs. Administrators reported that block scheduling seems to have positive impact on lower-performing students and on achievement scores for most students. The increases were found for both urban and rural schools.

Bryant and Claxton (1996) surveyed 55 high schools that had moved to block scheduling to assess the effects of the change on physical education. They reported that all comments were positive. Physical educators reported decreased absenteeism, improved student behavior, more teacher collaboration, and more planning time.

5. *Develop the curriculum plan.* The curriculum plan, using the design-down approach, can now be based realistically on the assessment of local conditions, the vision believed to be most salient to those local conditions, a series of outcomes aligned with that vision, and instructional practices and organizational arrangements that assist in achieving the outcomes.

6. *Implement the plan and assess the results.* In order to create a "live" curriculum that continually adjusts and improves, the planning group should agree to assessment measures that will provide evidence of the degree to which the vision is being achieved through significant outcomes. This allows for the best chance that physical educators will, indeed, get what they design.

THE NASPE CURRICULUM FRAMEWORK

Through NASPE leadership, physical education professionals have developed a national curriculum framework to help local physical educators think about and plan a coherent, meaningful physical education for their students. The first important step in this initiative was the Outcomes Project, which sought to answer the question, "What should students know and be able to do as a result of physical education?" An important contribution of the Outcomes of

Quality Physical Education (National Association for Sport and Physical Education, 1995) was a widely accepted definition of a physically educated person as the following:

- *Has* sufficient skill to perform a variety of physical activities
- *Does* participate regularly in physical activity
- *Is* physically fit
- *Knows* the benefits, costs, risks, and obligations of physical activity involvement
- *Values* the role of regular physical activity in the maintenance of a healthy lifestyle

The five components of this definition were further defined through the series of 20 more descriptive outcome statements shown in Chapter 1 (Box 1.3). For example, the "*is* physically fit" component was further defined as the capacity to assess, achieve, and maintain physical fitness, along with the capacity to design safe, personal fitness programs in accordance with principles of training and conditioning. In the early 1990s, a national education movement in the United States began to work toward goals and standards for all subjects in public schools. This culminated in 1994 when Congress passed the *Goals 2000: Educate America Act*. Title II of that act established a National Education Standards Improvement Council, which had the responsibility to work with various national professional organizations to develop voluntary content standards for their subject matter. NASPE took the lead in this initiative for physical education professionals.

In 1995, NASPE published *Moving into the Future: National Standards for Physical Education*. This document now represents the major curriculum planning resource for physical educators in the United States. Seven content standards were identified to provide curricular alignment with the vision provided in the NASPE definition of a physically educated person (Box 8.2).

The NASPE framework identifies specific examples of the content standards for every other grade level, starting with kindergarten (K, 2, 4, 6, 8, 10, and 12). For each content standard, the document specifically describes what should be emphasized, then describes sample behavioral benchmarks that would indicate progress toward the standard for that grade level. The sample benchmarks are followed by examples of assessment strategies and the criteria a teacher might use to assess whether the performance has reached the "good enough" level.

The NASPE curriculum framework has adopted a "distribution principle" that addresses all content standards at each grade level. The unwritten assumption of this framework is that all content standards are addressed *equally* at all grade levels—or, at the very least, this is what one might infer from examining the materials. Thus, the NASPE materials suggest multiple specific examples of the application of each content standard for each grade level. The NASPE framework and suggestions could be applied with different distribution principles. For example, you can take any one of the content stan-

---

BOX 8.2   NASPE Content Standards

The physically educated person:
1. Demonstrates competency in many movement forms and proficiency in a few movement forms
2. Applies movement concepts and principles to the learning and development of motor skills
3. Exhibits a physically active lifestyle
4. Achieves and maintains a health-enhancing level of physical fitness
5. Demonstrates responsible personal and social behavior in physical activity settings
6. Demonstrates understanding of and respect for differences among people in physical activity settings
7. Understands that physical activity provides opportunities for enjoyment, challenge, self-expression, and social interaction

Source: Reprinted from *Moving into the Future: National Standards for Physical Education* (1995), with permission from the National Association for Sport and Physical Education (NASPE), 1900 Association Drive, Reston, VA 20191-1599.

---

dards, start with an exit level of the standard, and, using the design down principle, develop a sequence of activities that would achieve the exit level. The NASPE materials do this, but they typically begin with the grade 12 exit standard and distribute the content standard examples across the K–12 spectrum.

The NASPE framework is an appropriate tool and guide for one using different distribution principles. For example, consider standards 1 and 2, which deal with competency in movement forms and applying concepts and principles to the development of motor skills. Although NASPE provides suggestions as to how these standards could be used at all grade levels, a group of physical educators might decide that standard 1 should be the guiding principle of curriculum in grades K–2, with perhaps a complementary focus on standard 5 (demonstrating responsible personal and social behavior in activity settings). Thus, the K–2 curriculum would have a clear *focus*. The design down principle would still be used, but in a different way than if one were working across the K–12 spectrum.

The planning group might also decide that the major *focus* of the curriculum in grade 6 should be on content standards 3, 4, and 6, which have to do with healthy lifestyles and a respect for differences. For that entire school year, the focus would be on physical activity, fitness, learning about differences, why it is important to respect them, and how respect can be shown in activity settings. Again, the design down principle would be used, but within a narrower developmental range. This is not to suggest that there would be *no* attention paid to other content standards—that there would be no effort to learn skills, no attention to responsible behavior, and the like. These would be attended to, but the main focus for choosing activities, deciding on instructional practices, and optimizing organizational arrangements would be on grade 6 outcomes for standards 3, 4, and 6.

The K–12 articulation plan might result in revisiting standard 1 (movement competency and proficiency) along with standard 7 as the curriculum focus for the second semester of the ninth grade. Here the focus might be on proficiency, and the entire 18 weeks of the term would be devoted to one sport, perhaps using the Sport Education curriculum model described in the next chapter. The focus would also include the investigation of where the sport is played in the community, who plays it, and what challenges and enjoyment they experience. Again, this is not to suggest that this ninth grade experience would not contribute, for example, to standard 3 (exhibits a physically active lifestyle). Indeed, by examining how a sport is played in the community and who plays it, students would inevitably come into contact with adults whose lifestyles include ongoing commitments to participation in a particular sport, what the costs are, and what the social aspects of the adult involvement look and feel like. The narrowed focus would better fit our design principles and enhance both the likelihood of achieving significant outcomes and the likelihood of capturing the enthusiasm of students to become fully engaged with the program.

The NASPE framework also allows for the incorporation of most of the goods cited earlier in this chapter. The key operational terms in NASPE's definition of content standards that lead to a physically educated person are "movement forms" and "physically active." These terms were purposefully chosen because they are sufficiently broad to encompass various definitions of the good that physical educators might develop in their vision for a curriculum. One could imagine that the content standards could all be achieved with a vision that focused solely on sports as the organizing framework for activity. Certainly, one can get and stay fit through sport. Certainly, different sport forms such as rhythmic gymnastics, volleyball, soccer, and the like provide a variety of physical, social, and aesthetic differences. Certainly, one could argue that sport provides a good vehicle through which personal and social responsibility can be learned and understanding and respect for differences can be achieved.

One could also imagine that a dance education program could achieve all the content standards. Jazz, ballet, aerobic, folk, and modern dance involve different skills and aesthetic experiences. Fitness and a physically active lifestyle are possible through dance. Likewise, recognition and respect for differences are eminently achievable through dance experiences, as are all of the qualities of personal and social responsibility.

Most physical educators would want some sampling of all those activities, along with, perhaps, some adventure activities and fitness activities. The issue is, how much can a curriculum "sample" and still achieve significant outcomes? We clearly have come down on the side of a more focused curriculum in which sampling is done in much larger chunks of curricular time.

The national movement toward subject-matter standards should not lead to a *standardized curriculum*. Not all students in all places need the same curriculum. The NASPE framework is sufficiently broad that physical educators can design curriculums that are sensitive to local needs and interests and *still*

achieve the exit standards associated with the definition of a physically edu-
cated person.

CURRICULUMS THAT SERVE STUDENTS EQUITABLY

Evidence presented in Chapter 2 shows that physical education curriculums have not served all students equitably. Thus, those who design curriculums must think about equity issues. Remember, you get what you design for! Sometimes curriculums do not serve students equitably not as a result of anyone intending that students be served inequitably, but rather because specific issues of equity are not considered during the design phase. The most significant factors in providing an equitable physical education for all children and youths are the instructional practices and learning environment developed and sustained by the teachers—issues dealt with extensively in Chapters 7 and 11. There are, however, questions that need to be asked at the curricular level to ensure that programs are equitable for all students.

The key question for curriculum designers is "What groups are best and most served by this curriculum?" Are males better served than females? Are more-skilled students better served than less-skilled students? Is the curriculum ethnically sensitive? Does it expand the students' capacities to live effectively in an increasingly multicultural world? Does it develop students' critical capacities to know when they are being manipulated by powerful economic forces in the health, leisure, and fitness industries? Does the curriculum inadvertently work to reproduce the inequities that exist in the worlds of sport, leisure, health, and fitness?

These are not easy questions to answer. What, for example, are the answers to curricular issues that involve gender? We know that girls have been traditionally disadvantaged in physical education, through both instructional arrangements and curricular offerings. Not too many years ago girls were offered gymnastics and dance while boys were offered touch football and basketball. Title IX was meant to eliminate that particular type of curricular inequity. We also know that even though activities are less gendered in society than they were a generation ago, many activities are still gendered. How do curricular designers in physical education deal with that issue? How do they ensure that boys and girls have opportunities to learn activities that may still have a gender association in the larger society? Answers to these questions require sound professional judgment. There are no "recipe answers," no quick fixes to the equity problems that have plagued physical education for some time. The first important step is to raise the questions—and keep raising them as curriculum is being designed.

We are strong advocates for bringing students into these discussions. Again, there is no magic formula for where and how students should begin to be given a real say in curriculum design. We suggest that the student voice be heard increasingly as the curriculum moves through the middle and high school years. Student voice can be incorporated in many different ways—and when it is heard and students understand that it is heard, we suggest that students will have a stronger sense of ownership of and loyalty to the physical education program. We also believe that, at some point in the high school years, students should be able to choose among activities, either electing courses within a requirement or being offered a wholly elective program.

SUMMARY

1. A curriculum is a set of objectives and outcomes that describe what students will achieve and the activities planned to achieve them.

2. A successful physical education requires a meaningful, relevant curriculum articulated across grade levels, effective teaching, and organizational structures that allow for meaningful engagements.

3. To participate effectively in curriculum planning, you must be able to use accurately terms such as outcome, objective, syllabus, graded course of study, content standards, authentic outcomes, and assessment.

4. Many PE curriculums are too broad in scope and include too many outcomes and activities that are seldom articulated across grade levels.

5. Curriculums should have a limited set of goods to achieve and a clear, limited set of important authentic outcomes; be designed down to achieve those outcomes; achieve alignment between goals, activities, and assessments; and be distributed to optimize effectiveness.

6. Values are important when you are designing curriculums and should be used to determine the goods that the curriculum is meant to achieve.

7. To design curriculums, teachers should know their students and context, have a clear program vision, define outcomes that represent that vision, assess how instructional and organizational practices help or hinder achievement of those outcomes, design down to alignment, and implement and assess the results.

8. The NASPE definition of a physically educated person is a broadly based definition of the good to be achieved through physical education.

9. NASPE content standards provide a framework for developing curriculums to achieve the good in that definition.

10. Equity issues of gender, skillfulness, and cultural relevance should be considered when planning curriculums.

CHAPTER 9

Main-Theme Curriculum Formats

The first question that needs to be asked when planning a curriculum is not: How can we plan more effectively or teach more effectively? It is: What curricula are worth planning? There is no point in doing more effectively what is not worth doing in the first place!

—DAVID PRATT (1994)

OVERALL CHAPTER OUTCOME

To describe what a physical education program would look like using each of the five main-theme physical education curriculum models and develop a coherent multimodel curriculum based on your perspective of the goods of physical education

CHAPTER OBJECTIVES

- To describe what is meant by a "main-theme" or focused curriculum

- To clarify how the development-refinement cycle has impacted the use of the main-theme physical education curriculum models

- To explain how most physical educators use these focused curriculum models

- To delineate the purpose, characteristics, beliefs, goods, and related NASPE K–12 content standards for Developmental Physical Education, Adventure Education, Integrated Physical Education, Physical Activity, Fitness, and Wellness Education, and Sport Education

- To explain the basis for developing a multimodel physical education curriculum

- To demonstrate how a group of teachers might go about designing a multimodel physical education curriculum

Selecting, planning, and implementing a meaningful curriculum are the most important issues to be addressed by physical education teachers. At this point, you should have reflected upon and answered some of the curricular questions posed in Chapter 8 related specifically to the children and youth with whom you might work. What is important to learn in physical education? What do you see as the needs for these students? What do your students view as most important? How does physical activity relate to their lives outside of school, and what problems do they encounter in accessing activity? What will motivate them to take part in your program? Are there current social and cultural problems that will impact teaching and learning? If so, how might a curriculum best facilitate the educational process in this setting?

In Chapter 8, we reviewed the principles of curriculum design and the curriculum framework that has been developed by the National Association for Sport and Physical Education (NASPE). Physical educators who want to design a curriculum "from the ground up" would use the material in Chapter 8. A real question is: Is the best curricular outcome achieved when physical educators start from scratch to build a wholly local curriculum? We think not.

Several curricular models have been developed, tested, refined, and further tested in a variety of school settings. The development-refinement cycle is no doubt responsible for the success of these curricular models and their widespread adoption by physical educators seeking to improve the impact of their curriculums. These models can be grouped under what we refer to as "main-theme" or "focused" curriculums. These models tend to have a narrower activity focus than the multi-activity model approach, and they tend to allocate more time to the narrower focus, thus allowing students to achieve important outcomes.

This is not to suggest that these focused curriculums are used simply as "recipes" and cannot be altered to meet local needs. They are models, not prescriptions. Physical educators who use them tend to adapt them to their own particular context, which is typically determined by (a) the type of students served, (b) the facilities, and (c) the equipment available. We are also not suggesting that the entire K–12 physical education curriculum have a singular theme. Quite to the contrary, we argue in this chapter that a K–12 curriculum can be created by adopting particular themes at particular points in the K–12 curriculum, but to do so in a way that allows for significant outcomes at each level.

No program can achieve all the goods in physical education. As you will see in the curricular models described in this chapter, well-designed and thoughtfully developed programs using a coherent curriculum may be able to achieve many of the goods in physical education across the K–12 curriculum. The outcomes and objectives and how they "play out" will be tempered by the local context in which they exist and the changing conditions that occur within the lives of students. Once you have determined what you believe are the goods in physical education, assessed their relevance to your students, and considered the context of your setting, you are in a position to determine which of the physical education curriculum models you will adopt. Each model attends to a set of specific goods and meets one or more of the NASPE content standards.

MAIN-THEME CURRICULUM MODELS

As noted in chapter 8, there appears to be no consensus within the profession on what constitutes the good to be achieved in physical education. The arguments against the more traditional multi-activity program have resulted from a renewed interest in what we call main-theme programs, that is, programs that have a clear sense of a more limited good and arrange sequences of activities to achieve that good. Main-theme programs develop because the physical educators responsible for them had a vision about what was the primary good to be achieved, considered the context in which they teach, and then developed content to achieve that vision using input and choices from their students. A main theme becomes an organizing center for the program—the central thrust around which content is developed to meet goals. The curriculum model becomes the main theme guiding development of a program. "The 'good' programs stood for something specific. We learned about good fitness programs, good social development programs, and good adventure programs. Each of the programs had a main focus that defined and identified the program" (Siedentop, 1987, p. 25).

We have chosen to highlight five main-theme curriculum models that have been developed in physical education. The five we have chosen have the elements to serve as main-theme models, with a different notion of good for students in each.

- Developmental Physical Education
- Adventure Education
- Physical Activity, Fitness, and Wellness Education
- Integrative Physical Education
- Sport Education

These exemplary models have been developed, promoted, and used successfully in various educational settings across the K–12 curriculum. Each model has a well-defined focus and a set of assumptions on which it is based as well as specific outcomes and implications for instructional practice. In addition, each model encourages and promotes alignment among intended outcomes, learning experiences, and assessment and has been successfully implemented in different contexts. Each model is also aligned to the NASPE K–12 content standards.

Each of these five models represents a different vision of how the good in physical education should be conceptualized and developed into a program. The actual implementation of these models may look quite different when delivered in different settings that consider and respect the perspectives of the students for whom they are designed. The idea is to fit the model to the context. There has been a growing consensus nationally, however, that not all goods can be achieved in any one program—and that trying to achieve too many goals results in too little achievement in any area.

As you read the model descriptions, you will note that we identify the NASPE content standards that appear to have the most emphasis for each. This emphasis does not suggest that these are the only standards addressed by a given model to the exclusion of the others. Rather, we identify the standards that form a major part of the model framework, and learner outcomes will reflect them.

Developmental Physical Education

Pairs of children are spread throughout the gymnasium and can be seen crawling, kneeling, stretching, and composing movement. They move from walking in straight lines to running in curved pathways, from moving like lumbering bears to tiptoeing like deer, or from swaying like branches in trees to falling like leaves loosened by the wind. Gentle music is playing in the

---

BOX 9.1   Physical Education Developmental Objectives

Physical development	Concerned with the program of activities that builds physical power in an individual through the development of the various organic systems of the body
Motor development	Concerned with making physical movement useful and with as little expenditure of energy as possible and being proficient, graceful, and aesthetic in this movement
Mental development	Concerned with the accumulation of a body of knowledge and the ability to think and interpret this knowledge
Social development	Concerned with helping an individual in making personal adjustments, group adjustments, and adjustments as a member of society

Source: Wuest & Bucher, 1995.

---

background while the teacher moves among the children providing comments, encouragement, and support for individual and partner effort. These children are working on a class project in which they will demonstrate their individual understanding of concepts of space presented in a creative movement collage.

Developmental Physical Education is built around the individual learner with the curriculum designed to meet each learner's developmental needs and unique growth patterns. The intent is to provide a holistic education that emphasizes cognitive, affective, and psychomotor outcomes within each individual, rather than achievement of content-specific goals. Gallahue (1998) suggests that, in the developmental model, there is an interactive relationship between the individual, his or her environmental circumstances, and specific objectives of learning tasks in which the learner is engaged. The developmental model, when done well, is age related, not age dependent. What, when, and how to teach depend on each individual, rather than age group appropriateness (Gallahue, 1998). This implies that physical skills be introduced and developed in a progressive and sequential manner consistent with the individual learner's current developmental level and learning needs.

Wuest and Bucher (1995) propose four objectives to guide Developmental Physical Education (Box 9.1). These objectives are in fact quite similar to those originally posed by Clark Hetherington in his 1910 work on education through the physical, which resulted in physical education programs that emphasized fitness, skill development, knowledge, and social development. Although we typically see Developmental Physical Education as an elementary-level curriculum model that emphasizes basic skills and movement, it is also reflected in multi-activity programs at the secondary level.

A physical education program based on a developmental curriculum model is designed in a sequential way that allows children to learn skills, achieve success, and improve their motor performance. A teacher organizing skill progressions developmentally and then challenging a child with appropriately designed tasks using a variety of teaching strategies would reflect a developmental perspective. Physical education programs are organized around developmental themes rather than specific movements and activities (Gallahue, 1998; Graham, Holt/Hale, & Parker, 1998).

An example drawn from Graham et al. (1998) demonstrates an appropriate developmental progression for striking using a popular skill theme approach (see Box 9.2). Striking is introduced in the early elementary school grades and focuses on the child attempting to make contact with an object using lightweight, short-handled implements. At this point, there will be no consistency, many instances of the object being missed, and inefficient skill attempts at striking the object. Appropriate tasks for this level include striking a diversity of objects tossed, dropped, or suspended using different directional strokes with modified lightweight paddles. As students gain in their consistency to strike the object, the teacher designs challenges that require the children to control the object they are striking. These challenges might include striking with varying amounts of force, repeatedly in succession, and in a specific direction or toward an object. Once children are successful with these types of tasks and can contact the object on repeated attempts and direct it in different directions with varying degrees of force, they are ready to move into more complex activities. In this progression, children will use a variety of implements, employ various strokes, and exchange hits with a partner. Success with these tasks indicates the child has developed a mature pattern of striking and has control over both body and implement in stationary and moving situations. The tasks would then move to gamelike activities in complex, changing environments.

Which NASPE content standards does the developmental model achieve? By comparing the NASPE standards with the Wuest and Bucher (1995) objectives, we identified three standards that appear to be a major emphasis: standard 2, the learner is able to apply movement concepts and principles to the learning and development of motor skills, and standard 5, the learner is able to demonstrate responsible personal and social behavior in physical activity settings, and standard 1, the learner is able to demonstrate competency in many movement forms and proficiency in a few. Although these three standards appear to be the most directly linked to this model, the others can also be a focus of planning or instruction for individual learners or an outcome of that instruction.

Adventure Education

A weekend orienteering trip to the mountains has been planned. Each small group of skilled high school orienteers is responsible for designing a 1.5-mile course for the middle school students. The high school students set about

Gwinnett County Public Schools Physical Education K–5 Curriculum

The fundamental objective of the physical education program is to provide opportunities for the development of motor skills and physical fitness.

Skill Themes and Fitness Concepts

Students in grades K–5 will experience a developmentally designed program of skill and fitness development, including educational games, educational dance, and educational gymnastics. The following motor skills and fitness concepts are included:

- body awareness
- balancing
- chasing, fleeing, dodging
- kicking and punting
- striking with implements (short and long handled)
- rolling
- throwing and catching
- traveling
- volleying and dribbling
- transferring weight
- jumping and landing
- cardiorespiratory endurance
- flexibility
- muscular strength and endurance
- fitness testing

Becoming physically educated is a developmental process that begins in early childhood and continues throughout life. The physical education program involves the total child and includes physical, mental, social, and emotional growth experiences. The physical education program provides instruction that will enable the pursuit of physical fitness and a lifetime of physical activity.

Source: Reprinted with permission of Gwinnett County Public Schools, Gwinnett County, Georgia.

studying the map of the territory, interpreting the three-dimensional nature of the symbols on the map, the contour lines that mark the hills and mountains, the blue markings representing either river or lake, the colored patches that mark the wooded areas of the territory, and the black lines that are actually trails, roads, and power lines. After examining the map for moderately challenging control points, the planners mark these points with a grease pencil on the plastic sleeve into which they have inserted the map. Attempting to keep in mind all they have learned about designing an orienteering course, they attempt to use environmental elevation, and water as the control points. As they make each decision, they attempt to ensure variety in the course, select route options that participants might select, and maintain a course that is challenging yet not too difficult.

Experiential learning that provides learners with the opportunity to challenge themselves physically and mentally, work cooperatively as a group to solve problems and overcome risks, and gain respect for, confidence in, and trust in themselves and their peers are all components of Adventure Education. These components form the basic philosophy of Adventure Education, rather than the activities that the teacher uses to achieve them. Project Adventure (Price, n.d., p. 1) articulates this a little differently when they suggest that adventure is about taking the following risks:

- self-motivated learning
- developing trust and confidence in ourselves
- learning how to navigate and achieve as part of a group
- discovering the potential for a lifelong learning adventure

As can be seen in Box 9.3, adventure in physical education can provide meaningful and challenging goals toward which students can strive, include problem solving and risk taking in order to achieve those goals, and provide opportunities for experiential learning within a safe environment. "Learning by doing creates an opportunity for greater depth of understanding; having fun along the way pushes productivity, creativity and achievement to a peak. As you are engaged and challenged, the learning is making an impact that will last" (Price, n.d., p. 23).

An Adventure Education curriculum will look quite different in terms of the concepts taught (communication, trust, problem solving, decision making, team building), the activities used as the vehicle to achieve these concepts (initiatives, rope courses, backpacking, games and play), and even the format of the program (lengthened class time, weekend experiences, extended week-long outings). Adventure Education will reflect such events as cooperative games, initiatives, individual and group challenges, climbing walls, and ropes courses.

Box 9.4 shows the adventure activities by grade level at Cedarwood Project Adventure Elementary School. In addition to these adventure activities, the program offers content outlined in the school district graded course of study (e.g., basketball, stunts and tumbling, volleyball, manipulatives); however, these activities have a different focus than they would have in a traditional physical education class. Here they focus on cooperation, teamwork, communication, trust, risk, and problem solving. The teacher debriefs the students at the close of a lesson to get them to reflect on what happened and what it meant relative to these concepts.

Regardless of how Adventure Education is delivered, one of the main foci is its experiential approach to learning, with physical activity as the means for individual and collective exploration and discovery. The challenges and risks inherent in adventure programming produce anxiety and stress. As these challenges are met, self-confidence and self-esteem increase. Many challenges require group effort that brings in the idea of a community of learners (see Chapter 6), team-building concepts, and group problem solving (see Box 9.5).

BOX 9.3   Devonshire Project Adventure

Through the nontraditional academic and physical education program, Devonshire Project Adventure educates the whole student through adventure-based experiences. These experiences allow students to challenge themselves mentally and physically to reach these goals:

Cooperation	Through group work and a supportive group atmosphere, the students will learn to work together cooperatively. Participants will communicate thoughts, feelings, and behaviors effectively through activities that encourage listening as well as verbal and physical cooperation.
Risk	Through the adventure approach, the students will make a commitment to take a risk displaying their talents and limitations, realizing that they will be accepted in a positive, safe environment.
Trust	Through attempting activities that involve some physical or emotional risks, students will trust their physical or emotional safety to others. Through a greater willingness to try new and different tasks, the students will learn to trust each other for ideas, encouragement, and support.
Challenge	The students will view mental and physical challenges as an adventure to be attempted and experienced. The activities will challenge participants to develop persistence and a resistance to frustration in attempting to reach a desired goal.
Problem solving	Group members will effectively communicate, cooperate, and compromise with each other through trial-and-error participation in a graduated series of problem-solving activities ranging from the more simply solved to the more complex.

Source: Robbins, K. 1998. Devonshire project adventure, Challenge by choice handout. Devonshire Elementary School, Columbus, OH. Reprinted by permission of the author.

Students learn to cooperate with and depend on each other to solve the problems presented to them. Adventure activities are one way to increase participants' self-esteem, reduce antisocial behavior, promote critical thinking, and improve problem-solving skills. The following excerpt outlines program guidelines designed to ensure student success in four areas (Price, n.d.):

Cedarwood Project Adventure
Peaks of Educational Commitment

Guidelines of Educational Commitment
Students, Staff, and Community

Project Adventure is a formal process to enhance self-esteem through a trusting atmosphere of cooperation, sharing, individual and group achievement in a climate where each child is given numerous opportunities to be successful.

BOX 9.4 Leveled Adventure Activities in Physical Education at Cedarwood Elementary School

	K	1	2	3	4	5
Cargo nets	X	X	X			
Ladders	X	X	X			
Treehouse	X	X	X			
Tire traverse	X	X	X	X		
Zip line		X	X	X		
Traverse wall			X	X	X	X
Rappelling				X	X	X
Inclined wall				X	X	X
Vertical climbs					X	X
Trapeze jump					X	X
Play pen					X	X
*Jungle nook	X	X	X			
*Initiatives				X		
*Initiatives XC					X	
*High ropes						X
*High elements						X

*Activities at the adventure education center.

Source: Price, P. Cedarwood project adventure school. Columbus, OH. Project Adventure [Online]. 9/4/99 from the World Wide Web http://www.pa.org. Reprinted by permission of the author.

Peak #1   Academic Excellence
- Developing critical, independent thinkers
- Acknowledging and accepting various learning styles and abilities
- Developing discipline, perseverance, and a motivation to learn
- Becoming lifelong learners

Peak #2   Personal Integrity
- Taking ownership of actions
- Treating others as you wish to be treated
- Making a commitment to grow, change, and learn
- Practicing honesty and fairness in work and play
- Finding the positive in all situations

Peak #3   Physical Wellness
- Making informed decisions that show respect for one's physical, emotional, and mental well-being
- Demonstrating a commitment to personal fitness goals
- Accepting yourself and others' physical and emotional abilities

BOX 9.5   Turn Over a New Leaf

Target group: varied
Group size: 6 to 15
Time: 15 to 90 minutes
Space: flat open space large enough for a tarp
Activity level: moderate

Challenge

Without touching the ground or stepping off the tarp, a group must turn the tarp over. Turning over a new leaf implies a new beginning, and the following rendition is a new beginning to an old activity. Turn over a new leaf is a standby offering a myriad of uses for diverse groups with varying needs. This activity is especially effective when creating a common group vision or direction with many types of groups.

Goals

Problem solving, creativity, communication, leadership, and fun

Props

One large tarp, blanket, or tablecloth to serve as the leaf, flip chart

Instructions

Ask all group members to stand on the leaf (tarp). Their task is to turn the leaf over without touching the floor or stepping off. Strategizing begins as the group stands together on the tarp. Tarp size is critical to the challenge level: the larger the tarp, the easier the challenge. Experiment with tarp size before you offer the initiative. About 2 square feet per person is a good rule of thumb. If the group accomplishes the turn easily, challenge them to fold the tarp smaller, then smaller, and smaller.

Framing

This is a good activity to use when creating a common group vision. Designate the top side of the tarp as the present, the underside of the tarp as the future, and the floor or ground surrounding it as the past.

- Accepting challenges that require extended risk taking to reach personal best

Peak #4   Community Pride

- Promoting a sense of family within the classroom, school, and home
- Taking responsibility for school and community improvement
- Recognizing accomplishments and excellence
- Providing charity and service to the community

There are many benefits to a well-developed and delivered Adventure Education program. Students develop social, personal, and decision-making skills,

BOX 9.5   Turn Over a New Leaf (*continued*)

Ask each person to write, on strips of masking tape, short descriptions of how he or she experiences the present. What is it like, what is happening now? Examples might be poor communication, doing the same old thing, afraid to make decisions, too many changes too fast. Tape them randomly to the top of the tarp.

After a group check-in to hear how people characterize their present experience, ask them to switch their minds from the present to the future. What would they create in their future? What do they need, wish, or desire in the group? Answers will vary widely, from individual to individual and from individual to group. Some groups will benefit from facilitator guidance to prevent unrealistic responses such as "a day off every other day." Seek descriptions of how an extraordinary group experience would look. What would need to be present for that to happen? Encourage single words or short, vivid, specific sentences where appropriate. The idea, at this stage, is to generate possibility. Stick descriptions of the future on the underside of the tarp. Then return the tarp to the present side. Begin with everyone standing together on top of the tarp.

When the players "turn over the new leaf" into the "future," ask each person to stand on a piece of tape other than his or her own. Ask each person to read the description of someone else's future and to connect that future wish with anything currently happening in this activity. Are any of the wishes already materializing? For whom? How? In this phase, the idea is to establish responsibility with the group members for creating their own futures and nurturing the idea that the future begins now, and in small steps.

Turn the tarp back to the "present" side, and invite players to consider any descriptions of their present they would like to transfer to the future. Tape these to the future side. The tarp now displays individual aspirations for working together. Plaster all tapes on the flip chart, and begin to create the common group vision, incorporating individual expressions from the tapes.

Source: Adapted from Faith Evans, Zip Lines, Summer 1998. Copyright © 1998 Project Adventure, Inc. Used by permission.

gain in self-confidence, and develop the interactive skills necessary for participation in activities that may carry over into their daily lives and future lifelong pursuits.

> Potential benefits [of outdoor adventure activities] . . . include skill development for lifelong recreational activities, and improved physical and emotional health components such as coordination, strength, cardiovascular response, and catharsis from the normal routine. Psychological and sociological benefits—self-concept, confidence, compassion for others, group cooperation, and respect for oneself and others—are often enhanced through outdoor adventure activities. (Ewert, 1986, p. 7)

As a result of reviewing the NASPE content standards in relation to Adventure Education, we suggest that standards 5, 6, and 7 are the most relevant. When working in groups toward a common goal, it is necessary to demonstrate responsible personal and social behavior, to understand and respect differences among people, and to appreciate that physical activity provides opportunities for enjoyment, challenge, self-expression, and social interaction. Again, keep in mind that other standards, such as standard 3, exhibiting a physically active lifestyle, may also be an outcome of the program.

Physical Activity, Fitness, and Wellness Education

Monday is the day for students to self-assess their cardiovascular fitness in the physical activity of their choice. Each student has set a personal goal and determined a training heart rate range necessary to reach that goal. Students enter the gymnasium from the locker rooms and pick up their heart rate monitors from the rack, get them on and secure, and begin to warm up in various activity groups. Those who have selected jogging head outdoors while the step aerobics group begins low-level stepping. The in-line skaters move to their workout area while the basketball players begin activity. They warm up until their heart rates reach their self-determined training zone and then attempt to maintain it for 20 minutes. Warm down is done as a group as students interact and talk about how they felt during activity. Students download their watches to the class computer, note on their own physical activity cards how many minutes they spent below, at, or above their training zone, and make notes in their physical activity journal.

Physical fitness has been regarded by some as the major goal of physical education. This goal was coupled with an emphasis on strenuous activity that adhered to frequency, intensity, and duration guidelines. More recently, our conceptions of fitness have changed and, as a result, so have the outcomes we expect from what was known as fitness education. The main goal of this more recent curriculum, which we refer to as Physical Activity, Fitness, and Wellness Education, is to provide children and youth with the skills and knowledge that will prepare them to develop and maintain lifetime physical activity. One way to do this is to take the stairway to fitness (Figure 9.1), which helps you to learn to make good physical activity decisions.

Lack of physical activity, rather than poor physical fitness, has been identified as a cardiovascular risk factor and therefore the emphasis of this health-related curricular focus. McKenzie and Sallis (1996) suggest that "reorienting school programs to promote physical activity could have a major impact on public health" (p. 224). In light of the recent surgeon general's report (1996) and others that identify the high numbers of our population living a sedentary lifestyle, this is a critical need in today's schools.

The surgeon general's report (U.S. Department of Health and Human Services, 1996) recommends that "all people over the age of 2 years should accumulate at least 30 minutes of endurance-type physical activity, of at least

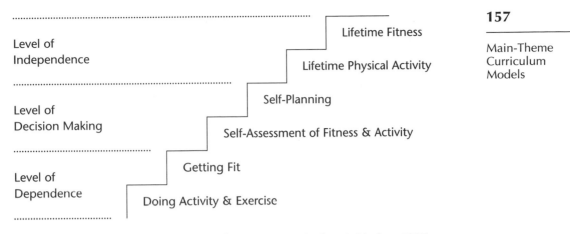

FIGURE 9.1   *The stairway to lifetime fitness (Source: Corbin & Lindsey, 1997, p. 12)*

moderate intensity, on most—preferably all—days of the week" (p. 28). This recommendation shifts the emphasis from strenuous exercise for fitness gains to development of physical activity for a lifetime. The Centers for Disease Control and Prevention (1997) (CDC) have published a set of guidelines for school and community programs to promote physical activity among young people. Physical activity programs for young people are most likely to be effective when they accomplish the following:

- Emphasize enjoyable participation in physical activities that are easily done throughout life
- Offer a diverse range of noncompetitive and competitive activities appropriate for different ages and abilities
- Give young people the skills and confidence they need to be physically active
- Promote physical activity through all components of a coordinated school health program and develop links between school and community programs

These guidelines suggest to us as physical educators that we must redirect our focus toward helping young people develop patterns of physical activity that promote and encourage lifestyle changes. This is critical if we are to help young people improve their own health and avoid becoming inactive adults. We know that physical activity patterns that are formed in children and adolescents carry over into adulthood. Ernst, Pangrazi, and Corbin (1998) provide a set of strategies to promote physically active lifestyles for all students through physical education programs:

1. *Emphasize process over product.* Promote and reinforce all types of physical activity throughout your program, instead of aiming at students just becoming physically fit.

2. *Teach personal evaluation of fitness.* Provide students with the knowledge and skill to assess their own levels of physical fitness in ways that are not threatening or unpleasant.

3. *Use self-paced activities.* To support the varying needs and desires of all learners, design activities that allow students to select the level of intensity they want to expend.

4. *Encourage success.* Generally, when we are successful, we tend to feel good about our effort and will choose to continue.

5. *Challenge, don't threaten, students.* Set challenges at an appropriate level so they are attainable rather than things students will avoid.

6. *Maximize activity time.* Get students active. Design lessons that allow physical activity development for at least 50 percent of the class time.

7. *Alternate high-intensity and low-intensity activities.* Provide students with recovery time between bouts of high-intensity activity using stations, circuits, or interval training.

8. *Discuss the value of physical activity.* Help students become knowledgeable about physical activity that will allow them to make good choices as they move through life.

9. *Promote personal interest activities.* If students are given the opportunity to participate in activities of interest to them, they are more likely to continue in an active lifestyle.

10. *Use effective class management.* Effective managerial skills will allow more time for students to be involved in physical activity.

11. *Promote nonschool physical activity.* Promote, encourage, and provide opportunities for students and their families to be involved with physical activity outside of school.

Three additional points for physical education teachers to consider when designing appropriate programs that support those just listed were identified by McKenzie and Sallis (1996):

- Give students more time in physical education to achieve physical fitness or physical activity objectives.

- Build a classroom instructional component into physical education in order to teach behavior change strategies and goal setting for learners to become physically active. (Box 9.6 provides an instructional component example.)

- Design physical activity and fitness programs in which families can be involved.

CDC guidelines provide several recommendations specifically for physical education programs (see Chapter 15) that are also consistent with the strategies just described. In addition, they suggest that physical education programs

BOX 9.6   Identifying Signs of Stress

All people experience some negative stress in their lives. Your body sends off certain signals when you are experiencing such distress. In this self-assessment, you will learn to identify some of the body's stress signals.

- Lie on the floor, close your eyes, and try to relax. Have your partner count your pulse and your breathing rate. Ask your partner to observe for irregular breathing and unusual mannerisms. Then ask your partner to evaluate how tense your muscles seem. Report "butterflies" or other indicators of stress to your partner. Write your results on your record sheet. Have your partner lie down while you record your observations about him or her.

- When directed by your instructor, all members of the class should write their names on a piece of paper and place the papers in a hat or a box. The teacher will draw names until only three remain in the container. The students whose names remain must give 1-minute speeches about the effects of stress. Observe your partner before and during the name drawing. Look for the signs and signals of stress. Record your results on the record sheet. Also, try to remember your feelings during the drawing. Finally, observe the people who were required to make the speech. Record this information on the record sheet.

- Finally, walk or jog for 5 minutes after your second stress assessment. Once again, work with a partner to assess your signs of stress. Write them in the third column of the record sheet. Notice that the exercise causes heart rate and breathing rate to increase. However, it may help reduce earlier signs of the emotional stress related to performing in front of the class.

Source: Corbin & Lindsey, 1997.

"follow the National Standards for Physical Education" (Centers for Disease Control and Prevention, 1997, p. 3). Four of the NASPE content standards appear to be a major focus of a Physical Activity, Fitness, and Wellness Education program. Standards 2, 3, 4, and 7 suggest that learners will apply movement concepts and principles to the learning and development of motor skills, exhibit a physically active lifestyle, achieve and maintain a health-enhancing level of physical fitness, and understand that physical activity provides opportunities for enjoyment, challenge, self-expression, and social interaction. For example, if students begin to use the physical activity pyramid (Figure 9.2), they can select the types of activities that will fit their individual health and wellness goals.

Integrated Physical Education

It is early fall, and students in the elective fitness and wellness course are in the midst of planning a year-long project they have had approved by their teacher

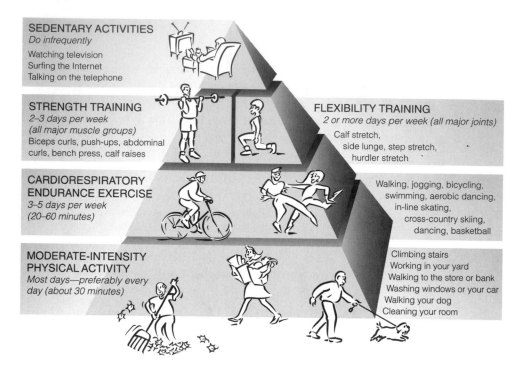

FIGURE 9.2 *The physical activity pyramid*

and the school administration. Small groups of seniors are gathered around the gymnasium, with the art teacher, shop teacher, or physical education teacher facilitating their discussions. The goal for this student-selected project is to design and develop a fitness course to be built around the campus and into the adjoining city park. The physical education teacher is providing advice on the fitness activities the students have chosen to include in the course, the art teacher is helping the students design clear and informative signs to guide participants in each activity, and students are seeking input from the shop instructor on how to build safe fitness apparatus for each station. These plans will go to the city engineers for actual development of the course, which is scheduled for a community grand opening in the spring.

Life is not compartmentalized by subject area. More and more educators have become aware of the need to provide learners the opportunity to integrate and connect their learning across the curriculum. An integrative education, often referred to as interdisciplinary learning, is the purposeful integration of two or more subject areas for the purpose of enhancing both and extending its application to real-life contexts. Central to this concept is recognition that each subject has its own unique content and place in the education of children and youth, yet when combined with other areas, it becomes more relevant to learners. "What integration does mean is that teachers can and should have such a clear understanding of the subjects they teach that they can expand on their knowledge to make references and applications beyond their own curricular framework" (Allen, 1996, p. 12).

Placek (1996) indicates that an Integrated Physical Education curriculum refers to integration both within physical education itself (internal) and between physical education and other content areas (external). Internal integration in physical education, according to Placek, suggests integrating the disciplinary base of physical education (exercise physiology, biomechanics, sport history, etc.) into elementary and secondary school physical education, as well as teaching social interaction, personal development, and thinking skills. Integrating disciplinary content has been seen most frequently in the area of fitness, in which exercise physiology concepts have been included in the content and activities in which children and youth engage. Vickers's (1992) academically based cross-disciplinary framework fits into this internal integration category, with its focus on either fitness or career development in the physical activity and fitness fields. Hellison's (1995) model for personal and social responsibility is certainly a prime example of the second form of internal integration specified by Placek. Hellison's model provides a set of goals/levels and teaching strategies that have been used effectively to teach children and youth how to take personal responsibility for themselves and their relationships with others. Cutforth and Parker's (1996) use of student journals to promote affective growth by encouraging students to write about what they do, how they react, and what their thoughts are in physical education provides an example of personal development within Placek's framework. Thinking skills are also becoming a priority in physical education. Schwager (1992) discusses how students are involved in the critical thinking skills of analyzing, comparing, and contrasting while providing performance feedback to peers during reciprocal teaching. McBride (1989, 1991, 1995, 1997) has endorsed and promoted the inclusion of critical thinking in physical education. He suggests that critical thinking involves reflecting on personal knowledge and understanding to make decisions. He provides numerous strategies for fostering these skills and includes designing challenging cooperative activities for students and using debriefing as a frequent teaching strategy. "Being a facilitator, using questioning, and promoting transfer all contribute to the critical thinking process" (McBride, 1997, p. 11).

Physical education has more often integrated other subjects than vice versa. Fogarty (1991) identifies four ways to integrate subject areas that may provide guidance in this endeavor: sequenced, shared, webbed, and threaded. *Sequenced integration* features two or more subject areas focusing on one topic simultaneously. *Shared integration* involves planning for content that overlaps subject areas. *Webbed integration* uses themes to guide instruction and learning experiences. A curriculum that is _threaded_ includes cognitive or social skills in all subject areas. Interdisciplinary teaching is a time-consuming model that requires a great deal of collaboration among teachers. Typically, we see other subject-matter educators questioning how physical education content can enrich their content, and what has generally been integrated into the classroom

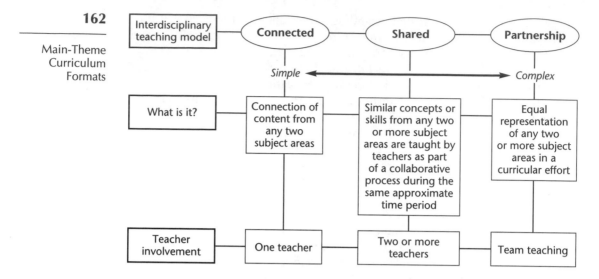

FIGURE 9.3 *Comparison of three selected interdisciplinary curriculum models (Source: Reprinted by permission from T. P. Cone, P. Werner, S. L. Cone, and A. M. Woods, 1998,* Interdisciplinary Teaching throughPhysical Education, *Champaign, IL: Human Kinetics.)*

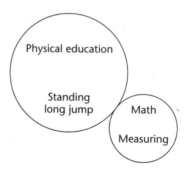

FIGURE 9.4 *Example of a connected interdisciplinary teaching model (Source: Reprinted by permission from T. P. Cone, P. Werner, S. L. Cone, and A. M. Woods, 1998,* Interdisciplinary Teaching through Physical Education, *Champaign, IL: Human Kinetics.)*

has related to games, sport, and dance, with little to no attention paid to other attributes or issues that might impact learning across various subjects.

Cone, Werner, Cone, and Woods (1998) developed three interdisciplinary models for integrating content from two or more subject areas that progress from simple to complex: connected, shared, and partnership (Figure 9.3). Their graphic representations of each of these models show how subject matter is related and developed (Figures 9.4, 9.5, 9.6, and 9.7). They have developed a set of active learning experiences to guide classroom teachers and physical education specialists in designing and delivering an integrated pro-

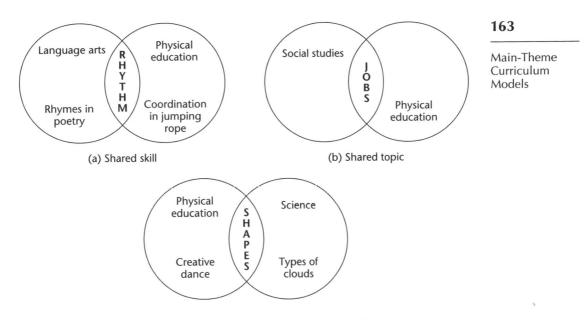

FIGURE 9.5 *Three examples of the shared interdisciplinary teaching model using (a) a shared skill, (b) a shared topic, and (c) a shared concept (Source: Reprinted by permission from T. P. Cone, P. Werner, S. L. Cone, and A. M. Woods, 1998,* Interdisciplinary Teaching through Physical Education, *Champaign, IL: Human Kinetics.)*

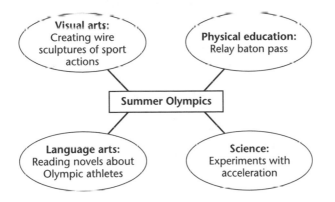

FIGURE 9.6 *Shared interdisciplinary teaching model using a theme (Source: Reprinted by permission from T. P. Cone, P. Werner, S. L. Cone, and A. M. Woods, 1998,* Interdisciplinary Teaching through Physical Education, *Champaign, IL: Human Kinetics.)*

gram using the different interdisciplinary models. We have selected two examples applied to the integration of physical education with math and science to demonstrate (see Box 9.7).

With the time and collaborative commitment it takes to design and deliver an integrated education, teachers might ask if it is worth the effort. Placek

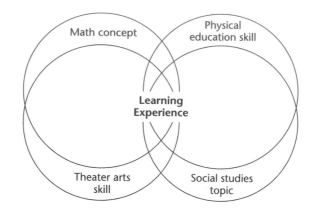

FIGURE 9.7 *Skills, topics, and concepts from various subjects are blended to create an interdisciplinary learning experience in this example of a partnership interdisciplinary teaching model (Source: Reprinted by permission from T. P. Cone, P. Werner, S. L. Cone, and A. M. Woods, 1998,* Interdisciplinary Teaching through Physical Education, *Champaign, IL: Human Kinetics.)*

(1996) suggests that integration allows schools to more efficiently include the increasingly large amount of content required within the limited time available, is more reflective of real life, combines subject matter into more meaningful and realistic segments, and provides students with a model from which to build their own critical thinking skills.

Cone et al. (1998) point out that none of the NASPE content standards speaks specifically to Integrated Physical Education, yet they believe, as we do, that there are indirect references that can be drawn. They point to the many scientific principles students learn in the science classroom that have application for motor skills. As students begin to apply these scientific concepts, they are certainly achieving standard 2—applies movement concepts and principles to the learning and development of motor skills. Cone and Cone (1999) point to standard 6—demonstrates understanding and respect for differences among people—as support for learning across, through, and about diverse populations and perspectives.

Sport Education

Students move to their team space in the gymnasium and begin warming up under the direction of their team trainer, who has designed stretches appropriate for the 25-day volleyball season in which they are participating. While students are warming up, team managers are reporting attendance to the teacher. As soon as all students are warmed up, they move into skill practice emphasizing the pass, set, and hit in a core drill formation under the direction of their team captain and with skill feedback from the teacher. After 15 minutes of varied skill practice, the team captains direct their teams to assigned courts for

BOX 9.7   Integrating Physical Education with Science and Math

Spaced Out

- Science: space, the new frontier
- Physical education: inventing a game, designing a movement experience
- Grade level: 3–5
- Create a movement sequence by going on an exploratory space mission. Begin with a rocket takeoff. Include a tethered space walk, landing on the moon, performing a work experiment, a computer glitch and technical engineering resolution, return flight, and landing back on the earth.
- Invent a new game that has never been played before. Play the game as if it were being played in weightless conditions. Write out the rules to the game. Describe how to play the game to some aliens that you meet in outer space. Play the game with the aliens.

It's Getting Complicated

- Mathematics: complex geometric shapes
- Physical education: body shapes
- Grade level: 3–5
- Under the direction of teacher challenges, have children make different geometric body shapes. Specifically, have the children assume shapes that create awareness of the concepts of concave and convex. Can they make concave and convex shapes while lying on the floor? Can they make concave and convex bridgelike shapes—back bend (belly up) and angry cat (belly down)—at a medium level? By hanging from rings or parallel bars, can they make concave and convex shapes? Can they make concave and convex shapes at high levels while standing?

- Have a large group of 10 to 12 children model a given shape and the parts of that shape. For example, a group assigned to create a circle could make the circumference, center, radius, and diameter. Height, length, depth, diagonal, or perimeter could be represented for a triangle, rectangle, or square.
- Create partner shapes that emphasize perpendicular, parallel, and intersecting lines. Create these shapes at low, medium, and high levels.
- While moving with a partner, show pathway lines that are parallel. Show a different way to move so that your pathways intersect.

Source: Text reprinted by permission from T. P. Cone, P. Werner, S. L. Cone, and A. M. Woods, 1998. *Interdisciplinary Teaching through Physical Education,* Champaign, IL: Human Kinetics.

a series of small-sided, three-versus-three volleyball games, which is the first round of games in the season competitive schedule. Officials and scorekeepers maintain the pace of the games to ensure that the first round is completed by the close of the class period. Prior to class dismissal, the duty team compiles the scores and records them on the publicity board while the team equipment managers collect the volleyballs. Members of each team select the member whom they feel displayed the most team effort for the day, and that individual's name is put on the fair play board.

In this scenario, students are actively engaged in the sport as it is actually played, working on skills in a realistic game-play situation, taking charge of various aspects of warm-up, practice, and game activities, and all under the direction of their selected team leaders. Students are interested and involved in their own sport experience, so their efforts toward improvement have a focus.

Sport Education defines the content of physical education as sport and provides direction on how sport can be introduced to all students within the context of physical education. Based on the assumptions that sport derives from play and is an integral part of our culture, within this model, sport is defined as "playful competition" (Siedentop, 1980). Sport Education is a curriculum and instruction model designed to provide students with an authentic, in-depth, and educationally rich sport experience within physical education. It is intended to move isolated skill practice through drills out of the curriculum and into sequential, progressive, and realistic gamelike situations in which students learn to organize and manage their own sport experience. The primary objective is the development of skilled and competent sport participants through which learners have the opportunity to develop the skills and understanding of strategies necessary to participate in sport successfully throughout life. Although content may be similar in some instances, Sport Education, when used well, does not fit into a multi-activity format of short units of instruction. Box 9.8 displays how one teacher has built Sport Education into her elementary school curriculum that has 50-minute class periods that meet every 4 days on a rotating basis.

Six features characterize Sport Education (Box 9.9) and distinguish it from more traditional forms of physical education: seasons, affiliation, formal competition, culminating event, record keeping, and festivity. Although these features are typically seen and experienced in after-school and organized sport, they are infrequently a part of physical education in schools. Sport Education evolved from the perspective that physical education was not teaching sport in ways that allowed students to experience an authentic sport experience. A major focus of this model is to help students become skilled sportspersons and provide opportunities for them to take responsibility for their own sport and physical education experiences. Figure 9.8 demonstrates the changing roles of the teacher, students, and community within the framework of Sport Education as it is delivered in Australia.

NASPE content standards 1, 3, 5, and 6 appear to hold the most relevance to Sport Education. Demonstrating movement competence, being physically

> **BOX 9.8   Building Sport Education into Elementary Curriculums**
>
> *Sports and level:* Soccer, volleyball, basketball, gymnastics, and track and field; upper elementary grades
> *Seasonal format:* Fitness unit followed by five Sport Education seasons
> *Team format:* Three teams per class; stay together for school year
> *Competition formats:* Modified games, tournaments, meets
> *Student roles:* Performer, captain, referee, scorekeeper, judge
> *Performance records:* Individual and team performance, managerial and instructional participation point system
> *Special features:* All-sport award, multiple awards, student notebooks, video-taping, performances at assemblies
>
> *Source:* Adapted from Siedentop, 1994.

active, taking responsibility for personal and social behavior, and respecting differences among people in sport settings are all inherent in the model. A well-designed and delivered Sport Education season should facilitate all students achieving these standards.

DESIGNING A COHERENT K–12 MULTIMODEL CURRICULUM

Individual teachers, or groups of teachers within one building, may select from these curriculum models and provide a successful and effective physical education program for their students. However, if children and youth are to leave our programs after high school as physically educated individuals, then *all* programs in which they participate must be designed to achieve this "physically educated" goal. Each of the curriculum models we described meets one or more of the NASPE K–12 content standards. None alone meets all the standards. This suggests that a coherent K–12 multimodel curriculum is designed to achieve all the standards and build upon the skills, knowledge, attitudes, and behaviors outlined within them.

A multimodel curriculum need not be restricted to schools and be under the direct supervision of physical educators. There is an abundance of resources and personnel in the community who are skilled, knowledgeable, and interested in working with children and youth in physical activity settings. Utilize those resources without giving up quality programming. Schools and community can work together to deliver physical education more effectively and thoroughly, and often in a more exciting way. Physical activity offerings not typically included in a physical education curriculum (snow boarding, canoeing, mountain biking) can become part of an off-campus program designed to meet an elective for interested students. Providing physical activity options

BOX 9.9	**Features of Sport Education**
Seasons	Seasons characterize how sport is organized, unlike our typical physical education units. These seasons are longer than our traditional units and include both practice and competition built into every session. This extended time reduces the number of seasons that can be offered in a school year yet allows more depth and time to develop skills and tactics of game play.
Affiliation	One critical feature of any sport experience is the social interaction that revolves around team membership. With this in mind and during any Sport Education season, students become members of a team and generally retain that membership through the entire season. A large part of what happens during the season occurs within teams and under the direction of team leaders: planning, practicing, supporting, competing, and celebrating. Appropriate means are necessary to guide team selection so that all players feel valued and essential.
Formal competition	The Sport Education season is built around a formal schedule of competition that is posted early to allow teams to anticipate and prepare for their opponents. This formalized schedule sets the stage for practices to become more meaningful, with students willing to take on skill and tactical practice in preparation for game play that runs throughout the season. As with organized sport, daily practice sessions progress from more emphasis on practice to practice interspersed with the formalized game schedule.
Culminating event	Generally, we see sport seasons closing in some type of culminating event or season finale. In Sport Education, it is critical that the culminating event involve all participants, rather than being focused on the more skilled players/teams. Maintaining a focus on play and success opportunities for all is a major focus of this aspect of Sport Education.
Record keeping	Keeping records and publicizing them is a feature that is paramount to organized sport and meaningful to participants. Sport Education offers this same opportunity to players and teams to receive recognition and identify successful and effective performances as a tool in goal setting and as a means of promoting the idea of team unity.
Festivity	We generally observe in organized sport environments a festive atmosphere that permeates from the players to the fans who come to observe the tournament. "In Sport Education, teachers and students work together to create a continued festival that celebrates improvement, trying hard, and playing fairly (posters, team colors, player introductions, award ceremonies, videotaping)."

Source: Adapted from Siedentop, 1998.

outside the school day allows students to participate for extended periods and often when they are physically more alert. When developing class schedules, think beyond physical education remaining within the traditional 8-hour day and examine options that might also work, such as evenings, weekends, or even weeks during school holidays. Students' voices can be solicited on these

FIGURE 9.8 *Changing roles and responsibilities in Sport Education*

issues, as well as about activity choices that best suit their personal needs and interests. These kinds of modifications broaden the scope of what we have typically seen in physical education and can be fit nicely into the goals of the curriculum models previously described. It takes creativity, a willingness to do things differently, and communication between teachers and facilitators available in the community.

Let's see how this might play out by examining what a group of teachers in District X came up with for their standards, aligned curriculum models, and links to the community. They began by envisioning what they see as meaningful 12th grade exit outcomes for students: Students will leave physical education with the desire, knowledge, and skills to be physically active throughout their lives. They will choose to participate in enjoyable activities that will challenge and promote physical well-being and a level of fitness in inclusive settings that respect all individuals. Working backward from this expectation, teachers select the standards, focus, and curriculum models that would allow them to achieve this outcome. It might look like Table 9.1.

MAKING IT WORK

Teachers in any school district can design a multimodel curriculum that reflects their perspective on where each standard is best emphasized to meet the varying needs and interests of their diverse populations. It takes communication among teachers within a school district across the K–12 program to achieve this outcome.

TABLE 9.1   Matching a Curriculum Model to Selected NASPE K–12 Content Standards

Grade Level	Standards	Focus	Curriculum Models
10 and 12 Elective program	Standards 1–7 Learners will select the curriculum that best meets their needs, desires, and goals for physical activity. They will design and monitor their participation within their choice of curriculum model.	Focus on learners as they apply content in physical activity setting and in all aspects of life Options offered over varying times and in school/community settings	Choices by semester of: • Fitness and Wellness Education • Sport Education • Adventure Education
9	Standards 2, 3, 5, and 7 Learners will exhibit a physically active lifestyle, apply movement concepts and principles to the learning and development of motor skills, demonstrate responsible personal and social behavior, and demonstrate understanding that physical activity offers opportunities for enjoyment, challenge, self-expression, and social interaction.	Focus on learners as they apply physical activity content to selves and others in all aspects of life. Learners will be involved in physical activity internships offered in the community, sharing their knowledge with younger children or seniors.	Integrated Physical Education; community with Fitness and Wellness Education
8	Standards 4 and 5 Learners will achieve and maintain a health-enhancing level of physical fitness and demonstrate responsible personal and social behavior in physical activity settings.	Focus on learners as they apply physical activity content to meet individual goals Activity options will be offered in schools or at local Y's and recreation centers.	Physical Activity, Fitness, and Wellness Education
6 and 7	Standards 3, 4, and 6 Learners will exhibit a physically active lifestyle, achieve and maintain a health-enhancing level of physical fitness, and demonstrate respect for differences among people in physical activity settings.	Focus on learners as they apply content in a physical activity setting Integration will extend beyond the gymnasium to the classrooms of other content areas. Parent involvement will be sought to support these efforts.	Integrated Physical Education

TABLE 9.1 Matching a Curriculum Model to Selected NASPE K–12 Content Standards (*continued*)

Grade Level	Standards	Focus	Curriculum Models
4 and 5	Standards 1, 3, and 6 Learners will exhibit a physically active lifestyle, demonstrate competency in many movement forms and proficiency in a few, and demonstrate an understanding and respect for differences among people in physical activity settings.	Focus on content applied to individual learners as they interact in a physical activity setting Sport Education will be offered in before-school and noon hour intramurals in addition to physical education class.	Sport Education
3	Standards 5 and 7 Learners will demonstrate responsible personal and social behavior in physical activity settings and understand that physical activity provides opportunities for enjoyment, challenge, self expression, and social interaction.	Focus on individual learners and their interactions with peers Initiatives offered through local adventure camps and parks departments	Adventure Education
K–2	Standard 2 Learners will apply movement concepts and principles to the learning and development of motor skills.	Focus on individual learners and their acquisition and application of content Parent involvement encouraged	Developmental Physical Education

How do we make it work? What steps do we need to take? Once teachers at each level have determined the goods of physical education, the NASPE content standards become the next step. As a group, teachers can reflect on what these standards might look like at the elementary school, middle school, and high school levels. Where should the emphasis be placed? Which are most appropriate for each level of learners? What is important or of interest to youth at each

BOX 9.10   Resources

Developmental Physical Education

Gabbard, C., LeBlanc, E., & Lowry, S. (1987). *Physical education for children.* Englewood Cliffs, NJ: Prentice-Hall.

Gallahue, D. L. (1996). *Developmental physical education for children.* Madison, WI: Brown & Benchmark.

Graham, G., Holt/Hale, S. A., & Parker, M. (1998). *Children moving: A reflective approach to teaching physical education.* Mountain View, CA: Mayfield.

Thomas, J. (Ed.). (1984). *Making sense of motor development: Interfacing research with lesson planning.* Minneapolis, MN: Burgess.

Adventure Education

Ewert, A. (1989). *Outdoor adventure pursuits: Foundations.* Worthington, OH: Publishing Horizon.

Journal of Experiential Education.

Journal of Adventure Education and Outdoor Leadership.

Rohnke, K. (1989). *Cowstails and cobras: A guide to games, initiatives, rope courses, and adventure curriculum.* Hamilton, MA: Project Adventure.

Rohnke K. (1989). *Silver Bullets.* Dubuque, IA: Kendall/Hunt.

Rohnke, K. (1995). *Quicksilver.* Dubuque, IA: Kendall/Hunt.

Physical Activity, Fitness, and Wellness Education

Corbin, C., & Lindsey, M. (1993). *Concepts of Fitness* (8th ed.). Dubuque, IA: William C. Brown.

Corbin, C., & Lindsey, M. (1997). *Fitness for Life* (4th ed.). Glenview, IL: Scott Foresman-Addison Wesley.

Journal of Physical Education, Recreation, and Dance Strategies.

Integrated Physical Education

Cone, T. P., Werner, P., Cone, S. L., & Woods, A. M. (1998). *Interdisciplinary teaching through physical education.* Champaign, IL: Human Kinetics.

Fogarty, R. (1991). *The mindful school: How to integrate the curriculum.* Palatine, IL: IRI/Skylight.

Fraser, D. (1991). *Playdancing.* Pennington, NJ: Princeton Book.

Journal of Physical Education, Recreation, and Dance Strategies.

Teaching Elementary Physical Education.

Sport Education

Journal of Physical Education, Recreation, and Dance Strategies.

Siedentop, D. (1995). *Sport education: Quality PE programming through positive sport experiences.* Champaign, IL: Human Kinetics.

TABLE 9.2 Standards by Grade Level **173**

Making It Work

Example 1

Elementary priorities Standard 2	Students should apply movement concepts and principles to the learning and development of motor skills.
Middle school priorities Standards 1, 5, and 6	Students should demonstrate competency in many and proficiency in a few movement forms, responsible personal and social behavior in physical activity settings, and understanding and respect among people in physical activity settings.
High school priorities Standards 3, 4, and 7	Students should exhibit a physically active lifestyle, achieve and maintain a health-enhancing level of physical fitness, and understand that physical activity provides opportunities for enjoyment, challenge, self-expression, and social interaction.

Example 2

Elementary priorities, K–3 Standard 2	Students should apply movement concepts and principles to the learning and development of motor skills.
Elementary priorities, 4–5 Standards 3 and 5	Students should exhibit a physically active lifestyle and responsible personal and social behavior in physical activity settings.
Middle school priorities, 6–8 Standards 3 and 6	Students should exhibit a physically active lifestyle and an understanding of and respect for differences among people in physical activity settings.
High school priorities, 9–10 Standards 3, 4, and 7	Students should exhibit a physically active lifestyle, achieve and maintain a health-enhancing level of physical fitness, and understand that physical activity provides opportunities for enjoyment, challenge, self-expression, and social interaction.
High school priorities, 11–12 Standards 1 and 6	Students should demonstrate competency in many movement forms and proficiency in a few and demonstrate an understanding of and respect for differences among people in physical activity settings.

level? Once teachers come to some type of collective agreement, they are beginning to describe the criteria that will guide program development at each level and allow selection of a curriculum model(s) to achieve its success.

Table 9.2 shows samples of what teachers might develop as a result of combining their collective perspectives on the importance of the NASPE standards across K–12. Clearly, the physical education programs delivering these will be quite different, with each intending to achieve a number of the goods identified for physical education. Every group of teachers attempting to develop a K–12 coherent curriculum could develop an equally varied yet important set of outcomes across or within each level.

Once a group of teachers (within a school or district) has determined its interpretation of a physically educated person and outlined which standards will be the focus at each level, it is ready to select the most appropriate curriculum model(s) to achieve these goals. Which curriculum model would be a best fit for standard 3? The goal of exhibiting a physically active lifestyle might best be achieved through a Fitness and Wellness Education curriculum, the main goal of which is to prepare children and youth for a lifetime of physical activity. This would include the knowledge, concepts, attitudes, and skills necessary to make appropriate activity choices and monitor participation in them.

The curriculum model(s) may be chosen at the elementary, middle, or high school level, rather than at the district level. Suppose you determine that an important set of outcomes for exiting middle school physical education is that students will be able to think critically, develop problem-solving strategies, demonstrate respect and support for their peers, and accept physical activity challenges. Which curriculum model might provide the most appropriate means to achieve such goals? Adventure Education, with its focus on personal and group challenges, problem solving, and risk taking, could meet these outcomes. Choice of a curriculum model provides a framework within which content decisions can be made and learning outcomes identified. Two curriculum models may be selected within one program, with students choosing the one that meets their interests and needs. There may also be three models selected to deliver physical education at one level. These might be mixed and matched as a means of meeting a set of goals that the students and teacher have identified as important. Each curriculum model has a place in physical education yet is designed to allow students to achieve very different types of outcomes.

There must be alignment between your beliefs about the goods of physical education, the curriculum model you select to achieve these goods, and the match between the two. For example, if you have determined that achieving and maintaining a level of physical fitness is most critical and then select Adventure Education as your curriculum model, you would not have much alignment between beliefs and practice. But if your focus is on providing children and youth opportunities to explore the relationship between physical activity, themselves, and the larger community within which they live and select the Integrated Physical Education model to facilitate this, you would have a strong alignment. Finally, if your intent is helping students to become competent, skilled, and self-motivated sport participants able to manage and direct their own sport experience and you attempt to achieve this through a multi-activity program, you would again not have achieved alignment between beliefs and practice. Had you chosen Sport Education to achieve this, you would have chosen well.

Physical education today is faced with a dilemma, the response to which will both promote and enhance our content in K–12 education or lead to its demise. Recycling our old curriculums that have been used repeatedly in the past will not help us solve the problems encountered by children and youth as they negotiate our programs. Teachers need to examine the context in which they teach, come to know and understand the students who live within that setting, and determine issues of greater significance that will impact these contemporary youth. Our task is to use our knowledge and expertise to guide the delivery of physical education content while leaving open options for youth to play a role in curricular decisions.

SUMMARY

1. Main-theme curriculums are narrowly focused and allocate considerable time to the focus that results in greatest learning for students.

2. Effective teachers who use the tested main-theme curriculums tend to adapt them to the needs of their particular context.

3. Developmental Physical Education assumes that all children move through cognitive, social, and physical developmental stages that impact what they are capable of doing and how we as teachers should design our programs.

4. Adventure Education provides meaningful and challenging goals for students and fosters problem solving and self-awareness through experiential learning.

5. Physical Activity, Fitness, and Wellness Education, when done well, develops students into individuals who can take responsibility for their own health and well-being by making good activity choices to guide them throughout life.

6. Integrated Physical Education is designed to educate students in a more holistic way by purposefully teaching the relationships and interactions between and among different subject areas and applying it to real-life situations.

7. Sport Education provides all students with the opportunity to experience sport in a realistic context and provides them with the skills and desire to take charge of their own sporting experiences by learning the rules, roles, rituals, traditions, skills, and strategies that make sport important in our culture.

8. A coherent K–12 multimodel curriculum is intended to provide students with the opportunity to achieve all of the NASPE content standards and experience the goods in each of the physical education curriculum models.

9. Multimodel curriculums should be developed across the school and community to draw on all possible resources for quality programming in physical education.

10. Mixing and matching the various curriculum models across the curriculum can be based on determining the value (good) placed on physical education, choosing the important content standards at each level, and then selecting the curriculum models to match these beliefs.

CHAPTER 10

Meaningful Assessment for Significant Learning Outcomes

The primary goal of assessment should be seen as the enhancement of learning, rather than simply the documentation of learning.

—NATIONAL ASSOCIATION OF SPORT AND PHYSICAL EDUCATION (1995)

OVERALL CHAPTER OUTCOME

To design authentic and meaningful assessment measures to demonstrate student progress toward and achievement of intended learning outcomes

CHAPTER OBJECTIVES

- To differentiate between assessment and grading
- To explain how learning tasks and assessment can be the same
- To differentiate between formal and informal assessment
- To distinguish between formative and summative assessment
- To describe alternative assessment
- To differentiate between a performance assessment and an authentic assessment
- To identify and describe a variety of assessment measures and when they would most appropriately be used
- To explain authentic ways to assess skill performance
- To demonstrate how reflection, such as journals, logs, or portfolios, plays a role in assessments
- To explain how and why student self-assessment is central to assessment
- To describe the role of technology in assessment
- To provide examples of how a grading system can match the outcomes of a program

In designing a tennis season, you determine that the expected outcome is for learners to be able to participate successfully in a game of doubles tennis. With this in mind, which of the following two assessments is more appropriate, relevant, and meaningful as a measure of this learning goal?

1. At the close of a 3-week tennis unit, a true/false and multiple-choice examination on rules and protocols is given, followed by a series of skills tests on key skills necessary for game play, including the serve, backhand, and forehand.

2. Several times throughout the 25-day tennis season, students work with a partner to assess and record their success on a set of skills (serve, forehand, backhand) when performed in one-and-one and doubles matches. Once per week, when students are playing in a tennis match, the duty team keeps records of their skill at playing (game statistics), interacting appropriately with their partner (verbal support and encouragement), selecting and performing game tactics (game statistics), following the rules governing tennis (violations tally), and enjoying the competition whether they win or lose

178

Meaningful
Assessment for
Significant
Learning
Outcomes

(verbal comments and demeanor). Finally, students maintain a progress journal highlighting aspects of the game they are performing well and areas that need improvement. They set goals for their performance in an attempt to improve their weaknesses and maintain their strengths.

If you selected the second assessment as being more appropriate, you are correct. This more authentic assessment provides a holistic picture of students in a real-life situation, as opposed to only a glimpse of what they can do in an isolated and controlled setting. The second scenario provides the learners with feedback to improve performance while allowing them to see where they stand in relation to the goal of playing successfully in a tennis match.

ASSESSMENT AND GRADING

When you hear the term "assessment," do you think of grades? They are in fact related, yet quite different. *Grades* are a reality of schools. Grades report a student's performance by attaching a mark to indicate the level of performance. The grade is generally calculated by averaging the results of several different assessment measures that occur throughout a grading period: homework, quizzes, projects, and so forth. Grades are intended to communicate to students how they are doing relative to course expectations and serve as a motivator for future effort, to inform parents of how their child is performing in a course, and to provide a yardstick for the administration to examine program effectiveness. Although the intent of grading is appropriate, most of those involved with the grading process (teachers, students, and parents) are not satisfied with how grades are used, especially in physical education. In physical education, grades are generally not based on a series of performance measures that spans an extended period of time; rather, they tend to reflect one-shot assessments that occur at the close of a unit of instruction. Teachers tend to grade students using a variety of variables other than skill performance or knowledge. Sometimes physical education teachers are prohibited from grading on performance or pass/fail is the standard. Most frequently, students are graded on participation, attitude, behavior, and attendance. In other words, physical education teachers tend not to grade on learning or performance. Not only do teachers not grade on learning; they typically do not assess students in physical education in any substantive way. Several reasons have been proposed to explain this lack of focus on achievement of worthwhile goals in physical education. These range from overcrowded classrooms and inadequate testing equipment to a lack of time to conduct ongoing assessment and teachers who believe testing is unnecessary. It has also been suggested that keeping students active is more important than their progress and that teachers have been inadequately trained to conduct meaningful and appropriate testing.

Assessment refers to a variety of tasks and settings where students are given opportunities to demonstrate their knowledge, skill, understanding, and application of content in a context that allows continued learning and growth. Although assessment and grading tend to go hand-in-hand and are frequently considered synonymous, you can see that they are not. To overcome this perception of sameness, we must learn to view and use assessment for purposes other than testing and evaluation. Teachers must be taught that well-designed and thought-out assessments can improve the quality of teaching and increase the amount of learning that occurs. Assessment can serve as a tool to track students' performance progress and allow them to take responsibility for their own learning and improvement. Tracking and regularly monitoring student progress results in greater motivation and achievement.

A NEW ASSESSMENT PERSPECTIVE

Educational reform has proposed changing the "how" and "what" of assessment so that it is more fully integrated into the teaching/learning process and provides documentation of student learning and achievement. This move emphasizes meaningful learning outcomes and performance-based assessments that are significant, reflect real-life situations, and involve students in worthwhile and relevant tasks.

As we emphasized in Chapter 8, the stronger the link between assessment and learning outcomes, the higher student achievement will be. This suggests that stating goals, providing learning experiences that allow students to progress toward those goals, and holding students accountable for achieving those goals by integrating assessment throughout the teaching/learning process will be most effective. Does this mean that you should teach toward the test (assessment)? If it is a good assessment that is relevant and directly measures the learning goal, then yes. For instance, if the intended outcome were for students to be able to design and perform a tumbling routine to music, then having them select the music to match their choice of tumbling elements would be appropriate. Allowing them adequate time to practice their developing stunts to music during mock performances would increase mastery of the skills and of integration of them into a whole. Finally, having a class performance of tumbling routines as the culminating event would match the intended outcome and would directly measure what they have learned and practiced. In another scenario, the learning outcome might be for students to recognize their feelings of anger or frustration in physical activity settings and to control/manage those emotions in a constructive way. We might select an assessment that allows them to reflect upon their feelings, identify them, and keep a journal of what brought those feelings on and how they handled the situation. This requires that students learn how to recognize their personal feelings and the behaviors and actions that reflect them and to develop a habit of noting in a daily journal occurrences of these instances and how they react to them.

Does this suggest that the learning experiences and assessment tasks are the same? Yes, but not exclusively. Students need to have opportunities to practice

180

Meaningful
Assessment for
Significant
Learning
Outcomes

what you want them to learn and what will be assessed (instructional alignment), yet practice of other innovative tasks can also be beneficial to and facilitate learning. In addition to practicing the final assessment in the previous example, students might be involved with such activities as developing a feelings collage that represents what they feel, learning to note the amount of frustration or anger they are experiencing on a feelings thermometer, or developing a series of flash cards that provide them with alternative solutions for handling their feelings.

Practicing the ultimate assessment allows a consistent accountability system to monitor student progress with interventions to improve student learning built into the process. The more realistic the performance assessment, the more students will be motivated to perform; and the result will be more learning, improvement, and success. All of this reinforces the current push toward assessment as an integral part of the teaching/learning process.

ASSESSMENT DEFINED

Assessment involves collecting, describing, and quantifying information about performance. In physical education, we typically see teachers assessing students on fitness tests, isolating skills in contrived settings, or awarding points subjectively for effort, dress, and participation. The recent focus on assessment that authenticates student achievement demands that teachers be able to show what students are learning in physical education. This goes beyond identifying the content covered in class and requires that we be able to demonstrate what students have learned, what they can do, how they have changed, how they can share their knowledge and skills, what real-life applications they can implement, and how their physical activity choices reflect their status as independent learners. How can all of this be shown? What tools do we have to measure these types of skills, knowledge, and behaviors? Assessing student data to demonstrate these learning outcomes requires ongoing or continuous assessment, a focus on various types of learning outcomes, viewing assessments as learning tools, utilizing both formal and informal assessment measures, and selecting a multitude of assessment tactics and strategies.

Formal and Informal Assessment

There is a spectrum of ways to assess student performance that includes both formal and informal means. These may be viewed on a continuum from standardized and controlled assessment (formal) on one end to less-structured assessments that are integrated into the learning process (informal) on the other end (Figure 10.1).

Formal assessments tend to be removed from real life and are contrived. These types of assessments may measure student performance, but that performance cannot be generalized to other situations. We frequently see the set in

Formal Assessments		Informal Assessments

Written exam
Skills test in isolation
	Teacher observation
	  using a checklist
	Self-scoring on
	  learning task
		Create portfolio
		Devise fitness activity plan
		Officiate game play
		Keep student journal
		Keep game statistics
		Teach senior aerobics
		Solve team initiative
		Design multimedia demo

FIGURE 10.1 *The assessment continuum*

volleyball assessed by the number of times a student can set the ball against the wall above a 6-foot line. Although this may demonstrate how many times the student can set the ball in this fashion, it certainly does not indicate how well the student will perform receiving a pass from a teammate and setting it to the hitter in a game of volleyball. Another student in volleyball may score well on a rules test but, when officiating a game, have difficulty recognizing violations or identifying the consequences for committing them.

Informal assessment is a means of using assessment as a learning experience to promote growth. Using our volleyball example, it would be possible to have our duty team in Sport Education keeping game statistics on the number of sets attempted as well as successful and unsuccessful sets for all students. This would provide information on what students are able to do in a game setting. As for learning and demonstrating knowledge of rules, we could have students involved in a three-versus-three game and, when a foul occurs, stop the game and have the teacher ask students to identify the foul and the consequence. This allows students to experience the foul and its consequence in a realistic game and provides an environment in which questioning and discussion can take place for clarification.

Formative and Summative Assessment

Two other terms that are related to formal and informal types of assessment measures are *formative* and *summative*. Both have their place in assessment, but there is a clear distinction between assessment that is intended to provide feedback to impact the ongoing instructional process (formative) and assessment that provides a final judgment on learning (summative). One demonstrates that learning is taking place, and the other determines whether it has or hasn't happened.

Formative assessment is used to provide continuous, ongoing information and feedback to both students and the teacher about progress toward learning goals. These types of assessments allow teachers to identify students who are struggling or experiencing learning difficulties so that they might provide them

182

Meaningful
Assessment for
Significant
Learning
Outcomes

with guidance to overcome these problems. Formative assessments suggest adjustments in instructional processes, help learners improve performance, tend to be informal in nature, and may also act as a learning experience or step in the learning process. The formative assessments themselves might be identical to those used in the summative measure of student learning, yet in the first instance, they provide students with practice and feedback on their progress rather than judging them as correct or incorrect. When assessment is used in this ongoing and continuous manner, it is directly linked to instruction and tends to motivate learners to want to improve and achieve. Formative assessment in this light seeks information to improve instruction and thus influence student learning. In summary, formative assessment serves three key purposes: It (a) provides feedback to both student and teacher to monitor learning and identify learning difficulties, (b) informs revision of teaching practice through assessment information, and (c) allows learners to assess their own performance, maintain a record of their progress, and identify their own weaknesses.

Summative assessment occurs at the end of an instructional sequence, tends to be formal in nature, and is intended to provide an evaluation of student learning for grading or comparative purposes. In other words, summative assessment determines exit success and how well students achieved the intended learning outcomes. In line with the current emphasis on student learning as an outcome of education, summative assessment is perhaps more critical than it has been previously. This importance suggests, however, that summative assessments be adequate measures of the intended outcomes so they truly reflect learning.

Alternative Assessment

There is a growing interest in assessment practices that are closer to teaching practice, and along with this movement, a set of assessment terms has evolved. These terms might be considered a means of viewing assessment differently and thus allowing us to link it more closely to learning. It is necessary to understand this assessment language in order to design and implement an effective assessment model.

Alternative assessment might be considered the umbrella term for all assessments that are different from the one-shot formal tools traditionally used in the past. It requires students to generate a response rather than choose from a set of responses. Ideally, alternative assessment involves students in actively solving realistic problems through application of new information, prior knowledge, and relevant skills. These alternative assessments might then be considered either as authentic or performance assessments, depending upon what the student is asked to do. An *authentic assessment* reflects real life, is performed in a realistic setting, and mirrors what students do outside of school. This might include submitting a scorecard to demonstrate competence on the golf course, monitoring and recording the percentage of time spent within training heart rate zone on a 30-minute jog using a heart rate monitor, or the entire class keeping daily training logs of their physical activity record.

A *performance assessment* requires students to create something using problem solving, critical thinking, application skills, reflection, or other learned skills to demonstrate learning. A student could design an orienteering course for his peers to navigate, another student might maintain a portfolio documenting her scores on successively complex gymnastics routines over the middle school years, other students might consult, collaborate on, and successfully complete a group initiatives project. In each case, tasks can be individual, with partners, or even in groups; assessment can reflect psychomotor, cognitive, or affective types of learning; scoring may be determined by the student or peers or be designed by the teacher; and feedback may be inherent in the task, self-imposed, or provided externally by peers or the teacher.

In line with the notion of assessment being ongoing, cumulative, and learning oriented, it must reflect formative, informal practices as outlined by alternative types of assessment. Whether you are selecting authentic or performance assessments, because we know that assessment and learning are closely related, assessment practices must mirror the learning process. If, as has been suggested, students only learn what will be assessed, then building assessment into the learning process should increase the amount of learning that occurs.

DESIGNING ASSESSMENT TASKS

Critical to good assessment is carefully matching the assessment task to the meaningful outcomes you identified to guide student learning. The tasks or student assignments can be numerous and varied as long as the choices closely reflect the intended outcomes and provide learners the opportunity to demonstrate their progress toward achievement of those outcomes. Herman, Aschbacher, and Winters (1992) provide six questions to guide development of effective assessment tasks that we have applied to a fitness example.

1. *Does the task match specific instructional intentions?* If you want students to assess their levels of fitness, determine their specific fitness needs, and design a fitness prescription to guide their fitness activity program, then having them do *exactly* that as the assessment task would be appropriate. Having them only identify the appropriate steps to complete this task would not be sufficient.

2. *Does the task adequately represent the content and skills you expect students to attain?* You need to determine exactly what it is you want students to be able to do and what content, knowledge, and skills it will require. In the previous example, students need to decide which fitness tests to use, evaluate their own levels of fitness based on test results and determine their needs for improvement, and be able to use fitness concepts to design an appropriate fitness prescription.

3. *Does the task enable students to demonstrate their progress and capabilities?* This requires you to determine whether the task is fair relative to expectations for prior knowledge and opportunities for students to have

184

Meaningful
Assessment for
Significant
Learning
Outcomes

learned and practiced necessary skills. Critical to the previous example would be whether students have been taught relevant fitness tests and concepts related to improving components of fitness. Depending upon your intent, you could ensure that all content has been taught or provide resources to challenge students to problem solve on their own.

4. *Does the assessment use authentic, real-world tasks?* We know that realistic tasks tend to motivate learners to achieve and also provide possibilities for transfer outside of the classroom to real-world settings. If we expect young people to maintain a health-enhancing level of physical fitness, then their ability to assess and monitor their own behavior is relevant and meaningful.

5. *Does the task lend itself to an interdisciplinary approach?* Frequently, realistic tasks cross over subject boundaries and require students to apply knowledge and skills from other domains. Fitness prescription includes determining target heart rate training range, which requires the calculation of percentages and other mathematical functions and thus asks the student to apply content from another subject area.

6. *Can the task be structured to provide measures of several goals?* Most programs identify goals for learners that come from the motor, cognitive, and affective domains, as discussed previously. Some tasks might assess students in two of these areas. During fitness testing, students may be required to interact with a partner or small group to successfully complete the selected tests. This would measure affective skills of collaboration, teamwork, and cooperation.

Alternative forms of assessment that include realistic and performance-based approaches are an ideal way to conduct continuous, formative assessment throughout the learning process. These approaches allow alignment of outcomes, instruction, and assessment, yet place new demands on both the students and the teacher. Students must take responsibility for demonstrating their learning, and the teacher must design realistic assessments to allow this to occur. Alternative assessments are established by determining meaningful outcomes prior to beginning instruction and then teaching toward and assessing the desired learning. The tasks should also provide a meaningful picture of student progress, rather than pieces of discrete information.

Consistent with our comments in Chapter 8 about how some content remains unspecified until the learners themselves interpret it, the same is often true of assessment. Not all knowledge, skills, behaviors, values, attitudes, or changes students make can be quantified and measured. As Kirk (1993, p. 252) indicated, "What students say, what they write, the adaptations and changes they make to their actions over time, are all appropriate and relevant evidence of learning."

We previously highlighted the need to ask, "What are the important outcomes?" rather than "What will my course/program cover?" Now we need to ask, "What must my students demonstrate to show they have a grasp of the content?" and "What will successful student understanding look like?" This again suggests that the final assessments and scoring criteria be thoughtfully developed and then become the focus of instruction and student learning experiences. We might also ask, "Are there ways that students can demonstrate their skill and knowledge in a way that is unique to them and their own personal style and ways of learning, or must all students show what they know in the same way?"

In recent years, physical educators have learned numerous methods to monitor student progress, retention, understanding, and physical performance that we demonstrate through the various curriculum models. Each of the physical education curriculum models provides abundant opportunities for authentic assessment to measure progress toward meaningful outcomes. But the teacher need not be the only one who assesses student performance. If assessment is designed as continuous and formative and to serve a variety of purposes, then the teacher, the student, or even a peer can play a role in the assessment process. We describe a variety of assessment tasks and link them to meaningful outcomes to clarify assessment tasks appropriate for use within the various models. Additional assessment strategies, tools, and applications can be found through a number of other resources, including the *Journal of Physical Education, Recreation, and Dance Strategies*. PE Central (http://www.chre.vt.edu/~/pe.central/) is continually publishing and updating a variety of assessment strategies. All of the strategies reported in these sources have been developed and used by teachers, graduate students, and professors from across the country.

OBSERVATION

You have heard the old saying that "teachers have eyes in the back of their heads." This suggests that teachers know what is going on in their classrooms (with-it-ness), which students are having difficulty, who is successful, and when an event pulls students off task. Experienced teachers frequently use observation in their classes as a means to provide feedback, to manage the classroom, to inform teaching practice, and as a tool for students to assess a peer's performance. As teachers become comfortable using observation, they are often able to convert their informal observations into criteria that they can then formalize and record using a checklist or rating scale. These tools ease the collection of information on student progress.

Checklist

A *checklist* is a list of statements, dimensions, characteristics, or behaviors that are basically scored as yes or no, based on an observer's judgment of whether the dimension is present or absent. A checklist may be used for process types of behavior (e.g., followed correct sequence of steps) or, more typically, as a product measure (e.g., critical elements performed). Whether process (sequence) or product (outcome) criteria are used to measure performance, the

186

Meaningful
Assessment for
Significant
Learning
Outcomes

Goal: Follow effective conflict resolution strategies to solve a problem in class

	Situation 1			Situation 2		
	Self	Teacher	Peer	Self	Teacher	Peer
A—Ask "What's the problem?"						
B—Brainstorm possible solutions.						
C—Choose the best solution.						
D—Do it.						

FIGURE 10.2   *Conflict resolution strategies checklist*

teacher, peer, or other observer determines whether the criteria were exhibited. A checklist makes criteria for performance public and allows students to clarify what they are expected to do and even to play a role in their own learning. A checklist, however, provides only limited information on whether a specific criterion was demonstrated and nothing about the quality of the performance.

The checklist shown in Figure 10.2 allows the student, teacher, or a peer to indicate whether the appropriate steps were taken in resolving a conflict situation in class. It does not provide information about the tone of voice or nonverbal mannerisms that might instigate problems. If students are unable to resolve their own problems in class after consulting the conflict resolution strategies checklist but the teacher finds that all the steps are being followed, then additional information is needed. This might be obtained by collecting anecdotal notes of what behaviors and language characterize the interactions during the process.

Checklists can also move the focus away from process and turn it toward outcome: Were the elements present or not present in the performance? Figure 10.3 shows such a checklist.

Checklists that are too complex and cumbersome may actually decrease the amount of accurate information that can be obtained, especially if they are being used for peer assessment or a student viewing his or her own performance on videotape.

Rating Scale

Whereas a checklist notes whether a specific criterion occurred, a rating scale indicates the degree or quality of that criterion. Degree may be noted numerically (1–5, with 5 being high), descriptively (always, most often, sometimes, rarely, never), or by level (beginning, intermediate, advanced). In the putting example, a descriptive or numerical rating scale could be easily applied to pro-

Goal: Develop a consistent putting swing

	First Putt		Second Putt		Third Putt	
	Yes	No	Yes	No	Yes	No
Balanced						
Square blade						
Comfortable grip						
Still body						
Eyes over ball						
Smooth, even stroke						

FIGURE 10.3 *Putting critical element checklist*

Goal: Develop a consistent putting swing

	Always	Most often	Sometimes	Rarely	Never
Balanced					
Square blade					
Comfortable grip					
Still body					
Eyes over ball					
Smooth, even stroke					

FIGURE 10.4 *Putting critical element frequency rating scale*

vide more in-depth information on the student's performance, as shown in Figure 10.4.

Because the rating scale requires two decisions (occurrence and quality), it generally takes more time and thought, which suggests that rating scales would tend to include fewer criteria for observation. Rating scales provide more complete and thorough data than a checklist and can be used by students to inform their own performance or by teachers to better determine learners' needs. In addition, the rating scale encourages students to focus on the quality rather than quantity of their performance, as the rating scale in Figure 10.5 shows.

188

Meaningful
Assessment for
Significant
Learning
Outcomes

Goal: Progress in skill performance from simple to complex and single skills to skill combinations

	Beginning	Intermediate	Advanced	Comments
Rolls Sideways				
Forward				
Backward				
Springs Upright				
Inverted				
Upright supports individual				
Partner				
Inverted supports headstand				
Transitional				
Handstand				

FIGURE 10.5 *Stunts and tumbling rating scale*

A final example of a rating scale/checklist was found on the PE Central Web site. Mark Manross suggests this cue checklist, shown in Figure 10.6, can be completed by the teacher while observing students and then used to guide instruction.

Peer Assessment Observation

We frequently see formal and informal peer observation experiences used in physical education to keep a record of the number of skill attempts, to provide feedback on students following a routine, or to indicate if critical features have all been included. Both the performer and the observer learn during a peer-directed task. If this type of assessment is going to be effective, students must know the criteria and what they look like when performed appropriately. In addition, students need to be taught how to observe, how to make appropriate judgments, and how to record or provide feedback to their peers. It is also imperative that students understand that their assessment of a peer is intended to provide feedback to improve performance. Teacher modeling of assessment is an appropriate place to begin training students to gauge performance. Fol-

Student name	Cue:	Cue:	Cue:

FIGURE 10.6 *Cue checklist (Source: http://www.pe.central.vt.edu)*

Task/Cue	Yes	Not Yet
1. Ball is held with the laces up and in an oblique position		
2. Kicking leg is slightly behind other leg		
3. Step is made by nonkicking foot		
4. Drop ball on top of foot		
5. Leg extends to the sky on the follow-through		

FIGURE 10.7 *Punting evaluation purpose sheet for sixth grade and up*

lowing this, they can gain practice observing and collecting data by counting a partner's skill attempts, timing some aspect of the performance, measuring the distance of an event, and then moving on to using a basic checklist and rating scale as previously described. An example posted on the PE Central Web site by Jim Krouscas demonstrates this (see Figure 10.7).

Figure 10.8 shows a more complex checklist in that it requires the peer to observe a series of motor skills in a routine and make judgments as they progress through the sequence.

Students can be taught to play a more critical role in assessing performance in realistic settings. In after-school sport, we frequently see students serve as statisticians and maintain the official statistics that serve as performance feedback to the coach and athlete and that make up the formal record of game performance. Students can be taught how to collect, compile, and summarize pertinent performance data. A simple set of statistics might be kept on students' performances on the badminton smash in either singles or doubles play, as shown in the form in Figure 10.9.

Name _____   Homeroom teacher _____

Check system:

−   Some problems with balance, falls, or performs with large/medium errors
+   Can perform skill, but has small form error
☺   Perfect performance

The "stars"		Top notch	
1. Acknowledge the judge		1. Acknowledge the judge	
2. Body wave		2. Straight body stretch	
3. Step forward into a lunge (hold 3 counts)		3. One-leg balance (hold 3 counts)	
4. Forward roll to stand:		4. Step into lunge (hold 3 counts)	
A. On incline mat			
B. On flat mat			
5. Arabesque (hold 3 counts)		5. Down into body sweep	
6. Chasse		6. Back walkover	
7. Pivot one half-turn on balls of feet		7. Pivot one half-turn on balls of feet	
8. Cartwheel to one-leg balance (hold 3 counts)		8. Back roll to stand	
9. Straight jump		9. Jump one half-turn	
10. Backward roll to stand (hold 3 counts)		10. Handstand (hold 3 counts)	
11. Stand—stretch to end		11. Forward roll to stand—stretch to end	
12. Acknowledge the judge		12. Acknowledge the judge	

FIGURE 10.8   *Gymnastics compulsory routine partner checklist*

A more complete yet complex set of statistics can also be kept accurately by students. The examples in Figure 10.10 can be used to keep one set of data (serve) on one student or that same set of data on all students. Once they become adept at maintaining this one set of data, students can move on to collecting two sets of data (serve and serve receive). This same procedure is followed for attack and set and finally the complete set of game statistics (serve, serve receive, attack, and setting) for all students using the combined statistics score sheet. This set of scoresheets can be modified for the age level and ability of students and adapted to whatever skills and combination of skills students are using in game play. This needs to be taught, modeled, and

Focus: Smash
        Assess each smash and record the outcome with a check mark in
        the appropriate space

Student name	Legal	Ace	Short	Long
Player 1				
Player 2				
Player 3				
Player 4				

FIGURE 10.9 *Sport Education badminton game statistics*

practiced until students feel comfortable collecting game statistics and until their peers feel that the data collected are accurate and reflect their performances.

PORTFOLIO

A portfolio is a collection of student work that documents the student's effort, progress, and achievement toward a goal or goals. It can either be representative or cumulative. A portfolio is a powerful tool that allows learners to take responsibility for demonstrating, monitoring, and displaying their own learning. Portfolios allow students to celebrate what they can do and display evidence to demonstrate their success. In order to select materials to reflect their progress, students must examine their work, reflect on what it represents, and assess it relative to the portfolio goal. This self-selection, reflection, and assessment process makes portfolio development an instructional tool.

A portfolio is not, however, an assessment until several issues have been considered and negotiated: (a) An assessment purpose is determined. (b) How and what to select for inclusion are defined. (c) Decisions on who may select portfolio materials and when they may be selected are articulated. (d) Criteria for assessing either the entire collection of materials or the individual aspects of it are identified (Herman et al., 1992). These issues are essential for designing a portfolio task, and student involvement in them is critical if students are to take ownership of their own learning and achievement. Perhaps most crucial are decisions related to what is to be included as samples of student work and then the criteria that will define and measure that body of work. Several questions that the teacher needs to consider relate to whether progress toward a goal or improvement will be assessed and, if so, how they will be measured. If the portfolio includes a variety of materials, how will these materials be weighted in the overall assessment? Issues related to how the portfolio will be

Serve & Serve Receive

Player	Serve				Serve receive			
	Ace	Legal serve	Illegal serve	Service %	Settable pass	Legal pass	Illegal pass	Receiving %

Serve

+ Serve results directly in point scored, opponent unable to make legal play on ball
0 Serve is legal & playable by an opponent
– Illegal serve, out of bounds, in net, or foot fault

Serve receive

+ Pass goes directly to setter & is ideal
0 Pass is legal & playable by opponent or teammate
– Illegal pass, out of bounds, or unplayable

Attack & Set

Player	Attack				Set			
	Kill	Legal attack	Illegal attack	Attack %	Assist	Legal set	Illegal set	Set %

Attack

+ Attack results directly in point scored, opponent unable to make legal play on ball
0 Attack is legal & playable by opponent
– Illegal attack, out of bounds, in net, or foot fault

Set

+ Set results directly in point scored by a kill
0 Legal set playable by opponent or teammate
– Illegal set, out of bounds, in net, or foot fault

Complete Game Statistics

Player	Serve				Serve receive				Attack				Set			
	A	LS	IS	S%	SP	LP	IP	R%	K	LA	IA	A%	A	LS	IS	S%

This statistics sheet requires the statistician to use the same scoring conventions as on the individual statistics sheets.

FIGURE 10.10 *Forms for data collection*

BOX 10.1   Sample Portfolio Assignments

Adventure Trust-Building Portfolio

- *Goal:* To become a group member who has learned to trust and is willing to actively participate as a member of the group.

- *Portfolio purpose:* After each group activity, prepare a summary report that describes the activity; what happened; the role you played in that activity; reactions, support, or other behaviors of your peers; and how these influenced your ability to trust and feel safe in the activity. At the close of the adventure experience, you will review your summary reports, reflect upon the growth you displayed developing trust and the behaviors of your peers that facilitated this growth, and share your perceptions on this process.

- *Portfolio evidence:* Summary report including what happened, your role, interactions with others, influences on your trusting, and perceptions on the trust-building process.

Moscow High School Wellness Portfolio

- *Goal 1:* Students will interpret and analyze effects of a variety of influences on their emotional health.

- *Goal 3:* Students will recognize the relationship between proper nutrition, fitness, and optimum wellness.

- *Portfolio evidence:*

  1. Write journal entries to communicate stress inventory results, identify consequences related to level, identify situations that result in stress level increases, and identify alternative responses for these situations.
  2. Role-play effective nonviolent strategies in potentially volatile situations, and provide a written reflection concerning personal growth as an outcome of this activity.
  3. Develop a personal fitness prescription that will address strengths and weaknesses in your personal fitness level, and monitor your progress toward reaching fitness goals.
  4. Develop and incorporate fitness and nutrition strategies for improving overall health.

Source: Karla Harman, Moscow High School, 1999. Reprinted with permission.

---

assessed are included in "Establishing Scoring Criteria—Using Rubrics" later in this chapter. Box 10.1 includes two portfolio assignments that may become assessments. The second was designed and implemented by a group of high school teachers who have revised their entire curriculum to meet the needs of their changing youth population. The two goals included in Box 10.1 (of the six identified in the Moscow High School curriculum) are also the goals for the portfolio assignment.

194

Meaningful
Assessment for
Significant
Learning
Outcomes

Portfolios today may take a variety of formats and utilize numerous tools. Electronic portfolios allow collection, organization, and storage of a variety of types of information into an electronic file. Information may represent digital pictures, rubrics from different assignments, digitized video segments, text, graphics, scanned photographs, and physical activity or fitness scores. There are numerous electronic portfolios designed for the teacher to collect, store, and even revise student work (e.g., Grady Profile).

More appropriate from our perspective are the programs that allow the students to create their own electronic portfolio (e.g., Link-way, HyperStudio, HyperCard). These programs and an accompanying portfolio assignment can be selected based on program goals or be left open ended for student choice. For example, MacVolleyball Complete contains a template for an electronic portfolio that includes specifications for volleyball skills and knowledge. Although this program is specific to volleyball, another program, MacPortfolio, allows the teacher to identify the standards to be achieved and leaves the choice of what evidence to include up to the student. How electronic portfolios are set up and arranged in each setting depends on the hardware and software available, how time is apportioned, and the teacher's skill and comfort in teaching the necessary technology know-how to students and arranging the environment to support this type of work. Karen Mendon, a teacher at Montebello Intermediate School, uses Mac-Health Related Fitness, a tutorial and portfolio program, for her students to maintain their own electronic portfolios. They have designed a fitness program with a 20-station cardiorespiratory circuit, a classroom, and a 6-station computer lab that the students rotate through. Students track their fitness levels, set goals, and monitor their progress as they proceed through the program. In addition, they create an individual fitness plan, calculate target heart rate zones, and conduct comparisons between calorie intake and exercise output.

Reflection is another skill that students need to be taught to help them take responsibility for their own learning and allow them to make sense of their progress. Reflection is the process of thoughtfully examining a situation, experience, the learning process, or personal feelings and attempting to make sense of them: What do they mean? What are their implications? How might I have behaved differently? Several assessment tools (e.g., portfolios, journals, self-assessments) require the learner to reflect upon some aspect of performance in order to respond thoughtfully.

JOURNALS

Journals allow students to reflect upon and share their thoughts, feelings, impressions, perceptions, and attitudes about their performance, an event, an assignment, or other learning experiences. A journal serves as a means of describing a situation, reacting to that situation, reflecting upon your actions, and using those reflections to learn and to grow. In this sense, the journal becomes a useful learning tool that can begin to demonstrate patterns, themes, and relationships that either facilitate or inhibit development. Journal writing may be conducted in class as a unit/season experience, linked to a specific aspect of instruction through a homework assignment, becomes a habit for students to develop as part of activity participation, or be a means of helping students examine their beliefs and attitudes toward a specific topic.

Journals can take a variety of formats and intents. They might be as "open" as "What were your feelings. . . ?" They may seek a response to a set of specific questions, or they may be an ongoing set of reflections on an issue or experience. To help them develop a sense of confidence in movement settings, students might be asked to keep throughout the year a weekly journal in which they write about their performance in each activity and identify where they felt successful and why. In another instance, students might be striving toward a series of fitness goals and maintain a journal noting their progress toward them, barriers they encountered, and their feelings about goal achievement. In each case, journal writing involves reflection: going back and recapturing thoughts, feelings, and events and interpreting what they mean personally.

Journal entries generally are not viewed as right or wrong and may include both positive and negative instances. Because journals reflect personal feelings, thoughts, and perceptions, they typically are not graded for their content. They may provide a record of student views on success and failure and information on how students process experiences. Journals can, however, be assessed for completion or by using a set of criteria that guided the journal writing itself. Care must be taken in scoring the student journal because it may tend to stifle reflection, honesty, and the sharing of personal feelings and perceptions. Box 10.2 shows a journal program that could be used to encourage students to reflect on and record their daily class activities.

EVENT TASKS

An event task simulates real life, allows multiple solutions and responses, is important, relevant, and current in an attempt to stimulate student interest, and can be completed in a single time frame. This could be reflected in the culminating event for a gymnastics season, successfully getting your entire team through a complex outdoor group initiative, organizing, implementing, and monitoring a wellness fair for the community, or each student designing a game that would use concepts of striking, speed, and accuracy. Although an event task can be performed in a single instructional time period, planning may take time out of class or over an extended period. An individual student or a group may perform an event task. Well-designed event tasks reflect learning outcomes, provide opportunities for learners to apply knowledge and skill

BOX 10.2　Sample Journal Assignments

Cooperation as an Integrative Theme

- *Theme:* Cooperation is a theme identified by an entire middle school as a necessary social skill that students need to master to function effectively throughout life.

- *Journal task:* Students will reflect upon how cooperation is used throughout life and from the perspective of different content areas. As they identify situations where cooperation is critical, they will describe it and discuss how and why it is critical and how well they feel they cooperate in each situation.

Seventh Grade Floor Hockey Trinity School

- *Goal:* Student journals were used to determine the students' ability to reflect upon their experiences during the Sport Education field hockey season.

- *Prompts*

  Entry 1: We have learned about fair play today. Why is fair play important? Who needs to play fair during game play? How does fair play help while participating in a game? How can you encourage fair play in others?

  Entry 2: Read the attached article and respond to it. Try to organize some thoughts and ideas that tie in with the things we have talked about in class the last couple of days.

  Entry 3: This article talks about Tracy winning the Little League Good Sport Award. Tracy says she tries to "spark her teammates" and "cheer them up." What can you say about being a good sport? Try to come up with some ideas to expand on this topic.

  Entry 4: Describe the importance of teamwork while playing offense and while playing defense. Are there similarities or differences between offensive and defensive teamwork?

  Entry 5: We have captains and managers on each team. These people fill the roles of the team leaders. What things does a team member look for in a leader? Is it possible for other team members to also be leaders? Explain and expand on this subject.

  Entry 6: The Reds have not had a captain since 1988. Why do you think they went this long without one? Think about what we have worked on in class, and respond to the following questions: Why does a team need a captain? Why are captains important in our class? Is it possible for a team to go without a captain? What would be the consequences of our teams not having captains? Explain and expand on your thoughts.

  Entry 7: Respond to the following statement: Winning isn't everything; it's the only thing.

  Entry 8: What would you tell a teammate who is making negative remarks? He might say, "I hate this game. I'm going to quit" or "I hate my team. No one passes me the puck."

  Entry 9: We started this season talking about fair play. As the season nears the end, do you think your team is still concerned with fair play? If not, what can you do to help your team remember to play fair? If your team is still playing fair, how did you help your team continue to play fair? Explain.

  Entry 10: Is the team leader in goals and assists (scoring statistics) always the best (most valuable) player or the fairest player on the team? Explain.

  Entry 11: Is fair play important as the season goes along? In other words, was fair play more important at the beginning of the season and now is winning more important at the end? Can winning and fair play be important to your team at the same time? Explain.

Source: Tom Gilbert, 1997, Trinity School. Reprinted with permission.

to a meaningful task, and allow learners to demonstrate level of achievement. Box 10.3 lists some event tasks for curriculum models for several grades.

197

Written Tests

WRITTEN TESTS

Probably the most typical form of assessment for cognitive concepts and general knowledge used in physical education is the written test. It is generally true/false, multiple choice, matching, and perhaps short answer. Typically, we see children and youth studying (or carrying around) a handout covering the rules, procedures, and etiquette that guide a sport or activity. Before play begins, students are tested on how well they know this information that will allow them to participate successfully. (This suggests a problem not only with the type of assessment, but also with the instruction that precedes it. That is a topic for Chapter 11.) Our initial chapter scenario provided a way of assessing this knowledge in a setting that reviewed, prompted, provided feedback, and stimulated learning of rules in a realistic game setting. However, despite our reluctance to encourage the use of written tests, they need not be *all* bad if designed in an applied manner that challenges students to critically think about the question (problem) in order to solve it. For instance, providing students with a game scenario to analyze allows them to demonstrate their knowledge of the rules and procedures governing an activity. Box 10.4 shows an archery example used in Mary Henninger's physical education class at Beechcroft High School that demonstrates this well.

Written tests are often a means of assessing whether students understand critical elements or performance cues that impact performance or know necessary safety procedures. Although this knowledge can be assessed most effectively in a realistic setting, there are ways of designing written tests to achieve this in a problem-solving and applied fashion. For example,

> Jim is taking part in a climbing unit in his fifth grade class. These two questions from his written exam relate to his knowledge of communication when climbing or belaying a climber.
>
> 1. Outline the set of commands that are used to initiate the backup belay. Explain what each command means.
>
> _____
> _____
> _____
> _____
>
> 2. What is the meaning of these commands?
> "tension" _____
> "slack" _____
> "falling" _____
> "slow down" _____

Another example of how to gain an understanding of what students have learned about concepts introduced to them can be done as an in-class assessment or used as a homework assignment. Reginald Kimball posted a written

198

Meaningful
Assessment for
Significant
Learning
Outcomes

BOX 10.3   Event Tasks

Sport Education, Grade 9 Acrosport, Partner Task

The culminating event for the season is a partner competition performed to music. Your task is to design a 90-second routine with a partner to music of your choice. The routine must include four different balance stunts, two locomotor and two nonlocomotor actions, two inversions, and weight transfers.

Fitness and Wellness Education Fun Run, Grade 10, Group Task

Organize and implement a fun run for faculty and students. To be included are a prerun meal, training workshop, maps to guide the runners, applications and run information, awards, and publicity.

Developmental Physical Education, Grade 2, Individual Task

Role-play examples of physical activity situations that might reflect hurt, anger, frustration, defensiveness, unethical behavior, or other emotions detrimental to performance or fair play. Students will then lead a discussion with the class to identify alternative types of behaviors to overcome these harmful ones.

The Culture of Sport, Personal Sport Culture, Individual Task

Students demonstrate their understanding of their personal sport culture by developing a biography of their sport and leisure involvement and the nature of those experiences. The individual experiences are presented as part of a "gallery walk" in which students display oral and pictorial perspectives of their lives in and views of sport and leisure activities (Kellum, Dixon, O'Sullivan, Kinchin, & Roberts, 1992).

Fitness & Wellness Education, Grade 9, Group Task

Students select a daily morning health message prompting students, teachers, and administrators about some aspect of health and wellness and arrange delivery of it over the school intercom. For instance, they might provide guidance related to nutrition and sound eating habits or be more specific about daily needs for physical activity.

Fitness and Wellness Education, Grade 3, Partner Task

Students work in pairs to make life-sized drawings of themselves participating in a favorite fitness activity. One student demonstrates an activity on a large piece of paper while the partner traces that activity. Students then display their activities and talk about which health- or fitness-related concepts are most critical to it.

Individual Task

Students demonstrate an activity they enjoy and identify the muscle groups used to perform it.

BOX 10.4   Archery Exam

1. Sally has just come outside to shoot. She reaches for a bow, immediately picks it up and checks it, then checks her arrows. After giving the command to check equipment, the teacher calls for bows up. Sally shoots her three arrows and hits the following: one in the blue, one in the black, and the final arrow splits the red and the yellow. After shooting her third arrow, Sally puts down her bow and begins playing around with her friends. They chase each other, hit each other, and wrestle. Once given the command to retrieve, Sally gets her arrows and returns to her line twirling them.
   - What did Sally score on each individual arrow? Total score?
   - What safety rules did Sally violate?

2. Bill has three arrows to shoot. On his first arrow, he hits the white. On his second arrow, he picks up the arrow, places it under the bow, places his three fingers on the string, draws, aims, and hits the blue, but it bounces off. On his third arrow, Bill places the arrow on the bow, places his three fingers on the string, aims, and releases. He hits the black. Bill is so excited that he runs out to get his arrows once the command is given to retrieve.
   - What did Bill score for each individual arrow? Total score?
   - What shooting steps did Bill perform incorrectly or forget to do?
   - What safety rules did Bill violate?

3. Tonya arrived late to class with a new hairstyle, new shoes, new gold hoop earrings, and a brand new Nike shirt with her name air brushed on it. After going through the proper shooting steps, Tonya hit the target three times. One arrow hit the white, one hit the blue, and her final arrow hit the bulls eye. She was so excited she ran out in her new shoes and stood by her target. When she arrived there, she noticed the arrow in the white only had two feathers. Tonya had just completed her best round of archery.
   - What was the score for each individual arrow? Total score?
   - What safety rules did Tonya violate?

4. Edward has four arrows to shoot. He hits the yellow, which bounces off, white, red, and his final arrow misses a passing squirrel. Once given the command to retrieve, Edward yanks his arrows from the target and returns to his line with the arrows in his back pocket.
   - What did Edward score for each individual arrow? Total score?
   - What safety rules did Edward violate?

Source: Beechcroft High School Archery Exam. Reprinted with permission from Mary L. Henninger.

---

assessment for fourth grade and up on the PE Central Web site. It includes the following:

Six-Week Assessment

1. When you use a hockey stick, the correct grip is to keep the hand that you write with on top of the stick, and the other hand goes below that hand.

200

Meaningful
Assessment for
Significant
Learning
Outcomes

   a. True
   b. False

2. When dribbling a ball with your hand, use your _____ so you can maintain control of the ball.
   a. Fingertips
   b. Palm
   c. Finger pads
   d. Whole hand

3. It is important to understand the difference between self-space and general space because:

   _____

   _____

4. When you are throwing the ball for distance, it is *most* important to:
   a. Step with the same foot you throw with
   b. Aim properly
   c. Step with the opposite foot you throw with
   d. Make sure you follow through with the hand you throw with

5. Mirroring is:

   _____

   _____

SELF-ASSESSMENT

The student's role becomes central in the new assessment process. If our intent is to make assessment an educative process to improve student performance, then students must be able to assess and modify their own performance. Because students do not have access to teachers at all times during the day, during summer vacations, or when they graduate from school, their ability to take charge of their own performance is critical. Students should not expect to achieve success the first time they attempt to perform a new task, so being able to assess and make corrections is crucial for them. Students must be taught the key tasks to achieve this self-assessment goal—the standards, the criteria, the know-how—and be given opportunities to practice assessing performance in such a way that they can make appropriate and necessary adjustments to be successful.

Student self-assessment can take a variety of forms, some of which we have already discussed. The intent of all self-assessment for students is to critically analyze aspects of their performance for comparison to their own goals, teacher-designed criteria, or peer performance standards. Self-assessment requires the student to reflect upon performance, learn to compare what a performance feels like to what it should look like (kinesthetic knowledge), and be able to analyze correct versus incorrect performance. Self-assessment can be as simple as recording the number of successful attempts on a checklist, ranking performance in comparison to progress toward target goals, or measuring and maintaining records of a personal fitness or activity profile.

Insight Media produces some excellent video and CD-ROM tools that can be used for classroom activity stations, for out-of-class work in a computer

Day	Time	Activity	How I felt physically

FIGURE 10.11 *Grade 11 personal fitness log*

center or library, or as supplemental to instruction. Personal Health Interactive (CD-ROM) provides numerous resources through a comprehensive wellness clinic. Students can learn to monitor their daily health behaviors or use this resource to access information related to numerous topics (healthy lifestyles, wellness concepts, and personal health risks).

Jambor and Weeks (1995) offer a video technique to help students take responsibility for improving their own performance. Interpersonal Process Recall (IPR) is most useful for students who understand what a motor skill should look like, have had some practice assessing their own performance, and are willing to interact with the teacher and peers on their performance. This technique puts students in the role of directing the viewing of their video and leading the analysis and discussion. The teacher becomes the facilitator, asking questions, seeking clarity, and prompting analysis of different movements. As students view the video, they may choose to stop it for discussion at any point to highlight what they see, how they felt, or what they consider significant or critical to them. The teacher's role during this discussion is to help the students delve more deeply into what they are viewing, their reactions to it, and the possibilities for changing a performance. Students must be allowed to work through this process with guidance rather than being told what is wrong and how to correct it. The collaborative nature of the interactions is intended to prevent students from getting defensive about their performance and to encourage them to identify errors themselves.

A student *log* is a record of performance on specific behaviors or criteria over a given period. A student log can be maintained by an individual (fitness or weight training log), partners (win/loss record in badminton), or the entire class (mileage record toward the goal of running across the country). Logs can be simple (activity performed) to complex (time of day, weight training exercises, frequency, intensity, and feelings about the workout) and utilize technology or the more traditional forms of documenting.

To use a log like that in Figure 10.11, students conduct a personal fitness assessment, identify fitness needs, establish short-term and long-term goals, select activities to meet those goals, design a weekly fitness plan, and develop the log to monitor progress. As they begin to participate in this fitness plan, they maintain a daily log of their progress.

Date	Fitness activity	Minutes	Resting HR	Exercise HR	Resting HR	Laps	Notebook	Rating scale

FIGURE 10.12   *Woodward High School activity log*

These logs can be maintained on computer in the classroom using spreadsheet software. If only one computer is available, individual students or the leader of a group of students can enter the data at the close of every class session. Raw data can be turned into a graph to reflect either individual or group work and posted (e.g., minutes of exercise with heart rate [HR] within training range).

Students in ninth grade at Woodward High School in Toledo, Ohio, are required to maintain an activity log that allows them to record and assess their participation level using the following rating scale:

1. Not much effort (no improvement on test scores)
2. Participated some of the time
3. Participated most of the time
4. Participated the entire hour

The log is shown in Figure 10.12

SKILLS TESTS

Skills tests tend to be isolated and do not reflect performance in a realistic setting. When designed to assess performance in an authentic way, they may be useful to determine performance level and provide feedback to learners. The Davis Bowling Skills Test (Davis, 1994) is an effective example of a skills test that also serves as a learning experience and can be used in an ongoing fashion. Students bowl one game of ten frames using two balls per frame unless they score a strike. The goal is to score 20 points (2 points per frame) on the skills test. Points are awarded only for the following:

- Hitting the headpin on the first ball
- Making a strike on the first ball
- Making a spare on the second ball

An open frame does not score points. One frame may serve as the entire skills test or be combined with a series of frames, with the entire set of scores or the

First trial		Date		Total score	
Student name			Class		
Frame	#1 Pin	Strike	Spare	Total	
1					
2					
3					
4					
5					
6					
7					
8					
9					
10					

FIGURE 10.13 *Davis Bowling Skills Test sample score sheet*

average score used to reflect performance. Figure 10.13 shows a sample score sheet.

ASSESSING GAME PLAY

Although collecting and summarizing game statistics provide a measure of individual and group game performance, other instruments provide a more complete picture of skill and tactical performance during game play. If the intent of game teaching is to improve game performance, then assessing game performance should include all aspects of game play in the context in which the game is actually played. This is quite different from the typical isolated skills tests we see administered in contrived, controlled, nongamelike settings in school physical education. We have selected the Game Performance Assessment Instrument (GPAI) (Mitchell, Griffin, Oslin, & Berkowitz, 1998) to demonstrate an appropriate alternative to these skills tests.

GPAI was designed to allow teachers to observe and code performance behaviors that demonstrate ability to perform effectively in games. These behaviors span different kinds of games and were determined in consultation with teachers knowledgeable in a variety of games. The components of game performance include the following:

Base   Appropriate return of performer to a home or recovery position between skill attempts

204

Meaningful
Assessment for
Significant
Learning
Outcomes

Adjust	Movement of performer, either offensively or defensively, as required by the flow of the game
Decision making	Making appropriate choices about what to do with the ball (or projectile) during a game
Skill execution	Efficient performance of selected skills
Support	Off-the-ball movement to a position to receive a pass
Cover	Providing defensive support for a player making a play on the ball or moving to the ball (or projectile)
Guard/mark	Defending an opponent who may or may not have the ball (or projectile)

Not all components apply to all games, and some components are more critical to one game than another. GPAI allows assessing all components of game play or selecting those that fit most closely with the game, purposes of instruction, and students working at different levels. This instrument uses a tally system to code appropriate and/or efficient and inappropriate and/or inefficient performances. Coding all four would provide the most complete picture of performance. Figure 10.14 demonstrates how you might code one student in ultimate Frisbee when the focus has been on maintaining possession and scoring.

Scoring criteria
  Decisions made
    Player attempts to pass to an open teammate
    Player attempts to score at the end zone
  Skill execution
    Reception—control of pass and set up of the Frisbee
    Passing—ball reaches target
  Support
    The player appeared to attempt to support the Frisbee carrier by being in/moving to an appropriate position to receive the pass

	Decisions Made		Skill Execution		Support	
Students	A	IA	E	IE	A	IA

Key	A = appropriate	IA = inappropriate
	E = efficient	IE = inefficient

FIGURE 10.14 *Form for coding in ultimate Frisbee*

Once data have been collected, they can be grouped for each component of game performance and overall game involvement. Performance measures can be computed using the totals of the different game components and inserted in the following formulas:

Game involvement = total appropriate decisions + number of inappropriate decisions + number of efficient skill executions + number of inefficient skill executions + number of supporting movements

Decision-making index (DMI) = number of appropriate decisions made ÷ number of inappropriate decisions made

Skill execution index (SEI) = number of efficient skill executions ÷ number of inefficient skill executions

Support index (SI) = number of appropriate supporting movements ÷ number of inappropriate supporting movements

Game performance = [DMI + SEI + SI] ÷ 3

ESTABLISHING SCORING CRITERIA—USING RUBRICS

Scoring criteria are the key to turning assessment tasks into true assessments, rather than just a series of learning experiences or tasks that students perform. A *scoring rubric* defines the criteria by which a performance or product is judged. Essentially, it consists of levels of performance (criteria) and a list of characteristics describing performance at each level. Rubrics can be used to judge performance for many assessment strategies, including portfolios, journals, group projects, and some event tasks. A rubric is, however, more than an assessment tool; it should also enhance instruction and facilitate learning. If an assigned task is accompanied by a scoring rubric, it provides students with a clear and specific goal. Rubrics make levels of learning public and thus promote good performance by showing that quality work is achievable and expected. In addition, because rubrics contain specific criteria for guiding and evaluating performance, they also provide the language and dimensions for useful and informative feedback.

Rubrics should be developed and shared before instruction begins so that both the students and teacher know expectations and so that the students can use the rubric to guide and assess their own work. There are two key steps for designing a scoring rubric:

1. Identify the performance task.

2. Define all criteria at the highest level, and then break those levels down into a four-point rubric. Design level 3 to reflect a performance that would be considered acceptable. Level 4 then would represent a student demonstrating above the accepted level of performance for the task. Each criterion must be teachable and represent a key attribute of the performance being assessed.

206

Meaningful
Assessment for
Significant
Learning
Outcomes

We strongly suggest obtaining copies of sample rubrics that others have used to serve as a guide to development of rubrics or to be adapted for specific needs. Numerous samples have been presented in several physical education journals, including the *Journal of Physical Education, Recreation, and Dance Strategies* and *The Physical Educator,* on the PE Central Web site, and in a variety of education journals. As rubrics are developed, they can be compared to samples of student work to see if the established criteria are appropriate. If not, make revisions and try again. The rubric must capture what is worth assessing and reflect quality work. Box 10.5 shows a sample rubric that was designed for a team-building experience in preparation for a high ropes initiative.

This next example uses different assessment criteria to judge performance. It also applies the use of technology to the assessment of student performance specifically related to the standards of the National Association for Sport and Physical Education (1995). This student project provides one way for tenth grade students to demonstrate their achievement of standard 2: applies movement concepts and principles to the learning and development of motor skills.

Student Project

Students will videotape themselves performing a sport skill, dance, or other physical activity of their choice, analyze the performance, and prepare a written report that includes one or more of the following: (a) listing all skills and strategies used; (b) analysis of personal performance of attributes observed for each skill; (c) a listing of the positive and negative performance attributes for each skill; (d) a listing of the critical elements for successful performance within the context of the activity; (e) suggested practice procedures that might be used to improve performance in the skills and strategies to improve overall performance in the activity; (f) suggest a conditioning program to enhance performance of the skills involved.

Criteria for assessment include:
a. Skills and strategies used in the activity are correctly identified.
b. Positive and negative aspects of personal performance are correctly identified.
c. Identified correctly the critical elements for successful performance within the context of the activity.
d. Describes appropriate practice procedures to improve skill and strategy of the activity.
e. Develops an appropriate conditioning program for the selected activity. (P. 78)

RELIABILITY AND CONSISTENCY

Whether you are using alternative assessment to provide feedback to learners, to inform the instructional process, or to reflect a student's progress, the measure must be reliable and consistent. This basically suggests that you score a student's performance the same way on successive trials or that, if two people are scoring the same performance, each gives the same score. This becomes a bit problematic with alternative assessment due to its reliance on teacher judgment. Alternative assessment must be equitable to all students. Teachers must

---

BOX 10.5 Sample Rubric

Goal: To work as a collaborative team to successfully get all members of the team safely over the electric fence

Scoring rubric:

- Works toward achievement of group goals

  4 Actively helps identify group goals and works hard to meet them

  3 Communicates commitment to the group goals and effectively carries out assigned roles

  2 Communicates a commitment to the group goals but does not carry out assigned roles

  1 Does not work toward group goals or works actively against them

- Demonstrates effective interpersonal skills

  4 Actively promotes effective group interaction and the expression of ideas and opinions in a way that is sensitive to the feelings and knowledge base of others

  3 Participates in group interaction without prompting, expresses ideas and opinions in a way that is sensitive to the feelings and knowledge base of others

  2 Participates in group interaction with prompting or expresses ideas and opinions without considering the feelings and knowledge base of others

  1 Does not participate in group interaction, even with prompting, or expresses ideas and opinions in a way that is insensitive to the feelings and knowledge base of others

- Contributes to group maintenance

  4 Actively helps the group identify changes or modifications necessary in the group process and works toward carrying out those changes

  3 Helps identify changes or modifications necessary in the group process and works toward carrying out those changes

  2 When prompted, helps identify changes or modifications necessary in the group process or is only minimally involved in carrying out those changes

  1 Does not attempt to identify changes or modifications necessary in the group process, even when prompted, or refuses to work toward carrying out those changes

Source: Adapted from Marzano, Pickerington, & McTighe, 1993.

---

be knowledgeable about content, design assessments that fairly and appropriately match the learning goal, select scoring criteria that adequately represent the performance to be judged, and make judgments as consistently as possible. There are no hard and fast rules to govern measuring the reliability of alternative assessment, yet the purpose for which results are used is important. It would be unfair to base a student's grade on assessments that do not measure

208

Meaningful
Assessment for
Significant
Learning
Outcomes

what they are intended to measure or on information obtained in an unfair or unreliable manner.

ASSESSMENTS WITH TECHNOLOGY TOOLS

Students can be assessed on meaningful content using a variety of technology tools, as you have seen throughout this chapter. These tasks might range from one-time event tasks, such as interacting with the technology using heart rate monitors, recording scores in a computer program, or coding their own performance from a videotape, to more extensive projects in which they design and present a multimedia project on selected physical education content. The extent to which these kinds of assessments can be implemented depends upon access to computers and other technology hardware within the school setting as well as teacher comfort with and training in the use of technology applications. Some schools may have computer labs for students to access; others may have one computer per teacher or department; still others may have only a computer for teachers to access through the library. There may be access to a variety of equipment (scanner, video camera, digital camera, Internet access, presentation programs, authoring programs) that can be scheduled on alternating or specific days, weeks, or even for a unit during which students rotate among equipment stations to develop their projects. These types of projects might be left wide open for student decisions or be more structured to meet specific intents of instruction.

For example, in a Sport Education soccer season, students performing the various roles for each team may be responsible for developing a presentation for the class to assist them with their responsibilities. The officials may access the Internet and search for examples of official score sheets, samples of how to keep game statistics, and a set of the official soccer rules. These materials could be pulled into HyperStudio from the Web and used to teach "how to" to the class with hard copies developed and printed from using Word. The publicists might design a newspaper template with Microsoft Publisher so they can publish stories on the soccer season as it progresses. Depending upon student access to computers, they could choose to publish their newspaper using PowerPoint instead. They might also find some helpful tools to design awards using clip art and banners to add festivity to the season. Captains and coaches might work together to design, print, and post daily practice workouts along with a checklist for students to note when they have completed tasks. Trainers may have their teams alternately wear heart rate monitors to assess and record the amount of time they spend within their training HR zone during activity. The possibilities go on and on.

Simons Middle School in Birmingham, Alabama, has integrated technology into its physical education program in numerous ways with assessments that appropriately meet the challenges they set (Chestnutt, 1997). They have developed a course that provides students the opportunity to select and conduct an in-depth technology-based study of a sport or activity of their choice, culminating in a multimedia presentation summarizing their results and learning. Students may select from a variety of resources to assist in their research or presentation: heart rate monitors, video editing, laser disc, digital cameras, interactive programs, and nutritional software. Students work individually and in small groups throughout the 9-week course, spending 3 days per week in activity and 2 in research on their sport. As students delve into their own sport, they create an electronic and written portfolio that includes a series of specific tasks designed to assist them in their analysis, including the following:

- Heart rate analysis of five activities utilizing spreadsheet, word processing, and HR monitors
- Analysis of one skill within their chosen sport/activity utilizing Hyper-Studio, videotaping, and laser discs
- One self-selected task chosen from such tasks as reading biographies, interviewing, videotaping, developing practice plans, and designing a conditioning or nutritional plan
- Five- to 7-minute final presentation to the class of a multimedia summary of research about the chosen sport/activity in video, HyperStudio, or slide format (i.e., PowerPoint, Persuasion)

Teachers' use of technology in teaching and assessing student performance is limited only by availability, access, and their own creativity and comfort with its use. Ask the students for help; you'll be amazed at what they already know and can do.

GRADING

Early in this chapter, we suggested that grading was a requirement of most schools and that physical education teachers tend to grade students based on participation, attitude, attendance, and behavior. If, however, grades are intended to communicate to students how they are doing relative to course expectations and serve as a motivator for future participation, then they must be based on learning outcomes and performance that demonstrates that learning. In other words, grades should not be based on misbehavior, presence in class, or participation. These are managerial issues that can be attended to through a well-designed preventive management system and consistent use of effective discipline strategies (Chapters 4 and 5). This is not to say that participation should not be a part of the grading system. If our intent is for students to become physically active throughout their lives, then participation is critical. When participation is identified as one aspect of the grading system, it must be defined, specified, associated with specific outcomes, and measured in meaningful ways. Kovar and Ermler (1991) provide ideas on how to build participation into the teaching/learning process and thus give it a meaningful outcome for students:

210

Meaningful
Assessment for
Significant
Learning
Outcomes

- Stating clear participation expectations
- Having no uniform requirements for participation (except decent attire that allows the student to participate)
- Allowing students to choose activities within the class
- Soliciting student input on activities included in the curriculum
- Contracting for certain grades
- Introducing new activities frequently
- Practicing old skills in new ways to stimulate interest

If grades are going to be meaningful and useful to students, the criteria behind them must be explicit and shared with learners before instruction begins. This will allow them to understand the expectations and provide them with the opportunity to set their goals toward achieving them.

The grading system must match program outcomes. This suggests that teachers identify the learning outcome categories to be included in the grading system, determine how they will be weighted, and define the criteria that will form the basis for each portion of the grade. We have already indicated the importance of selecting assessment strategies that measure what students are expected to learn and reflect an accurate picture of their progress.

Every grading system will look different. Each is based on a specific set of learning outcomes and expectations. Table 10.1 provides an example of grading systems specific to the Sport Education curriculum model. This is not to say that Sport Education is always graded in this fashion. The teacher and students will have a voice in determining what will best meet their needs and the direction they are moving within this model.

TABLE 10.1 Sport Education Grading System

Learning Outcomes	Weighting	Criteria	Measurement
Competent sportsperson	40%	Sufficient skill performance	GPAI
		Strategy execution	Skill checklists/rating scales
		Knowledgeable games player	Game statistics
Literate sportsperson	25%	Demonstrates responsibility in team roles	Officiating duties
			Role assessments
		Team player	
Enthusiastic sportsperson	25%	Fair player	Journals
		Active participant	Participation log
		Optional activity	
Independent learner	10%	Responsibility for own progress	Goal setting and maintenance log

TABLE 10.2   Adventure Education Learning Outcomes

Standard	Emphasis	Criteria	Assessment
1: Demonstrates competency in many forms and proficiency in a few movement forms	10%	Safely participates in adventure activities Demonstrates adequate skill to be successful in tasks	Safety checklist Skill performance rubric
2: Applies movement concepts and principles to the learning and development of motor skills	10%	Applies skills in adventure environment	Support skill rating scale Application of concepts checklist
3: Exhibits a physically active lifestyle	10%	Actively participates in tasks	Teacher and self-assessment profiles
4: Achieves and maintains a health-enhancing level of physical fitness	10%	Fit enough to successfully complete adventure tasks	Fitness progress on tasks to match needs of activities
5: Demonstrates responsible personal and social behavior in physical activity settings	20%	Demonstrates cooperative, responsible, and caring behavior to peers	Peer assessment Self-assessments Journal Solving team initiatives
6: Demonstrates understanding of and respect for differences among people in physical activity settings	20%	Shows respect for all peers, provides support to each group member, and seeks to involve everyone in tasks	Social behavior rubric Interactive activities checklists
7: Understands that physical activity provides opportunities for enjoyment, challenge, self-expression, and social interaction	20%	Accepts challenges and demonstrates, thinks critically, problem solves, and displays enthusiasm in interactions with peers and the tasks	Problem-solving rubric Activity profile and log

Table 10.2 breaks Adventure Education learning outcomes down using the NASPE physical education standards. Weighting is determined according to the emphasis of the curriculum model, and criteria are identified based on the teacher's interpretation of how those would play out in the program. Assessments are then selected to reach those criteria and outcomes.

If helping students take responsibility for their own learning and their own physical activity experience is a program goal, then allowing them to take part in their own assessment would be important. Using a contract system for grading would be an appropriate strategy. It requires students to set personal goals,

212

Meaningful
Assessment for
Significant
Learning
Outcomes

Goal: Over the course of the semester, I will improve my mile time to under 12 minutes, be able to increase my running distance to 3 miles, and enjoy participating in running activities

I _____ will fulfill the following contract to earn an A in the fitness component (three times per week) of my semester (16 week) grade.

1. Warm up and warm down as part of my activity each day

2. Walk/run the cross-country circuit three times per week during class

3. Increase my running distance each day until I can run the entire 3-mile course

4. Monitor my workouts each day using the heart rate monitor and maintain my heart rate in my training zone (60–80 percent of my maximum) for the running portion of my workout

5. Set short-term goals for every 2 weeks to guide me through my workouts, for example
   End of week 2   Continuous run without stopping or walking
   End of week 4   Reduce 30 seconds from mile run time
   End of week 6   Reduce 15 seconds from mile run time

6. Maintain a log of my time running versus walking, 3-mile running times, weekly 1-mile time, and HR above, below, and within training heart rate zone

7. Maintain a journal of how I am feeling each week, relating how I feel to the improvement (or lack of improvement) I am making each week

FIGURE 10.15   *Sample fitness contract*

determine how to achieve them, and design the criteria to which they will be held accountable for success. Determining the expectations for each step along the way and identifying what reflects a grade at each step are up to the student. How to measure progress toward their goals can either be determined exclusively by the students or in conjunction with the teacher. Contract grading sets the stage for the learner to interact with the teacher in determining appropriate goals and how to measure them. It gives teachers the opportunity to encourage students to analyze their own performances and determine how they might improve.

Figure 10.15 is a fitness contract developed by a 15-year-old high school student who wants to feel better, improve his best mile time of 14 minutes, and increase the distance he can run comfortably to 3 miles three times per week.

Regardless of the grading system you select, accurate records of student performance must be kept. A comprehensive system of maintaining these records can be created either manually or through the use of a computer program. Several grading programs are available for the teacher to maintain student grades using computer software. MicroGrade and Easy Grade Pro are two such programs that allow a variety of ways for the teacher to keep a record of student progress and design ways to improve performance. Other programs that can be used for grading and recording purposes are ClarisWorks or Microsoft Works. In addition, the various grids, rows, and columns can be used to maintain grades using spreadsheet software.

SUMMARY

1. Authentic assessment provides a holistic picture of student performance in a real-life situation while giving the learners feedback on how to improve.

2. Grades are intended to communicate to students how they are doing relative to course expectations, motivate them for future effort, inform parents of how their child is performing, and provide a yardstick for the administration to examine program effectiveness.

3. Assessment allows students to demonstrate their knowledge, skill, understanding, and application of content in a context that allows continued learning and growth.

4. The new assessment perspective attempts to change the how and what of assessment so that it is more fully integrated into the teaching/learning process and documents student learning and achievement.

5. Learning experiences and assessment are the same to the extent that they allow learners the opportunity to practice what you want them to learn and what will be assessed.

6. There is a continuum of assessment measures from standardized and controlled assessment on one end (formal) to less-structured assessments that are integrated into the learning process (informal) on the other end.

7. Two types of assessment refer to that which is intended to provide feedback to impact the ongoing instructional process (formative) and assessment that provides a final judgment on learning (summative).

8. Alternative assessment is an umbrella term for all assessments that differ from the traditional one-shot formal tools traditionally used in the past. Ideally, it involves students in actively solving realistic problems through application of new information, prior knowledge, and relevant skills.

9. Authentic assessment is performed in a realistic setting and mirrors what students do outside of school. Performance assessment requires students to create something using problem solving, critical thinking, application skills, reflection, or other learned skills to demonstrate learning.

214

Meaningful
Assessment for
Significant
Learning
Outcomes

10. An assessment is good to the extent that it matches the intended outcome and learning experiences. A series of assessment design questions allows determining whether the intended outcome is relevant and meaningful and the learning experiences are aligned with it.

11. Teachers become skilled at observing student performance and are often able to convert their observations to checklists and rating scales in an attempt to obtain written data of what occurred.

12. Peers can learn from assessing one another and, when trained, are able to provide useful feedback using rating scales and checklists or by maintaining game statistics.

13. A portfolio is a useful form of self-assessment that puts the responsibility on the students to demonstrate their own learning. It documents a student's effort, progress, and achievement toward a goal(s) and involves student reflection on personal growth and progress.

14. A journal allows students to reflect upon and share their thoughts, feelings, impressions, perceptions, and attitudes about their performance, an event, an assignment, or other learning experiences. A log is simply a record of performance on a specific behavior or criterion.

15. Written tests can be designed so that students must think critically about a problem in order to solve it and may thus strengthen the physical response in the more realistic setting.

16. If assessment is to be truly an educative process, then self-assessment is a critical component in which students must be trained to assess and modify their own performance.

17. Maintaining game statistics or assessing game performance is necessary if a teacher really wants students to be able to play a game, rather than perform skills in isolated situations.

18. A scoring rubric defines the criteria by which a performance or product is judged and can be used for a number of assessment measures: portfolios, journals, activity logs, group projects, event tasks, or individual routines.

19. A series of steps to guide teachers in developing scoring rubrics to meet their assessment needs has been identified.

20. A variety of assessment measures for physical education using computer technology, video and audio tools, and numerous other physical activity technologies can be designed by either students or teachers.

21. To be meaningful, grades must be designed to match the physical education program with the criteria shared with learners prior to the onset of instruction.

CHAPTER 11

Designing Task Progressions To Achieve Learning Outcomes

We cannot teach everything we know to be of value so we must teach students to continue questioning and seeking new knowledge and skill.

—G. WIGGINS (1989)

OVERALL CHAPTER OUTCOME

To design appropriate learning progressions and instructional tasks to achieve learning outcomes using a skills approach and a tactical awareness of games approach

CHAPTER OBJECTIVES

- To describe the role of learning tasks in instructional alignment
- To clarify what makes an activity appropriate
- To enumerate how the "less is more" principle relates to program goals
- To explain what teachers need to know about their content
- To describe what is meant by a learning progression
- To demonstrate how teachers explain progressions to learners
- To differentiate between informing, refining, extending, and applying tasks
- To distinguish between within-task progressions and between-task progressions
- To clarify the refining-extending cycle and when you know it is appropriate
- To explain the primary focus of the tactical approach to teaching games
- To describe planning considerations for using the tactical approach

Outcomes are the significant learnings that are the intent of instruction. Outcomes are the first step in instructional alignment (Chapter 8). Assessment is the second and perhaps most important step (Chapter 10) because it provides continuous learning opportunities and feedback while informing both the teacher and student when learning has occurred and what remains to be mastered. In Chapter 10, you learned that teaching toward an assessment is desirable if that assessment matches the intended outcomes and those outcomes are valid, meaningful, and relevant. The learning tasks that students experience are what facilitate learning and move students toward those outcomes. This third step, designing a progression of learning tasks, is the focus of this chapter. We discuss planning aspects of the instructional process and the design of learning tasks to serve as the necessary link between outcomes and assessment. In Chapter 14, we examine the delivery of those tasks to learners.

CHOOSING CONTENT
TO MATCH THE CURRICULUM MODEL

Once the main-theme curriculum models have been selected and meaningful learning outcomes specified, you must choose the activities that will form program content; design learning experiences for learners to practice application of relevant skills, strategies, and knowledge; and design aligned assessment measures to determine if the outcomes have been achieved. The selection of activities, however, is the point at which program planning often breaks down. Activities are sometimes chosen because they are "neat" or because it is "that time of year," rather than for the degree the activities lead to expected outcomes. Keep the following points in mind before beginning to plan for and select program activities:

1. *An activity is appropriate because it contributes to program outcomes.* "Appropriate" in this case is a relevant term. If your main theme is Sport Education, then team handball and tennis are appropriate activities. If you have an Adventure Education theme, then rappelling and climbing are appropriate activities. Golf would be an appropriate activity for Sport Education, but not for a fitness curriculum. Orienteering might be appropriate for an Adventure Education program and can also be done in a cross-country Sport Education season. Any number of activities could be linked across the curriculum in an Integrated Physical Education model, just as a skill theme would be appropriately taught within a Developmental Physical Education model.

2. *Successful programs accomplish goals.* If you are to err in planning, it is wise to err in the direction of trying to achieve too little rather than too much. This was emphasized in the "less is more" principle in Chapter 8. Limited goals—a fewer number of activities—are easier to achieve than a large set of goals and many activities. Doing activity units well takes time. There is reason to question whether an exposure program accomplishes anything of lasting value. If you want your program to be successful, choose a limited number of outcomes, and develop a limited number of activities to achieve them. This assumes, of course, that the outcomes you are trying to accomplish are *learning* oriented, relevant, and meaningful, rather than merely keeping students busy.

3. *Know what you are doing.* The activities you choose become the content of your program. Teachers should *know* their content well because without that knowledge they cannot develop the appropriate progressions for learning content thoroughly. "Knowing" refers to both the content and how to apply it to specific learners. Choosing activities with which you have limited experience results in inadequately developed content. How much space does the activity take? How can it be modified? How are the skills and strategy best refined? How should equipment be modified? To answer these questions typically requires that you know the activity well. This suggests that, if you include an

activity you don't know well, you take the time to research the content and thus enable yourself to design appropriate sequences and learning experiences.

If you choose activities that do indeed contribute directly to the goals implied in your curriculum model, if you know your activities well enough to develop content appropriately for the learners you serve, and if you provide sufficient time for those learners to make meaningful gains in performing the activities, then you will have taken huge strides toward establishing a successful program of physical education.

DEVELOPING PROGRESSIONS OF INSTRUCTIONAL TASKS

Keep in mind what you learned in Chapter 1, that effective teachers take time to find out what their students understand about what they are going to learn. In other words, what meanings do they attach to a particular content, and what are the implications for you in your planning? Once you know where you are headed and what you want learners to achieve, you must determine how to meet your goals. To understand how to get there, you should first know your starting point; that is, what will be the students' levels of skill, understanding, and experience when they enter the program? As a trained professional educator, you will know part of this in a general way from your study of motor development, elementary school physical education, and secondary school physical education. This general knowledge will allow you to develop content by planning task progressions that lead to important outcomes. *Progressions* are learning tasks that move students from less complex and sophisticated tasks to more difficult and complicated tasks by adding complexity and difficulty. The eventual result is the kinds of meaningful performances that represent the intended outcomes of the program. The application of these progressions, however, will always be *specific* to the students taught in any particular setting, the experiences students bring with them, and the time available. Experienced teachers know that you can teach two fifth grade classes in consecutive time blocks and require very different progressions to adequately meet the developmental differences in each. Nonetheless, designing progressions becomes an important technical skill in developing content. Developing progressions is where knowledge of content and knowledge of teaching come together—what Shulman (1987) has called *pedagogical content knowledge,* that unique blend of content and pedagogy that is the special expertise of the teacher.

Teachers communicate progressions to students through a series of instructional tasks within a lesson or unit and, from year to year, across units in the same activity or category of activities. Rink's (1985, 1993b, 1998) model for developing progressive instructional tasks is widely used in physical education. Initial tasks *inform* the student of a new skill or strategy. Subsequent tasks

218

Designing Task
Progressions
To Achieve
Learning
Outcomes

refine the quality of the performance, *extend* the performance by altering it slightly, and *apply* the skill or strategy (Rink, 1985).

1. *Informing tasks.* These are the initial tasks to begin a lesson and a sequence of learning tasks. From this initial task, the teacher develops the lesson and the subsequent content to be mastered.

2. *Performance refinement quality.* Perhaps the most neglected, yet most important, kind of progression is the sequence of learning tasks through which students improve the technical quality of a skill or strategy performance—what Rink (1985) calls *refinement tasks.* Each skill or strategy task that the teacher introduces will need to be refined. In refining tasks, the conditions of practice do not change. Only the focus of student attention changes as different technical elements or strategy are emphasized. Teaching third grade students to juggle using the cascade technique provides an example. Tossing or "popping" a scarf can be introduced with a demonstration and explanation of four or five critical performance elements that define the skill (*informing task*). Students can then practice this skill daily as they progress through the juggling unit. However, the skill must be refined if the student is to move on to juggling with three or more implements. Students may tend to break the wrist when they pop the ball, as they should do in other kinds of throws, but not in the juggling pop. The pop must be quick, sudden, and short, with no follow-through. Students may try to mimic a juggler who has a smooth, flowing rhythm, yet when learning, they must have sharp and definite movements, sometimes known as marcato or marked rhythm. It is through a series of refining tasks that students become more aware of the technical components of a good pop so that this critical aspect of juggling improves. Success in skill and strategy requires quality performance, and that should be the teacher's goal. Refining tasks can't always be anticipated. Teachers must use information about the performance of their students to develop progressive refining tasks.

3. *Within-task progressions.* Both skills and strategies need to be simplified to begin with and then gradually made more complex. Think of building content in one of the track and field events, for example, the shot put. The basic task—putting the shot—will not change, which means that, right from the outset, a legal put rather than a throw is taught. However, few would begin to teach the shot put by having students start from the back of the circle and then teach the glide or spin in their mature forms. Instead, a series of *within-task progressions* is taught. Rink (1985) refers to this as *intratask development.* You might begin with an implement that is lighter than a standard shot and with students in the final putting position, focusing on hip and shoulder rotation to provide force to the put. Regardless of where you begin, you would have to refine the skill demanded in *that* task before you extend the skill with a slightly more complex task, which would again require

refinement before moving to still another more complex task. Rink (1985) refers to within-task progressions as *extending tasks,* those that change the complexity of performance. At the end of this chapter, we identify a series of methods to modify task complexity, which is essentially a means of extending the movement task. The *refining-extending cycle* repeated over and over again forms the central core of content development in physical education. Box 11.1 provides an example of appropriate and inappropriate progressions for the overhead set. Knowing what to refine and how much to extend—for the specific learners you are working with—is perhaps the most important ingredient of expert planning. Box 11.2 provides examples of refining and extending tasks for a one-hand shot in basketball.

4. *Between-task progressions.* When planning a program that begins with either novice learners or young learners, consider progressions between related tasks. For example, moving from a scissors jump to the Fosbury style in developing high jump content, from a horizontal traverse to a vertical climb in developing climbing content, or from a three-versus-three strategy in soccer to a full-sided game with more players in a larger space all represent different tasks rather than variations of one major task. The progressions among them become important building blocks in developing content for a program. Between-task extensions need to be thought through carefully. Teachers sometimes assume that tasks are progressions when they are not. To be a progression, one task would have to be related to another in terms of common critical performance elements (see "Content Analysis" in Chapter 12). For example, we would argue that the underhand serve in volleyball is not a progression for the overhand serve, even though the underhand serve might be used for young or novice volleyball players. The technical demands of the two skills are too different for them to be a skill progression. But the scissors style of high jump contains virtually all the beginning technical elements that students will need when they eventually learn the Fosbury style, so those two form a legitimate progression.

5. *Application tasks.* Providing students with the chance to apply their skills and use strategies in more authentic ways is the intent of application tasks. Application tasks therefore allow students opportunities to participate in the movement through an applied experience or to assess their skill/strategy performance. A small-sided game puts students in a setting where they must select and perform skills and game strategies. One partner might be asked to assess the performance of the other partner during a gymnastics competition or to double-check the reading on a heart rate monitor, thus assessing one aspect of his or her own mastery of content. Students might be asked to monitor the number of legal forehand strokes they can perform during a pickleball partner rally. Each of these is an applied task students can perform once they gain adequate skill and confidence. Application tasks need not wait until the

BOX 11.1 Appropriate and Inappropriate Progressions for the Overhead Set

In each lesson, the teacher has explained and demonstrated the overhead set and begun practice with having students set the ball back to a partner from a short toss. The students have practiced the forearm pass before the set in a previous lesson.

Teacher A—Inappropriate Progression

Task 1: Toss the ball to your partner with a high toss from about 10 feet. Your partner sets the ball back to you and you catch it.

Task 2: Now let's use the overhead set in a game. You must use two hands to set the ball to another person to forearm pass before you can send the ball back over the net.

How this progression looks when graphed:

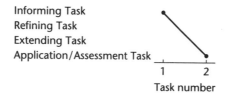

Teacher B—Appropriate Progression

Task 1: Toss the ball to your partner with a high toss from about 10 feet. Your partner sets the ball back to you and you catch it.

Task 2: This time, as you practice, try to get yourself in the "get set" position before you hit the ball. Get there and get ready.

Task 3: If your trajectory isn't high on the ball after you set it, what does that mean for where you are hitting it? How can you get a high trajectory? O.K., this time get under it more.

Task 4: When you and your partner can both set the ball five times in a row with a high and accurate trajectory, take two or three steps back and make your toss higher and try it.

Task 5: Now let's try the set from a forearm pass. Toss the ball to your partner. Your partner will forearm pass the ball to you; you will set it back and your partner will catch it. The sequence becomes toss-forearm pass-overhead set and catch (toss-pass-set-and catch).

Tasks 6 and 7: When you can do this five times in a row, move farther away from each other, and see if you can still make it work.

Task 8: In groups of three, one person serves the ball, one does a forearm pass, and one sets the ball. Start with an easy serve, and make the serve more difficult as you are ready.

How this progression looks when graphed:

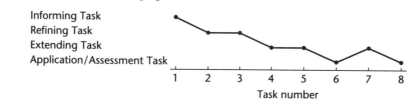

Source: Adapted from Rink, 1998.

BOX 11.2   Examples of Refining Tasks and Extending Tasks

Situation: Basketball, one-hand shooting, novice or young learners. Initial informing task: Square to basket, ball in possession, stationary position, close to basket.

- Refining tasks
  Spread shooting hand behind ball.
  Support with off hand (not pushing or letting go too early).
  Turn elbow toward basket (not toward side).
  Keep ball at head level (not brought down).
  Bend knee to generate force (rather than just with arms).
  Press toes to generate force (keep ball high).
  Emphasize wrist snap with ball "rolling" off fingertips.
  Coordinate knee bend and toe press.
  Extend wrist and flex elbow as knees are bent.
  Keep eye on rim.

- Extending tasks
  Pivot away, pivot back to square up position, and shoot.
  Receive pass from teammate, square up, and shoot.
  Shoot from different angles, but always squared up.
  Gradually extend distance from basket.
  With back to basket, pivot, square up, and shoot.
  Move to spot, receive pass, square up, and shoot.
  Dribble to spot, square up, and shoot.
  Shoot from spot, move to next spot, receive pass, square up, and shoot.

Keeping a class shot chart on which students keep track of their shooting practice each day can produce the accountability needed to keep students on task.

---

final task in a progression; they can be incorporated along the way as a means of providing feedback and allowing students to experience skills and strategies in applied ways.

DEVELOPING TASKS FOR TACTICAL AWARENESS IN GAMES TEACHING

Although Rink's model (1985, 1993b, 1998) may be effectively applied to the teaching of games and game tactics, other approaches have also been used with success. Two are the Teaching for Understanding, a six-stage model developed by Bunker and Thorpe (1982), and the Tactical Games Approach, a three-stage model developed by Griffin, Mitchell, and Oslin (1997). The major focus of Rink's model is designing progressions of skill performance. It begins with an informing task and then utilizes refining, extending, and applying tasks to build skill progressions during content development. The primary

222

Designing Task
Progressions
To Achieve
Learning
Outcomes

focus of the tactical approach is on the strategic aspects of performance, rather than on skill components of the game. Motor skill performance is a critical aspect of playing a game, yet knowing what to do and when to do it are equally important. For instance, as students begin to develop their ability to maintain possession of the ball in soccer, they must understand the concept of providing support to their teammates and passing to an open player. As golfers begin to make decisions about hitting the ball the proper distance, they must understand the conditions surrounding the shot: distance from the hole, lie of the ball, and any obstacles between the ball and the hole. The decisions players make prior to the shot (club selection and swing length) are just as important as execution of the shot itself if the ball is to successfully reach the target. These each require tactical knowledge and motor skill to execute. Often, we see physical education classes in which students are taught and practice motor skills yet lack the knowledge of when to use them in a game situation.

Planning for this approach requires identifying tactical problems for different games and getting students to where they know they need the skill to solve the problem. Two critical questions that will help identify these tactical problems have been suggested by Griffin et al. (1997):

1. What problems does the game present for scoring, preventing scoring, and restarting play?

2. What off-the-ball movements and on-the-ball skills are necessary to solve these problems?

This approach emphasizes components of game performance beyond execution of motor skills: decision making, providing support, marking or guarding, covering teammates, adjusting position as the game evolves, and using a base position to ensure court/field coverage (Griffin et al., 1997). The model has three stages that produce a learning cycle (game-practice-game) for game performance: (a) game form (representative and exaggerated), (b) tactical awareness (what to do), and (c) skill execution (how to do it).

1. *Game form.* This approach begins with a modified version of the game and is exaggerated to present tactical problems to students. Let's use net games as an example and the tactical problem of creating space. In tennis, students may be set up to play a one-point, half-court singles game on a short-narrow court with the goal of becoming aware of space on either side of the net. Conditions require students to alternate serves and use only ground strokes during the game. In this case, the game resembles the full-court game of tennis, yet the narrower court requires students to play to the back and front of the court to create space and a complete advantage (Griffin et al., 1997).

2. *Tactical awareness.* As previously suggested, the game is modified or exaggerated in such a way that students must determine what to do to succeed in this situation. These conditions must be carefully thought through and developed if they are to encourage students to think in a tactical way. Part of your role as a teacher is to pose to the students questions that will prompt them to problem solve and think both criti-

cally and tactically. Planning for questions that will guide students to solve tactical problems takes knowledge of the game and planning. Ask questions about the goal of the game: *What* must they do to achieve that goal (necessary skills)? *Why* are specific skills/movements necessary? *How* can they perform the skills they have identified (Griffin et al., 1997)? The following question-answer example demonstrates the process.

Q. What was the goal of the game as we designed it for this practice?

A. To become aware of where there is space on both sides of the net

Q. What did you have to do to win a point?

A. Hit to an open space

Q. What spaces are there on your opponent's side of the net to which to hit the tennis ball?

A. Front and back, side to side

Q. How do you return the ball if it does not come to your forehand side?

A. Backhand

This line of questioning should lead students to understand the importance of the backhand ground stroke and set the stage for skill instruction and practice on this stroke (Griffin et al., 1997).

3. *Skill execution.* Through game play, teacher questioning, and problem solving, students come to recognize the need for specific skills, and these then become the focus of the lesson. During the skill execution phase of the lesson, the specific skills can be taught, teaching cues can be emphasized, and skill practice can be designed. We again use the tennis example, but focus now on backhand ground strokes. Students might be set up with a tosser and a hitter. The tosser tosses or hits the ball to the hitter, who uses a ground stroke to return it. The ball is stopped and each partner repeats the skill five times. The student, teacher, or partners can use the cues previously emphasized to prompt performance.

4. *Game.* To end skill practice, reintroduce students to a game in which they have the same goal as in the original game. The intent is for them to solve the tactical problem using the skills they have just practiced. In our tennis example, students are put back into a half-court singles game on a long and narrow court with the goal of becoming aware of space on either side of the net. They now know how to return a ball that has been hit to a space on their court that is away from their forehand.

HOW ALIGNMENT FITS INTO PLANNING TEACHING PROGRESSIONS

Progressions should be thought of as instructional tasks that lead to learning outcomes. Earlier we argued for the development of learning outcomes that

224

Designing Task
Progressions
To Achieve
Learning
Outcomes

are meaningful and relevant to students outside the instructional setting (that is, playing games well, negotiating wilderness settings, participating in fitness activities, and the like). As tactical problems are posed to students or refining and extending tasks are designed to help their progress toward these meaningful outcomes, instruction must be aligned so that students have the best chance for success.

Instructional alignment exists when there is a match between the intended outcomes, instructional processes, and assessment. In other words, instructional alignment requires a match between goals, practice, and testing. Substantial evidence suggests that well-aligned instruction produces achievement results that are two to three times stronger than results of nonaligned instruction (Cohen, 1987). The concept of instructional alignment requires teachers to think seriously about the nature of the goals they have for their students and how they can arrange task progressions that meet those goals. Using assessment procedures that are closely aligned with the goals helps ensure a better match. "Teach what you assess and assess what you teach" is an old adage in education. It is often violated in physical education.

To effectively refine student performance of skill and to carefully align conditions of outcomes, instruction, and assessment, you must know a great deal about the activity for which you are planning. As Cohen (1987) suggests, this need to know quite well the subject you teach brings us full circle to the issue that began Part Three.

> Teaching what we assess, or assessing what we teach seems embarrassingly obvious. The fundamental issue is: *What's worth teaching?* This is the same question as: *What's worth assessing?* We can either know what we are doing, or not know what we're doing, but in either case, we'll be doing something to other people's children. Do we not have an ethical obligation to know what we're up to? (p. 19)

If instruction is well aligned with goals and assessment procedures, it will allow students many opportunities to practice relevant skills and strategies and solve tactical problems in *situations similar to those in which they will be used*. Rink (1985) refers to these kinds of tasks as "applying tasks." A particular instructional task can refine a skill or strategy and still be an applying task; that is, the stimulus conditions of practice can be such that they are aligned with outcomes, even though the major purpose of the practice might be to refine or extend the performance of a skill or strategy. Thus, both refining and extending tasks can be defined so that they serve as applying tasks, too. When they do, instructional alignment is more likely.

MODIFYING TASK COMPLEXITY

Whether you are planning progressions for use with the skill or the tactical approach, designing tasks so they progress from simple to more complex allows students to initially achieve success and become progressively more challenged with increasingly difficult tasks. The teacher needs to identify fac-

---

BOX 11.3   A Modified Game of Tennis

Basic problem of game	To strike the ball with a racquet so it crosses over the net on the fly and lands in bounds in such a way that the opponent cannot return it
Modifications	
Space	Court divided in half (long and narrow)
Equipment	Use shorter racquet for ease in handling Use lighter ball to slow pace Use "old" tennis balls Raise the net to slow pace
Rules	Eliminate serve; bounce-hit from midcourt
Scoring	Four-point game Alternate serves every point

---

tors that impact task complexity, be able to apply them in appropriate learning experiences, and then be able to plan for a progression of experiences that move from simple to complex. We discuss five factors to consider to reduce or increase complexity: space, equipment, number of participants, rules, and conditions/tactics/problems. Box 11.3 describes one way to modify a tennis game.

Space

Moving the volleyball service line up, practicing high jump "backovers" from a raised takeoff platform rather than the floor, shortening or lengthening a playing field, or designing a flat orienteering course with few obstacles all reduce the complexity of an activity. These examples demonstrate how performance complexity can be manipulated by modifying the space or playing area of an activity. One issue relates to the performance level of students. A full-sized playing area is inappropriate for most beginners. Modify it to achieve the skill and strategy objectives of instruction. A smaller surface makes a game less strenuous for the novice or less-fit student. If the instructional goal is for students in a three-versus-three soccer game to provide support to the ball carrier, a shortened field will allow them to achieve this without undue fatigue; in fact, they will be able to practice longer. Changing the dimensions of a playing area can increase the complexity as well. Lengthening a court forces front and back movement and placement opportunities. Added width forces lateral movement and skill in one aspect of a game. In a game of badminton, players can be challenged by shuttle placement tasks that are the only conditions whereby they can score. Modifying space requires that players learn to get into position for a successful response.

226

Designing Task
Progressions
To Achieve
Learning
Outcomes

Equipment

Using racquetball rackets for tennis, softballs instead of a shot for putting, larger targets when working on shooting skills, and smaller and lighter balls for basketball; designing an incline climbing wall; and lowering the volleyball net for spiking reduce task complexity. Changing the size or weight of an implement allows progressively more complex tasks to be developed. Novice volleyball players may begin with a balloon and progress to skill practice and game play with a beach ball. The volleyball net can be lowered, then raised as students become more skilled. These modifications slow down the game, give students time to move to get under the ball, and allow them to get into position to be ready to perform the skill. As they become more skilled, they might move to a large, soft trainer volleyball and eventually use regulation volleyballs. As skills and game tactics develop, task complexity does also.

Number of Participants

One sure way to increase complexity is to add participants. A soccer player may be successfully dribbling and shooting on goal until defenders are added to the game and the tactical demands increase. It is suddenly more difficult to achieve consistent shots when faced with opposition and adapting to others, as opposed to playing on an open field unchecked. Likewise, having to plan for and get eight team members over an adventure obstacle adds more challenges than if the team had only five members. Practicing a skill alone is generally easier. Complexity may be added progressively by increasing the number of participants and thus the difficulty. Skill practice or application of a strategy in a three-versus-three field hockey setting allows more opportunities and fewer players with whom to contend than a six-versus-six or full game.

Some skills are difficult or impossible to practice alone. In these instances, the complexity can be altered to achieve the goal. Returning a toss from across the net with a forearm pass is easier than returning a serve. A well-taught toss that is placed accurately and at a constant speed is more easily controllable for the receiver than either an underhand or overhand serve.

Small-sided games allow more student involvement and opportunities. They also set the stage for students to determine what to do and how to do it. Game formations and spatial arrangements can be modified to allow the design of games with a specific focus or adapted for ability levels of students. A set of small-sided games could have a different focus in each game, from basic skills and tactical problems for the novice players to more complex skills and tactics as skill and experience increase.

Rules

Rules are conditions placed on a game to set boundaries for performance. Primary rules define the main problems to be solved and thus the nature of the game. In field hockey, the main problem to be solved is how to pass and receive the ball with the stick while attempting to put the ball in the opponent's goal. Primary rules should remain intact. Secondary rules, however, can be altered to reduce inhibiting factors and to exaggerate features, strategies, and skills to be learned. These are the rules that can be modified without changing the main problems to be solved in the game. Secondary rules can be modified to change the complexity of the game and opportunities to practice. Offside in soccer and the 3-second rule in basketball are examples of secondary rules. Adjusting how points are scored is a means of modifying rules that has implications for motivation and skill practice, yet does not change the game itself. For example, in tennis, deuce games and four-point or no-ad games can be used. Restarts can be modified so as to speed up play and allow a focus on other skills and strategies.

Conditions/Tactics/Problems

All games have tactical problems that must be solved and associated skills that need to be mastered. The tactical complexity of a game must match the developmental level of your learners. Adding tactical complexity to a game as students' awareness, understanding, and skills increase can do this. Levels of tactical complexity can be identified so that lessons can be designed using appropriately complex tasks for the learners At the novice level, learners may be required only to understand the importance of maintaining possession of the ball, attacking the goal, and restarting the game and to possess the on-the-ball skills (e.g., passing, receiving, shooting) necessary to solve these problems. As students become more skilled, they can be introduced to the idea of providing support and defending space/goal and the aligned on-the ball skills (goal keeping) and off-the-ball movements (marking/guarding) necessary to solve these problems. As the tactical level increases, so do the skills and movements that students must learn and practice.

CLOSED AND OPEN SKILLS

Most sport performance, as well as fitness and adventure activities, require efficient execution of both skills and strategies. If the execution of skill and strategy is important content in your sense of appropriate physical education programming, the distinction between *closed skills* and *open skills* should affect how you develop that content.

- Closed skills are performed in a fixed environment in which the conditions are unchanged during the performance. These skills tend to be self-paced, repetitive, and routinized. The shot put is a good example. The size of the ring, the weight of the shot, the dimensions of the sector into which the shot is put, and the rules for putting are all fixed.

- Open skills are performed in an ever-changing environment with conditions that are variable. These skills tend to be externally paced. Responding effectively to the changing environment becomes the most

228

Designing Task
Progressions
To Achieve
Learning
Outcomes

Closed	Closed with Varying Environment		Open
Shot put	Golf		Soccer dribble
Volleyball serve	Free weights		Scuba diving
Universal lifting			Lacrosse pass
	Juggling	Tennis forehand	
	Bowling	Vertical climb	

FIGURE 11.1 *The closed-open skills continuum*

important factor when performing an open skill. A basketball guard dribbling down court to initiate an offense is a good example. The guard contends with differing defensive configurations, each of which might cue a different set of offensive options. Defensive pressure changes, as do the conditions of the game itself—time remaining, score, and the like.

- Some skills have stable conditions, yet the performer is often required to perform the skill in different environments. Perhaps the best example of this type of skill is golf, where the basic stroke is the same, yet the player must adjust to different lies on the course, club selection (woods, irons), surfaces (fairway, green, bunker), and distance to the hole.

The closed-open distinction is best understood as a continuum, with the skills performed under most constant conditions at one end and skills performed under most variable conditions at the other. Skills are placed on the continuum according to the conditions under which they are performed, as shown in Figure 11.1.

Developing content of closed and open skills differs markedly. The more closed the skill, the more emphasis will be on refining technique that is performed invariably. These skills require consistency in practice so they become routinized and predictable. The more open the skill, the less time will be spent on technique, and the more time will be spent extending tasks that cover the variety of situations in which the skills will be used. The goal is to develop performance that is appropriately responsive to the varying demands of an ever-changing setting. One of the major errors—an error in instructional alignment—physical educators make when developing content for open skills is treating them as if they were closed skills, with the conditions of practice constant instead of variable.

SUMMARY

1. Well-designed learning tasks link outcomes and assessment.

2. An activity is appropriate when it contributes to program outcomes.

3. To be successful, a program should focus on a limited number of learning-oriented, relevant, and meaningful outcomes and include a limited number of activities to achieve those outcomes.

4. Teachers need to know their content and how to apply it to specific learners.

5. Progressions are learning tasks that move students from less complex and sophisticated tasks to more difficult and complicated tasks by adding complexity and difficulty and eventually to the kinds of meaningful performances that represent the intended outcomes of the program.

6. Teachers communicate progressions to students through a series of instructional tasks within a lesson or unit and, from year to year, across units in the same activity or category of activities.

7. Informing tasks are the initial tasks to begin a lesson and a sequence of learning tasks. Refining tasks refine the technical quality of performance. Extending tasks change the complexity of the task. Applying tasks allow students to apply their skills in more realistic ways.

8. Within-task progressions consist of tasks that move skill and tactical performance from simple to complex. Between-task progressions refer to the progressions that are necessary between related tasks.

9. Repeating the refining-extending cycle over and over is one means to develop content.

10. The primary focus of the tactical approach is on the strategic aspects of performance.

11. Planning for the tactical approach requires identifying tactical problems for different games and getting students to where they know they need the skill to solve the problem.

12. There are two critical questions to assist with identifying tactical problems: (a) What problems does the game present for scoring, preventing scoring, and restarting play? (b) What off-the-ball movements and on-the-ball skills are necessary to solve these problems?

13. The three stages of the tactical learning cycle (game-practice-game) are game form (representative and exaggerated), tactical awareness (what to do), and skill execution (how to do it).

14. Factors to consider when modifying task complexity include modifying space, equipment, number of participants, rules, and conditions, tactics, and problems.

15. Closed skills are performed in a fixed environment in which the conditions are unchanged during the performance. Open skills are performed in an ever-changing environment with variable conditions.

16. The more closed the skill, the more emphasis needs to be placed on consistency in practice and on refining the technique until it becomes routinized, whereas the more open the skill, the less time needs to be spent on technique as opposed to practicing it in variable situations through more complex tasks.

CHAPTER 12

Developing Effective Units of Instruction

Most students (perhaps over 90 percent) can master what we have to teach them, and it is the task of instruction to find the means which will enable our students to master the subject under consideration. Our basic task is to determine what we mean by mastery of the subject and to search for the methods and materials which will enable the largest proportion of our students to attain such mastery.

—BENJAMIN BLOOM (1980)

OVERALL CHAPTER OUTCOME

To design a unit plan and accompanying lesson plans to guide delivery of a unit of instruction

CHAPTER OBJECTIVES

- To discuss reasons teachers plan
- To distinguish between plan-dependent and plan-independent teachers
- To describe strategies for determining entry and exit levels
- To explain the purpose of a content analysis
- To conduct appropriate procedural and hierarchical analyses
- To develop appropriate game frameworks
- To differentiate between the task analysis question for procedural and hierarchical analysis and a tactical analysis
- To describe practical factors related to unit planning
- To outline a well-constructed generic unit plan
- To specify planning considerations for each of the physical education curriculum models
- To describe a well-constructed daily lesson plan

The focus of this chapter, which is planning units of instruction, was chosen for three reasons. First, most teachers consider unit planning to be their most important planning task (Clark & Yinger, 1979). Many teachers work on a daily basis from their unit plan, rather than having individual daily lesson plans. Second, teachers who prefer to plan at the daily lesson level typically do so by planning all the daily lessons for a *unit*. Thus, the unit again appears to be the most functional way to think about planning. Third, focusing on unit plans requires that you think about progressions that build across daily lessons and move toward the achievement of unit objectives. Even though a unit is taught to students through the daily lesson, it is the series of daily lessons (the unit) that should make sense as a whole.

WHY TEACHERS PLAN

There are four main reasons teachers devote time and attention to planning for instruction (Clark & Yinger, 1979; Stroot & Morton, 1989).

1. To assure that a progression is followed both within and between lessons

2. To help the teacher stay on task and use time as planned

3. To reduce teacher anxiety and help him or her maintain confidence while teaching

4. To fulfill a building or district policy

Not all teachers plan for all these four reasons, nor do all these reasons influence teachers in the same way. Some principals require that teachers leave lesson plans for the next day on their desk when they leave school in the afternoon. This is done because teachers, owing to illness or some unforeseen emergency, may need substitutes the next day.

In their study of effective elementary physical educators, Stroot and Morton (1989) found what many have noted from observing teachers work: Some teachers are very dependent on plans; others seem to be nearly independent of plans. They referred to these two extremes as *plan-dependent* and *plan-independent teachers*. For example, one teacher in their study said, "I would feel incredibly uncomfortable if I did not have them (plans), and I carry them around on my clipboard everywhere I go" (Stroot & Morton, 1989, p. 219). Another teacher taped the daily plan on a wall of the gymnasium where it could be referred to easily if needed, even though observation indicated that the teacher seldom referred to it. Still other teachers go through an entire day's teaching without referring to plans, needing only to glance at them in the morning to remind themselves about what they intend to do in their classes that day. The difference between plan-dependent and plan-independent teachers seems to be one of personal comfort, reduction of anxiety about lessons, and maintaining confidence as the teaching is actually done. Remember, in this study, these were all *effective* teachers, so there is no suggestion here that plan-dependent teachers are more or less effective than plan-independent teachers. It seems a matter of personal style, although less-experienced teachers tend typically to be more plan-dependent. The plan-independent teachers do their work from mental recall of their previous planning and experience with the activity being taught.

The same study found, as have most others, that somewhere back in time all the effective teachers had worked hard to plan good units of instruction. The work they did when they initially planned units of instruction is similar to what will be presented in this chapter. Thus, no matter whether the teachers were, at the moment of the study, plan-dependent or plan-independent, they had all gone through extensive planning when initially developing units—and they frequently upgraded and modified those initial plans based on their experiences teaching them. If the teachers perceived themselves to be in an activity unit in which their own background was "weak," they tended to become more plan-dependent than in those units where their own skills and experiences were stronger.

The great problem of planning physical education units, especially when students are grouped only by grade level, is that some students will have all the limitations described previously, but others will have the physical capacity, skills, and experience for higher-level instruction. Most teachers tend to plan their units at or just below what they consider to be the average for their classes and then attempt to adjust the instructional task system so that it accommodates students who vary markedly in their readiness for those tasks. Many of the instructional strategies described in Chapters 7, 13, and 14 are relevant to meeting the needs of diverse learners within the same class.

Recalling from Chapter 11 that effective programs accomplish real goals, it makes sense to plan units so that ample time is provided for limited goal accomplishment. Many students will need a large number of successful repetitions to develop skills to the point where they can be used in applied settings. Strategic concepts will have to be practiced to the point where students can execute them reliably in modified game settings. Repetitions of skill and strategy practice take class time, often more than planners are willing to allocate. The result, far too often, is classes that rush through skill and strategy practice so quickly that the skills can't be performed well in applied settings and the strategies are nowhere to be seen once game play begins. Of particular interest at this point is the research in physical education (Marks, 1988; Son, 1989) that reveals that teachers seldom use refining tasks during their skill instruction. Again, recalling from Chapter 11, it is through repeated cycles of refining and extending tasks that skill develops and the execution of strategy becomes reliable. This refining-extending cycle takes time, especially if all students are to get enough repetitions to be able to perform the skills and strategies in applied settings.

The choice of instructional outcomes is important because they form the basis of unit planning. Therefore, those outcomes should be defined with entry-level status of learners clearly in mind and with realistic appraisal of what can be accomplished in the time available.

CONTENT ANALYSIS

In Chapter 8, we talked about designing curriculums backward from authentic outcomes that are ultimately assessed through a final performance. This is true at the unit level as well. In other words, whether you are using a Physical Activity, Fitness, and Wellness Education; Adventure Education; or Sport Education curriculum, your first task is to assess your instructional goal to determine where you are going and what you want learners to achieve. Frequently, we see teachers who are not sure where they are going and so teach the wrong thing or misalign what they teach and what they assess as having been taught (Cohen, 1987).

Content analysis is a technique to determine all aspects of your instructional goal (outcome) necessary for its achievement: physical, tactical, social, and cognitive. Each of these components will also be broken down to allow the development of instructional sequences and the design of learning experiences. Box 12.1 provides an example using a track and field season in Sport Education.

BOX 12.1   Content Analysis in Sport Education

Goal: Using the flop technique, students will be able to achieve a height commensurate with their height and weight during a class track meet

Assessment: A class track meet where students compete in field events by ability flights

At this point, I need to ask myself the task analysis (TA) question: "What does the learner have to do to perform this task?" The answer will come from my *content analysis*.

Physical	*Tactical*	*Social*	*Cognitive*
Technical skill performance	Where to move	Team player	Rules
	When to pass	Officiating	Etiquette
		Fair play	Ritual

This begins to identify the aspects of the units that need to be planned. Each can now be broken down further with task specificity determined by asking the TA question for each component.

Goal: Long jump with proper approach, takeoff, and landing

Running Approach ⟶ Last Stride and Foot Plant ⟶ Take Off from Board ⟶ Flight ⟶ Landing

FIGURE 12.1   *Long jump procedural analysis*

Two kinds of content analysis are used in planning: the *procedural analysis* and the *hierarchical analysis*. A procedural analysis describes a chain of events that together define a meaningful unit of performance. Activities such as bowling, cascade juggling, vaulting in gymnastics, running a three-lane fast break in basketball, and the long jump in track and field are typical of those skills for which a procedural task analysis is useful. Procedural analyses of the high jump and fast break are shown in Figures 12.1 and 12.2.

For skills in which a procedural task analysis is useful, the individual elements of the chain (the foot plant, the takeoff, and so on) can be learned somewhat independently and then put together to form the chain. Usually, the individual elements of the chain are fairly easy to learn. The putting together represents the crucial aspects of the instruction. The final outcome requires that each element of the chain be performed smoothly and in an integrated fashion. A breakdown at any element tends to ruin the entire performance.

A procedural task analysis is useful for identifying the points at which instruction should be focused, both in identifying the elements of the chain and in pinpointing the crucial spots at which the elements have to be linked smoothly for a skilled performance. The long jump represents a short, fairly

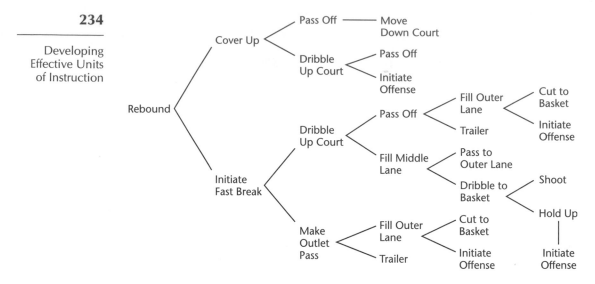

FIGURE 12.2   *Some possible fast-break behavior chains for a basketball player rebounding*

simple chain; rebounding and initiating a fast break in basketball represents a considerably more complex set of elements. A procedural task analysis of a fast break is shown in Figure 12.2. Notice how the analysis allows the designer or planner to identify the important learning tasks (the elements of the chain) and also the points at which they need to be put together smoothly for a skilled performance.

Hierarchical analysis is a description of all the subskills that must be learned to perform the terminal skill. In a hierarchical analysis, there is a necessary relationship between the skills. One skill must be learned before the other can be learned (unlike in the procedural analysis, in which elements can be learned independently). In a hierarchical analysis, the planner starts with the instructional goal and asks the TA question: "What will the students have to be able to do in order to accomplish this task?" This question is asked again and again until the basic entry skills for the tasks are learned. A hierarchical analysis is shown in Figure 12.3.

The hierarchical analysis identifies only those skills necessary for accomplishing the higher-level skill. With practice, designers and planners become able to identify subskills and adjust the size of the subskill steps to best suit learners' needs. The size of steps from one subskill to another is crucial to the success of the design. If the steps are too large, students will experience failure too often and lose interest and enthusiasm. If the steps are too small, they might become bored. The planner works to establish steps that are large enough to be continually challenging and small enough so that students achieve frequent success.

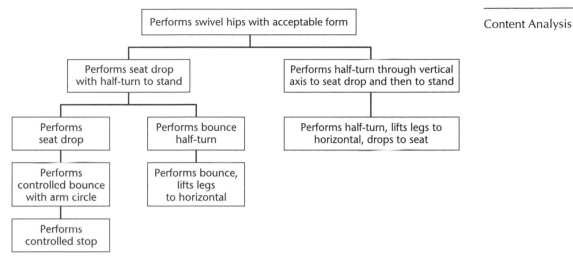

FIGURE 12.3 *Hierarchical analysis*

Social and cognitive goals are likely to require a hierarchical rather than a procedural analysis. If the goal is that students will correctly call their own fouls and violations in modified games without arguing, the teacher has to ask herself what tasks need to be designed to achieve that goal by the end of the unit. The goal involves a cognitive component because the students must know the fouls and violations and the appropriate consequences when they are committed. The goal also involves a social component in that the students are willing to make calls on each other without arguing. The teacher might decide that students will routinely call their own violations and fouls in all skill drills. This introduces the need for students to know the rules and to become accustomed to acting in less-intense situations than an actual game.

A *tactical analysis* can take either of the forms just described. If you are using the tactical approach for teaching games as described in Chapter 11, developing game frameworks to identify and break down tactical problems would be more appropriate. A game framework identifies the tactical problems that must be solved in three categories: scoring, preventing scoring, and restarting play. In addition, each tactical problem will involve off-the-ball movements and on-the-ball skills that are critical to success in game play. Table 12.1 provides an example of a game framework for soccer.

The choice of tactical problems depends upon the readiness of your students and the level of their tactical understanding and skill in a game. Griffin, Mitchell, and Oslin (1997) suggest that the TA question in this case become, "How tactically complex do I want the game to be?" Asking this question allows the planner to develop levels of tactical complexity to meet the needs of

TABLE 12.1 Tactical Problems, Movements, and Skills in Soccer

Tactical Problems	Off-the-Ball Movements	On-the-Ball Skills
SCORING		
Maintaining possession of the ball	Supporting the ball carrier	Passing—short and long Control—feet, thigh, chest
Attacking the goal	Using a target player	Shooting, shielding, turning
Creating space in attack	Crossover play Overlapping run	First-time passing—1 versus 2 Crossover play Overlapping run
Using space in attack	Timing runs to goal, shielding	Width—dribbling 1 versus 1, crossing, heading Depth—shielding
PREVENTING SCORING		
Defending space	Marking, pressure, preventing the turn, delay, covering, recovery runs	Clearing the ball
Defending the goal	Goalkeeping—positioning	Goalkeeping—receiving the ball, shot stopping, distribution
Winning the ball		Tackling—block, poke, slide
RESTARTING PLAY		
Throw-in—attacking and defending		
Corner kick—attacking and defending		
Free kick—attacking and defending		

Source: Reprinted by permission from L. Griffin, S. Mitchell & J. Oslin, 1997, *Teaching Sport Concepts and Skills: A Tactical Games Approach* (Champaign, IL: Human Kinetics), p. 11.

the students and outlines a progression of tactical complexity to follow in designing instruction (Table 12.2).

Once you have identified instructional goals and completed relevant analyses, most of the actual content for the unit is developed. If you are using a skill progressions approach, the subskills and elements identified become the informing and extending tasks for the unit. Most tasks will require refining along the way. Applied tasks should be inserted regularly to sustain the students' enthusiasm and show them how their developing skills and strategies

TABLE 12.2 Levels of Tactical Complexity for Soccer

Tactical Problems	Levels of Tactical Complexity				
	I	II	III	IV	V
SCORING					
Maintaining possession of the ball	Pass and control—feet	Support		Pass—long Control—thigh, chest	
Attacking the goal	Shooting	Shooting Turning	Target player		
Creating space in attack			First-time passing	Overlap	Crossover
Using space in attack				Width—dribbling, crossing, heading	Depth—timing of runs
PREVENTING SCORING					
Defending space		Marking, pressuring the ball	Preventing the turn	Clearing the ball	Delay, cover, recover
Defending the goal		Goalkeeper position, receiving, throwing			Making saves, kicking/punting
Winning the ball			Tackling—block, poke	Tackling—slide	
RESTARTING					
Throw-in	Throw-in				
Corner kick	Short kick		Near post		Far post
Free kick			Attacking		Defending

Source: Reprinted by permission from L. Griffin, S. Mitchell & J. Oslin, 1997, *Teaching Sport Concepts and Skills: A Tactical Games Approach* (Champaign, IL: Human Kinetics), p. 13.

are put to use. If employing a tactical approach, you must design a game form to present students with the tactical problem that is the focus of a lesson. You should also frame questions to guide students toward critical thinking so they will begin to identify what they need to do to solve a problem and why specific skills are necessary for success. At this point, when the many tasks needed to achieve success in the instructional goal have been identified, planners realize how much there is to be done in the time allotted. The great temptation is to include too many tasks and not plan for sufficient time to achieve them at each point in the progression. The inevitable result of succumbing to this temptation is that the instructional goal becomes impossible to attain.

PRACTICAL FACTORS RELATED TO UNIT PLANNING

The most important instructional design goal for unit planners is to identify relevant content through content and tactical frameworks and to develop sequential learning tasks (Chapter 11) for a particular set of students to achieve success in the major tasks. However, you may also consider certain practical factors as you translate those unit-level tasks into daily instructional tasks for students. You need to identify the skills for which practice routines can be developed, envision how equipment could be modified, think about the use of space, consider the ratios of equipment to students, figure out how to modify applied performance conditions, and design effective accountability mechanisms.

1. *Build routines for fundamental skills.* Nearly every unit of instruction will have skills that are fundamental to success in the activity. It is often difficult for students to participate successfully in applied activities unless they have achieved a certain level of mastery in the fundamental skills. For example, passing, catching, and pivoting are fundamental to success in basketball. It is difficult to imagine how a student could experience success in a modified basketball game without being able to perform those skills quite well. To achieve an adequate level of performance in applied settings, fundamental skills must be practiced often. One way for teachers to accomplish this in units is to develop routines for practicing fundamental skills. *Skill routines* are designated ways of practicing skills. These are like managerial routines in the sense that students can master them quickly and correctly with only minimal instructions. Three or four skill routines might be developed in a basketball unit, perhaps one for the passing/catching/pivoting combination, one for shooting, one for dribbling, and one for defensive movement. On a simple command, students would immediately organize and begin the routine. If groupings were sufficiently small (partners, triads, and so forth), students could practice each routine for 30 seconds. In 2 minutes, a rather large number of successful repetitions could be achieved. Like managerial routines, however, these skill routines have to be performed both quickly and accurately to achieve their intended effect, which is a great deal of good practice in a short time.

2. *Modify equipment to achieve intended outcomes.* Instructional tasks can be made easier or more difficult by modifying the equipment students use. Successful repetitions are often difficult to achieve with full-sized equipment. It is much easier to learn good stroking skills with rackets that are shorter and lighter. Slightly deflated soccer balls or

foam balls make it easier to learn kicking and trapping. Even a commercially produced elementary school discus is typically too large for fourth or fifth graders to grip and hurl—a shuffleboard disc is more appropriate. Any game or activity that requires students to anticipate the flight of an object can be made much easier by slowing down the object or causing it to stay in the air longer. Students can often execute skills in controlled settings (partner pass), but not when the action goes more quickly. The problem is that they don't have enough experience to anticipate the flight of the object and move to be in position to execute the skill. Thus, using beach balls for beginning volleyball-type skills or raising the net in badminton-type games to keep the object in the air longer gives students more time to anticipate and move to the proper position. The overall point is that student performance outcomes for units often depend on the equipment used.

3. *Design space-skill relationships to emphasize success.* The difficulty of learning skills is often related to the space the skill is performed within. In ball-striking games, a very small court requires too much control of shots for many successes to occur. Activities requiring guarding are often easier in larger spaces. Activity or game spaces that are too large often result in only a few students participating. Teachers should try to design spaces that produce an optimum level of challenge and success relative to the skill levels of the students. As students increase their skillfulness, the spaces can be modified to continue to make the activity challenging.

4. *Optimize equipment/student ratios.* Few instructional factors influence student response rates as much as the ratio of available equipment to students. More good responses lead to more achievement. Other things being equal, students in class with a 2:1 equipment ratio will get twice the number of response opportunities as those in a class with a 4:1 ratio. The equipment/student ratio should be a major factor in planning unit performance outcomes. The higher the ratio, the less you can expect to achieve. This is an especially important factor for all individual skill practice. When skill practice purposely takes place in groups, then the appropriate consideration is the equipment/group ratio. This factor needs to be kept in mind when designing applied tasks such as games.

5. *Modify applied performance conditions to ensure high, successful participation.* Teachers must plan tasks that are challenging and plan appropriate culminations for task development progressions. This is especially true for game playing because, in many units, games will represent the most frequent kind of applying task. How many "hits" does a sixth grader get in a six-versus-six volleyball game that lasts 12 minutes? According to research (Brown, 1985; Lawless, 1986; Parker, 1984), the answer depends on how skilled the student is relative to others in the class. A relatively skilled student will get a reasonable number of hits. A less-skilled student will get very few hits, often no more than

one or two decent hits per 20 minutes of game play. Games like softball produce even more disastrous response rates for most players. Modifying applied performance conditions requires planners to consider together the issues described in points 2, 3, and 4, that is, equipment modifications, space arrangements, and equipment/student ratios. The "best" kind of volleyball game is probably a three-versus-three game with net height, court size, and ball modified to fit the skills of the students. Most experts argue that volleyball is a series of three-person strategies, so the three-versus-three configuration preserves the fundamental nature of the game and allows for more hits per unit of time.

6. *Create accountability mechanisms to ensure high rates of on-task behavior and achievement of goals.* Two kinds of accountability need to be considered when planning: daily accountability aimed at on-task behavior and unit-level accountability aimed at achievement of end-of-unit objectives. Teachers need to hold students accountable for staying on task on a daily basis. Some activities, such as a checklist for gymnastics stunts, lend themselves to peer monitoring of performance. Some activities lend themselves to group challenges with resulting public recognition. Some teachers rely on active supervision, prompts, and feedback to keep students on task. Although daily on-task behavior is crucial to goal achievement, teachers would do well to consider a unit-level accountability system that is contingent on achievement of end-of-unit objectives. In some cases, this might take the form of a test, such as a fitness test at the end of a fitness unit. For other activity units, students might work toward awards, such as performance awards for various events in a track and field unit. In a Sport Education format, teachers have had great success developing seasonal awards based on performance throughout the sport unit—awards such as a fair-play award, most improved award, best out-of-class practice record award, coaches' awards, as well as team championship awards. Children enjoy signing their names to posters that reflect goal achievement; for example, a poster at the end of a horizontal climbing wall can be signed when the wall is negotiated appropriately. In Chapter 3, we showed that accountability drives instructional task systems. Strong motivational and incentive schemes, tied to unit objectives, can create the necessary climate for a high degree of goal achievement.

CONSTRUCTING THE UNIT PLAN

There is no best way to actually write a unit plan. Eventually, teachers adopt formats that prove to be most useful for them in their daily teaching. Remember, it is the class lesson that gets taught to students. The unit plan, therefore, should be constructed using a format that provides the necessary guidance at the lesson level. There are two sets of guidelines to guide the design of a unit plan: a generic set appropriate for any curriculum model and a second set that is specific to the needs and requirements of the model you are using.

Generic Guidelines

To be most helpful to teachers who will use unit plans again and again, the plan should include the following elements:

1. *Entry and exit outcomes to guide class time boundaries and allow activity.* Getting into the gymnasium and involved in activity quickly has proven effective for many teachers. An entry routine is one of the best ways to achieve this. For a given unit, for example, children might enter the gym, pick up their jump rope, go to their home base, and begin warming up using a jump rope routine previously taught. Other classes may see students entering the gymnasium and beginning warm-up under the direction of their team trainer, attaching harnesses to peers for climbing, obtaining their personal activity journals that provide the daily workout, or selecting from among the options provided on the week's fitness board. Equally important is how class is brought to a close. Adventure Education typically involves a debriefing in which students have the opportunity to reflect upon the day's lesson and how they feel about it. Bringing closure to a fitness lesson by having students record in their daily log will provide feedback relative to their performance and set the stage for the next lesson. To be effective, each of these must be thought about, planned for, and taught to students.

2. *Authentic outcomes and matching assessment.* The best way to ensure a high degree of instructional alignment is to have the performance goals match the assessment measures. As you have learned, designing authentic outcomes allows students to strive for assessments that are worthwhile and relevant. If teachers have skill, tactical, social, and cognitive goals, these should be included at this point with a means of assessing when they are achieved. Decisions about both process and product goals can be made here.

3. *Content analyses and tactical frameworks that reflect what is considered necessary to achieve the unit outcome.* These should be completed for all aspects of the content: skill, tactical, social, and cognitive.

4. *Needs assessment.* Complete as detailed a needs assessment as possible for each unit. Identify factors that must be considered when beginning this unit, from available equipment and the range of student ability to understanding students' interest in the content and its relevance to them.

5. *Block plan.* You cannot construct a good unit by simply starting at the beginning of the content analysis and moving toward the end. Remember, the unit is a series of lessons. Each lesson should make sense, too.

The unit plan should have anticipated instructional tasks blocked by lesson so that day-to-day teaching progressions will be clear, and each lesson can be judged as an independent entity as well as being part of a series of lessons comprising the unit.

6. *Specification of special managerial routines for the unit.* Are there specific managerial routines needed for this unit that go beyond those in operation throughout the school year? In gymnastics, for example, many teachers establish routines for rotating among apparatus. With limited equipment, you might need a special routine for sharing.

7. *Anticipating safety issues and establishing special rules.* When planning an archery unit or a gymnastics unit, you will have special safety considerations specific to that activity. Your regular class rules will need to be expanded for that unit. Remember, these will be new rules, and they will require teaching and vigorous enforcing at the outset until they become established.

8. *Organizational arrangements to save time.* For most instructional tasks, there will be a preferred organizational arrangement (practicing alone in self-space, partners, triads, and so forth). Moving from one organizational arrangement to another takes time. Planning tasks within lessons, therefore, should take into consideration the transitions between organizational arrangements. Moving from self-practice, to partners, to quads represents a series of easy transitions that should take little time. Grouping practice tasks within one organizational framework also makes sense, for example, doing a series of practice tasks using partners before moving on to a different organizational arrangement.

9. *Accountability materials.* Do you need posters, charts, ribbons, or homemade certificates? The unit plan should include both a list of materials and a copy of each.

Specific Model Considerations

Developmental Physical Education.   When you are using this model, perhaps the most important concept to keep in mind is that all children have their own individual patterns of growth and development. When we apply this to planning, it suggests that the teacher plan for the individual child rather than for grade level or content. This implies that the teacher must be able to accommodate for differences between and within groups of children at the same age level. For example, if a small group of children, or one child, is not prepared to perform skills in complex situations, they are provided with opportunities to respond and challenges in environments that are appropriate for their abilities. A growing body of literature provides us with guidance in making these planning and instructional decisions. The Council on Physical Education for Children (COPEC) has developed a document that highlights appropriate and inappropriate practices for physical education programs (Table 12.3 provides selected components of this document). This document provides physical educators with a yardstick by which to measure their own programs and the quality of the physical education they are delivering to children.

COPEC suggests that all children should have access to quality daily physical education, which it defines in its 1992 document, *Developmentally Appropriate Physical Education Practices for Children:*

> Quality daily physical education is both developmentally and instructionally suitable for the specific children being served. Developmentally appropriate practices in physical education are those which recognize children's changing capacities to move and those which promote such change. A developmentally appropriate physical education program accommodates a variety of individual characteristics such as developmental status, previous movement experiences, fitness and skill levels, body size, and age. Instructionally appropriate physical education incorporates the best known practices, derived from both research and experiences teaching children, into a program that maximizes opportunities for learning and success for all children. The outcome of a developmentally and instructionally appropriate physical education is an individual who is "physically educated." (p. 3).

Adventure Education.   When using the Adventure Education curriculum model, the teacher becomes a facilitator who supports students in learning and developing in an experiential setting. In order to do this, the teacher must set *boundaries* that challenge students yet allow participation in a safe environment, establish *trust* and commitment to the group, demonstrate *energy* to motivate and keep the group moving in a positive direction, and transfer applications drawn from the experience into *meaning* in the "real" world (Rohnke & Butler, 1995). Rohnke and Butler (1995) outline five steps that are critical for planning and leading a group (Figure 12.4). Although not specific to a physical education setting, these steps can be adapted and applied to the planning process: *assessing* your learners and your goals, *planning* how to meet the goals you have outlined, *preparing* the materials necessary to deliver the program, *leading* the students through the experience, and *evaluating* what needs to be revised while it is occurring or for the next time.

Pat Price, the physical educator at Cedarwood Project Adventure Elementary School, highlights the following decisions she makes when planning for the Adventure Education model.

- What is the active decision-making role for the students?
- What are the risk factors, and are they developmentally appropriate?
- What are the emotional factors, and are they emotionally appropriate?
- Is there an element of perceived risk?
- Are goals and challenges student driven?
- Do goals and challenges require the physical and emotional support of classmates?
- Is the activity fun?

TABLE 12.3 Appropriate and Inappropriate Physical Education Practices for Children

Component	Appropriate Practice	Inappropriate Practice
Curriculum	The physical education curriculum has an obvious scope and sequence based on goals and objectives that are appropriate for all children. It includes a balance of skills, concepts, games, educational gymnastics, rhythms and dance experiences designed to enhance the cognitive, motor, affective, and physical fitness development of every child.	The physical education curriculum lacks developmental goals and objectives and is based primarily on the teacher's interests, preferences, and background rather than those of the children. For example, the curriculum consists primarily of large-group games.
Development of movement concepts and motor skills	Children are provided with frequent and meaningful age-appropriate practice opportunities that enable individuals to develop a functional understanding of movement concepts (body awareness, space awareness, effort, and relationships) and build competence and confidence in their ability to perform a variety of motor skills (locomotor, nonlocomotor, and manipulative).	Children participate in a limited number of games and activities in which the opportunity for individual children to develop basic concepts and motor skills is restricted.
Cognitive development	Physical education activities are designed with both the physical and the cognitive development of children in mind. Teachers provide experiences that encourage children to question, integrate, analyze, communicate, apply cognitive concepts, and gain a wide multicultural view of the world, thus making physical education a part of the total educational experience.	Instructors fail to recognize and explore the unique role of physical education, which allows children to learn to move while also moving to learn. Children do not receive opportunities to integrate their physical education experience with art, music, or other classroom experiences.
Affective development	Teachers intentionally design and teach throughout the year activities that allow children the opportunity to work together to improve their emerging social and cooperation skills. These activities also help children develop a positive self-concept. Teachers help children experience and feel the satisfaction and joy that results from regular participation in physical activity.	Teachers fail to intentionally enhance the affective development of children when activities that foster the development of cooperation and social skills are excluded. Teachers ignore opportunities to help children understand the emotions they feel as a result of participation in physical activity.

TABLE 12.3 Appropriate and Inappropriate Physical Education Practices for Children (*continued*)

Component	Appropriate Practice	Inappropriate Practice
Concepts of fitness	Children participate in activities that are designed to help them understand and value the important concepts of physical fitness and the contribution they make to a healthy lifestyle.	Children are required to participate in fitness activities, but are not helped to understand the reasons why.
Physical fitness tests	Ongoing fitness assessment is used as a part of the continuing process of helping children understand, enjoy, improve, and/or maintain their physical health and well-being. Test results are shared privately with children and their parents as a tool for developing their physical fitness knowledge, understanding, and competence. As part of an ongoing program of physical education, children are physically prepared so they can safely complete each component of a physical test battery.	Physical fitness tests are given once or twice a year solely for the purpose of qualifying children for awards or because they are required by a school district or state department. Children are required to complete a physical fitness test battery without understanding why they are performing the tests or the implications of their individual results as they apply to their future health and well-being. Children are required to take physical fitness tests without adequate conditioning (e.g., students are made to run a mile after "practicing" it only one day the week before).
Assessment	Teacher decisions are based primarily on ongoing individual assessments of children as they participate in physical education class activities (formative evaluation), and not on the basis of a single test score (summative evaluation). Assessment of children's physical progress and achievement is used to individualize instruction, plan yearly curriculum and weekly lessons, identify children with special needs, communicate with parents, and evaluate the program's effectiveness.	Children are evaluated on the basis of fitness test scores or on a single physical skills test. For example, children receive a grade in physical education based on their scores on a standardized fitness test or on the number of times they can continuously jump rope.
Regular involvement for every child	Children participate in their regularly scheduled physical education class because it is recognized as an important part of their overall education.	Children are removed from physical education classes to participate in classroom activities, as punishment for not completing assignments, and/or for misbehavior in the classroom.

TABLE 12.3 Appropriate and Inappropriate Physical Education Practices for Children (*continued*)

Component	Appropriate Practice	Inappropriate Practice
Active participation for every child	All children are involved in activities that allow them to remain continuously active. Classes are designed to meet a child's need for active participation in all learning experiences.	Activity time is limited because children are waiting for a turn in relay races, to be chosen for a team, or to play with limited equipment or playing games such as Duck, Duck, Goose. Children are organized into large groups in which getting a turn is based on individual competitiveness or aggressive behavior. Children are eliminated with no chance to re-enter activity, or they must sit for long periods of time. For example, activities such as musical chairs, dodgeball, and elimination tag provide limited opportunities for many children, especially slower, less-agile ones, who actually need activity most.
Gender-directed activities	Girls and boys have equal access to individual, partner, small-group, and team activities. Girls and boys are equally encouraged, supported, and socialized toward successful achievement in all realms of physical education.	Girls are encouraged to participate in activities that stress traditionally feminine roles, whereas boys are encouraged to participate in more aggressive activities. Boys are more often provided with leadership roles in physical education class. Statements by physical education teachers reinforce traditional socialization patterns that provide for greater and more aggressive participation by boys and lesser and more passive participation by girls.
PE and recess	Physical education classes are planned and organized to provide children with opportunities to acquire the physical, emotional, cognitive, and social benefits of physical education.	"Free play" or recess is used as a substitute for daily, organized physical education lessons. Free play, in this case, is characterized by a lack of goals, organization, planning, and instruction.

- Does the activity increase student's self-confidence?
- Is there personal accountability and responsibility for skill acquisition and strategy?

Kelly Robbins at Devonshire Alternative Elementary School would add a couple of items to Pat Price's planning list. She suggests that, to use the Adventure Education model, teachers must design hands-on activities based around the

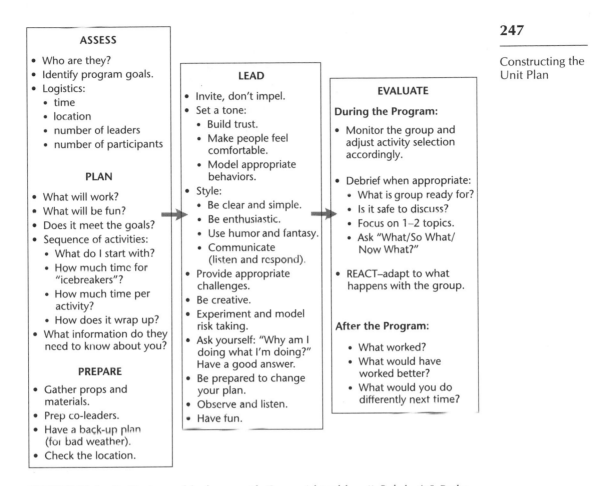

ASSESS

- Who are they?
- Identify program goals.
- Logistics:
  - time
  - location
  - number of leaders
  - number of participants

PLAN

- What will work?
- What will be fun?
- Does it meet the goals?
- Sequence of activities:
  - What do I start with?
  - How much time for "icebreakers"?
  - How much time per activity?
  - How does it wrap up?
- What information do they need to know about you?

PREPARE

- Gather props and materials.
- Prep co-leaders.
- Have a back-up plan (for bad weather).
- Check the location.

LEAD

- Invite, don't impel.
- Set a tone:
  - Build trust.
  - Make people feel comfortable.
  - Model appropriate behaviors.
- Style:
  - Be clear and simple.
  - Be enthusiastic.
  - Use humor and fantasy.
  - Communicate (listen and respond).
- Provide appropriate challenges.
- Be creative.
- Experiment and model risk taking.
- Ask yourself: "Why am I doing what I'm doing?" Have a good answer.
- Be prepared to change your plan.
- Observe and listen.
- Have fun.

EVALUATE

During the Program:

- Monitor the group and adjust activity selection accordingly.

- Debrief when appropriate:
  - What is group ready for?
  - Is it safe to discuss?
  - Focus on 1–2 topics.
  - Ask "What/So What/ Now What?"

- REACT–adapt to what happens with the group.

After the Program:

- What worked?
- What would have worked better?
- What would you do differently next time?

FIGURE 12.4 *Facilitation model reference guide (Source: Adapted from K. Rohnke & S. Butler, Quicksilver: Adventure Games, Initiative Problems, Trust Activities, and a Guide to Effective Leadership, © Project Adventure, Inc. Used by permission.*

themes (challenge, risk, problem solving, trust, and cooperation) and create a sense of community rather than competition. She also uses adventure language (What? So what? And now what?) related to these themes in directions and conversations and when utilizing the debriefing (student reflection) at lesson closure. She feels that, if the activity can be personalized and made meaningful to all students, they will remember it.

Would adding a climbing wall to your program make it an Adventure Education model? Generally, no. Adventure Education embodies a philosophy rather than just being an adventure activity. Unless that philosophy is infused throughout the program, a climbing unit, although enjoyable and even a learning experience, will not provide a total Adventure Education experience. "Climbing is a multi-dimensional activity consisting of intense physical, emotional, cognitive, and cooperative objectives" (Pat Price, personal communication, 1999).

Integrated Physical Education. Planning using an integrated model varies, depending upon whether you are using a connected, shared, or partnership model. Both the shared and partnership models require collaboration with another teacher(s). To implement a shared model, teachers need to determine themes and time lines and how to sequence the content in both classrooms. The partnership model requires the additional step of team teaching in one setting. Perhaps the first step would be to attempt integration on your own using the connected model. This requires that you independently determine what content you want to integrate and identify how you will gain the information to support your planning and delivery of that content. Cone, Werner, Cone, and Woods (1998) identify seven strategies for developing interdisciplinary learning experiences:

1. Review curricular guides, scope, and sequences to inform you of what content will be taught during the school year at each grade level in all subject areas.

2. Select content (themes, topics, issues) to be the focus of an interdisciplinary experience.

3. Gather content information to provide guidance in planning.

4. Decide on the interdisciplinary teaching model(s): connected, shared, or partnership.

5. Create lesson plans and determine specific activities that will allow students to reach the goals of the experience.

6. Determine scheduling, materials, equipment, organization, and facilities.

7. Decide how to assess student learning in ongoing and authentic ways.

Physical Activity, Fitness, and Wellness Education. If the intent of a physical activity, fitness, and wellness program is to help students take responsibility for their own healthy lifestyle and be able to make good activity choices to achieve this, then perhaps one of the most critical tasks is to get students to buy in to physical activity. This suggests designing programs that are both *relevant* to learners and the student culture within which they live and *motivational,* which translates into providing activities that are fun and personally challenging. If these two objectives are achieved, then developing or adapting a program to introduce students to the steps necessary for becoming skilled and knowledgeable individuals able to make personal fitness and activity decisions is critical. As you learned in Chapter 9, the stairway to lifetime fitness will move students through a process of *performing* activity and exercise, *getting fit, self-assessing* their fitness and activity levels, and learning to *self-design* their own fitness programs that will result in their valuing physical activity and choosing to continue to be active throughout life (Corbin & Lindsey, 1997).

Sport Education. Planning for Sport Education must consider sport selection, students' levels of involvement, materials necessary for the season to function, and strategies to make the season festive. Siedentop (1994) provides an entire chapter on planning a Sport Education season. Here are some highlights from that chapter:

- *Sport selection.* Sports can be chosen from any of the game categories (invasion, net/wall games, target games, fielding/run scoring). When first attempting to implement the Sport Education model, select a sport that you know well so you can respond to the many questions that arise and lend an air of excitement for a sport about which you are confident. The season must be long enough to achieve the goals of Sport Education and make learners competent and knowledgeable players in a variety of roles.

- *Student involvement.* Movement from a teacher-directed to a student-directed format will vary, depending upon your style and comfort with students' taking responsibility for their own sport experience. Decisions about student roles and team selection must be made early in the planning stage because how much the students will take on will determine the depth and specificity of your planning.

- *Preparation of materials.* Development of materials to manage the sport season can be an overwhelming task, so allowing students to take on some of this responsibility may prove useful. Teachers often develop a coaching notebook to guide much of the season. This can include roles and responsibilities; score sheets; statistics sheets; competition schedule; information on skill, strategies, rules, etiquette, rituals, and traditions; entry forms; point systems; directions to captains on guiding practice; and any other of an assortment of necessary forms.

DEVELOPING LESSON PLANS FROM THE UNIT PLAN

For many experienced teachers, the unit plan, if it has instructional tasks blocked by lesson, will be sufficient for teaching each lesson. For some experienced teachers and nearly all beginning teachers, a daily lesson plan will prove very helpful, particularly to help them stay on a time schedule and to create the confidence that comes with having a good plan to refer to when needed.

Teachers need first to consider what they want to accomplish on a given day. What are the expected outcomes? This requires analyzing the tasks required to achieve these outcomes: How many tasks will it take? How many repetitions do kids need to perform the task well? How much time is available? Once teachers have this information, they can begin to determine how much can be accomplished and what a time schedule might look like to include all the tasks necessary for success. Frequently, teachers plan for the skill and tactical components of a lesson and put little thought or planning into the social or cognitive aspects. We suggest that your lesson plans include instructional tasks for all aspects of what you want learners to achieve. If you

Tactical Problem: Winning the point

Lesson Focus: Spiking (crosscourt and down the line)

Objective: To use attack variations

A. **Game:** 6 versus 6
   Goal: Winning the point by attack
   Conditions: Regulation court; regulation rules. Initiate game from a free ball. Free ball toss
   from server position, rally score.
   Note: Teams can implement the no-ace serving rule as a variation.

   Questions
   Q: *What do you ultimately want to do when you attack (spike) the ball to win a point?*
   A: Kill the ball; spike so players cannot return
   Q: *What are the different types of spiking?*
   A: Tip, crosscourt, down the line, roll shot

B. **Practice Task:** Attack variations
   Goal: Hitters get four trials, then rotate.
   Conditions: Two teams and three or four balls. Tosser tosses a good pass to setter 1, then
   tosses a pass to setter 2. Setter 1 sets a high outside for hitter to spike, down
   the line, crosscourt, tip, roll shot (see diagram).

C. **Game:** 6 versus 6
   Goal: Same as initial game
   Condition: No-ace serve game or regulation

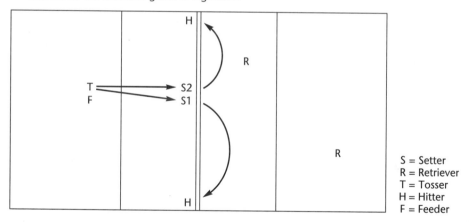

S = Setter
R = Retriever
T = Tosser
H = Hitter
F = Feeder

FIGURE 12.5   *Activity component of the lesson (Source: Reprinted by permission from
L. Griffin, S. M. Mitchell, & J. Oslin, 1997, Teaching Sport Concepts and
Skills: A Tactical Games Approach (Champaign, IL: Human Kinetics)*

want to teach managerial routines, include student practice tasks in your lesson plan. When you expect students to learn how to perform specific roles in
Sport Education, plan for them, design practice tasks, and build them into
your lesson plan. When teaching students fitness concepts, plan how they will
be implemented and linked to activity, and include them in your lesson plan.

Once you have determined what you want to achieve in a given lesson,
document it. We suggest developing a lesson plan that has two sides: one that
reflects the activity component of the lesson (Figure 12.5) and the other that

details specific instructional tasks designed to meet the expectations of a particular curriculum model (Table 12.4).

There is no perfect format for lesson planning. Format to reflect specifics of a particular curriculum will look as different as the characteristics of each model. Our suggestion is to design a format that meets your needs and includes space for you to document and highlight information that will guide your teaching and student participation. For instance, when teaching Adventure Education, conduct a "debriefing" to bring closure to an experience. This means you need to determine the issues you want to pursue, develop a series of questions that will generate discussion, or outline the method you want to use to get participants to reflect on and discuss what occurred. The format you use to do this need not be prescribed and could certainly vary by teacher as well as across adventure experiences.

When focusing on the activity component of a given lesson, most teacher educators would agree that a lesson plan should reflect the following:

1. The anticipated progression of tasks with a time allotment for each task (It is most helpful to the teacher if the time allotment is listed cumulatively for the length of the lesson.)

2. Descriptions for how each task will be communicated to students (Some feel that, at the outset, the exact words should be written on the lesson plan.)

3. The organizational arrangements for each task

4. Any teaching cues or prompts the teacher wants to remember to help the students master the task (These might be critical elements of skills or just reminders to "speak slowly and enunciate clearly" if you have been experiencing difficulty with students understanding your explanations and directions.)

5. Some way of recording reactions to what took place so that the next time the lesson is taught or when the unit is revised, you have information about what went well or what might be changed

We have chosen to provide examples of two lesson plan formats to fulfill the activity component. Each provides the necessary space to include instructional decisions to reflect and the resulting tasks for students to complete. The first is geared toward Rink's model of content progression (Table 12.4) and attends to the points just outlined. The second reflects decisions necessary when teaching for tactical awareness (Figure 12.5) and is presented in a more holistic type framework.

TABLE 12.4 Sample Lesson Plan: Instructional Plan

Anticipated Progression of Tasks	Anticipated Time	How Task Will Be Communicated	Organizational Arrangements	Goal Orientation
Introduce schottische step.	2 min.	Demonstration with music		
Do part one of schottische step. / Step is teacher-paced. / Step is self-paced.	2 min.	Demonstration with cue words (step, step—step, hop—step, step—step, hop)	Individual students are scattered, facing teacher; dance is teacher-paced with cues.	Perform part one with proper rhythm.
			Dance is self-paced; students move forward within own area.	
Do part two of schottische step. / Practice repeatedly. / Step is teacher-paced. / Step is self-paced.	4 min.	Demonstration with cue words (step, hop—step, hop—step, hop—step, hop)	Individual students are scattered, facing teacher; dance is teacher-paced with cues.	Perform accurate step pattern.
			Dance is self-paced; students move forward within own area.	
Combine parts one and two. / Practice repeatedly.	5 min.	Walk-through with teacher cueing	Same as above.	Make smooth transition from part one to part two. Have ability to repeat pattern.
Do schottische step with music. / Listen to music first. / Perform to music at slow speed.	5 min.	Teacher explanation only	Individual students are scattered, facing teacher; students move anywhere within the group; dance is paced by music.	Adjust to music.

TABLE 12.4 Sample Lesson Plan: Instructional Plan (*continued*)

Anticipated Progression of Tasks	Anticipated Time	How Task Will Be Communicated	Organizational Arrangements	Goal Orientation
Use direction changes. Alternate forward and backward movement. / Add turns, sideways movement, and music when ready.	7 min.	Teacher explanation and demonstration	Individual students are scattered.	Make changes without interrupting the flow of the pattern.
Design a pattern using directional turns.				Decide on what step to make the turn.
Do the step with a partner (step is initially teacher-paced and then self-paced). / Go forward. / Go backward. / Combine forward and backward. / Add sideways movement and turns. / Add different partner relationships.	7 min.	Teacher explanation and demonstration	Partners are scattered.	Start fast and lead partner. Develop versatility to perform step in a variety of ways.
Do the buggy schottische. Do part one (no music). Do part two (no music). Combine parts one and two (no music).	4 min.	Listen to music demonstration Teacher explanation only	Partners are scattered. Sets of two partners are scattered; students have choice of partners.	Accurately reproduce dance.
Do self-designed dances. Create a dance sequence in sets of two partners using the schottische criteria (change in pathway; change in direction; at least two different relationships with others).	10 min.	Teacher explanation and demonstration of an example	Sets of two partners are scattered.	Develop versatility in use of schottische. Understand phrasing and dynamics of choreography.

(Rink, 1998, pp. 240–241)

1. Teachers plan to ensure progressions within and between lessons, to use time efficiently, to reduce anxiety and build confidence, and to fulfill building or district policies.

2. Although teachers may be plan dependent or plan independent as they teach, evidence suggests that all effective teachers originally plan units thoroughly.

3. Determining entry and exit levels is the starting place for unit planning.

4. Ample time should be allocated for limited goal accomplishment.

5. End-of-unit outcomes should describe both goals and the means for assessing them.

6. Outcomes should be written for the physical, tactical, social, and cognitive.

7. A content analysis is a technique to determine all aspects of your instructional outcomes necessary for its achievement.

8. A procedural analysis describes a chain of events that, taken together, form a meaningful unit of performance.

9. A hierarchical analysis is a description of all the subskills necessary to perform the instructional goal.

10. Unit plans are more practical when routines for daily behaviors and fundamental skills are taught; equipment is modified to achieve outcomes; space-skill relationships ensure success; equipment/student ratios are optimized; applied-performance conditions ensure high, successful participation; and accountability mechanisms ensure high rates of on-task behavior.

11. Elements such as entry and exit outcomes, authentic outcomes with matching authentic assessments, content analyses and tactical frameworks, needs assessments, a block plan, anticipated safety issues and related rules, time-saving organizational arrangements, and accountability materials should be in the generic unit plan.

12. Specifics related to each physical education curriculum model should be specified in the unit plan.

13. If concepts such as fair play and effort are important outcomes, they should be included in the unit and daily lesson plans.

14. Daily lesson plans might have two sides: one that reflects the activity component of the lesson and the other that speaks to the needs of a specific curriculum model.

15. Elements such as task progressions, task communication, organizational arrangements, teaching cues, and reactions for purposes of revision should be present in a daily lesson plan.

PART FOUR

Skills and Strategies for Effective Teaching in Physical Education

All the knowledge about effective teaching and all the good planning for an exciting, challenging physical education eventually depend on your ability to engage students in sustained, meaningful contact with the content—that is, they depend on effective instruction. Certain skills and strategies are common to all instructional formats, even though those formats differ markedly in terms of how students are organized and your role as a teacher. Because time in class is seldom sufficient to accomplish all the goals of physical education, this section shows you how to extend your program to engage students in nonattached school time, after school, in the community, and with their parents.

You will understand the differences among instructional formats and their relative strengths and weaknesses for teaching situations you might encounter. You no doubt will have a favorite that will become your main format—and that is O.K. This section also includes important observation instruments you can use to help you improve your teaching skills and strategies, regardless of what instructional format you use.

CHAPTER 13

Generic Instructional Skills and Strategies

The teacher's job involves many roles besides that of instructing students. At times the teacher will serve as a parent surrogate, an entertainer, an authority figure, a psychotherapist, and a record keeper. All of these are necessary aspects of the teacher's role. However, they are subordinate to and in support of the major role of teaching. Important as they are, they must not be allowed to overshadow the teacher's basic instructional role.

—Jere Brophy & Thomas Good (1974)

OVERALL CHAPTER OUTCOME

To observe a physical education class and accurately evaluate the degree to which the lesson reflects appropriate instructional strategies

CHAPTER OBJECTIVES

- To explain the role of deliberate practice in learning
- To describe how teaching is best evaluated
- To explicate lessons as arrangements of tasks
- To differentiate between teacher-mediated and student-mediated formats
- To describe the features of a safe, challenging, and meaningful learning environment
- To explain the purpose of guided and independent practice and the teacher's role
- To designate how modified games can form a learning progression and the teacher's role during applying tasks
- To list the prerequisites for effective student-mediated learning
- To enunciate options for holding students accountable
- To describe the functions of an effective closure
- To explain the importance of lesson pace and momentum

Chapters 13 and 14 focus on teaching, particularly the various ways instruction is delivered to students. Effective instructional task systems come in many varieties, ranging from direct teaching to self-instructional models, with many variations in between. In Chapter 13, we consider the main instructional functions that are necessary for effective teaching, no matter what format a teacher adopts. Regardless of whether you choose to utilize a direct, active-teaching format, a small-group problem-oriented format, or a cooperative learning format, you still need to effectively communicate instructional tasks and help students learn to organize for effective practice. You also have to ensure a safe and challenging instructional climate. These and other instructional functions have to be planned and delivered effectively for any instructional format to achieve its goals. In Chapter 14, we focus on the specifics of the various formats being utilized in physical education.

Research on teaching has shown clearly that teachers can make a difference. Who your teachers are and what they do in class will affect how much you learn, how you feel about the subject, and how you feel about yourself as a learner. Teachers can, on occasion, also touch the lives of students, influencing them in very profound ways. We cannot forget, however, that the primary purpose of schooling is to help students learn and grow in ways that eventually lead to productive work, leisure, and citizenship. The main role of teachers in achieving that primary purpose, as the opening quote to this chapter suggests, is their role in developing and sustaining an effective instructional system. Through this role, physical education teachers provide an equitable quality education for all students.

Although Chapters 13 and 14 focus on instruction, we should not forget that an effective managerial system provides the foundation for effective teaching (see Chapter 4). An effective preventive management system produces the time and order necessary for students to engage purposefully in the content. Never underestimate the importance of an effective class management system—it provides the opportunity for an instructional system to work. Without it, students are unlikely to engage seriously with the learning tasks, regardless of how well those tasks are planned and delivered.

TEACHING AND LEARNING

What is at the very heart of effective teaching and learning? Educational psychologists, whether from a behavioral or cognitive perspective, seem to agree that *for students to get better at anything, they have to engage in sustained, deliberate practice.* In Chapter 1, we argued that the "learning student" was the key to an effective physical education and that learning students needed to get "plenty of perfect practice" (see Box 1.2). We know a lot about the conditions that define what psychologists call "deliberate practice" or what we have referred to as "perfect practice." The information in Chapters 13 and 14 is intended to show you how physical education teachers can arrange the conditions for deliberate practice in a variety of formats. Information in Chapters 6 and 9 was intended to help you understand some of the conditions necessary to sustain students in useful practice, through meaningful curriculum choices and facilitative organizational features. As we have said repeatedly, it is the quality and quantity of student involvement that reveals the effectiveness of an instructional task system.

Effective teaching, therefore, is best evaluated by observations of students—their work involvement (process) and what they achieve (outcome or product). When teachers substantially increase the amount of Active Learning Time in Physical Education their students are accruing on a daily basis, they have, other things being equal, improved their effectiveness. This represents a process approach to evaluating teaching and learning. If students can perform a nearly flawless floor exercise routine at the end of a gymnastics unit, this represents an outcome or product measure of effective instruction. The same is true for students who not only can successfully present folk dances at the end of a unit, but also demonstrate new knowledge about the countries in which the dances originated. If the students ask that the folk dance unit be extended

---

BOX 13.1   How Much Time? How Much Information?

Situation. A junior high instructor is introducing some advanced tumbling skills (handsprings). As the class begins, the instructor asks a student to bring over a projector and then threads a film loop. The students are shown an assisted handspring while the instructor explains and discusses the skill. Then the students are shown two other film loops on the other handspring skills. During each showing, the instructor details the execution of the skill.

Results. The students are given far too much information, and far too much time is spent in the presentation.

Analysis. The equipment is not ready. The need for repeated showing of film loops is questionable. The verbal explanation is probably far too detailed for an introduction. No live demonstration is given. Students have to sit for a long time. The question is, "When they finally get up to try the skill for the first time, will their attempts be much better because of the detailed presentation?" The answer is probably no.

Prescription. The students need to have an overall visual impression of what the handspring looks like, with their attention drawn to the two or three crucial aspects of execution. Then they need specific beginning objectives to get them started practicing the skill and specific feedback about their performance. The presentation gives the illusion of high-level teaching, but is actually contrary to principles of effective instruction.

---

because it's so much fun, this too is evidence of effective instruction. Finally, if students take their teams from a Sport Education volleyball season and enter the school intramural volleyball league, this is important evidence that effective instruction has occurred.

Evaluating instruction only through observations of the teacher can be misleading (see Box 13.1) Well-explained tasks and a pleasant rapport with students that do not translate into high rates of work involvement are of little value from an achievement perspective. Do not misunderstand this caution. How teachers instruct is important because it has been shown that some kinds of instruction are more likely to produce effective student work involvement, and effective work involvement has been related to achievement and attitude gains. The point is that evaluating instruction must include evidence about what students do as well as evidence about what teachers do.

Teachers teach; students learn. Teachers cannot learn for the students. Students learn through their involvement with the content—and they get better through purposeful practice. What teachers can do is influenced by the kind of work students do and the intensity and duration of their engagement with the learning tasks. This involvement, on a lesson-by-lesson basis, is the key to understanding effective teaching. This is true whether the student engagement is related to motor skill, tactical, cognitive, or social objectives. It is also true regardless of whether the instructional format is direct or indirect, group, small group, or individualized.

If you want to improve your students' motor skills, fitness, knowledge, social skills, or attitudes, influence the quality and quantity of their involvement with content in class (and out of class, too). But in attempting to influence the nature of their involvement, always remember that how students react to instructional tasks, through modifications, will influence the potential for learning (see the several discussions of negotiations in Chapter 3). This is why we have advocated that teachers strive to develop a learning climate that is characterized by cooperation—and, where possible, over time to build a learning community (see Chapter 6).

LESSONS AS ARRANGEMENTS OF TASKS

Lessons should be viewed as arrangements of tasks. This is a useful way to view lessons because it focuses on what students *do* in the lesson. Every lesson has managerial and instructional tasks, and teachers should never forget that students always have social tasks to accomplish (see Chapter 3 for an explanation of task systems). Students will enter the gymnasium or need to move to an outdoor space (transition tasks, entry tasks, initial activity tasks). They will have to be informed as to what content will be practiced for the lesson (informing, refining, extending, and applying instructional tasks). They may have to organize differently for different instructional tasks (transitional tasks, equipment replacement tasks). At some point, they may have to gather and disperse to receive instruction and return to practice. The lesson will eventually culminate in closure, and students will move to their classrooms or locker room. How all these tasks are implemented determines the success or failure of the lesson from an instructional point of view.

Students engage in instructional tasks regardless of the instructional format utilized. What does differ in various instructional formats, and in a sense defines their categories, is how tasks are *mediated* in the teaching/learning process. The two primary categories are (a) formats in which teachers mediate instruction and (b) formats in which students mediate instruction. Teachers can mediate tasks directly, as in group-oriented active teaching formats; indirectly, as through a task or station teaching format; or indirectly, through self-instructional formats. Many teachers are experimenting with instructional formats in which much of the instruction is mediated by students, as in peer or reciprocal formats, small-group instruction, Sport Education teams, or a cooperative learning format. We focus on these various formats more completely in Chapter 14. What is important here is to understand that our focus for viewing a lesson as a series of tasks requires you to think first about what students will do in that lesson—and this focus helps you see the degree to which you are facilitating the purposeful practice that will lead to important student outcomes.

TABLE 13.1   Main Elements of a Typical PE Lesson

Student Task	Instructional Function
Enter gym and engage in initial practice task.	Development and teaching of entry routine for practicing familiar tasks
Gather for instruction and receive instruction for a new skill.	Gathering routine and well-planned demonstration that culminates in clear communication of informing task
Practice the informing task.	Guided practice
Disperse for independent practice, and practice task.	Dispersal routine and supervision of independent practice
Refine task being practiced.	Attention routine, clear refinement communication
Extend task by changing conditions of practice, followed by practice.	Attention routine, clear communication of extending task, followed by active supervision
Refine task and continue practice.	Attention routine, clear refinement communication, followed by active supervision
Gather students to explain applying task.	Attention and gathering routines, well-planned explanation and demonstration
Explain organizational format for applying task, and disperse students for practice.	Dispersal routine followed by guided practice
Apply task practice for 10 minutes.	Active supervision
Gather for closure.	Gathering routine followed by closure

Table 13.1 contains the main elements of a typical physical education lesson, showing the tasks students would perform, and the important instructional functions that the fulfillment of those tasks contribute to an effective lesson. The lesson shown assumes a direct, teacher-mediated format consistent with what we have called "active teaching."

Some instructional functions get repeated throughout the lesson. The important managerial and routine functions were described in Chapter 4. The instructional functions of explanation/demonstration, task communication, guided practice, active supervision of independent practice, and closure are addressed in this chapter.

A similar analysis can be made of a format such as Sport Education, in which many of the instructional and managerial tasks are mediated by students (Table 13.2). The instructional functions are similar to the teacher-

Student Task	Instructional Function
Enter gym, go to team space, engage in warm-up skill or skill practice.	Development and teaching of entry routine, teaching student coaches how to guide and supervise practice
Teams meet for discussion of strategy for next round of competition.	Gathering routine, teaching coaches how to lead discussion and involve teammates
Transition to first game is made. Players go to appropriate game spaces. Referees/ scorers get equipment and move to assigned spaces.	Transition routines, teaching team managers how to organize equipment and assignments
First game is played.	Students fulfilling multiple roles
Game ends and transition to next game is made. New teams, referees, and scorers are named. Results are turned in.	Transition routines, managers guiding team members to appropriate places
Second game is played.	Students fulfilling multiple roles
Game ends and transition to next game is made.	Transition routines, managers guiding team members to appropriate places
Last game ends. Teams return to home place. Statisticians gather all game results. Managers put away all equipment. Coaches debrief teams.	Routines for gathering at home place, game results, and equipment, all roles previously taught
Class gathers for closure: recognition of performance, fair play, and student roles.	Routine for class closure

mediated example, but in Sport Education, most of the actual instructing and managing is done by students with the help and guidance of the teacher.

ENSURING A SAFE LEARNING ENVIRONMENT

A major responsibility of every physical education teacher is to provide a safe learning environment for students. Safety should be considered when planning, but it is in the implementation of a lesson that safety must be foremost. Whenever a potentially hazardous activity is being undertaken, the teacher should emphasize clearly the *rules* that have been established with regards to the hazard. These rules should be described and prompted often, and students should be held accountable for obeying them. To do less is to risk both student injury and a lawsuit. Boxes 13.2 and 13.3 discuss legal liability for teachers.

BOX 13.2   Key Issues in Protection from Liability

Traditionally, teachers have been conscious of legal liability because they work in settings where there are physical risks. What is new in liability is the need to protect oneself against *educational malpractice,* which results from inappropriate prior instruction that leads to an injury. The following principles provide a good checklist for teachers to use to ensure that they have acted responsibly.

- Be at the site—don't let students warmup unsupervised.
- Know the activity you are supervising—make sure you have a supervision plan that is specific to the activity.
- Understand the numbers—teacher to student ratios related to age, student experience, and level of risk in the activity.
- Inspect equipment before students use it.
- Review safety rules with students before each class—post them conspicuously.
- Know your students' strengths and weaknesses so you don't place them in situations unsafe for their experience and skill levels.
- Be a strong supervisor—make sure all students are aware that you are present and in control.

Source: Adapted from CAPS, 1997.

This is not to suggest that activities involving risk should not be used in the physical education program. Quite the contrary, one goal of the program should be to help students learn to take some risks and want to participate in activities. Many sport activities have the potential for injury. What needs to be emphasized are the rules regarding safety in terms of the specific activity and the space within which it is practiced and played.

Psychological safety is also important for a good learning environment. Students not only need to *behave* safely, but they also need to *feel* safe about what they are doing. This means they should feel comfortable about their participation, should be willing to participate fully. They will have psychological safety to the degree that their efforts are supported and are not met with ridicule and negative comment.

Students will also feel comfortable, and tend to behave safely too, if they have experienced an appropriate progression to shape their skills and if they have a background of related successes. If they have experienced the proper progressions, they will be challenged by current tasks and feel able and willing to perform them safely.

Finally, the teacher must be constantly alert to unsafe student behavior. Students are not mature adults. Often, in the excitement of an activity, they do not behave in fully mature ways. Teachers need to be aware of student behavior that jeopardizes the students' own safety or the safety of others. Unsafe behavior should be desisted immediately, and specific feedback should be

263

Ensuring a
Challenging and
Meaningful
Learning
Environment

BOX 13.3 Terms and Concepts Related to Legal Liability for Teachers

You cannot acquit yourself responsibly as a teacher regarding issues in liability unless you understand some basic terms and concepts that are fundamental to laws related to liability.

- *Liability* is the breach of a duty, most often through a negligent act.

- *Negligence* is conduct that falls below an established standard of care to protect others against unreasonable risk. Negligence can occur through acts of commission or omission.

- The *but for* test refers to establishing negligence as a causal factor in injury; that is, the injury would not have happened *but for* the negligent act.

- *Duty* is the responsibility to protect others from unreasonable harm and to avoid acts of omission that produce harmful situations.

- Being a *professional* means you undertake to provide services in the practice of a profession and that you are required to exercise the knowledge and skill typically demonstrated by members of that profession who are in good standing in similar communities.

Risk is typically assigned on the basis of the facts and circumstances involved in the individual situation. In school cases, the level of risk is a function of the interaction among the following issues:

1. The person exposed to the risk (the student) is considered to need the most protection.
2. The reason for taking the risk; that is, did the student undertake the activity voluntarily with knowledge of the potential consequences, or was the student doing what the teacher said to do?
3. The magnitude of the risk, which relates to the potential for physical harm.
4. The utility of the risk.
5. The necessity of the risk; that is, was there some other activity that might have produced the same instructional outcome with less risk?

Source: Adapted from Drowatzky, 1978.

given as to why the behavior is unsafe. Active supervision (discussed later in this chapter) is the best strategy to help teachers keep in close contact with what their students are doing.

ENSURING A CHALLENGING AND MEANINGFUL LEARNING ENVIRONMENT

What makes a lesson challenging and meaningful to students? There are several important answers to that question. First, we argued in Chapters 8 and 9 that curricular choices and curricular design are important for a successful physical education. We also argued that curricular choices were always contextual; that is, they were for a particular group of students in a particular setting. Curricular planning should allow for a sufficient amount of time in units for students to achieve significant progress toward meaningful unit goals, which we have argued should be defined in authentic terms.

Curricular choices should take into account the cultural relevance of activities to the students' lives and help extend students' perspectives of what activities might be relevant to their lives. This is tricky territory. For some students, especially in urban settings (Cothran & Ennis, 1998), sports such as basketball and football may be considered relevant, but activities that are newer to them, such as team handball or lacrosse, may be considered irrelevant. It takes tremendously skillful teaching, and the development of a cooperative spirit in classes, for teachers to satisfy what students perceive to be their immediate interests, yet also help them extend those interests. This certainly cannot be accomplished without a class climate in which student voices are heard and open discussion and trust define relationships.

A challenging learning environment will develop when unit goals are authentic and when teachers design tasks (or work cooperatively with students to design tasks) that continually provide challenge but also allow for success. Because not all students will have the same skills or background in any activity, provision of challenging tasks that allow for success must include a variation of task difficulty within tasks. The inclusion format, described in the next chapter, allows students to select from a range of difficulty levels with a basic task framework, thus helping to ensure that all students are challenged and all students can be successful. When students are consistently challenged by meaningful tasks and successfully accomplish them, their learning is positively affected, their interest in the activity is strengthened, and their motivation to persist in getting better is increased.

Teachers are able to design more meaningful instructional tasks when they take the time to find out what a particular activity or skill means to students at the outset of a unit. Teachers make a mistake when they assume that activities and skills mean the same things to students as they do to the teachers who design them. What do students think the purpose of volleyball is? What does it mean to them to strike a ball with their forearms? What does it mean to them to be able to hit the ball with their forearms and direct it toward a target? We know that students construct meaning from their involvement with an activity, that they build meaning on existing knowledge. We also know that, if the knowledge they start with is inaccurate or incomplete, the meanings students construct are likely to be inaccurate and incomplete (Resnick & Williams-Hall, 1998). Thus, teachers must take the time to assess what meanings and understandings students bring to a particular content and then work to ensure that their knowledge and understandings are accurate as they use instructional tasks to build on that base.

The physical education learning environment should also be intellectually challenging. There is no reason to "dumb down" PE. There are nuances to skill development and tactical play. There are aesthetic dimensions to sports and dance. There is a wealth of health-related information and meaning to exercise. Students should be encouraged to ask questions, to seek answers. They should be encouraged to explore the ideas that grow from engagement in physical activity. They should be encouraged to express themselves and their reactions to developing arm strength or playing a zone defense. Teachers who find ways to let students know that they value expression, questioning, and the interplay of ideas contribute to a climate of openness in which student voices are respected—and improve the intellectual climate of the class.

COMMUNICATING TASKS TO STUDENTS EFFECTIVELY AND EFFICIENTLY

Both managerial and instructional tasks must be communicated to students. If the tasks are informing tasks, the communication will sometimes be fairly extensive. Task communications should be evaluated by their effectiveness and efficiency. *Effective task communication* means that students will attend to and comprehend the information you present and that information will be sufficient for them to initially do the task as it has been described. *Efficient task communication* means that only as much time as is necessary will be used to ensure effective communication.

Most physical education teachers probably spend more time than is necessary in task communication. They often provide more information than students can use when they begin to practice the task. Most experts agree that students learn most effectively when they have a good general idea of what is to be accomplished and are aware of major technical features of the skill or strategy, but not the details. The details of task development are mastered through a series of refining tasks, not by including them all in the informing task.

Motor skill and strategy tasks should be introduced by establishing the importance of the task or linking it to previous work. Students should then see what the whole task looks like. They should be told what to look for in terms of the few elements being emphasized for that task practice. Teachers often have students passively watch these task presentations, but there is much to be said for having the students actively involved. Particularly in skill tasks, students can be "shadowing" you as you describe the elements being emphasized.

Before beginning practice, you should check to see if the communication was received accurately. Students can respond as a group or individuals can be chosen to show or describe an element. This check for understanding will serve not only as a signal to you that the task has been communicated effectively, but also as an accountability mechanism to keep students attending to your presentation. This check for understanding should include both the elements of the skill or strategy to be practiced and the organizational conditions for practice.

The following are suggestions for developing effective task communication skills:

1. Be sure about your information. Know your content. Understand what is most important to tell and show students—and what is less important.

2. Use language students understand. Take into account their age level and experience with the activity. Teach technical terms carefully so that, when they are used, students understand them.

3. Show enthusiasm, but speak clearly and slowly. Students don't know the content as well as you do. They need time to process new information.

4. Use metaphors and analogies to bring the new information closer to the student experience. This is what pedagogical content knowledge (PCK) is all about: being able to transform your technical knowledge of content and deliver it to students in ways they can easily assimilate and use.

5. Demonstrate (or have demonstrated) the skill under conditions as close as possible to how it will be used in the applied setting. Demonstrate the set pass near the net, goal-keeping skills at the goal. When it is important for students to see the skill from more than one view, provide the appropriate views. For example, to emphasize the appropriate shooting arm elbow position for basketball, show it both from the side view and the front view.

6. Make sure the demonstration and explanation are accurate. The demonstration doesn't have to show perfect technique, and the explanation doesn't have to be overly technical. But the critical elements shown and explained should actually be the critical elements and should be shown accurately.

7. Remember, you are not demonstrating just a skill or tactic, but also the manner in which you want students to practice it. You should end by demonstrating the practice task itself. Students should know what to do and how they will know if the task is completed successfully.

8. As much as possible, involve students during the demonstration/explanation. Passive observing is not as good as shadowing the movements.

9. If safety is a particular issue with the task, make sure the dangerous elements are emphasized and appropriate safety rules and routines are clearly understood (e.g., no high-sticking in floor hockey or rules about using parallel bars).

10. Check to see if students understand what they have seen and heard *before* you disperse them for practice.

Tasks must be communicated both to students gathered to receive the information and, on other occasions, to students dispersed in some practice format. You should usually gather students for tasks that require new information or more lengthy explanations and demonstrations. This means that these tasks will be preceded by attention and gathering routines. Most refining tasks and some extending or applying tasks can be communicated to students at their dispersed positions, without first gathering them. Communicating tasks to a dispersed class requires you to place yourself where all students can see and hear the explanation. Dispersed task communication also requires that you use a good, strong voice. If the conditions of task practice have been changed, as they often are with extending tasks, then you should check that the students understand them before they return to practice.

EMBEDDING RELEVANT TASK INFORMATION IN THE ENVIRONMENT

Learning time is a precious commodity that should be used judiciously. Much of the information communicated from teacher to student during class time could be communicated just as effectively in another manner without using class time. Mimeographed handouts are inexpensive, provide the learner with a permanent record of instructional intent, and reduce the possibility of students misunderstanding a verbal presentation. Instructional objectives, rules, diagrams of playing fields, diagrams of defensive and offensive maneuvers, and other matters can be communicated to students through handouts. Of course, it is useless to provide handouts for students if there is no mechanism in your instructional system to ensure that they use them. An informal method of ensuring this is to intermittently ask students questions that pertain directly to the handouts. If you provide a handout listing instructional objectives at the end of Monday's class, at the start of the next class, you might ask several students what the criteria for certain objectives are. If you hand out a diagram of a badminton court, you can ask a student to show the back boundary line for the doubles serve. Students' understanding of the material should be formally assessed only if the handout is of sufficient importance to warrant taking time for this. Thus, you might administer a short rules test before beginning actual game competition in a new activity. If students have a handout on the rules and if they must pass a short quiz in order to gain access to the game, then chances are they will learn the material. Thus, the game can proceed at a much higher level because the situations in which rules will need to be clarified will be minimal.

Posters using cue words to describe the critical elements of the skills that are being practiced can be placed around a gym so that students can look at them when they need them. Pictures of players with the critical elements emphasized can provide another source of information. Diagrams of strategic movements can also be used. Thus, when students need to have this information, they can get it without taking the time of the whole class. For example, if one group is having problems practicing a particular skill, it could be sent briefly to a poster and picture to refresh members about which elements to emphasize and see what those elements look like in action.

GUIDED PRACTICE

When a new task has been introduced (informing task) or when the conditions for task practice have been changed substantially (extending task), a period of guided practice should occur after the new task has been communicated. *Guided practice* is a period of group practice that functions to (a) correct major errors in performance, (b) reteach if necessary, and (c) provide sufficient practice so students can participate in independent practice successfully (Rosenshine & Stevens, 1986). In teacher-mediated instruction, guided practice is most effectively accomplished through teacher-led, whole-group practice. In student-mediated instructional formats, guided practice occurs similarly, except that students lead the practice.

Guided practice usually occurs in a whole-group formation with the teacher in a position to see and be seen by the entire class. As students practice the task, the teacher provides prompts and cues to emphasize the major technical features of the task and the way the task is to be practiced. The organizational format allows the teacher to check to see if major errors are being made. If so, time is taken to reteach the skill or strategy, emphasizing the elements related to the errors. Checks for student understanding are frequent, both by visually monitoring performance and by asking questions.

Teacher feedback during guided practice typically focuses on the technical aspects of performance, particularly the critical performance elements emphasized during the task communication. Feedback relative to these critical elements should be specific, and you should strive to achieve a balance between correcting errors and reinforcing appropriate performance (see Box 13.4 for an explanation of various forms of feedback and Box 13.5 for correctives related to student errors). You should also ensure that the conditions for student practice are being followed, that is, student practice is congruent with the task description. For example, if the practice task requires a "feeder," a player delivering thrown or passed sets to practice spiking, the type of feed should be monitored also, with supportive or corrective feedback provided for students feeding correctly and incorrectly.

Response rates during guided practice should be as high as possible, and there should be enough practice trials for you to feel confident that students can be successful when shifted to independent practice. If initial student responses during guided practice result in too many errors, then you should either reteach, emphasizing the elements being performed incorrectly, or shift practice to an easier task that will act as a building block for the current task. Once you are sure that tasks can be performed successfully as intended, then students can be shifted to independent practice.

INDEPENDENT PRACTICE

The purpose of *independent practice* is for students to integrate the new task into previously learned material and to practice the task so that it becomes automatic. Students need sufficient practice so they can use the skills confidently and quickly in conditions under which the skill or strategy will eventually be used. Time is a precious commodity in physical education, and many teachers feel that they have to cover a large number of activities. Subsequently,

BOX 13.4 Subject-Matter Feedback: Types and Examples

- *General positive feedback:* Purpose is to support student effort and build a positive learning climate.

Nice shot.	Good effort.	That's the right idea, Mary.
Tough defense, Jim.	A-1, Roberto.	Tremendous pass, Bob.
That's better, Jill.	Very nice.	Squad 1 did really well.

- *Nonverbal positive feedback:* Same purpose as above. Can accompany verbal statements.

Clapping hands	Thumbs-up signal	Pat on the back
The "OK" sign	Scruffing hair	Raised, clenched fist

- *Positive specific feedback:* Purpose is to provide specific information about what was done appropriately.

  Good feed, Bill, it was exactly the right speed and height. That was nice. Your circle was different from anybody's. Beautiful! You really had your knees tucked that time. Everybody in this circle made the switch to the step-hop exactly on beat. Much better. Your front arm was straight throughout the backswing. Well done, squad 2. Your timing on the cuts was good.

- *Corrective feedback:* Purpose is to correct errors with specific information.

  Denise, you need to keep your position longer before you move. Start from the legs, Joe. You're just shooting with your arms. OK, but you did that last time. Try to find a different way now. Squad 3 needs to cover the wings of the zone better. Anticipate! Jane, you had an open alley and should have tried a passing shot.

- *Specific feedback with value content:* Purpose is not only to provide information, but also to connect performance with outcome.

  Way to help on defense, Pat. When you cover like that, we can take some chances.
  That's better. When your head is up, you can see your teammates.
  Good effort, Jane. When you work hard like that, you will improve very quickly.
  Thanks, Wanda. When you provide that kind of help, Jesse's going to learn a lot.

teachers often do not allow enough time for students to practice tasks to the point where they can do them successfully and automatically. The result is that students have covered many skills, strategies, and activities, but can't do any of them well enough to enjoy the context they are used in. Students need to have sufficient command of skills and strategies to utilize them effectively in game settings. Students need to know dance steps and transitions well enough to do the dances to music without prompts. They also need to be strong and fit enough to perform sustained strength or aerobic activities.

BOX 13.5 **Feedback Related to Student Responses**

Although it seems logical to suggest that teacher feedback should be directed at the main elements of tasks being practiced, it doesn't always happen that way. Occasionally, teachers prompt a student to focus on one element of performance, the student responds successfully, and the teacher corrects another error rather than reacting positively to the successfully performed element. Some have referred to this as the "correction complex" in teaching physical education. Here are some types of student responses and hints for relating your feedback more appropriately:

1. Student responses that are correct, quick, and firm: Support positively with brief reactions that do not disturb the momentum of practice.
2. Student responses that are correct, but hesitant: Support positively with brief reactions, but add some specific information related to technical elements.
3. Student responses that are "careless" errors: Briefly correct the error and prompt better concentration or effort.
4. Student responses that show lack of knowledge or skill: Give corrective feedback targeted to specific elements and support for continued effort. Take time to reteach or reassign to component tasks if necessary.

Source: Adapted from Rosenshine & Stevens, 1986.

Independent practice should provide the successful repetitions necessary to allow students to use the skill or tactic confidently and appropriately in an applied setting. Guided practice is used to correct major errors and ensure that students can profit from extended practice; independent practice is used to achieve high rates of successful repetitions of the task. The teacher role (teacher or student) during independent practice is very different than during guided practice. Typically, students are dispersed for independent practice, using all the space and equipment available. The major instructional function during independent practice is *active supervision*. The major purposes of active supervision are to (a) keep students on the assigned task and (b) provide supportive and corrective feedback where necessary. The following are the key features and elements of active supervision, whether mediated by teachers or students:

1. Keep all students within sight. Moving around the perimeter of a space is usually better than moving through a space, especially at the outset when you are trying to establish a strong on-task focus.
2. Scan frequently. Don't get caught up for too long with any student or group. Briefly scan the entire class frequently.
3. Don't get predictable. Moving down a line of tennis courts or clockwise around a gymnasium gets predictable. Some students, when they can predict you are far away, will be more likely to go off task.

4. Use your voice across space. It is important that students know that you are aware of their behavior even though you are not near them. Quick prompts and feedback across space help to accomplish this goal. Try to balance the supportive and corrective comments; that is, don't respond only to the off-task students all the time.

5. Be aware of unsafe or disruptive behavior and stop it immediately.

6. Try to distribute your attention equitably. Make sure that time and interactions are not predictable on the basis of gender, race, or skill level.

7. Use opportunities to build expectations for a successful learning-oriented climate.

MODIFIED GAMES AS LEARNING TASKS

It is possible to utilize small-sided, modified games as learning tasks, that is, to use games rather than skill or tactics drills to provide independent practice for students to improve. Students enjoy games, and their motivation to participate is usually higher in games than in drills. We need to emphasize that, to be useful as learning tasks, games must be sufficiently small sided to allow for many response opportunities and sufficiently modified that those repetitions can largely be successful. An example of using a progression of small-sided games as learning tasks is provided by Bell and Darnell (1994) in their Sport Education soccer season in elementary school physical education.

Teams (usually three for a class of 24 to 27) are introduced to the skills of dribbling, shielding, shooting, and tackling by their coaches with the help of the teacher. They are also introduced to the tactical concepts of defensive space (stay between your person and the goal) and shooting angles (the goal becomes smaller or larger, depending on the shooting angle). The first competition of the season is a one-versus-one competition played much like half-court basketball. A scrimmage session is held to ensure that students understand the rules and procedures for the game. Play is initiated with a dribble from the back line. As many as eight games are played simultaneously in an elementary school gymnasium. The games all start and stop at the same signals and are typically of short duration (e.g., 3 minutes). Transitions happen quickly so that the next group of eight games can begin quickly. In a 40-minute period, as many as six or seven groups of eight games can be completed. A round-robin tournament is utilized with points for games won accumulating for each of the three class teams.

The one-versus-one competition is followed by a two-versus-two competition in which the skills of passing and trapping are added and the tactical concepts of tandem defending and offensive spacing are introduced. Again, a scrimmage session is used to ensure that students understand the game and can use the skills and tactics (much like a guided practice session). The round-robin proceeds as in the first competition, with game length extended to 6 minutes (two 3-minute periods to allow for changing defensive position in the tandem).

The next competition is three versus three, and throw-ins, corner kicks, and goal kicks are added. Goalie play is also introduced. Most elementary school gyms can accommodate three "pitches" of sufficient size for the three-versus-three competition. Students experiment with various defensive and offensive combinations, such as two forwards and a defender; one goalie, one defender, and one forward; or two forwards and a defender-goalie.

The season ends with a five-versus-five minitournament in which each team competes as a whole. The entire gym space is used, and substitution rules ensure that all players get equal playing time and equal opportunity to play different positions. The amount of time in team practice is kept to a minimum, typically in the first 10 minutes of class, when students enter the gym. Because all players also have to referee and keep score, they tend to learn the rules early and well.

What is important is that you see this approach in the same way you would view a progression of skill tasks that lead up to a five-versus-five soccer game. The series of progressively more complex games provides the independent practice necessary for students to learn the new skills and tactics. Rather than practice each new skill separately in a drill, this approach makes the game a task and gradually adds to the skill and tactical base as the game grows slightly more complex.

TEACHING WHILE APPLYING TASKS

Many teachers plan to have a culminating applying task for each lesson. Units are often planned so that they build to a series of applying tasks toward the end of the unit. Applying tasks can be games, dances, gymnastic performances, and the like. With the approach to planning advocated in this text, the entire unit should be devoted to getting students ready to participate successfully in the applied contexts for which the skills are relevant.

There is evidence, however, that many teachers design applying tasks, such as games, and then refrain from any teaching while the students are practicing the task (Metzler, 1979; Ormond, 1988). To consider what teaching functions might be accomplished during applying tasks, first distinguish between the concepts of scrimmage and game. A *scrimmage* is a set of conditions that are very like those of an applied context, such as a game, but in which the teacher stops and starts action to engage in brief teaching episodes and also engages in interactive teaching. A *game* is an applied context in which the stops and starts are determined by the nature of the activity rather than the teacher's judgments. In this general sense, the concepts of scrimmage and game are applicable to activities such as gymnastics and dance. That is, a scrimmage for a folk dance lesson would be to perform the dance to the musical accompaniment, but with brief stops and starts for the teacher to provide instruction; the game would be the folk dance performed in its entirety without breaks.

What we described as a scrimmage occurs infrequently in physical education. Most physical education classes move from practice tasks into game conditions without the intervening benefit of scrimmage situations. Curiously, the evidence for interschool sport teams is nearly opposite (Ormond, 1988; Rate, 1980). In those settings, coaches use scrimmage very frequently.

In both physical education and coaching settings, frequent prompting may be the best teaching function during scrimmages and games (Ormond, 1988). A *prompt* is a teacher intervention that guides performance in one direction rather than another. Prompts are often brief, typically single cue words or phrases. Think, for example, of the prompts used in teaching a folk dance. Handclapping or a drumbeat can be used to accentuate the underlying beat that cues the various steps in a dance. Teachers also often use verbal prompts to cue the steps, especially during initial practice. Transitions from step to step are often highlighted verbally. Although these prompts are gradually faded as students get more proficient and come under the control of the musical prompts, they do not have to be eliminated completely.

Game play, culminating activities, gymnastics routines, and dances are meant to be fun and exciting. Students typically look forward to them, often asking when they enter the gymnasium, "Are we going to play a game today?" There is no reason, however, for teachers to abandon their instructional role during these applying activities. Quite the contrary, these are the activities in which performance needs to be polished and elements put together so that the entire performance is successful, be it a game or a dance. Teachers can prompt behavior and support successful performance without interfering in the activity itself. Likewise, scrimmage tasks can be arranged when game conditions are present, but frequent yet brief teaching episodes can be interspersed to emphasize key points and correct key errors.

PREREQUISITES FOR EFFECTIVE STUDENT-MEDIATED INSTRUCTION

Earlier in this chapter, we distinguished between teacher-mediated instruction and student-mediated instruction (peer tutoring, reciprocal teaching, small-group work, teams, cooperative learning). Formats that rely on student-mediated instruction are becoming increasingly popular with teachers, and for good reason. Advocates of student-mediated instruction claim that it is effective because it results in the following (Cohen, 1994b):

- More, active engaged, task-oriented behavior than individual work
- More feedback to struggling students
- More opportunities for purposeful practice for students of all skill levels

- Better prosocial behavior development among students
- Strong within-group forces that help students avoid drifting off task
- Better motivation and allegiance to the class because of increased peer interactions
- Equal-status interaction among students

If all these were present, both content and social outcomes would be positively affected.

Effective use of the student-mediated instructional formats requires that teachers prepare students to be able to take part in them effectively. This is especially true if the students' previous school experiences have been primarily in teacher-mediated, whole-group instructional formats. The younger the students, or the less experience they have had working in pairs or groups, the more important is an effective training program as prerequisite for participation in student-mediated instruction.

The goals of a training program are twofold: (a) to develop the specific skills students will need to participate effectively in student-mediated instruction and (b) to establish special behavioral norms for working in pairs and groups. The teacher should make it clear to students why student-mediated instruction is important and what they might expect to gain from participating in it. The specific skills needed to participate typically include the following (Cohen, 1994a; Houston-Wilson, Lieberman, Horton, & Kasser, 1997):

- Student capacity to be aware of different ability and interest levels of their peers
- Communication techniques such as listening skills and providing clear explanations
- Teaching skills such as prompting, showing, observing performance, and giving feedback
- Reinforcement techniques (see Boxes 13.4 and 13.5)
- Ability to see critical performance elements and common errors in the skills practiced

The behaviors necessary for effective participation in student-mediated instruction group around three important norms: (a) Everyone should contribute. (b) No one should dominate. (c) All should be sensitive to student status within the group. The contribution and dominance-avoidance norms are typically achieved by helping students be willing to express their ideas, listen to others so all have a chance, ask others for their ideas, and discuss and give reasons for their ideas. It is also helpful if some means for conflict resolution is taught to students as the appropriate strategy for resolving the differences and disputes that inevitably arise in these instructional formats. Students must recognize all the status issues that can marginalize them in physical education—gender, skillfulness, race, body type, height and weight, and the like. The norm of "all getting a fair chance" cannot be achieved without students being fully aware that these status issues often work to the detriment of some of them.

These behavioral norms are identical to those teachers establish as they move from compliance to cooperation to community (see Box 4.1), regardless of what instructional format is utilized.

Cohen (1994a) says the skills and behavioral norms needed to participate effectively in student-mediated instruction cannot be learned simply through reading about them or listening to someone explain them. She suggests that students best learn these skills and norms through participating in skill builders—games and practice activities designed to allow students to learn to work together.

ACCOUNTABILITY AND MONITORING STUDENT PERFORMANCE

In Chapter 3, we showed that instructional task systems are driven by formal and informal accountability and that, in the absence of accountability, the instructional task system can be suspended. What happens in the total absence of accountability for performance in the instructional task system depends on two things: (a) the focus of the managerial system in which students might have to look like they are making an effort and (b) the interests and motivations that the students have for the subject being taught.

Accountability refers to all the practices teachers use to establish and maintain student responsibility for task involvement and outcomes. The clearest form of accountability is the grade-exchange opportunity—what we typically refer to as *testing* or *assessment*. Grade exchanges occur infrequently in most physical education classes, often only at the end of a unit. Effective teachers utilize many different kinds of accountability mechanisms to keep students strongly on task and motivate them to improve their performance. Among these accountability mechanisms are the following:

- Public challenges with result reporting, such as "Shoot from the six spots with your partner rebounding" and then "How many made 3? 4? 5? 6?"

- Recording scores, such as keeping records of time on a fitness circuit and recording daily results on a class poster

- Carefully supervising practice and noting successes publicly, such as monitoring the practice of a volleyball bump-and-set drill and, at the end, noting the several practice groups that did particularly well

- Carefully supervising practice and providing specific feedback and general support, such as monitoring the practice of a serve-and-return tennis practice task and providing support for students working hard and technical feedback to students making errors in critical elements of the skills

- Building accountability into the practice task, such as designing a dribble, pass, trap, and tackle soccer task into a minigame by providing students a way to keep score

Teachers need to build accountability into their task progressions if they expect students to stay on task and be motivated to improve their performances. Accountability should not be thought of as an extra but, instead, should be integrated with the instructional task itself. Eventually, if instructional tasks are designed so that practice conditions are aligned with meaningful terminal goals, students will become more and more motivated by performing the task itself—which is typically referred to as *intrinsic motivation*.

Accountability and monitoring can also be embedded in curriculum models when they are designed as authentic experiences. For example, in Sport Education, student scorekeepers provide records of performance for every competition. Team statisticians have the task of compiling and updating these records and posting them in the gymnasium. Because teams are typically working to accumulate points toward a championship (by practicing well, playing fairly, and competing successfully), the statistics and point totals have a meaning that is embedded in the curriculum model. Students mediate the monitoring, with the teacher ensuring that student performance in scorekeeping and compiling statistics is done well. When accountability is embedded clearly in the unit design, the teacher has to do less with daily efforts at informal accountability.

Active supervision of student practice is the most widely used form of monitoring and accountability by physical education teachers. Active supervision is an important teaching skill, but if it is also the major form of accountability, then, inevitably, instructional task systems will be weakened. The need for active supervision, as a monitoring and accountability mechanism, is *inversely* related to the strength of a content-embedded or formal accountability system; that is, the stronger the overall accountability system, the less need there is for teachers to use their active supervision for accountability purposes. This is a tremendously important difference. Teachers who use their active supervision to provide feedback and encourage students find their teaching to be more enjoyable and their relationships with students more pleasant. Teachers who have to use their active supervision primarily to keep students on task are acting more like police than teachers. Because teachers spend a large portion of class time actively supervising practice, the policing function gets terribly tiring. This suggests that, in planning units and lessons, teachers should take great pains to build monitoring and accountability into the activity itself so that students have incentives to practice purposefully and teachers have built-in means for monitoring progress. Then they can attend to the more important interactive functions of supporting and helping students.

THE FUNCTIONS OF AN EFFECTIVE CLOSURE

Closure refers to the end-of-class time when teachers bring together the parts of a lesson to make it whole for students, to make sure students understood the important elements learned in the lesson, to reestablish the importance of the elements, and to assess and validate students' feelings relative to the lesson.

Many teachers do not plan for or implement closure because they feel it is not important, don't want to waste time with it, or simply run out of time before they get to it. We believe closure is an important ingredient of a lesson and that it should be planned for and implemented carefully.

An effective closure can accomplish many things. Although not all of them should be attempted for every class closure, the following represent some goals and strategies for effective closures (Jensen, 1988; Marks, 1988):

1. *Closure means completion.* Students should be made aware of what was accomplished in the lesson. This can often be done by asking a few pertinent questions, using the answers both to check students' understanding and to underscore their important accomplishments.

2. *Closure is an opportunity for recognition.* How did the class as a whole do? What students did well? What students provided help to others?

3. *Closure is an opportunity to check students' feelings.* Which activity was best liked? How do students feel about their progress? Use this opportunity to make sure that students feel good about their real accomplishments.

4. *Closure can be a review.* What critical elements were learned today? Have a student demonstrate how the cartwheel is done correctly. Students can respond verbally, but they can also *do* the task to show their understanding.

5. *Closure can provide a transition from intense activity to locker room or classroom behavior.* Lessons often culminate with an applying task, which is often very active and intense. Students then have to go to a locker room to change or return to their class. In either case, closure provides a transition time for students to "cool down" physically and psychologically.

MAINTAINING THE PACE OF A LESSON

Every lesson has a pace—the forward momentum of the various managerial, transitional, and instructional tasks, as well as the smoothness of those events. The pace can be very slow to very fast. Smoothness can range from being very jerky to very even. A strong, smooth pace is important to effective teaching (Kounin, 1970).

Clearly, effective planning is an aid to creating and maintaining smoothness and momentum. Knowing where you are headed and how much time each lesson element should take will increase your chances for effective pacing. A briskly paced, smooth lesson conveys the message to students that this is an orderly, important learning environment. Regardless, however, of how well lessons are planned, it is in their implementation that pace is established and maintained. Especially important to pace is organization and transitions.

Managerial routines (see Chapter 4) are important to briskly paced lessons because they get things done quickly with as little fuss as possible. Transitions between instructional and practice elements of the lesson should be made quickly. Teachers should expect students to hustle during transitions, and non-compliant students should be held accountable. Equipment changes should be accomplished without producing down time, which means they have to be planned for so that equipment will be ready and easily accessible to students.

Practice tasks should be such that students remain active. Waiting for turns to practice and doing activities that produce down time for students means that you risk losing lesson momentum. More and less intense practice activities can be sequenced so that students can continue to practice without having fatigue produce slowdowns that destroy the lesson's pace.

The biggest enemy of lesson pace is student waiting. In Chapter 2, we showed that waiting time typically accounts for the single largest chunk of time in physical education, sometimes accounting for half the lesson time. However, research on effective physical education teachers has also shown that waiting time can be less than 7 percent of lesson time (Eldar, Siedentop, & Jones, 1989). Lessons with high amounts of waiting time cannot possibly have the brisk pace required for teacher effectiveness. Teachers need to communicate expectations that students hustle, support those who do, admonish students who don't, and generally convey a sense of energy to the students.

SUMMARY

1. Purposeful student practice is the key to effective teaching, which suggests that observation of students is the best way to evaluate teaching.

2. Lessons should be viewed as progressions of tasks that lead to meaningful outcomes.

3. Instructional formats can be categorized as teacher mediated or student mediated.

4. Each task in a lesson requires different instructional functions.

5. Teachers need to ensure a physically and psychologically safe learning environment.

6. Teachers need to ensure a challenging and meaningful learning environment with meaningful goals and challenging tasks that allow for student success.

7. Effective task communication requires knowledge, enthusiasm, use of metaphors, and appropriate and accurate demonstrations that involve students.

8. Task information can be embedded in the environment through handouts, task posters, task cards, videos, and the like.

9. The purpose of guided practice is the ensure that students understand and can perform a task sufficiently well to benefit from independent practice.

10. The purpose of independent practice is to engage in a sufficient number of successful repetitions to be able to use the skill appropriately in an applied context.

11. A series of small-sided, modified games can be used as a learning progression.

12. Teachers should approach applying tasks as if they were scrimmages, with appropriate feedback and prompts to ensure progress.

13. Students need to be prepared to take part effectively in student-mediated formats, which includes the particular skills (observing, feedback, etc.) and the appropriate behavioral norms for cooperation.

14. Teachers need to monitor student performance and find a variety of ways to hold students accountable for achieving task objectives.

15. Closure is an end-of-class task in which teachers complete the lesson, recognize student performance, check student feelings, review critical learning, and change from a more to less active mode.

16. Effective lessons have a brisk pace that is not slowed down but maintains forward momentum, especially during transition and management tasks.

CHAPTER 14

Instructional Formats

Teaching functions are usually performed within an instructional framework—a delivery system for getting content to the learner. This instructional framework is called a teaching strategy. Many factors influence the choice of a teaching strategy, including the content itself, the characteristics of the learner, and the objectives and preferences of the teacher.

—JUDY RINK (1985)

OVERALL CHAPTER OUTCOME

To design instruction using a variety of instructional formats

CHAPTER OBJECTIVES

- To describe Mosston's spectrum of teaching styles
- To match various formats to context issues
- To differentiate between instructional format and teaching style
- To distinguish between teacher-mediated and student-mediated instructional formats
- To describe and analyze active teaching
- To explain and characterize task formats
- To delineate and examine teaching through questions
- To define and consider peer and reciprocal teaching
- To describe and analyze small-group teaching and cooperative learning
- To explain and examine self-instructional formats

Various approaches for teaching physical education continue to be discussed, promoted, debated, and analyzed. These approaches to teaching were first referred to as "teaching styles" by Muska Mosston (1966) when he introduced the spectrum of teaching styles. This work suggests that teaching is based on a series of decisions teachers make about their teaching behavior and learners are invited to make about their learning behavior. As teachers and learners interact in the teaching/learning process, behavior patterns emerge; these define the different teaching styles that form a spectrum. According to Mosston (1966) and Mosston and Ashworth (1994), a teacher's choice of instructional format then is determined by the series of decisions made, who makes them, how they are made, and for what purpose. These decisions are organized into three sets: decisions about intent that are made prior to face-to-face interaction (preimpact), decisions about action that are made during a lesson (impact), and decisions about evaluation that will inform subsequent lessons (postimpact). Depending upon who makes these decisions, the spectrum is divided into two clusters of what we refer to as instructional formats: those that seek replication of knowledge and those that seek discovery or creativity.

BOX 14.1   Style and Format: What's the Difference?

It is not uncommon for laypersons to confuse teaching style with instructional format. As used in this text, *instructional format* refers to the different ways teachers organize for the delivery of instruction and, particularly, how the student role changes as a result of the changing format. We describe several formats in this chapter.

Teaching style refers to the instructional and managerial climate for learning; it is often most easily seen through the teacher's interactions. The climate for teaching can range from clearly negative to clearly positive, with a neutral climate in the middle. Teachers can be "upbeat" or "laid-back." They can be frequent interactors or infrequent interactors. They can be very challenging or very supportive, or even both at the same time. Students experience the teacher's style through the interactions the teacher has with the class as a whole, with groups, and with individuals. The amalgam of these many interactional features produces each teacher's distinctive style. Terms such as *warm, caring, businesslike, demanding,* and *aloof* are used to describe teaching styles.

Format and style are basically unrelated phenomena. It is easy to imagine a quietly supportive and laid-back teacher succeeding in active teaching as well as in task or problem-solving formats. It is just as easy to imagine an upbeat, energetic teacher succeeding with different formats.

What is your style? How would you describe yourself as a teacher? Do you think that makes you better suited to one format rather than another?

There has been a tendency to confuse "teaching style" with "instructional format" (see Box 14.1). As used here, *instructional format* refers to the way a teacher organizes and delivers instruction and provides practice for students. *Teaching style* refers to the managerial and instructional climate of the learning environment, especially as reflected in the interaction patterns of the teacher with the students.

MATCHING INSTRUCTIONAL FORMAT TO CONTEXT

Education is most effective when teachers adapt instructional formats to the contexts within which they teach. Instructional formats should reflect sensitivity to (a) personal skills and preferences of teachers, (b) characteristics of the learners being taught, (c) the nature of the content being taught, and (d) the context within which teaching takes place. Some teachers feel more comfortable with some formats than others. Personal preference is a legitimate factor in the teacher's choice of which format to adopt, especially when that preference derives from a professional belief in the validity of a format. Teachers no doubt tend to perform better when they work from a format that they believe to be effective, one with which they are comfortable. Nothing is worse for teachers than to feel they are being forced to adopt an instructional format they do not believe in and cannot employ adequately. Teachers' beliefs about instructional formats can change, and teachers can learn to utilize new formats—often easily when they become convinced that a different format will better help them achieve their goals. These changes, however, should be the result of professional development and reflection, not administrative imposition.

The choice of instructional format should be sensitive to the characteristics of the learners. Clearly, when learners have had substantial experience in an activity, you will approach the teaching of that activity differently than if the class were all beginners. Well-behaved students give teachers more options for choice of format than do students who require more attention to managerial and behavioral issues. Children with disabilities may require a direct format or warrant consideration of a peer teaching (Chapter 7) or cooperative learning format. Students for whom English is a second language may benefit from a technique called total physical response (Asher, 1977), in which all instruction is through physical demonstration followed by a student physical response, or mirroring. Appropriate terminology may be added to the demonstration so that learners pick up the vocabulary along with the physical skill.

Content is also a factor. Gymnastics, climbing, soccer, and folk dance might lend themselves to different instructional formats. Teaching basic skills in any activity is a different issue than teaching higher-level strategies to learners who already have mastered the basic skills. For example, fitness problem solving is best preceded by acquisition of basic knowledge about fitness and basic techniques for measuring it. Thus, a teacher might change from a whole-class, active teaching instructional format for basic knowledge and skills to a group-oriented problem-solving format for higher-order knowledge and skills, all within the same fitness unit.

The context for teaching is also important to the choice of format, particularly the facilities. If the facility for teaching tennis consists of six courts, all in one row, then the problems of gathering and dispersing along that row of courts might compel a teacher to use a task or individualized format rather than an active teaching format. Safety issues in a beginning archery class taught outdoors might suggest active teaching with visible teacher control at the outset. If one teaching format is better than another, however, it is better only within a particular context, and then only because it matches the needs of that context in a particularly effective way.

The effectiveness of any instructional format must be judged in terms of student process and outcomes. Do students achieve the goals of the unit? Are there large amounts of academic learning time in the lessons? Do students grow in their appreciation of the activity and their desire to participate? Answers to these questions should determine whether the teaching format meets the needs of the context in which it is used.

INSTRUCTIONAL FORMATS

As we indicated in Chapter 12, how tasks are mediated in the teaching/ learning process defines the two categories of instructional formats: teacher mediated and student mediated. There is no hierarchy of formats; each is appropriate for a given context, the outcome and objectives of a lesson, what you want learners to achieve, the content to be introduced, the expectations you hold for learner behavior and growth, and your expertise. These issues will guide your selection of format within either the teacher- or student-mediated format.

Teacher-Mediated Instructional Formats

Teachers in an instructional setting generally work with groups of learners. Learning should occur for each member of the group. When designing group instruction, the teacher must decide how to meet the needs of all individuals to facilitate learning: design similar experiences for all learners, provide all learners with appropriate explanations and demonstrations when they need them, effectively intervene with each learner when needed, and optimize opportunities to respond to all learners.

Active Teaching. The dominant format for effective teaching in U.S. schools, especially for children and beginners at any level, is active teaching. In *active teaching,* teachers provide direct instruction, either to a whole class or small groups, followed by guided practice in which major errors are corrected, followed by independent practice in which student work is actively supervised, all within a supportive climate in which high, realistic expectations are set for student work and students are held accountable for performance. In active teaching, content is communicated by the teacher, rather than through curricular materials. The pacing of the lesson is brisk and teacher controlled. Students get many learning opportunities and experience high success rates. Active teachers are skilled managers, relying on managerial routines to optimize time for learning and reduce opportunities for off-task and disruptive behavior. The review of research on teaching effectiveness in Chapter 2 presented more complete descriptions of active teaching.

Active teaching is also referred to as *direct instruction* (Rosenshine, 1979), *interactive teaching* (Rink, 1985), and *explicit instruction* (Rosenshine & Stevens, 1986). Active teaching also provides the main components for instructional theory into practice, popularly known as the Hunter model (Housner, 1990).

Active teaching has been shown to be differentially more effective than other instructional formats for well-structured subjects, such as reading, mathematics, and physical education. Part of the success of active teaching can be attributed to the organizational and supervision aspects of the format that allow teachers to manage student engagement.

In active teaching, the teacher chooses the content and arranges the progressions, which are typically sequenced in small steps. Feedback and evaluation are done by the teacher, with active supervision as the necessary intermediate function.

> **BOX 14.2   Station Teaching in a Fifth Grade Climbing Unit**
>
> Students are initially introduced to and have the opportunity to practice a set of climbing-related activities. Following this introduction and practice, these activities become stand-alone stations set up around the teaching stations. Each day throughout the 4-week climbing unit, students rotate among the six stations.
>
> cargo net
> zip line
> climbing wall
> horizontal wall
> soft or mohawk walk
> electric fence
>
> Task cards pictorially demonstrate each task and prompt spotting and safety. At the close of each lesson, a debriefing is conducted focused on various aspects of student participation: group support, spotting, fear, conflict resolution, leadership, or enjoyment.

Task Teaching.   Teachers often find it useful to have students practicing more than one task at the same time. This is typically accomplished through a task-teaching format. *Task teaching* refers to organizing the learning environment so that different students can engage in different learning tasks at the same time. Task teaching has also been referred to as *station teaching* (Mohnsen, 1995; Rink, 1998), although we would argue that station teaching is a subcategory of task teaching because there are ways of doing task teaching without stations. The availability of a climbing wall to accommodate an entire class is an example of task teaching that might prompt a teacher to design a set of related tasks for students to rotate among (see the example in Box 14.2).

Task teaching is not confined to situations in which limited equipment is the dominant contextual factor. Consider the possibilities for teaching a strength development or a golf unit. In strength development, several major muscle groups must be worked on regularly. In golf, several different strokes fundamental to the game must be practiced regularly. Both of these could be accomplished through an active teaching format with the teacher pacing students through the series of strength and skill tasks, all students doing the same task at the same time. Both could also be accomplished through a format in which various strength and stroke task stations are spread throughout the learning space and students rotate among the task stations during the lesson.

In task teaching, it is usually inefficient for a teacher to communicate the content of each task to students. Teachers sometimes try to describe and demonstrate each task at the outset of a lesson, but this strategy, to be effective, requires that tasks be simple and easily remembered. Introducing new tasks is difficult in a task format. Sometimes teachers use active teaching to introduce tasks in the early lessons of a unit and use task teaching to practice

---

SPRINT STARTS

Split your foursome into two groups of two. One group has a timer and starter/recorder, and the other group has two runners. Time only the two full effort tasks. Groups switch roles after running group has finished each task. This will give you time to rest before the next running task.

Task 1. 3 starts plus 15 yards at a shuffle
Task 2. 3 starts plus 30 yards at a stride
Task 3. 3 starts plus 60 yards at full effort
Task 4. 3 starts plus 15 yards at full effort

FIGURE 14.1 *Task card for sprint starts*

these tasks as the unit progresses. Students then know the tasks and can practice them without lengthy teacher explanations and demonstrations.

Most teachers who use task formats design task cards for students or task posters for each station. These communicate the task through brief, simple descriptions. Task posters can also use pictures or drawings. The student reads the task description, perhaps looks at the picture of correct technique, and begins to practice the task. This approach lends itself to either simple tasks or ones with which students are familiar. Figure 14.1 shows a sample task card.

One advantage of the task format is the possibility of accommodating different skill levels at one station. A major problem in teaching large groups of students is that they often have marked differences in ability and experience with the activity. In active teaching, the teacher typically communicates one task and students respond. Occasionally, very effective teachers find ways to communicate variations in the task that accommodate different skill levels. For example, students could be given the option of serving from the end line or center line in volleyball, depending upon their skill level. Stations, however, are perhaps a more effective way of providing for varying skill levels.

Designing tasks that have multiple levels of performance and allow students choices in selecting their entry levels characterizes a special case of task teaching called *inclusion*. Within a given task, there might be options on skill progressions, physical performance criteria, choice of various implements, size of targets, or number of required repetitions, and students would select how and where to begin the task, depending upon their skill level. In juggling, for example, stations might be set up sequentially, moving students from juggling one implement to cascade juggling with three implements. Students would be directed to move up or down the task sequence using scarves, balls, hoops, or clubs, as their skills allow. Tasks could be communicated through task cards or self-instructional materials.

Another advantage of task formats is that teachers can set up their physical space ahead of time in ways that help learners master content. In badminton, for example, a teacher might want specialized learning aids to help students acquire specific skills. In an active teaching format, these aids would have to be set up and taken down as the tasks changed throughout the lesson. With a task format, they can be set up for the entire lesson, with students rotating through the task stations. One station might be for the short and long serve, with a string stretched above the net to provide feedback for the short serve and target areas on the floor. Another station might have similar aids to the clear and drop shots. These stations could be used for individual student practice or set up to allow team practice in three-versus-three game conditions. A final station might be a computer with an interactive badminton CD to provide students practice at shot selection based on the tactical problem posed.

Task progressions between stations are more difficult and represent a general weakness of this format. The problem is that, with six stations and five students per station, all stations have to be used at the outset, with students rotating throughout the lesson. If stations 1 through 6 represent a progression, then some students will be starting at the last part of the progression and moving to the early part. Thus, the task format is typically used for tasks that do not represent progressions.

Most teachers who use task formats signal changes in stations and have student groups rotating on signal. It is possible, however, to have students rotate after having met some particular performance criterion, whether it be volume of practice (25 trials) or quality of practice (five consecutive hits above the line). The problem with criterion-based rotation is that several stations tend to get crowded, with resulting problems of equipment sharing and active involvement.

To use task formats well, students need to have good self-control skills. Teachers can actively supervise task environments just as they would independent practice of any kind. They can provide more feedback and teaching, however, if students are generally well behaved and on task. Task formats work best when tasks are clearly described (a situation for performance, the performance itself, and qualitative or quantitative indicators of success or completion) and when there is a strong accountability system other than teacher supervision, such as accumulating points toward individual awards or competition among the rotating groups based on collective scoring.

Teaching Through Questions. *Teaching through questions* refers to an instructional format in which tasks are communicated to students through questions that pose problems that guide student activity toward particular goals or questions that pose problems to be solved. In physical education, this approach has been widely used in teaching young children, especially when the focus has been on movement and movement concepts. Teaching through questions when teaching movement to children is really a variation of active teaching because a whole-group format is typically used and teachers tend to control the pacing of the lesson by presenting a sequence of tasks through questions. The questions most often represent refining and extending tasks (Chapter 11), but ones that allow students to explore options rather than reproduce a skill as shown by the teacher.

The distinguishing characteristic of this format is the way in which the task is presented to students and how that changes the student's role in the learning process. In active teaching, tasks are described carefully, including the conditions for practice, the task itself, and some measure of success. In teaching through questions, the common strategy is to describe conditions for practice and some measure for success, but to leave the performance itself open for student exploration and interpretation. For example, a teacher says, "Maintaining your self-space, can you find a different way to balance on three body parts?" Balancing on three body parts indicates the successful completion of the task, but there are several ways students can be successful. The nature of the task presentation encourages students to explore different combinations. One solution might be followed by the question, "Can you find another way to do it?" The decision of what to do to fulfill the task is left to the student, who does not try to reproduce what the teacher has explained and shown as the right way to do a task. When teachers prepare a series of task questions that help students progress toward specific skill goals, the format represents what Mosston described as *guided discovery* (Mosston & Ashworth, 1994).

With older students, teaching through questions can be used in connection with most instructional formats to add a problem-solving component to the learning environment. When teaching through questions is used in connection with other teaching formats, the result is most often referred to as a *problem-solving approach*. In Chapter 10, we saw how teachers can use questioning to get students to solve problems and think critically and tactically. Most activity units could be taught using the teaching through questions format. Box 14.3 shows questions and examples from a basketball unit. In some instances, teaching through questions is intended to achieve cognitive goals that are often at least as important as motor skill or strategy goals. Figure 14.2 shows this approach for part of a high school unit on cardiovascular endurance.

Student-Mediated Instructional Formats

In Chapter 13, we introduced the notion of student-mediated instructional formats, in which students fulfill many of the teaching functions performed by teachers in active teaching formats. We also explained the prerequisite skills and behavioral norms that teachers have to establish among students in order for student-mediated instruction to be fully effective. The question is how effective student-mediated instruction is when it is done appropriately. The answer is clear: Students can teach and learn from each other effectively, and they enjoy it (Cohen, 1994b; Cooke, Heron, & Heward, 1983; Smith, Markley, & Goc-Karp, 1997). There is also evidence that important social skill benefits are achieved through use of these formats (Dyson & Harper,

BOX 14.3   Types and Examples of Questions

Questions can be organized into four types according to the cognitive activity involved. Questions from each category are used for different purposes. To use questions as part of an instructional format, make sure they are consistent with the purposes for which they are used.

1. *Recall questions.* These require a memory-level answer. Most questions that can be answered yes or no are in this category.
   - Where should your eyes be when you are dribbling?
   - Which hand should be up on defense against a right-hand dribbler?
   - Which foot should you push off from when cutting?
   - Should you keep your elbow out while shooting?

2. *Convergent questions.* These aid analysis and integration of previously learned material, require reasoning and problem solving, and typically have a range of correct and incorrect answers.
   - Why should you stay between your opponent and the basket?
   - What are your responsibilities if your opponent shoots and moves to the right to rebound?
   - What should you do if the defender steps out to guard you on a pick and roll?

3. *Divergent questions.* These require solutions to new situations through problem solving. Many answers may be correct.
   - What ways could you start a fast break off a steal?
   - What could you do if caught defending a taller player in the post?
   - What passing options do you have when double teamed?
   - What strategies would you suggest when three points ahead with 2 minutes left in a game?

4. *Value questions.* These require expressions of choice, attitude, and opinion. Answers are not judged as right or wrong.
   - How do you react when you are fouled but the referee doesn't call it?
   - How do you feel about intentionally fouling opponents at the end of a game?
   - What gives you more enjoyment, scoring a lot or playing on a winning team?

1997; Strachan & MacCauley, 1997). The instructional formats that are most common within the category of student-mediated instruction are (a) peer tutoring and reciprocal teaching, (b) small groups and cooperative learning, and (c) teams.

Peer Tutoring and Reciprocal Teaching.   As learning groups get smaller, achievement increases (Bloom, 1984), with the most dramatic achievement gains resulting from tutoring. Instructional formats that utilize pairs or triads of students as the basic instructional unit are typically referred to as *peer tutoring* or *reciprocal teaching*. These formats are particularly useful for

Problems:

1. What effect does posture and speed of movement have on heart rate?

2. What is your minimum threshold of training?

3. What activities best develop cardiovascular (CV) endurance?

Directions: Perform all activities with a partner. Activities except calisthenics and volleyball, which will be done as a class, can be done separately. Perform each of the activities, then immediately calculate your working heart rate at the end of the activity. Rest between activities so that your heart rate returns to normal.

Activities (take pulse and calculate heart rate after each):

1. Lie down for 5 minutes and relax.

2. Sit up, then take pulse after 1 minute.

3. Stand rigidly at attention for 2 minutes.

4. Slow walk for 2 minutes.

5. Fast walk for 2 minutes.

6. Slow jog for 2 minutes.

7. Medium run for 2 minutes.

8. Sprint for 30 seconds.

9. Jump rope for 1 minute.

10. Perform calisthenics for 5 minutes.

11. Play a volleyball game for 5 minutes.
    - What happens to your heart rate as you change body positions?
    - How did your heart rates differ from those of members of the opposite sex in class?
    - What is your personal target zone for a CV endurance work?
    - What might your target zone be if you were 45 years old?
    - How do the heart rates you achieved compare to yours in daily activities?
    - What options might you have to get an appropriate CV workout each day?

FIGURE 14.2 *Laboratory task sheet for cardiovascular fitness (Source: Adapted from Lawson & Placek, 1981)*

achieving the goals of guided practice, which is fundamentally important to putting students in a situation in which they can benefit from independent practice. They are also useful for creating conditions in which students can utilize higher-order thinking skills to solve problems.

As suggested in Chapter 7, in relation to teaching students with disabilities, peer tutoring is typically of two types. One is when higher-skilled students tutor lower-skilled students for the primary purpose of boosting the performance of the latter. This format might prove useful in certain limited situations for short periods of time, but it does not represent a sufficiently general format for use in day-to-day teaching. The more useful, general format is referred to as classwide peer tutoring (CWPT), in which all students serve as both tutors and tutees (Houston-Wilson, Lieberman, Horton, & Kasser, 1997). CWPT has a long history in physical education, where it is more commonly referred to as reciprocal teaching (RT) (Mosston, 1966; Mosston & Ashworth, 1986, 1994).

CWPT or RT is typically highly structured, using teacher-developed materials to guide the progress of the tutorials. Tutors benefit from having to teach skills, knowledge, and tactics to classmates. Tutees benefit from individualized attention and feedback. The tutorial pair can progress at a pace conducive to the mastery of content. The key to successful CWPT-RT is the quality of the instructional materials, evaluation, feedback, and encouragement provided by the tutor. An additional benefit to CWPT-RT is that students acquire important interactive skills and also gain knowledge about the learning process through their responsible roles in it.

There is no strong evidence suggesting how student pairs should be formed. Contrary to conventional wisdom, there is evidence that higher-skilled students benefit from peer tutoring as much as lesser-skilled students; thus, mixed-ability pairs might be most useful. What is clear is that tasks assigned to students should be well structured, unambiguous, and challenging (Cohen, 1994a). When students are in pairs (or triads for certain activities), their roles should be clearly defined and understood. When students are tutors, they are teachers. When students are tutees, they are learners. For this format to work, the tutors must be able to evaluate and control their partner's work. Tutors have to have the skills to teach, and students must work cooperatively. When student pairs stay together over extended periods, they can develop a cooperative working relationship of mutual respect. When pair combinations are rearranged within a class, students get new opportunities to learn and teach with other classmates. Thus, there are benefits both to sustaining pairs and switching pairs, and some combination of each is likely to provide the best long-term benefit.

CWPT-RT requires that teachers spend time preparing appropriately structured materials. A series of steps guides development of task cards or sheets (Mosston & Ashworth, 1994). These include the following:

1. Clearly defined description of the task, including specific steps
2. Critical points to guide observation by peers
3. Drawings, sketches, or pictures of the task
4. Feedback cues to prompt appropriate performance

Figure 14.3 shows a tennis task sheet for use with pairs. Figure 14.4 shows a soccer task sheet for use with triads. Once students have been taught to perform the instructional functions and the necessary managerial routines have

Acc. = Accomplished n.t. = Needs more time	doer 1				doer 2			
	1st set		2nd set		1st set		2nd set	
Task/Criteria*	Acc.	n.t.	Acc.	n.t.	Acc.	n.t.	Acc.	n.t.

1. Stand with left side turned to the net, with weight on the right foot. (If left-handed, do the opposite.)
2. Swing the racket back at about hip height after you throw the ball upward. Keep eyes on the ball.
3. Transfer your weight onto the front foot, and swing the racket on a fairly straight line to the ball.
4. Watch the ball until it is hit by the racket. Bend the knees slightly through the stroke.
5. The racket contacts the ball when it is even with the front foot.
6. Keep wrist firm and swing with the whole arm, from the shoulder.
7. Rotate the trunk so that the shoulders and hips face the net on follow-through.
8. Follow through with the racket, upward and forward in the direction of the hit.

1   2   3

*In some tasks, the specific description of the "parts" constitutes the "points to look for."

FIGURE 14.3 *Criteria sheet for pairs in tennis (Source: M. Mosston and S. Ashworth,* Teaching Physical Education, *4th ed., 1994, p. 71. Copyright © 1994 Allyn & Bacon. Reprinted by permission.*

been established, the teacher's role during the lesson is to supervise the tutoring process, providing feedback and encouragement to both tutors and tutees. In RT, perhaps the most widely used form of student-mediated task teaching in physical education, one student takes the role of performer while the other is observer and coach (Ernst & Pangrazi, 1996). This relationship continues until the task is completed or a signal is given to switch roles; then the task is

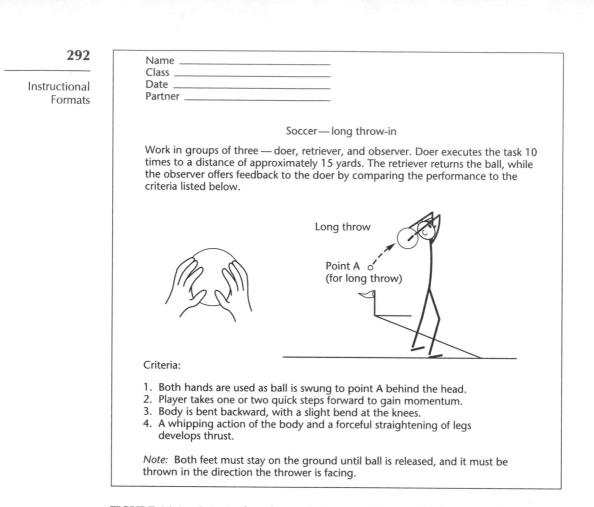

Name _____

Class _____

Date _____

Partner _____

Soccer — long throw-in

Work in groups of three — doer, retriever, and observer. Doer executes the task 10 times to a distance of approximately 15 yards. The retriever returns the ball, while the observer offers feedback to the doer by comparing the performance to the criteria listed below.

Long throw

Point A
(for long throw)

Criteria:

1. Both hands are used as ball is swung to point A behind the head.
2. Player takes one or two quick steps forward to gain momentum.
3. Body is bent backward, with a slight bend at the knees.
4. A whipping action of the body and a forceful straightening of legs develops thrust.

Note: Both feet must stay on the ground until ball is released, and it must be thrown in the direction the thrower is facing.

FIGURE 14.4 *Criteria sheet for triads in soccer (Source: M. Mosston and S. Ashworth,* Teaching Physical Education, *4th ed., 1994, p. 95. Copyright © 1994 Allyn & Bacon. Reprinted by permission.*

repeated with the roles reversed. Ernst and Pangrazi (1996) suggest the following "pairing principles":

- For effective outcomes (communication skills, cooperation, etc.), allow students to choose partners they regard as supportive.

- When feedback and coaching are important, pair students of higher and lower ability.

- For maximum interaction (problem solving or game strategy), pair students who are compatible.

- For cognitive and affective tasks, gender and ability are not relevant, so pair students based on other factors.

- For tasks that involve pairs against one another, partners should be of similar size, strength, and ability.

Always pair students in ways that do not leave marginalized students to the final pairing; indeed, pairing should be done in ways that advance the community nature of the learning environment and contribute to the goals of antibias teaching (see Chapter 6).

A form of reciprocal teaching from classrooms (Rosenshine & Meister, 1994) offers a variation on this format that combines some of the features of active teaching with the benefits of CWPT-RT. In this format, the teacher provides whole-group guided practice to begin a task—a basic explanation and modeling of the skill or tactic, inviting student comments and questions as they make initial attempts to perform the skill or tactic. As it becomes clear to the teacher that students basically grasp the task, the format is shifted to CWPT-RT, so students continue to practice under conditions of ample response opportunities and evaluative feedback. This variation requires fewer prepared materials, although it still necessitates the planning of well-structured, unambiguous tasks that have an appropriate degree of challenge.

Small Groups and Cooperative Learning. Educators are always on the lookout for instructional formats that improve achievement while having important social benefits for students. Small-group formats, including cooperative learning, seem to provide those benefits. We use the descriptor *small groups* as the overall label for a variety of formats, of which cooperative learning is a special case.

Cohen (1994a, p. 1) defines small group formats as "students working together in a group small enough so that everyone can participate on a task that has been clearly assigned." Small-group work is also defined by having these tasks carried out without the direct and immediate supervision of the teacher. Group work, as an instructional format, is not the same as ability grouping, nor is it a strategy for teachers to gather special groups of students for short-term intensive instruction. Group work is a fundamental way to organize students for everyday instructional purposes.

There are two key features of small-group work (Cohen, 1994a). The first is that the teacher delegates authority to the group to fashion the nature of its work to accomplish the task the teacher has assigned. The learning process is still controlled by the teacher because he or she evaluates the group's final product, but the manner in which students fulfill the task is a function of the dynamics within each group. Because of this feature, the teaching functions within the group are largely guided by group decisions and mediated by the students themselves. The fact that the teacher evaluates the final product is the key to the accountability mechanism of group work.

The second feature is that members need each other to complete the task; that is, they can't complete the task by themselves. Group members have to interact to decide how the task assigned by the teacher will be accomplished and who will do what. This requires substantial communication within the group and is the reason communication skills should be pretrained before extensive use of this format. Students will have to listen, ask questions, criticize, disagree, and make collaborative decisions. This process enhances both their thinking and their collaborative social skills. Cohen (1994a) suggests that groups of five are optimal for interactive and participatory purposes.

Group work requires interdependence of various sorts. Goal interdependence exists when individuals can achieve their goals only when other group members achieve theirs. Resource interdependence exists when individuals can achieve their goals only when other group members provide needed resources. Reward interdependence exists when rewards to the group are based on contributions of each individual group member. Individual accountability is also important, so that group recognition and rewards are clearly attributable to the cumulative contributions of each group member. The notion of a group reward to which contributions of each member are absolutely clear is especially important for instructional tasks that involve collective or collaborative individual work. When the instructional task is a challenging and interesting group task that requires all group members to contribute to the outcome, the need for individual accountability tracking by the teacher is reduced because the accountability to keep students involved and working hard is embedded within the task itself.

Group work can be powerful in learning for several reasons. The student-to-student interaction within groups requires that all members pay attention and respond. Students also tend to care about the evaluations of their classmates, so they tend to be more task oriented. Members seem not to want to let the group down by not carrying their fair share of the load. Working toward the group goal encourages members to help one another, providing assistance when something isn't understood, resources are needed, or technical help with skill or tactics is appropriate.

Groups don't just coalesce and function smoothly on their own. The pretraining for skills and behavioral norms, suggested in Chapter 12, is necessary. It also helps if group members have specific roles designed to help the group function more effectively. These roles are as follows (Cohen, 1994a):

1. *Facilitator.* Groups need leadership, but not domination. The facilitator does not control discussion, but instead sees that all have a fair chance to participate, helps keep the group on task, and helps the group make clear decisions.

2. *Harmonizer.* This person is attentive to the feelings of group members, helps them reach decisions through compromise, and generally helps ease potential and real interpersonal conflicts.

3. *Resource manager.* This student knows what the task is, what resources are needed to complete it, and where to get those resources.

4. *Recorder and reporter.* If the task requires producing a record along with a product, this student records the progress of the group and is prepared to report it when called upon.

Each of these roles requires some training, with modeling, feedback, and clear criteria for how the job is done well.

Cooperative learning is a special variation of small-group work. It has developed as a much utilized format both in classrooms and physical education. The use of cooperative games (in which outcomes are determined by team members cooperating to achieve a goal) is common in elementary school physical education. But cooperative learning really refers to an instructional format, rather than the activity being pursued (Kagan, 1990).

Cooperative learning is treated here as a special variation because of the specific cooperative learning structures that have been developed and widely tested in schools. Three common cooperative learning formats are the *pairs-check, jigsaw,* and *co-op, co-op* formats (Kagan, 1990). In the pairs-check format, students work in groups of four with two-partner pairs in each group. Student pairs work on an instructional task with one coaching the other, as in peer teaching. The two pairs then get together to check to see if they are achieving the same goal, solution, or outcome, with further feedback and practice as a result. In the jigsaw format, each student on a team becomes an "expert" at one element or skill by working with members of other teams who are experts on the same element or skill. They then return to their own teams, and experts teach other team members the element or skill they have learned. Thus, all the bump or set experts in a volleyball unit might work together to master that skill and then return to their own teams to teach it to their teammates. In the co-op, co-op format, students work together in groups to produce a particular group product to which each student makes a contribution that can be evaluated. The groups then present their work product to the rest of the class. The format might be successful in developing acrosport demonstrations or learning folk dances.

These cooperative learning formats allow learners to be active in their own learning by seeking and clarifying content from and for their peers. Frequently, students who need further explanation of a task or concept will be able to grasp it more easily if it is explained by another student, rather than the teacher. Regardless of the learning format used, students are generally assigned a task, a problem, or a goal to be solved or achieved as a group. Success at achieving the given task will be determined in part by the students' cooperative skills and willingness to work as a team. These, like any other skills, need to be taught and practiced.

Cooperative learning is intended to produce social and affective outcomes as well as content mastery outcomes. When used appropriately, cooperative learning results in social gains among racial groups and across skill levels, as well as in more acceptance of students with disabilities and increased friendships among students in general (Slavin, 1990). Teachers often use cooperative learning formats for student practice of instructional tasks after having used an active teaching format for initial instruction. Cooperative learning, which contains some elements of peer teaching, could also be used in a task format. The Sport Education curriculum model represents a form of cooperative learning in the context of sport, and it could easily be adapted to become a full-fledged cooperative learning model.

Size of group is important for cooperative learning. Smaller groups, even pairs, maximize participation and involvement. Keeping the groups small allows more time to practice speaking, listening, and making choices. A variety of techniques can be used to form small groups: self-selection, structured categories procedures, and mixed ability grouping. Depending upon the intent of the cooperative tasks, the number of students in your class, and their interactive skills, each of these strategies can be useful. In cooperative learning, student work is structured so that it requires interdependence in the achievement of group goals but also provides individual accountability for group members. One common feature of coop learning formats is the notion of student teams.

Teams are a special type of group that we need to mention here because they are frequently used in physical education. Although generally composed of larger groups than those described previously, if done well, teams provide many of the social benefits described for small groups and also allow students to take responsibility for their own experiences, thus moving teams into the self-instructional formats. One of the strengths of the Sport Education model (Chapter 9) is the meaning that students derive from the sport experience as a result of being a member of a team and the personal growth that comes from being affiliated with the same group of individuals over time. As students begin to develop an affiliation with their team and its members, they begin to feel an allegiance to and responsibility toward their peers and the team effort. To allow students to take responsibility for their sport experience, the Sport Education model has roles that team members take on and fulfill throughout the season. These roles tend to be more clearly defined because the team is formed for the purpose of competition. These roles include that of participant (everyone), captain or coach, referee, scorekeeper, statistician, and even publicist, manager, trainer, and a sports board. Although each of these roles should be defined so that students know their responsibilities to the team, the decision on who will define them may vary by teacher, experience of students, and context. Box 14.4 provides an example of roles and responsibilities for high school touch rugby and tennis seasons.

Self-Instructional Formats. *Self-instructional* formats allow students to progress through a sequence of learning activities without the physical presence of a teacher. These are really a family of formats that share the common feature of allowing the students to work without the immediate direction and supervision of the teacher. Among the formats in this family are individualized instruction, contracting, and personalized systems of instruction (PSI). Self-instructional formats embed all the teaching functions in materials and typically use a formal accountability system. Teachers who plan self-instructional formats spend a great deal of time developing and improving those materials and maintaining records of student performance in an accountability system. As Box 14.5 indicates, self-instruction is one of the instructional formats that puts students at the center of the learning environment.

Self-instructional formats can be used within a traditional class setting, or they can be used for students to pursue learning independently from a class setting. Self-instructional formats are widely used in high school physical education for courses that take place away from the school, such as in a local bowling alley, indoor tennis arena, or area golf course. The nature of physical education content results in self-instructional formats that often require stu-

**BOX 14.4   Roles and Responsibilities for High School Touch Rugby
and Tennis**

The sports board was responsible for the organization and control of events throughout the season. Duties of the sports board included the following:

- Planning the competitions with the teacher
- Dealing with disputes or student requests
- Meeting with the teacher to share ideas and feedback from students
- Providing positive role models for teams
- Planning the culminating event
- Ensuring the smooth day-to-day functioning of the program

Whether playing touch rugby or tennis, managers, coaches, and captains had the following roles.

Manager

- Support the coach
- Organize equipment for team practice
- Ensure that players know who, where, and when they are playing
- Check for appropriate uniforms, numbers, and so forth
- Arrange for substitutes for absent players
- Report concerns to the coach and teacher
- Organize the team when it is on duty

Coach

- Be fair to all players on their team
- Involve all players in practice and competition
- Listen to players' ideas
- Plan active practices, seek advice of the teacher
- Discuss ideas with the manager and captain
- Make substitutions during contests

Captain

- Liaise with the coach about practice and game strategies
- Make on-court or on-field decisions for the team
- Represent the team to the referee during competition
- Lead the team in congratulations and postcompetition rituals
- Be an example of fair play

Source: Reprinted by permission from B. Grant, 1995, *Quality P.E. through Positive Sport Experience: Sport Education* (Champaign, IL) Human Kinetics, p. 87.

BOX 14.5   When Teaching Least is Teaching Best

When we think about teaching, our first thoughts typically are about the things teachers do in class. Too often when we think about evaluating teaching, we think about watching what the teacher does. A consistent message in this book has been that the best evaluation of teaching comes from watching what *students do*. Teachers do not have to be at the center of the stage for good instruction to take place. Indeed, arguments can be made that, for students to become responsible, independent learners, the teacher must move off stage, so that the students themselves can occupy the central roles. There are several instructional formats in this chapter that can accomplish that goal better than others.

Responsible, independent learners can no doubt develop from many of the variations of peer teaching and self-instructional formats. Although responsibility and independence are important qualities, one might also argue that learning to work together toward collective goals is also an important, humanizing experience. Some peer formats and most cooperative formats would be appropriate for this goal.

It is O.K. for teachers to get off and stay off center stage in the instructional format. Enough is now known about classroom management for teachers to work gradually toward implementing instructional formats that not only promote independence and responsibility, but also require collaboration and responsibility for others and allow students to experience the multiplier effect that can be achieved through communal effort toward collective goals.

The formats through which these goals can be achieved are not easy to implement. Teachers need highly developed class management skills to develop an orderly environment in which students can learn to function effectively in these student-centered formats. Even then, active teaching might sometimes still be the preferred format because format needs to be adapted to goals and context.

---

dents to work in pairs, triads, or small groups to complete the learning tasks. Thus, self-instructional formats are often used in conjunction with peer teaching formats. Also, because of the need to develop clear and explicit materials for learners, self-instructional formats take on many of the characteristics of task teaching.

The strengths of self-instructional formats are the flexibility allowed learners and the possibility of matching learning tasks to student abilities more than is possible in a whole-class, active teaching format. The flexibility of good self-instructional materials is that they can be used within a class or outside a class. There is also much to be said for students having the responsibility of completing a learning sequence on their own by following the materials prepared by the teacher.

Self-instructional formats rise or fall on how specific and appropriate the materials prepared for students are and the degree to which the accountability system motivates the students to complete the tasks. The self-instructional materials need to be complete and explicit, providing students with the help

---

VOLLEY

Purpose:

To redirect an aerial ball strategically.

Skill Analysis:

1. Align body part with approaching ball.
2. Focus eyes on approaching ball.
3. Move total body and body part toward ball.
4. Apply firm body part to center of ball.
5. Follow through toward intended flight direction.

Kinds: Foot, knee, shoulder, and head.

Task Learning Experiences:

1. In partners, A throws the ball toward B's shoulder, and B volleys the ball, executing a shoulder volley. Repeat five times from a distance of 10 feet. Reverse. Repeat from 15 feet.
2. Repeat task #1, preceding the volley with two or three steps. Reverse.
3. Repeat tasks #1 and #2, directing the ball to the left, right, and toward center.
4. Repeat tasks #2, #2, and #3, executing a knee volley.
5. Repeat tasks #2, #2, and #3, executing a foot volley.
6. In partners, A throws the ball underhand so that it arches and drops toward B's head. B executes a head volley. Repeat three times from a distance of 10 feet. Reverse.
7. Repeat task #6, directing the ball to the left, right, and toward center.
8. Stand 10 to 15 feet from a wall and kick the ball into the wall. Volley the rebound with different body parts according to the level of rebound. For a more forceful rebound, precede the kick with two or three steps. Different levels of rebound can be achieved by contacting the ball at various points below the center. Repeat ten times.

FIGURE 14.5   *Self-instructional materials for volleying in soccer (Source: Reprinted by permission from D. Zakrajsek and L. Carnes, 1986,* Individualizing Physical Education: Criterion Materials, *2nd ed. (Champaign, IL: Human Kinetics), p. 186.*

they need at the point when it is needed. Figure 14.5 shows self-instructional materials for the skill of volleying in soccer. These materials are typical of self-instructional materials to be used within a class.

Contracting is a form of individualized instruction in which students sign a learning contract to complete a sequence of learning tasks according to a predetermined set of criteria. Contracting is a popular self-instructional format for physical education courses completed at sites other than the school and under the jurisdiction of persons other than the physical educator. Thus,

Requirements:

1. Practice at a local course for a total of 20 hours.
2. Complete test on golf rules at score of 90 percent or better before playing on course (test is available in PE office).
3. Play 36 holes of golf and turn in completed score cards.
4. Maintain a diary describing problems encountered in skill practice and play. Turn in at completion of unit.
5. Play a final 18 holes at the end of the unit.

Practice Tasks (20 hours minimum):

1. On practice range, hit 9 iron, 5 iron, and 1 or 3 wood 20 times each. Utilize critical element checklist for each practice. If possible, have a partner observe and complete checklist.
2. On practice green, hit 25 9-iron pitch and chip shots. Utilize critical element checklist as you practice.
3. On practice green, putt 50 putts of varying lengths and slopes.
4. As you improve, spend more time practicing the tasks you are having most difficulty with.
5. Have practice times attested by a partner or course employee.

Playing Tasks (minimum of 36 holes):

1. Play at least nine holes at a time.
2. Play following all official and local rules.
3. Complete score card and have score attested.
4. Record thoughts and reactions in your diary.

Grading Criteria:

C = Completion of all requirements.
A or B = Negotiated on basis of improvement in score from practice rounds to final 18 holes.

FIGURE 14.6 *Self-instructional golf contract*

students might complete a golf unit or a bowling unit at local sites on their own without the supervision of the teacher. The contract specifies the learning tasks to be completed, the amount of practice required, and the criteria for performance necessary for a particular grade or fulfillment of a requirement. An example of a learning contract is shown in Figure 14.6.

Personalized systems of instruction (PSI) is a self-instructional format in which content is divided into small units students must master before moving on to other units. PSI formats require developing specific instructional tasks and clear mastery criteria. Students then practice the tasks until they meet the criteria; they then move on to the next task. PSI allows for individual progress through a series of learning tasks. At the end of a PSI unit, students will differ

---

Unit 4—Rules and Rally

Terminal Objectives

1. Student will demonstrate knowledge of tennis rules by scoring 80% or more on a written test.
2. Student will demonstrate the ability to move from a ready position to the forehand and/or backhand ground strokes so that a rally is continued for 6 consecutive hits, and the balls remain within a singles court.

Learning Tasks

1. Student will read handout provided and answer questions on a worksheet.
2. Student will participate in "home base" drill so that six consecutive balls are hit between singles boundaries.
3. Student will participate in "ground stroke" scramble until six consecutive balls are hit within singles boundaries.
4. Student will participate in "two-on-one" drill until the student can rally six consecutive times within singles boundaries.

FIGURE 14.7 *Learning task from a high school tennis unit (Source: Tousignant, 1983, p. 34. Reprinted with permission from the* Journal of Physical Education, Recreation and Dance. *The Journal is a publication of the American Alliance for Health, Physical Education, Recreation, and Dance, 1900 Association Drive, Reston, VA 22091.)*

in terms of *how much* they have learned rather than *how well* they can perform. Grading is typically done in terms of how many tasks are completed within the time constraints of the unit. PSI could also be used away from the time demands imposed by class periods during school days. If so, students who need extra time to master a series of tasks could do so. Figure 14.7 shows a single task from a PSI tennis unit. The unit is composed of a series of such tasks.

SUMMARY

1. Instructional formats refer to how a teacher organizes instruction and delivers practice to students. Instructional style refers to the managerial and instructional climate of the learning environment.
2. Mosston's spectrum of styles describes ways of teaching based on a series of decisions that teachers make about their teaching behaviors and the decisions learners are invited to make about their learning behavior.
3. The instructional format should match the context for teaching, which reflects the teacher's personal preferences, the learners' characteristics, the content, and the context within which the teaching takes place.

4. Active teaching is a direct format in which the teacher controls the pace of the lesson, providing ample guided and independent practice, producing high rates of successful student participation in a supportive climate.

5. Task teaching is a format in which different students are engaged in different tasks at the same time, typically rotating among task stations throughout the lesson.

6. Teaching through questions is a variation of active teaching in which student responses are not prescribed, typically taking a guided discovery or problem-solving approach.

7. In peer tutoring and reciprocal teaching formats, students take on instructional roles, typically in pairs, triads, or small groups, and are prepared to assess peer performance and provide feedback.

8. Small group and cooperative learning formats involve student work that is structured so that it not only requires interdependence in the achievement of group goals, but also provides individual accountability for members of learning groups.

9. Teachers do not have to be center stage; good instruction and learning often take place with students occupying more central roles.

10. Self-instructional formats allow students to progress through a sequence of learning activities without the immediate presence of the teacher, with teacher-prepared materials important to successful implementation.

11. Contracting and PSI are self-instructional formats used both in regular classes and independent study.

CHAPTER 15

Extending the Physical Education Program

These physical activity guidelines address school instructional programs, school psychosocial and physical environments, and various services schools provide. Because the physical activity of children and adolescents is affected by many factors beyond the school setting, these guidelines also address parental involvement, community health services, and community sports and recreation programs for young people.

—CENTERS FOR DISEASE CONTROL AND PREVENTION (1997)

OVERALL CHAPTER OUTCOME

To design a proposed expanded physical education program that uses nonattached school time, links students to community programs, and involves parents

CHAPTER OBJECTIVES

- To explain why an expanded physical education requires more than increased class time in the school schedule
- To clarify the public health interest engendered by the surgeon general's report and the CDC guidelines
- To describe the multifactored approach suggested by the CDC guidelines
- To outline options for using nonattached schooltime
- To delineate options for using out-of-school time
- To describe ways of linking school PE programs to activity opportunities in the community
- To enunciate the features of comprehensive approaches to school-based physical activity and health programs
- To illustrate the common features of efforts to extend physical education

In Chapter 8, we said that all the experiences students have in physical education while they attend a particular school represent that school's *program*. Normally, we think of the program as what happens in physical education classes. Although time in PE class might represent the heart of a school program, if that is the extent of the program, the likelihood of achieving important goals is reduced. In this chapter, we address how to extend the physical education program beyond what goes on in the regular class schedule.

Most of our profession's efforts to expand physical education have been directed toward securing more time for physical education in the regular school timetable, that is, more classes per week. This effort is most clearly seen in the campaign for "quality, daily physical education" that our profession has waged for many years. Indeed, the United States Congress passed House Concurrent Resolution 97 in 1987, calling for quality, daily physical education classes in schools. Many state legislatures have passed similar resolutions. A resolution, however, is not a law requiring anything to happen. Thus, in this era of legislatures "resolving" to support quality, daily physical education, the net effect has been a loss of time devoted to PE in the weekly schedule and a corresponding loss of presence in the school curriculum. These losses are due mostly to the pressures on schools for increased emphasis on reading, mathematics, science, and technology.

We support the movement for quality, daily physical education—but we also believe that we can't just wish for it or wait for it to happen. If we can't expand physical education by securing more class time in the daily schedule, then we have to find other ways to do it that move beyond the daily class schedule. That is what this chapter is about.

EXPANDING PHYSICAL EDUCATION TO BUILD PUBLIC TRUST

Why has physical education lost time and presence in the school curriculum in an era when health and physical activity have become so important in society? There are many reasons, no doubt, but we find two arguments particularly relevant. First, many parents and other adults did not have particularly good experiences in physical education, at least not to the degree that they have become champions for an expanded PE. Too many adults found their physical education experience unchallenging, boring, and largely irrelevant to their education and lifestyle. The second reason is that many parents and caregivers are using the private and community sectors to involve their children and youth in sport and physical activity programs with adult supervision; thus, *their* health and physical activity goals for their daughters and sons are being achieved in programs outside the school.

Your first reaction may be to say that our main agenda should be improving physical education classes in schools—and we find no fault with that argument. Indeed, this entire book is devoted to exactly that agenda. *We have to make physical education classes better*. To expand an effort that is of low quality will win us no friends and will not help us achieve our goals for children and youth. However, better teaching within physical education classes is not enough. As we improve the quality of teaching and learning in PE, we also have to expand its influences beyond scheduled classes. When children and youth experience quality physical education within classes and have it expanded through out-of-class experiences, we will earn widespread public support.

To understand our argument, you have to be aware of the degree to which the physical education profession has moved in the past decade toward a single, overarching purpose for school physical education: to help children and youth adopt habits that lead to physically active lifestyles as adults. We are not suggesting this is the *only* purpose currently advocated, but it is clearly the most commonly cited global purpose. The increasing consensus within the physical education profession around this purpose is the result of the surgeon general's report (U.S. Department of Health and Human Services, 1996), which clearly established the relationship of *physical inactivity* to a host of health problems among adults. There is now convincing evidence that adults who lead lives that include regular, moderately intense physical activity (PA) are at much less risk for a host of degenerative diseases. Given the enormous costs of health care in our society, it is understandable that the physically active lifestyle has become important to policy makers and education professionals. It is not easy to work with children and youth in ways that actually influence their lifestyles as adults. A program would have to have a tremendous impact on boys and girls for it to move them into patterns of activity and sustain them in those activity patterns so as to form lifelong habits. We believe that the time devoted to physical education in most school timetables is insufficient to attain this goal, even if that time is in high-quality classes.

In 1997, the Centers for Disease Control and Prevention (CDC) published a series of policy guidelines to establish a comprehensive approach to promoting lifelong PA among children and youth. The basic rationale for this comprehensive program approach is described in the quote that opens this chapter. The CDC guidelines recognize that a comprehensive approach, involving school, community, and parents, is necessary if we are to impact the lives of young persons. Furthermore, the CDC guidelines were developed with the underlying assumption that the K–12 school system should be the focal point from which a comprehensive program develops. In other words, the "ball is in our court," and it is our responsibility to expand the concept of school physical education to meet the demands of the age in which we live. It will become clear in this chapter, however, that the "our" in the previous statement refers not only to physical educators, but also to health educators, school nurses, classroom teachers, and school administrators. To make that clear and to introduce you to the meaning of a comprehensive programmatic approach, we now turn to those CDC guidelines.

CDC RECOMMENDATIONS FOR LIFELONG PHYSICAL ACTIVITY

Ten policy suggestions make up the CDC guidelines. The full guidelines can be downloaded from the Division of Adolescent and School Health (DASH) home page on the World Wide Web at http://www.cdc.gov/nccdphp/dash. After accessing the DASH home page, click on "strategies," then select "School Health Program Guidelines." Table 15.1 shows the main features of the guidelines.

A review of the guidelines reveals what must begin to happen for a truly *comprehensive* program to develop. These are the most important issues relative to an expanded physical education:

- Physical education and health education must complement each other and work together.
- Nonattached time in the school day (before school, noon break, recess, and after school) should be used for PA programs.
- Schools should work to provide students access to safe space/facilities in school and the community.

TABLE 15.1 CDC Youth PA Recommendations

1. Establish *policies* that promote enjoyable, lifelong PA.
   - Require daily physical education K–12.
   - Require health education K–12.
   - Commit adequate resources to PA instruction and programs.
   - Hire professionally trained persons.
   - Require that PA programs meet the needs and interests of children.

2. Provide physical and social *environments* that encourage PA.
   - Provide access to safe spaces/facilities in school and community.
   - Prevent PA-related injuries/illness.
   - Provide time in the school day for unstructured PA (to accumulate a significant percentage of weekly PA requirements).
   - Do not use PA as punishment.
   - Provide health promotion for school faculty.

3. Implement planned and sequential *physical education* curriculums that emphasize participation in PA and that encourage students to develop the knowledge, attitudes, motor skills, and confidence needed to adopt physically active lifestyles.
   - Make PE curriculums consistent with national standards.
   - Impart knowledge of PA to students.
   - Develop students' positive attitudes toward, motor skills for, and confidence in participating in PA.
   - Promote participation in enjoyable PA in school, community, and home.

4. Implement planned and sequential *health education (HE)* curriculums that encourage students to develop the knowledge, attitudes, and behavioral skills needed to adopt physically active lifestyles.
   - Make HE curriculums consistent with national standards.
   - Promote collaboration among PE, HE, and classroom teachers for PA instruction.
   - Develop students' mastery of the behavioral skills needed to adopt and maintain positive lifestyle behaviors.

5. Provide *extracurricular PA programs* that meet students' needs and interests.
   - Provide a diversity of developmentally appropriate PA programs for the largest number of students.
   - Link students to community PA programs, and use community resources to support extracurricular PA programs.

- Inclusive, attractive extracurricular PA programs should be developed.
- Parents and other caregivers must become involved and become advocates for their children's involvement in PA programs.
- School personnel should help students become involved in community PA programs.
- Because these suggestions are to be *school* initiatives, school administrators and classroom teachers must become involved and supportive.
- The regular physical education program should be of high quality.

How do physical educators begin to develop a more comprehensive PE program that is designed to promote enjoyable PA in the school, community, and home? The remainder of this chapter is devoted to answering that question,

TABLE 15.1   CDC Youth PA Recommendations *(continued)*

6. Include *parents and guardians* in PA instruction and extracurricular PA programs, and encourage them to support their children's participation in enjoyable PA.
   - Encourage parents to advocate for high-quality PA instruction and programs for their children.
   - Encourage parents to support their children's participation in appropriate, enjoyable PA.
   - Motivate parents to be role models for PA and to plan family activities that include PA.

7. Provide PE, HE, recreation, and health-care professionals with *training* that imparts the knowledge and skills needed to effectively promote PA among youths.
   - Through higher education, provide preservice training for education, recreation, and health-care professionals.
   - Teach educators how to deliver PE that provides a significant percentage of each student's weekly PA.
   - Teach the active learning strategies needed to develop knowledge about, attitudes toward, skills in, and confidence in PA.
   - Create environments that enable youths to enjoy PA instruction and programs.
   - Qualify volunteers who coach sport and recreation programs for youths.

8. Provide *health services* that assess PA among youths, reinforce PA among active youths, counsel inactive youths and refer them to PA programs, and advocate for PA instruction and programs for youths.
   - Regularly assess PA, reinforce active youths, and refer inactive youths.
   - Advocate for school and community PA instruction and programs.

9. Provide a range of developmentally appropriate, noncompetitive *community sport and recreation programs* that are attractive to youths.

10. Regularly *evaluate* school and community PA instruction, programs, and facilities.
    - Conduct process evaluations to determine how policies, programs, and training are implemented.
    - Conduct outcome evaluations to measure students' achievement of PA knowledge, behavioral skills, and motor skills.

Source: Adapted from Centers for Disease Control and Prevention, 1997.

primarily by showing you the many efforts of school districts, schools, and physical educators to respond to the national concern about the physical activity habits of children and youth and how those habits can be sustained through the life span.

EXTRACURRICULAR PROGRAMMING IN NONATTACHED SCHOOLTIME

Many physical educators are developing attractive PA programs for students to participate in during nonattached schooltime. A sampling of such efforts follows.

Elementary and Secondary School Models

The Citrus County Fitness Break (Bradford-Krok, 1994) allows classroom teachers in elementary schools in Floral City, Florida, to take short PA breaks with their children each day. A series of videotapes was developed, each emphasizing a fitness component or concept, combined with a short activity session. Each tape was made as a "skit" to hold the attention and capture the enthusiasm of the students.

At the Ravenal Elementary School in Sineca, South Carolina (Carpenter, 1994), a daily morning exercise program was developed with the support of the school principal. Fifth grade students were assigned to each homeroom in the school and trained to lead exercise routines. Each routine was designed with the help of a professional aerobics instructor. The exercise program began at 7:55 a.m. and ended at the school's tardy bell at 8:05 a.m. Homeroom teachers assisted both by helping to maintain order and also by participating with the students.

At the Maryland Avenue Elementary School in Bexley, Ohio (B. Siedentop, 1998), during the lunchtime recess, students can participate in "options," an intramural program related to the regular curriculum. Because they have already learned skills and tactics of various activities, the options program allows students extended time to participate in those activities.

At the Edison Elementary School in Grandview Heights, Ohio (Eichner, 1996), students have the opportunity to participate in a morning PA session several times a week before the beginning of the school day. As many as 70 to 80 join in each of these sessions. The gymnasium is typically set up as a series of stations with fitness activities. Children rotate among the positions on signals from the teacher.

The Herbert Hoover High School in San Diego, California, operates a 2,800 square foot fitness center (Samman, 1998) used for PE classes, sports teams, staff members, and the community. Modest monthly fees are charged for membership ($2 for students, $3 for alumni, $5 for staff/community). The center is open 6 days per week for 10 hours per day. Drop-in activity for students is encouraged. An after-school fitness club is open to all students, faculty, and staff.

Many high schools that have developed fitness facilities offer drop-in activities for students during the school day. Students typically take advantage of these opportunities during study hall time and other breaks in their schedules. They can drop in to use these facilities, and group aerobics sessions are scheduled during the day.

Many teachers who utilize the Sport Education curriculum model (see Chapter 9) extend its impact during nonattached school time (Bell, 1994). They do this in a number of ways. First, class teams can earn points toward a particular championship when their coach presents a recess practice plan and gathers the team at recess to practice skills and strategies for the Sport Education season. Second, seasons are often extended through intraclass competitions at the noontime recess (for example, when after a gymnastics season all the students who competed in the balance beam competition within class come together for an intraclass competition at one noonhour intramural time, followed all week by other intraclass competitions for other apparatus).

Cross-Age PE Teaching

Clovis High School in California has an elective physical education course for seniors in which they earn their credit by teaching children in the district's elementary schools (Samman, 1998). Students are placed in pairs and assigned to an elementary classroom under the supervision of the classroom teacher. They teach four 1-hour lessons each week. A district physical education specialist rotates among the schools to serve as a resource person for the students and to observe their teaching.

Recess

In elementary schools, the major source of nonattached time is recess. Many elementary schools have a morning, noon, and afternoon recess, each typically 15 minutes long, with the noon recess sometimes longer. There is controversy in the elementary education literature as to whether recess should be structured in some way to ensure certain kinds of activity or whether it should be left unstructured so that students can engage in free play.

Research in physical education shows that girls are less active than boys (Sarkin, McKenzie, & Sallis, 1997), even in schools where they are as active as boys during physical education classes. Teachers interact differently with girls and boys as early as kindergarten, both in classes and on playgrounds during recess (Colvin, 1995). One doesn't have to observe children at play on too many playgrounds during recess to understand that some children are marginalized (based on gender, skillfulness, appearance, and other irrelevant factors). Many children who most need to be more involved in regular PA are probably least likely to be involved during recess. This leads us to believe that recess should be structured, and the best way to do it is as an adjunct to the physical education curriculum, so that students have extra time to practice the skills they are learning in PE classes.

OUT-OF-SCHOOLTIME PROGRAMS

PE Homework

One of the best ways to help students increase their weekly PA, and also learn more about the content of physical education, is to assign homework. Homework can be built around skill development, fitness, or knowledge (Docheff, 1990). Homework that focuses on activity tasks can be monitored by (a) having students sign an "affidavit" attesting to their activity, (b) having a parent or caregiver attest to the fact that an activity assignment has been completed, or (c) through an honor system. Activity homework should be related to the skill development goals of the unit the students are engaged with, such as practicing basketball shooting or working with a friend on soccer dribbling and tackling. Activity homework that is related to accumulating a specified amount of moderate to vigorous physical activity (MVPA) can be done by recording bicycle rides, walks, runs, and the like in a journal.

Homework that focuses on knowledge and understanding can focus on current events, using the daily newspaper, magazines, or the library. Homework can also require students to observe an event and report their responses and perceptions of it following some question guides prepared by the teacher for the assignment. This kind of homework is particularly well suited to the goals of antibias teaching (see Chapter 6). Students could prepare antibias gender projects that focus on how women are portrayed in sports advertising, how announcers describe female play and appearance differently than male play and appearance, or how much space a local newspaper gives to women's sports as opposed to men's.

Homework assignments in physical education should extend the PE program by contributing to curricular objectives through assignments that are enjoyable for students rather than repetitive busywork (Arbogast & Misner, 1990). Homework assignments should have a specific purpose, with a sufficient amount of structure that students know what to do, how well it should be done, and when the assignment is completed. Finally, encouraging parents to be aware of and supportive of PE homework assignments is a good way to build cognizance of physical education and even involve parents with their children in physical activities.

After-School Clubs and Projects

There are many ways to help students think about their after-school and weekend physical activity. One example is a 100-lap run campaign held at an elementary school (Wilkerson & Werner, 1994). All children are encouraged to walk/run 1 lap per school day until the 100th day of school, when a school assembly is held to celebrate their accomplishments with 100-lap ribbons given to all who reach the goal. Students who miss days can make them up with extra laps.

A similar program was conducted for an entire school year in Columbus, Ohio, where fourth and fifth grade students at an elementary school planned and completed "trips" to other cities in the United States that were also named Columbus (Eichner, 1996). Students accumulated miles by walking, running, and cycling. They made class goals about which city they wanted to travel to, then kept track of their progress on maps in the school hallways. As part of this program, students also measured the distance from their homes to school so that walking or cycling to school each day could count in their accumulated totals.

Walking clubs have become more and more popular as people understand the value of walking as a form of moderate PA and enjoy walks, particularly through scenic areas. Walking routes can easily be established in and around a school (Gym Shorts, 1995). Walking is a great activity because it can be done individually or in groups. Goals can be set up, and progress toward achieving them is easy to measure and record. Recess walks, lunch walks, or after-school walks can be organized. Teachers can walk with students, which lends a strong measure of support to such a program. Advanced students can try power walking, and activities such as orienteering can grow from this activity.

Performance Groups

Performance groups are another way to extend the physical education program. They are particularly popular at the elementary school level, where basketball skills groups, jump rope clubs, and unicycle groups practice in order to perform at local events. The idea of a performance troupe could logically encompass many different physical education activities (Steller, 1994). A performance troupe uses movement and skill activities in a choreographed group performance. The fact that troupes perform in public at local events lends a seriousness to the enjoyable activity and helps students gain poise and confidence through successful performances. Such performances typically combine some skill elements with an obvious fitness workout, all done through choreography to music. The logistics of practicing and performing will, of course, differ markedly in terms of how old the students are and the specifics of the local context.

Intramural Programs

Intramural programs have been the traditional approach to extending sport and recreation opportunities to students beyond their regular physical education programs. In recent years, however, intramural programs have been greatly reduced. There appear to be two reasons. The first is that many students are bussed to school, and busses leave after school, eliminating opportunity for many students. Second, the increase in interschool sports opportunities, particularly for girls, has put an added stress on scheduling time in school gymnasiums and playing fields. Nonetheless, intramural programs are sustained in many schools.

COMMUNITY LINKS

PE-Community Connections Through Curriculum Innovation

Seattle's 25 high schools have added activities to their programs by partnering with community, professional, and private sector sport, health, and fitness organizations (Turner, 1995). Each high school is challenged to add an activity in conjunction with an outside group. For example, some have taken advantage of the U.S. Tennis Association's program providing equipment, assemblies, and instruction. Some schools have arranged to participate in the "First Swing" golf program sponsored by the Professional Golfers Association and mediated by local golf club professionals. Fire department paramedics have taught CPR classes. The Seattle Parks and Recreation Department, in cooperation with U.S. Rowing, has provided free rowing instruction. One of the benefits of this program is that students learn where to engage in such popular activities and how to gain access to them.

Community-School Facilities and Programs

Indoor and outdoor facilities for physical activity are typically expensive to build and maintain. Many communities are trying to utilize their facilities to the fullest by making them school-community facilities. In Perry, Ohio, the community built a new high school that includes a comprehensive community sport and recreation center (Schmid, 1994). Part of the facility is a 185,000 square foot Community Fitness Center, a joint-use facility for community residents and students at Perry High School. Residents and students can join the center for a modest annual fee. The center is open for community use 30 hours each week and is used for school programs the remainder of the time. The school district and the community share the costs of equipment, maintenance, and employee salaries.

Other districts have experimented with allowing any adult resident to participate in any regular physical education class at the high school level and allowing high school students to gain their physical education credit through participation in community programs. Adults joining high school students in physical education classes—either in school or in the community—extends our notion of what physical education can be and how students can learn with and from participation in PA with adults.

Solving the Intramural Problem Through Collaboration

The West Des Moines School District in Iowa has developed an intramural program for seventh and eighth graders in conjunction with a local YMCA and the local parks and recreation department (Samman, 1998). Three junior high schools are served with an extensive program headed by school intramural directors assisted by YMCA and park district personnel, who organize adult volunteers to serve as coaches, officials, and mentors. The program is jointly financed.

Links to Parents and the Community

As we work to raise the quality of physical education and extend the program in ways described in this chapter, we should link to parents and the community as advocates for our program and for the benefits of a physically active lifestyle (Boyce & Markos, 1995; Mize, 1990). Many different types of advocacy programs have been developed by physical educators. Newsletters and brochures are sent home to parents. Local TV stations show tapes of special programs and events. Parents' nights are held, focusing on the PE program and often involving parents in activity. Health and wellness fairs, where assessments, programs, and information are made available to parents and community members, are common. Family sports days, fun runs, and skill clinics are held. Youth sport fairs are organized to introduce parents to the variety of programs available to their children and youth and to educate the parents about what to look for to provide a quality sports program. School assemblies are organized around themes such as the Olympics, Women's Sports Week, or Fitness Week.

At Cabell Midland High School, a 6-week evening program called "Family, Fun, Fitness" is offered to families and community members (Samman, 1998). The school auditorium, gymnasium, and fitness center are used. Speakers provide information. Assessments such as diet analysis, body composition, and lung capacity are available. Activities are planned, local wellness agencies participate, and the whole effort is designed to help families learn more about health and fitness and how to keep active together.

COMPREHENSIVE PA AND HEALTH PROGRAMS

Healthy Lifestyles Elementary School Program

There is some evidence that school physical education programs are becoming more comprehensive in conception and scope. Virgilio (1996) has described a comprehensive healthy lifestyles elementary school program, the fundamental basis of which is based on the premise that time allotted to physical education is insufficient to meet PA goals for children. The program emphasizes learning lifelong skills and participating regularly in MVPA. Children develop a personal portfolio of their learning and activities that they carry with them through their elementary school years. The model has a strong parent education component, and classroom teachers include health, nutrition, and cardiovascular fitness content in their curriculums. Classroom teachers are also responsible for seeing that the children in their classes get at least 30 minutes per week of MVPA in addition to their physical education and recess time.

Parents are encouraged to become very involved. A parent newsletter is regularly distributed. Parent-teacher conferences and PTA programs are used for progress reports and to gain support for parental involvement. A parent resource room containing videos, computer software, cookbooks, cassettes, and educational games that can be used by the family at home is developed at the school. Parents also serve as aides in physical education classes, monitor playground activity, and serve on a school advocacy committee.

A home-based activity program is offered, and families are encouraged to commit to a family contract to exercise together using a schedule they develop. Children are assigned fitness homework, and their parents are encouraged to help them complete it. The nutrition component of the program involves both school lunch programs and nutrition content in classrooms, but it also extends to the family through parent education and family activities designed to improve the nutritional content of family meals. The parent committee meets with the school lunch staff to ensure that school meals have reduced sodium, fat, and sugar levels. School cafeterias are decorated to promote healthy choices in food selection. Finally, the physical education teacher works with the parent advisory committee to establish links with community agencies that offer physical activity programs for children. Special projects such as sport fairs and community health fairs are developed. The entire program is designed to affect lifestyle choices, and the total environment of the child—school, home, and community—is enlisted in that effort.

CATCH

A similar program was developed for the Child and Adolescent Trial for Cardiovascular Health (CATCH), the largest multicenter, multicomponent research experiment ever undertaken to focus on PA and health among children (McKenzie et al., 1996). The CATCH program includes a physical education curriculum that emphasizes PA and skills, a classroom curriculum promoting cardiovascular health, a food service intervention using the school cafeteria, an antismoking curriculum backed by antismoking school policies, and a home/family component.

Classroom teachers, physical education teachers, food service personnel, school administrators, and parents were involved in this comprehensive model, which was tested in 96 schools in four states over a 3-year period, with more than 5,100 children participating. The goals of the project were to increase PA, reduce fat and sugar intake, reduce the chances of children beginning to smoke, increase students' knowledge of cardiovascular health, and generalize the effects through communication with and help from parents.

Districtwide Wellness Initiatives

The CDC guidelines reviewed at the start of this chapter could not be achieved solely by the efforts of a physical educator in a school or a group of physical educators, even though our examples throughout this chapter speak to the extraordinary ways some physical educators have found to expand their programs. A truly comprehensive approach requires leadership at the school level or, even more important, at the school district level. The following two approaches show us the real possibilities for an expanded physical education.

The Escambia County Schools have a districtwide wellness initiative that has four goals (Samman, 1998):

1. Incorporate wellness throughout the curriculum and in the school environment.
2. Help students, faculty, and staff develop healthy lifestyles.
3. Form partnerships with the community to promote wellness for students, faculty, and staff.
4. Involve parents in developing student and family wellness.

What is interesting here is the effort to build a total environment dedicated to wellness. For the faculty and staff, there is a monthly newsletter, indoor and

315

Common
Features of
Efforts To Extend
Physical
Education

outdoor walking paths, exercise classes after work, an annual wellness fair, and special events such as fun walks and challenges. For students, there is a 3-day wellness fair that focuses on wellness and fitness assessments. With the help of the school wellness team, each student develops an individual wellness plan that involves nutrition and physical activity. The fifth graders put on plays about wellness. Parents meet with their children and the wellness team to design a summer family wellness plan.

Local hospitals and health agencies participate in the school programs and make every effort to extend their services and programs to the students and their families. A Parent Distance Learning project offers a series of 15-minute videos that parents can use to learn how to be better role models for their children. The videos are available at each school and are shown on a local public access cable channel. The wellness teams at each school are composed of administrators, school nurses, cafeteria managers, building janitors, classroom teachers, physical educators, parents, and community members.

The Clay County School District has developed a comprehensive wellness program that serves students, faculty, staff, and community members (Samman, 1998). A community-based coalition was formed consisting of health administrators, school principals, an assistant superintendent, health and physical education teachers, a town council member, a parks and recreation council member, a 4-H leader, and several local business leaders. This coalition board made a district assessment and established short-term and long-term goals for the program. The involvement of many sectors of the community resulted in substantial ownership for the program throughout the community and no doubt is a main reason for its success.

The program has not only increased the quantity and quality of time students spend in physical education classes, but has also built a better physical activity infrastructure by creating more physical activity spaces and programs. There are worksite fitness programs for staff at each of the district's schools. The school year begins with a health fair, which offers assessments and counseling for individualized wellness plans. A Six Weeks to Wellness program offers school employees incentives to adhere to their wellness plans.

The district has invested in sufficient numbers of teaching positions to offer daily physical education to students. Parents are involved through family fitness nights and an incentive program to plan and engage in family fitness activities. The district's middle and high school both have wellness centers. Schools are tobacco-free, and their food service programs have been scrutinized to ensure they contribute to the wellness goals of the district. The coalition board is now planning to add after-school programs that promote physical activity and nutrition.

COMMON FEATURES OF EFFORTS TO EXTEND PHYSICAL EDUCATION

These many examples give us a glimpse of how bright and successful our future might be. Is there any doubt that the public trust in and support of physical education are high in the communities in which these schools are located? How could parents and community leaders not respond favorably to such efforts? These many successful ventures not only show us that it can be done, but give us some strong evidence of what contributes to the success.

- The lines between physical education and health education are blurred.
- The regular class program is extended through after-school and summer initiatives.
- Comprehensive school programs have the support of administrators, classroom teachers, and school staff.
- Activities and programs to involve parents with their children are provided.
- The psychological and physical climates of the school support the effort.
- Efforts are made to extend services to the community and to gain its support.
- Programs for faculty and staff are commonplace.
- Assessments and counseling are available to students, staff, faculty, parents, and community members.
- Special events are frequent and are meant to be educational and enjoyable.
- Communication of program goals and events is frequent and widespread.

These features are all consistent with the CDC policy guidelines reviewed at the beginning of this chapter.

Achieving an expanded physical education in more schools and communities is hindered by two pervasive problems. First, few PE teachers have been prepared to do the kind of community building, program planning, and entrepreneurial work necessary to build and sustain programs of the kind described in this chapter. Many physical educators are prepared to teach their classes skillfully and to develop relevant, successful curriculum plans; that is, they are prepared to perform well in the regular class timetable. To develop and sustain programs in nonattached school time and after-school time, to link with community programs, to offer and promote family programs, and to work with classroom teachers, health educators, school cafeteria personnel, and school nurses toward a comprehensive approach require different skills and strategies. Our state and national organizations should sponsor workshops that focus on these skills, particularly how to develop the local network of professionals and community persons that is necessary to design and support expanded programs for children and youths.

The second obstacle to expanding physical education is that PE teachers already have full-time jobs. An elementary school PE specialist might teach 6 to 12 classes a day (depending on length of class), with no time in between classes and perhaps one planning period per week. Secondary school PE teachers often teach 5 classes per day and might have some extra duties as well.

School districts that want to take these issues seriously and strive to develop expanded school-community programs should seriously consider giving the physical education teachers either (a) reduced class commitments or (b) a supplemental contract to allow them to have the time to do the planning and networking necessary to begin such ventures.

SUMMARY

1. Quality daily physical education is a worthy goal, but we must try to expand physical education through other means if we are to build the public trust.

2. The surgeon general's report and the CDC guidelines focused physical education on the major goal of influencing students to develop and sustain a physically active lifestyle.

3. The CDC guidelines offer a comprehensive, multifactored approach to physical activity programming that includes school, home, and community.

4. Extracurricular programming in nonattached school time can help expand physical education for children and youth.

5. Extracurricular programming in out-of-school time is an effective way to expand physical education for children and youth.

6. Establishing and sustaining programmatic links with the community can increase physical education opportunities.

7. Comprehensive physical activity and health programs have been developed at the school and district levels using a multifactored approach to engaging students in physical activity at school, at home, and in the community.

8. Involving parents with their children in physical activity programs at school, at home, and during the summer is a necessary component of a comprehensive approach.

9. Common features of successful efforts to expand physical education include blurring lines between health and PE, extending PE to nonattached schooltime and summers, involving school staff and parents, changing the psychological and social climates of the school to support PA, linking school PE programs to activity opportunities in the community, and providing assessment and counseling, along with frequent communication.

CHAPTER 16

Instruments for Assessing Teaching Effectiveness

To recapitulate, recording is the terminal event of a complex series that begins with defining the response class of interest, proceeds through observing, and culminates in creating a permanent record of the behavior. . . . The permanent record that remains after defining, observing, and recording have taken place is the only evidence that measurement actually occurred, and the quality of the entire process cannot exceed the characteristics of that record.

—J. JOHNSTON AND H. PENNYPACKER (1980)

OVERALL CHAPTER OUTCOME

To use an existing observation instrument or create a new one, to gather reliable data on teacher and student behavior

CHAPTER OBJECTIVES

- To define *reliability* and explain its importance in systematic observation
- To designate strengths and weaknesses of traditional methods for assessing teaching and its outcomes
- To outline and provide examples of systematic observation methods
- To combine observation methods into a system to accomplish a specific purpose
- To list the steps necessary to develop an observation system
- To describe how observers are trained
- To calculate the reliability of observational data accurately
- To differentiate among purposes of various observation systems
- To observe teacher and student behavior reliably

Teaching skills will improve to the extent that trainee teachers have a chance to practice specific skills and get reliable feedback about progress toward goals. To expect such improvement without feedback is wishful thinking. The research literature in teacher education is not very helpful when it comes to the outcomes of intern experiences such as student teaching. There is no evidence to defend the proposition that merely putting trainee teachers into a real setting will *automatically* improve their teaching. There is evidence to support the notion that the teaching skills of student teachers actually (in terms of the skills emphasized by the training program) deteriorate.

For teaching skill to improve, there should be goals, feedback on a regular basis, and a chance to improve. This implies that practice teaching experiences need to be supervised, at least in the sense that the experiences must be observed and data collected in order to provide feedback for the trainee teacher. But supervision must also include the *systematic* collection of data if it is to be useful. Supervision that is done intuitively, with little more than note taking to collect data, is unlikely to be powerful enough to account for improvement. That is not just an opinion. It is a statement of fact backed by a substantial body of research. The research on traditional forms of supervision is so dismal that Mosher and Purpel (1972, p. 50) concluded their review of it with the statement that "the inescapable conclusion to be drawn from any review of the literature is that there is virtually no research suggesting that supervision of teaching, however defined or undertaken, makes any difference."

Systematic observation of teaching is necessary for improvement to occur. Frequently, the primary responsibility for observation is on the university supervisor in a field experience or a student teaching experience. There is ample evidence, however, that the school cooperating teacher can do the observations just as well. There is also evidence that students can observe each other if they are placed in pairs or triads in schools for their practical experiences. We need to underscore, however, that observations produce records of, rather than judgments about, what went on. Women and men preparing to teach need records of their performances and those of the students they are teaching. Records in the form of observational data can then be used in many ways, including conferences with the supervisor, triad conferences with the supervisor and cooperating teacher, and self-evaluation. Records are what is needed, not judgments.

In recent years, it has become clear that teachers can improve their teaching, often dramatically and quickly (Metzler, 1990; Randall, 1992; Siedentop, 1986). To do so, however, they have to have specific teaching goals, observations of their behavior and that of students that is relevant to those goals, and feedback from the observations. The observational data become a record used by the student teacher, the supervisor, and the cooperating teacher to review the performance and suggest ways of improving it. The number of observation instruments available is substantial, so much so that a textbook focusing solely on instruments for various purposes in physical education and sport is available (Darst, Zakrajsek, & Mancini, 1989).

The appropriate strategy to optimize the influence of observation and supervision is (a) to decide on specific goals for teaching that can be related to observations of teacher or student behavior, (b) to create an observation protocol that is specifically related to those goals, (c) to ensure reliable observations, and (d) to use the observational record to reflect upon the achievement of the goals and to suggest further strategies for improvement. This process is one of the most fundamentally important for a successful teacher education. Box 16.1 shows a range of variables that have been clearly shown to be related to teaching effectively. These variables can all be observed through the instruments suggested in this chapter.

THE RELIABILITY OF OBSERVATIONAL DATA

Reliability in observational data collection is of great importance. The term *reliability* has many meanings in scientific literature; we define it as the degree

BOX 16.1   What To Observe:
Assessment of Teaching and Its Outcomes

The variables listed below have all been shown by research to be related to teaching effectively. You should also review "Assessing Teaching and Learning as They Happen" in Chapter 1.

Teacher Process Variables

Managerial prompts per managerial episode
Positive/negative behavior reactions
Distribution of attention—boy/girl, high/medium/low skilled
Expectation statements
Skill feedback analysis
Time spent in explanations of skills and strategies
Number of managerial routine prompts at beginning of school year
Clarity of instructional task statements
Sequence of refining, extending, and applying tasks

Student Process Variables

Time spent waiting
On-task time during management, instruction, and practice
Responses to instructional tasks (congruent, modified, off task)
Analysis of skill responses (appropriateness, success, etc.)
Instances of disruptive behavior
Appropriate help and support for fellow students

Teaching Units

Managerial episodes
Accuracy of prompt–student response–teacher feedback cycle
Latency and congruency of initial student task responses
Relationship of supervisory patterns to on-task behavior

Criterion Process Variables

Academic learning time–physical education
Opportunity to respond (appropriateness and success of responses)

Student Outcome Variables—Short Term

Scores on Physical Best fitness test
Game statistics from end-of-unit class tournaments
Scores on knowledge tests

to which two people, using the same definitions, looking at the same person, at the same time, record the same behavior. Why is reliability important? Suppose that a peer or instructor observes your teaching during the first week of a teaching experience and records the behavioral interactions and feedback statements you make to your students. This becomes your baseline performance. Suppose another observation is taken the next week, and your interaction and feedback rates are considerably lower. Now the question is "Who changed—you or the observer?" If the observer changed (perhaps interpreting the definitions differently or perhaps just not being as accurate), then you will get misinformation and maybe even a poor evaluation. That is why it is important for the data collected on teaching to be reliable—so it can reasonably be assumed that the data reflect faithfully what actually happened during the teaching episode. This chapter discusses techniques for collecting reliable information on teaching.

Most data gathering in science is accomplished by automatic recording systems. Exercise physiologists automatically record the heart rate of subjects prior to, during, and after exercise. The behavior in this case is the heartbeat, and it is made observable by placing electrodes on the skin and transmitting the impulse to a machine that continuously and automatically prints out the fluctuations in heart rate. Kinesiologists collect data on action of the muscles in much the same way. These data are accurate and reliable and provide a convenient permanent record of some crucial aspects of human behavior. But the behaviors of importance in teaching cannot be recorded by transmitting impulses via electrodes. Most often the behaviors in question must be observed by another human being. Most socially significant behavior is seldom convenient, in that it is not easily observable, and this lack of convenience creates measurement problems that often demand the use of human observers.

When one human is used to observe the behavior of another human, steps must be taken to ensure the reliability of the observations. If psychology has told us anything in the past 50 years, it is that the facts and our perceptions of the facts may differ considerably. If I observe your teaching skills, I may be viewing them from my history of experience and interpret things differently than someone else. If during subsequent observation sessions I detect some change in your teaching performance, I must assure myself that the change occurred in your teaching performance and not in my observations. We all tend to see what we want to see, and we are particularly susceptible to the influence of suggestion. If your cooperating teacher tells your supervisor that you have "really improved" in some aspect of your teaching, all evidence indicates that your supervisor will tend to see you as improved whether or not any change has occurred. Therefore, it is important to collect data that give reliable evidence of your progress and are not susceptible to the whims of suggestion or the distortions of perception that so commonly plague inadequate observation systems. Methods for assessing the reliability of observations are presented later in this chapter.

For many years, teacher educators and teaching researchers attempted to assess teaching and its outcomes through a variety of methods such as intuitive judgment, eyeballing, anecdotal records, checklists, and rating scales. In teaching research, these methods have long been abandoned because they were shown to be unreliable and not valid as measures of teaching. But for some reason, they are still widely used as methods for gathering data on teaching for supervisory purposes. Even though experts and texts consistently caution against using such methods, they are still employed more often than systematic observation.

Intuitive Judgment

What we call *intuitive judgment* implies that a supervisor or cooperating teacher watch you teach, then make an overall judgment about what was seen. If the observer is experienced both in teaching and observing, such summary judgments are often accurate. The question is: Are they valuable for improving teaching? We think not. Trainee teachers do not need overall estimates as much as they need specific information about the details of their performance. We also believe that intuitive judgment is the result of too much focus on the teacher and not enough focus on what students are doing in class. This is not to suggest that highly experienced and thoughtful observers cannot make good global judgments, but rather that such judgments are useful only when they are used in addition to a record developed from systematic observation.

Anecdotal Records

If an observer keeps notes on what goes on during an observation session and uses these notes to discuss the session with you, the method is referred to as an *anecdotal record*. Anecdotal records can be very useful if the observer carefully describes events and avoids interpreting them. Good anecdotal recording is systematic, but in a qualitative, rather than quantitative, fashion. Anecdotal records that fall below this standard are less useful and become simply a more systematic version of eyeballing.

Quality anecdotal recording is particularly useful for the latter stages of a teacher education program, when teacher trainees have already gotten a lot of systematic feedback on their teaching skills and the students they teach. Quality anecdotal recording, done by an experienced professional, can reveal the subtle and complex elements that contribute to successful lessons. This information is often valuable to trainees who have already improved their basic teaching skills and are ready for more complex information about events in class. Anecdotal recording, however, should still be related to the trainee's goals for a particular lesson, except the goals can be broader and more complex than for more specific teaching or student behavior.

Checklists and Rating Scales

323

Traditional
Methods for
Assessing
Teaching

In the past, the most common method of systematic observation was the use of checklists. A *checklist* is a list of statements or characteristics about which an observer makes a judgment. The judgment is often a yes or no decision. Sometimes it involves use of a scale so that the space between the yes-no points is graded to allow for a range of possible responses such as *often, sometimes, infrequently, never.*

Eyeballing

The most common form of feedback used in preparing teachers is what we refer to as *eyeballing.* The supervisor or cooperating teacher simply watches you teach for a period of time. No notes are taken; no checklist is used; no data are recorded. After the session, the supervisor discusses the teaching performance with you. Some very specific incidents may be brought up. Some very valuable information may be brought to your attention, but it is unlikely that any information will be passed along that will help you improve your teaching skills systematically. As an observation method, eyeballing is very susceptible to errors in perception due to misconceptions, previous history, or suggestion. Far too often feedback generated from eyeballing is insignificant and useless for improving teaching skills.

Eyeballing can be a valuable technique if it is used in addition to a systematic method of observing and recording behavior. Eyeballing has potential value because the observer is usually a trained professional, a master teacher, who can see complexities of interaction during teaching that are too subtle to be picked up by a systematic observation program. But if eyeballing is the primary observation source from which feedback is generated, then a sufficient amount of reliable information will probably not be made available to you.

The checklist method has one dubious advantage and a number of very serious drawbacks. The advantage is that it provides the appearance of a true data-based approach to the improvement of teaching skills. By using a checklist as a terminal evaluation instrument, the supervisor is giving a pseudoscientific wrapping to a very casual approach to evaluation. If the checklist is used in successive observation sessions as a learning tool rather than strictly as a terminal assessment tool, the same advantage is gained. The benefit gained from the use of checklists is derived primarily by the supervisor; it provides a false sense of security, the illusion that the feedback given the intern is based on some hard evidence rather than mere eyeballing.

Checklists are notoriously unreliable. The statements or characteristics on the checklist are not defined sufficiently to ensure reliable observations. To make a rating on the initiative shown by an intern is virtually impossible unless the characteristic labeled *initiative* is defined so that the intern, the supervisor, and other interested parties have some common understanding of its meaning and some examples of initiative and lack of it.

Rating scales are often thought to be more precise and sophisticated if they involve a large number of choice points. The rating scale shown here has nine choice points ranging from always to never.

Always   1   2   3   4   5   6   7   8   9   Never

This kind of rating device is highly unreliable. The illusion of greater precision and sophistication is gained at the cost of reliability. The fact is that the fewer the choice points, the more reliable the ratings. However, this is balanced by the fact that fewer choice points provide less-precise information. One is left with a dilemma: a choice between reliable, imprecise information and more precise yet less-reliable information. Neither is acceptable as a primary data collection format for a program that is serious about helping interns improve their teaching skills.

Rating scales are useful when information generated from simple choice points is of sufficient value to help improve teaching skills. In this case, rating scales are quick, efficient, and reliable. Checklists are useful for recording tasks completed. They serve as good reminders of the number of tasks to be completed, the nature of those tasks, and the time at which they are completed. But this use of checklists is little more than record keeping and should not be seen as a substitute for actual data collection.

SYSTEMATIC OBSERVATION METHODS

The systematic observation of teachers teaching has revolutionized teaching research and has led to important discoveries about the nature of effective teaching (see particularly Chapter 2). Systematic observation is the foundation on which teaching research has been built. It should also be the foundation on which teaching skills are developed. Systematic observation is simple to do—it requires only some basic understandings and a little practice. The data produced through systematic observation become the information used to help teachers improve. In most cases, a simple summary of the raw data is all that is needed. No sophisticated statistical analysis is necessary. Adding, subtracting, and dividing are all that is required to develop very meaningful and useful information about teaching. The primary techniques of systematic observation are event recording, duration recording, interval recording, group time sampling, and self-recording and lesson-embedded data collection.

These methods for observing and recording behavior have been used extensively in many areas of research dealing with human behavior. Because they have been used extensively, their reliability is well demonstrated. These methods are included also because they are easy to learn and easy to use. They require no apparatus more sophisticated than a tape recorder or a stopwatch. They have been used reliably by researchers, teachers, and students (Siedentop, 1981).

Reliable use of these methods depends on how well the various performance categories are defined. Given adequate definitions, the methods are easy and reliable. They can usually be learned in one or two practice sessions. Most difficulties in using the methods arise more from problems in definition of performance categories than from technical errors associated with the observation systems.

Event Recording

Once a performance category has been defined adequately, it can be observed most simply by making a cumulative record of the number of discrete instances that it occurs within a specified time period. This results in a frequency count of the events as they occur (Hall, 1971). Your supervisor may record the number of your positive interactions with students. Your cooperating teacher may count the number of times students break specified class rules. You may count the number of trials that two students have at a skill during a class session. Event recording produces a numerical output that can easily be converted to a rate per minute. The value of converting to rate per minute is that performances from different occasions can be compared because they are classified in common units—that is, rate per minute.

Event recording is one of the most useful methods of collecting meaningful data; any action or reaction of a student or teacher and any aspect of interaction between student and teacher that can be defined can be measured by counting the number of times it occurs. Concepts such as cooperation, competition, competitive effort, sportsmanship, and aggressiveness can be given new meaning by defining them in terms that can be observed and then by counting them as they occur.

Event recording can be done continuously; that is, several categories of teacher behavior can be observed via event recording for an entire teaching session. The length of a session is easily determined, and the data can be converted to a measure of rate per minute. Often it is too time-consuming and fatiguing to do event recording for an entire session. Also, other observations may need to be made. A valid measure of teacher behavior can be obtained by doing event recording for a short time period and repeating it at intervals throughout a teaching session. For example, it is usually quite satisfactory to do 3-minute periods of event recording and to do five such intervals in a teaching period. If the five recording intervals are spaced throughout the period, a valid sample of the teacher's behavior is gained even though only 15 minutes of the session are devoted to the data collection. This concept of sampling behavior rather than recording it continuously is important to any data-based approach to the improvement of teaching.

Duration Recording

Event recording is useful if the most meaningful understanding of a behavior can be gained by having some idea about the frequency with which it occurs. For example, one way to better understand the efficiency of a learning environment is to have some idea about the number of trials that students need to practice a skill. Event-recording intervals placed periodically throughout a session give valid and reliable information that can be seen as number of trials per minute.

Sometimes, however, the frequency of a behavior does not yield the most useful information. Suppose that you want to get some measure of the degree to which a student is participating in your class. The first task would be to define participation and nonparticipation. It would not be appropriate to use event recording to study participation. One single participation (an event) might last for a long time, and another single participation (another event) might last for a short time. To know that two events occurred would not help you understand a student's rate of participation. It would be far better to record the amount of time a student spends in activity that you have defined as participation. A stopwatch could be turned on and off according to a student's participation; the resulting cumulative time would be the most accurate measure of participation.

Duration recording uses time as a measure of behavior. The raw data derived from duration recording is expressed in minutes and seconds. A student might participate for a total of 21 minutes, 30 seconds in a 30-minute class. These raw data can be converted to a percentage figure that permits comparisons among students and among various sessions. The data are converted by dividing the total time of a recording session into the time derived from duration recording. The resulting measure is expressed as a percentage of total time spent in participation.

As with event recording, it is often inefficient to do duration recording continuously for an entire teaching session; samples can be taken with duration recording. Three 5-minute samples of duration recording spaced periodically throughout a teaching session provide valid information about the percentage of time spent in any defined behavior. In this case, the percentage figure is derived by using the total time of the recording intervals rather than the total time of the class. The output is still in percentage of time spent in a defined behavior category.

Duration recording is useful for any behavior category in which the length of time spent engaged in the behavior provides the best estimate of the importance of the behavior. This is true for both teacher behavior, such as the amount of time spent giving instructions to the class, and student behavior, such as the amount of time spent in managerial activity or participation.

Interval Recording

The term *interval recording* refers to observing behavior for short time periods (intervals) and deciding what behavior best characterizes that time period. For example, the total time period might be divided into 10-second intervals. In the first interval, the teacher is observed. In the second 10-second interval, the observer records the behavior category that best represents what he or she just observed. In interval recording, consecutive intervals are used first to observe and then to record. Intervals should be small, usually no longer than 20 seconds and sometimes as small as 6 seconds. The observation interval does not have to be of the same length as the recording interval. Usually, the recording interval can be shorter, especially as observers grow more skilled or when a small category system in which fewer decisions are necessary is used.

The data generated from interval recording are expressed as a percentage of intervals in which each behavior occurs. However, because the intervals represent a precise measure of time, the interval technique can also be used to estimate time involvements. Interval recording has the advantage of being highly reliable. The instructions such as when to observe and when to record can be preprogrammed on a cassette and the observer cued through an ear jack on the tape recorder.

Interval recording has been used successfully to observe teacher behavior, student behavior, and measures such as academic learning time. Observers should strive to use as short an interval as possible to have reliable data. The only problems usually encountered using interval techniques are when the intervals are so long that several behaviors can occur and the observer has a difficult time deciding which behavior to record. A short interval (6–12 seconds) normally avoids that problem. If a 10-second observe and 10-second record interval system is used, there will be one data point gathered every 20 seconds, 3 per minute, and 90 per 30-minute teaching episode. The total of 90 data points is usually sufficient to ensure the validity of the behavior being observed; that is, what is recorded faithfully represents what actually happened in the setting.

Group Time Sampling

One technique used to gather periodic data on all members of a group (typically a class or specific subset of a class) is *group time sampling*. Group time sampling has also been referred to as *placheck recording* (planned activity check). At regular intervals throughout the observation session, the observer quickly scans the group and counts the number of students engaging in the behavior category of interest. This scan typically takes no more than 10 seconds, even for a fairly large class. A smaller group could be scanned in 5 seconds. Once a student is counted, the observer does not return to that student even if her or his behavior changes. The goal is to observe each individual at a moment in time and to record the number of the total group engaged in a particular behavior category. Behavioral observations for categories such as effort, participation, productivity, and appropriate behavior lend themselves well to the group time-sampling technique. Periodic measures of criterion variables such as academic learning time could also be taken in this way.

The group time-sampling method is used as follows. The observer always scans in a specified direction, usually from left to right. A specified amount of time is taken for the scan (usually 10 seconds). However, this is dependent on the total number in the group because with larger groups progressively more time is required to complete the scan. The number of people engaged in the behavior category is counted. It is always easiest to rate the behavior category in which the fewest are engaged. For example, if you are rating productive and unproductive behavior and most students are engaged in productive behavior, it is easier to count those engaged in unproductive behavior. The number engaged in productive behavior can be calculated simply by subtracting the number engaged in unproductive behavior from the total. Again, it is best to convert these raw data into a percentage figure. This is done by noting the size of the total group and dividing the total into the appropriate figure. Thus, a percentage of students engaged in productive behavior can easily be calculated by dividing the total number of students into the number engaged in productive behavior.

Group time samples should be spaced periodically throughout a class session. Because they take only 10 seconds to complete, they need not prevent the observer from making other observations during the time between intervals. Eight group time samples spaced evenly through a 40-minute session will take only 1 minute, 20 seconds of observation time, yet they will yield valid information concerning the behavior of the group.

Self-Recording and Lesson-Embedded Data Collection

Information about the teacher and his or her students can be collected as a regular part of the teaching process. This is particularly true for estimates of student involvement. Students who record their own or their peers' opportunities to respond (OTRs) related to instructional tasks produce a useful record. The peer tutoring and reciprocal teaching models (see Chapter 14) create situations in which students can record partner efforts at completing a task. Small-group formats often include a "recorder" who could function for this purpose. Sport Education formats include regular collection of game performances that can be used for supervision purposes. Because we have advocated throughout this book that effective teaching is best analyzed in reference to student involvement in the lesson, these lesson-embedded sources of data can be powerful indicators of teaching improvement.

Teachers can also self-record behaviors—and do it in ways that do not detract from teaching. A small tape recorder can be used to record your verbal behavior during a lesson. Later you can code the tape to produce a record of skills such as task descriptions, prompts, feedback statements, and supportive comments. Most schools have videotape machines. Occasionally producing a videotape of a class can help you learn about yourself and your students. When using a video system, use a wireless microphone to capture your verbal behavior on the tape. Wrist chronographs can be used to time important lesson segments, allowing for an overall record of management, instruction, and practice time. You can keep tallies of events on a clipboard or in a small notebook. Some teachers use wrist counters to tally events.

COMBINING OBSERVATION TECHNIQUES INTO ONE SYSTEM

The choice of an observation technique should make sense in terms of the behavior being observed. Feedback from a teacher to a student is best observed with event recording—the most meaningful measure of feedback is either as a rate (number of feedbacks per minute or per 30-minute teaching lesson) or as a ratio (percentage of total feedbacks that were delivered accurately or percentage of total feedbacks that had specific information content). Useful information about feedback can also be developed through an interval format. But duration recording doesn't give useful information about feedback. Knowing the length of a feedback interaction doesn't tell us much about it.

Student learning opportunities can be gauged as a measure of time using duration recording or interval recording. Thus, total amount of time spent in active learning is a very meaningful piece of information. So is the percentage of intervals in which a student was engaged in academic learning time. Student learning opportunities can also be observed through event recording, accrued by counting the number of trials per 30 minutes that occur among members of a class.

Variables such as student on-task behavior can be observed in a number of ways, through event recording (number of instances of off-task behavior), duration recording (percentage of total time spent on task), interval recording (percentage of total intervals spent on task), or group time sampling (percentage of students off task). The choice of which one to use will most often be dictated by considerations such as reliability and economic use of the observer's time. The goal should be to get the most reliable data possible with the most efficient use of the observer's time (using less time to get reliable data on on-task behavior leaves more time to observe something else).

Many observation systems incorporate more than one kind of observation technique. This can be done quite easily through sampling the various behaviors in question. The goal should be to sample them regularly and to have the samples spread out across the entire time period. If all the teacher behavior data were collected in the first 15 minutes of a teaching episode and all the student behavior data in the second 15 minutes, the data would not yield a true picture of what went on throughout the entire period. It is much better to sample a small amount of teacher behavior, then move to student behavior, then back to teacher behavior, and so on throughout the entire observation period. For example, the following 4-minute cycle of observations uses event recording for teacher behavior and group time sampling for student on-task behavior and student learning time:

10 seconds	Group time sample number of students off task
10 seconds	Record
10 seconds	Group time sample number of students in ALT-PE
10 seconds	Record
20 seconds	Rest
60 seconds	Event record teacher behavior
10 seconds	Group time sample number of students off task
10 seconds	Record
10 seconds	Group time sample number of students in ALT-PE

10 seconds	Record
20 seconds	Rest
<u>60 seconds</u>	Event record teacher behavior
4 minutes	Total time

With this format, the 4-minute cycle could be repeated seven times in a 30-minute observation period, leaving 2 extra minutes for rest. The seven cycles would produce 14 group time samples for off-task behavior, 14 group time samples for academic learning time-physical education, and 14 minutes of event-recorded teacher behavior data. Because each cycle was distributed well across the total time, together they represent a very faithful picture of what actually happened.

This is all accomplished with just one observer. That observer is aided tremendously (and the data made more reliable) if the particular patterns of observe and record are preprogrammed on a cassette tape with simple cues such as "Observe student off-task behavior," "Record student off-task behavior," "Begin 1 minute of teacher behavior event recording," "End teacher behavior event recording," and "Begin 1 minute rest." An ear jack should be used so that the cues are heard only by the observer and therefore are not intrusive in the setting where the observations are taking place. Ideally, a very small tape recorder could be placed in a pocket, so that the entire apparatus would be as unobtrusive as possible. The tape recorder should be battery powered so that the observer is free to move about. Batteries should be checked often so that the time intervals on the tape are as accurate as possible.

By sampling behavior rather than observing it continuously and with the development of multitechnique observation systems, the amount of information collected by one observer can be substantial. This observer can be an instructor, a peer intern, a helping student, a cooperating teacher, or the teacher if the session is videotaped.

IMPORTANT DECISIONS IN DEVELOPING AN OBSERVATION STRATEGY

An observation system should serve a specific purpose. Often, a teacher, or students and faculty in a teacher education program, may want to produce information on a few specific teacher or student variables. If so, a small, specific system should be tailored to the goals of the experience. On other occasions, a more comprehensive observation system is needed, but it too should be developed so that it produces information relative to the more comprehensive goals. The point is clear: You should develop an observation system to produce information about established goals, rather than choosing an existing system and then letting the goals develop from that choice.

Once the observational techniques of event, duration, interval, and time sampling are understood and mastered, adapting existing observational systems or developing new systems becomes quite easy. If proper attention is paid to appropriate behavior sampling and if the categories are well defined, observation systems from the very basic to the complex can be developed and refined. These are the steps that should be followed in developing observational systems:

1. Define the goals the observational data will be used for. The more carefully and specifically this is done, the easier will be the remaining steps in the process. Suppose you want to get information about teacher feedback. Should you attempt to assess the accuracy of the feedback (for example, the degree to which the information relayed to the student was based on an accurate performance diagnosis)? Are subcategories of general positive, positive specific, and corrective sufficient? Do you want to further subdivide to find out how many feedback statements are directed to boys and girls or high- and low-skilled students?

2. Decide what teacher and/or student behaviors will give the most valid information relative to your goals. This step is fairly easy if the goal is to produce information relative to class time spent in managerial and transitional activities. It is more difficult if you want to produce a measure of class climate or teacher enthusiasm. In this part of the process, very explicit, behavioral definitions are extremely important. Problems in producing reliable observations are almost always related to incomplete or "fuzzy" definitions of behavior categories.

3. Decide what observation technique to use. Some behaviors, such as teacher prompts, clearly lend themselves to event recording; others, such as student waiting, lend themselves to duration recording. Interval recording can be used for almost all behavior categories. Thus, as the number of goals to be achieved through an observation system increases, decisions have to be made about the combination of observation techniques that best produces a valid record of behavior related to those goals. The coding format for advanced management skills (see Figure 16.7) and the general supervision instrument shown later in this chapter (see Figure 16.10) both utilize several observation techniques combined to produce a number of different data sets.

4. Decide how much can be observed reliably. The complexity of observation is related to the number of decisions the observer has to make relative to his or her experience in observation. A 5-category teacher behavior system is quite easy, even for a beginning observer. A 24-category teacher behavior system is much more difficult because every time the teacher does something, the observer has to decide from among many categories which category to use to record that behavior. If duration and event recording are being used, the complexity increases because the observer's attention may be focused on two things at once. Generally, it is more important to produce less data that are highly reliable than it is to produce more data with lower reliability. The generally accepted convention in applied research is that independent observers should achieve 80 percent agreement for data to be considered reliable.

The first step in building a system is to choose the variables to be observed. This process was explained in the preceding section. The second step is to choose the observation technique, that is, to decide whether the variables chosen would best be observed through event recording, duration recording, interval recording, or group time sampling. This decision is made on the basis of two factors: (a) the *match* between the technique and the variable and (b) the integrating of the various techniques into a total system. If the observation system is small, limited to only one or a few variables, then the match between the technique and the variables should guide the decision. This means, first, that most teacher behaviors are best observed through event recording. Second, certain analytic units such as managerial episodes are most meaningfully observed through duration recording (merely counting the frequency of managerial episodes doesn't reveal much of interest—it is their length that counts). Third, an overall criterion process variable such as Academic Learning Time–Physical Education (ALT-PE) is best observed through interval techniques in which the intervals are quite short.

But if there are several variables to observe, then the system must be built in a way that allows one observer to do several things. In this case, measures of ALT-PE might best be gathered with group time sampling because it requires less observer time than does interval recording. The time saved can be used observing other variables through other techniques.

Once variables have been chosen and carefully defined and observational techniques have been chosen, the next step is to develop the actual coding instrument. A coding instrument is a record sheet that enables an observer to record observations most efficiently. Several examples of coding instruments appear in this chapter. They should be developed for observer efficiency, which means that they make the process of transferring the observation to the coding sheet as easy as possible. For example, after several years of using duration recording and transferring durations to coding sheets in columns, one research group discovered a much easier process, that of building a *time line*. The use of a time line enables an observer to make a simple mark across the line to show when one kind of activity stops and another starts. This was not only simpler for the observer, but also provided a much more useful *picture* of what had happened and was more easily interpretable to the person for whom it would become feedback.

A portion of a time line is shown in Figure 16.1. This time line is 6 minutes long and is divided into 10-second units. The observer merely draws a line through the time line when one activity, such as a management episode ends and an instruction activity begins or when a transition activity ends and a practice activity begins. Later the time line can be examined to calculate total time spent in the various activities. This method is simple and efficient. It also is a useful format for providing feedback because the teacher can then actually *see* the flow of activities as they occurred in the lesson.

Like observation instruments, coding sheets should be developed for specific, local purposes. It is unlikely that a coding sheet developed in one place

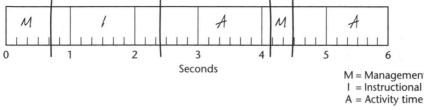

M = Management time
I = Instructional time
A = Activity time

333

Important
Decisions in
Developing an
Observation
Strategy

FIGURE 16.1 *Time line*

will be exactly what is needed in another place. The point is to develop an instrument that reflects as precisely as possible the decisions made concerning the goals of the teaching episode and the techniques through which the variables will be observed.

Coding sheets such as the general supervision instrument shown in Figure 16.10 provide a large amount of information on one sheet. Several techniques are used, and a place is provided in which to summarize the information. This provides useful feedback for the teacher and a convenient way of storing collected data on teaching for future reference. There should always be an area on the coding sheet itself (either at the top or on the back) to provide relevant information such as that concerning the teacher, the setting, students, and the duration of the total observation period. If this information is included, the completed coding sheet becomes a valuable record that can be used for feedback, for research, and for eventually establishing realistic goals and expectations for future experiences.

Making the Observations

Choosing relevant variables, matching observation techniques to the variables, and developing the coding sheet for transferring the observations to a permanent record represent the actual building of an observation instrument. What remains is to put it into use, to ensure that it can be used reliably.

Preprogramming an audiotape to cue the observer is an important contribution to systematic observation, especially for systems that use different techniques, sample behavior, or are interval systems. Of course, if you are simply using a five-category event-recording instrument to monitor teacher feedback, the audiotape feature is unnecessary. But if observers need to sample behavior, switching from the observation of one variable to another or switching from teacher to students, the cues on a preprogrammed tape can greatly simplify the task for the observer and thus increase the chances of obtaining reliable data.

The observer should be as unobtrusive as possible and still be in position to get the necessary data. If teacher verbal behavior is being observed, then the observer should plan to move around, keeping in close proximity to the teacher, yet staying as inconspicuous as possible. Students will react to the presence of an observer, but will react less and less the longer the observer is in the setting. Teachers too will react—and tend at the beginning to be on their "best behavior." Across time, however, the demands of teaching are such that teachers will tend to behave more normally, attending to the needs of their students and the immediate situation rather than thinking constantly about being observed. Still, unobtrusive observation should be sought.

The observer should have all that is needed to complete the observations, including (a) extra coding sheets, (b) extra pencils, (c) a clipboard or some other firm surface on which to place the coding sheet, (d) strong batteries if a portable tape recorder is being used to provide preprogrammed cues, and (e) copies of all definitions for categories under observation. The observer should be at the setting in plenty of time to be prepared for the beginning of the teaching session. The data can be summarized while the teacher is ending the class and taking care of after-class supervision. The data can then be used as feedback when the teacher has the time available to study them and react to them. Supervisory conferences should be based on the data and use it as a foundation from which to examine and interpret what went on.

Training Observers

We have emphasized that observational skills are easily acquirable and that reliable observations can be made by peers, instructors, cooperating teachers, supervisors, or teachers themselves if the teaching sessions are videotaped. In each instance, the observer, no matter who it might be, needs to have sufficient training to ensure the collection of data that meet minimal reliability standards. Most of the observation techniques described in this chapter and the observation systems shown as examples can be learned to an adequate degree of reliability in a short period of time, often as little as 2 to 4 hours. More complex systems will take a little longer. The steps in training observers are clear-cut and are widely accepted in the literature concerning systematic observation:

1. Observers learn definitions from printed materials. Definitions should contain sufficient examples so that distinctions among categories are clear. Good definitions are the single most important ingredient in collecting reliable data. When observers are having problems, the difficulty is almost always traceable to definitional problems.

2. Observers study a written transcript of a teaching lesson and categorize the behaviors from the transcript. This process can be done as "homework" and tends to eliminate many errors and remedy major misconceptions.

3. If useful, observers discuss the categories, the examples, the transcript, and other issues.

4. Observers practice observations on a videotape. The tape should have been coded by an experienced observer so that the trainee can compare his or her data with that of an experienced observer. This process helps

to establish observer accuracy. The term *observer accuracy* refers to the degree to which an observer agrees with a precoded standard.

5. Observers practice in the field. Observers should always practice in pairs so that interobserver reliability can be calculated. The term *interobserver reliability* refers to the degree to which two independent observers working with the same definitions viewing the same subjects at the same time record similar data. The two (or more) observers can then discuss discrepancies and resolve issues.

6. Throughout the training process, a decision log should be kept. A *decision log* is a record of observer disagreements and how they were resolved. Periodically, the definitions should be reviewed in light of the information developed through the decision log and changes made to fit the decisions concerning how to handle various situations.

7. Observers practice until they have met a minimal reliability standard. In behavioral observation research, using interobserver agreement calculation techniques (see next section), a criterion of 80 percent is typically required before observers can begin to collect data that are used for research. A slightly less stringent requirement is no doubt acceptable if the purpose of the observation is to generate feedback for teachers in training.

8. Reliability should be checked often to ensure that observers are applying the code accurately. This is analogous to calibrating a weight scale regularly. The observer needs to be "calibrated" too.

Calculating the Reliability of Observation Data

There are several reasons why it is important to ensure that observations are reliable. First, reliable observations indicate whether or not the definition of a teacher or student performance category is sufficiently clear and adequate. A poorly defined teacher or student performance category almost guarantees unreliable observations. When a reliability check indicates a low reliability, the situation is most often remedied by clarifying the definition of the performance categories.

A second reason for estimating reliability is to make sure that changes noted in teacher or student performance are due to the teacher or student and not to the observer. Observers often tend to see what they want to see, either consciously or unconsciously biasing the observations by their feelings about how they want the experience to turn out. This does not mean that an observer is unprofessional or incompetent. It does mean that all of us are subject to this tendency.

A third reason for checking reliability is to ensure that the changes noted in the observations do indeed reflect what is going on in the class. If observations indicate that a teaching intern decreases management time from one week to the next, he or she can take pride in the improvement to the degree that the observations are known to be reliable. If they are not reliable, then the results hardly differ from those generated by eyeballing.

We emphasize a data-based approach to improving teaching skills. If this model is used and certain improvements occur in your teaching skills, it is crucial that you, the school in which you teach, and the college or university at which you study have confidence that these improvements are real. Such confidence is directly related to the reliability of the recordings made during the intern experience.

The term *reliability* refers to the degree to which independent observers agree on what they see and record. In this sense, the term *independent observers* can be taken to mean that one observer could not detect recordings being made by another observer. This criterion is usually satisfied by having observers placed far enough apart so that no visual or auditory cues could be used to detect the observations being made. If a tape recorder is used for a coding format, reliability checks can be made by splicing an extra ear jack into the ear jack line and allowing for sufficient cord to have the observers sit approximately 10 feet apart.

The general formula for computing reliability is

$$\frac{Agreements}{Agreements + Disagreements} \times 100 = \% \ of \ agreement$$

For event recording, duration recording, and permanent produce measurement, reliability can be calculated by dividing the data of the observer who has the lower number of instances or time by that of the observer who has the higher number of instances or time.

If event recording is being used to judge the number of social interactions that a student has during a period, and one observer records 14 while a second observer records 12, the reliability would be computed as follows:

$$\frac{12}{14} \times 100 = 86\% \ reliability$$

If duration recording is being used to measure the amount of time a teacher spends verbalizing to the class, and one observer records 12:30 while a second observer records 13:10, the reliability would be computed as follows:

$$12:30 = 750 \ seconds$$

$$13:10 = 790 \ seconds$$

$$\frac{750}{790} \times 100 = 95\% \ reliability$$

If attendance is being self-recorded by students as they enter class, the teacher, student helper, or observer can unobtrusively check the students as they record their attendance. If such an observer agreed with each student as he or she checked in, the reliability would be 100 percent. If, in a class of 30 students, the monitor disagreed with the check-in of 2 students, the reliability would be computed as follows:

TABLE 16.1   Sample Data from Independent Observers for Two Students   337

	Observer A		Observer B	
Interval	Student 1	Student 2	Student 1	Student 2
1	U	P	U	P
2	U	U	U	P
3	P	P	P	P
4	U	P	P	P
5	P	P	U	U
6	P	P	U	P
7	P	U	P	U
8	P	P	U	P
9	U	U	P	U
10	P	P	P	P
11	P	P	P	P
12	U	P	P	P

Note: P = Productive
        U = Unproductive

$$\frac{28}{30} \times 100 = 93\%$$

For interval and group time-sampling recordings, reliability is determined by estimating the degree to which the independent observers agree or disagree for each interval or sample recorded. Suppose that interval recording was used to rate the degree to which two students were engaged in productive learning behavior during a physical education class. The raw data of the time sample might appear as in Table 16.1.

To compute reliability, the observations by interval for each student must be compared. Any interval for which the observers have recorded the same rating indicates agreement. Any interval for which they have recorded different ratings indicates disagreement. If the raw data are rearranged so that the observations of the two observers for each student can be compared, the agreements and disagreements become immediately apparent.

Table 16.2 shows observations that are clearly in disagreement. For student 1, the 7 circled intervals indicate seven disagreements. For student 2, the 2 circled intervals indicate two disagreements. There are 12 intervals, so the reliability would be computed as follows:

TABLE 16.2 Sample Data Scored for Disagreements Between Observers

	Student 1		Student 2	
Interval	Observer A	Observer B	Observer A	Observer B
1	U	U	P	P
2	U	U	U	P
3	P	P	P	P
4	U	P	P	P
5	P	U	P	U
6	P	U	P	P
7	P	U	U	U
8	P	U	P	P
9	U	P	U	U
10	P	P	P	P
11	P	P	P	P
12	U	P	P	P

Reliability for student 1

$$\frac{5}{5 + 7} \times 100 = 42\%$$

Reliability for student 2

$$\frac{10}{10 + 2} \times 100 = 83\%$$

There is clearly some problem with these data. A reliability of 80 percent is usually considered necessary for research purposes. With a low number of intervals (12), a reliability of 75 percent would probably suffice. But these data indicate a substantial discrepancy and must be considered unreliable. The observers should attempt to clarify the definitions of productive and unproductive learning behavior, using examples of each to come to a greater agreement about the performance category they are observing.

Reliability for group time sampling (GTS) is determined by computing how much the independent observers agree for each group time sample recorded. Suppose that you want to check the degree to which your students are engaged in active learning. After defining what you consider to be active learning, you could conveniently sample this category using GTS. Suppose that you do one group time sample every 3 minutes during a 30-minute period. This would provide ten samples per period and would give you a good idea of the degree to which your students were involved in active learning. Let's assume that you have 24 students in your class and that your cooperating teacher is doing a reliability check. The raw data for the group time sample recordings might appear as in Table 16.3.

Reliability is computed most easily by counting the disagreements for each GTS. Because you recorded 12 active learners in the first GTS and the cooperating teacher recorded 14, there were 2 disagreements; because there are 24 students in the class, there were 22 agreements. In the 10 GTSs shown, there is a total of 8 disagreements, which subtracted from the total possible of 240

TABLE 16.3   Group Time Sample Data

339

Examples of
Observation
Systems

	Your Observation	Cooperating Teacher
GTS 1	12/24	14/24
GTS 2	18/24	19/24
GTS 3	17/24	17/24
GTS 4	14/24	14/24
GTS 5	10/24	12/24
GTS 6	12/24	10/24
GTS 7	14/24	14/24
GTS 8	20/24	21/24
GTS 9	22/24	22/24
GTS 10	20/24	20/24

(10 × 24 class members) shows 232 agreements. The reliability is computed as usual:

$$\frac{232}{232 + 8} \times 100 = 97\%$$

This shows a very high reliability, which should give you confidence that your observations of the degree to which your students are engaged in active learning are accurate. Incidentally, the hypothetical data show that, during the middle portion of the class session, the percentage of students engaged in active learning was barely 50 percent, a fact that might encourage you to examine what in the organization of the class caused half the students to be inactive for such a substantial portion of the instructional time.

EXAMPLES OF OBSERVATION SYSTEMS

What follows are examples of various systematic observation instruments. The coding for these instruments will be *event, duration, interval, time sampling,* or some combination thereof. The observation protocols have been chosen to show a variety of these recording techniques and to show systems that focus on a few basic behavioral categories as well as more comprehensive systems.

1. *Student time analysis.* Information concerning how students spend time can be useful for making judgments about the general effectiveness of a class. Time analyses require duration recording. Figure 16.2 shows a simple, three-category time analysis in which blocks of time spent are listed in the appropriate columns of *teacher talk, management,* and *active learning.* Data such as these are best expressed as a percentage of

Record of Time Allotment in Class

Class: *9th Grade/Mr. Allen*   Date: *1/9*   Time: *2:00   2:40*

Teacher Talk (demonstration and instruction)	Management	Active Learning
3:06	1:17	6:18
1:08	1:24	5:20
4:30	0:46	3:50
2:06	0:40	4:25
1:10	2:50	___
___	1:50	19:53
12:00	1:00	
	0:20	
	___	
	9:07	

FIGURE 16.2   *Student time analysis in columns*

total class time, thus allowing for comparisons across classes of differing lengths. You will notice in this example that the total of teacher talk and management is more than the time spent in active learning.

2. *Student time analysis using a time line.* The example in Figure 16.3 uses five categories, thus allowing for a more detailed analysis of time than was possible in the previous example. Also, the use of a time line preserves a visual record of the sequence of various blocks of time across the lesson. Teachers can look at a completed time line and see immediately where the management blocks occurred and where in the lesson students spent time waiting. But the data on the time line are slightly more difficult to count and summarize than the simple column approach shown previously.

3. *Teacher reaction analysis using event recording.* Teachers respond to students often during classes and in many different ways. These events occur so frequently and often so quickly that teachers seldom have a good idea about the general pattern of their reactions. Thus, it is often helpful to record these events and provide the feedback to the teacher. We have found it useful to distinguish between reactions to social/managerial behavior and reactions to substantive, subject-related behavior such as skill attempts or game play. Examples of these can be found in Box 5.3 and Box 13.4. Event recording systems could be developed to observe any combination of these behaviors. The example in Figure 16.4 uses four important categories, two for skill feedback and two for behavior feedback. This systematic observation of teacher reac-

Teacher _____ School _____ Activity _____ Date _____

Grade Level _____ Time Begun _____ Finished _____ No. in Class _____ No. Participating _____

Time Analysis

Wait (W)	Periods of no activity and no movement between activities
Transition (T)	Periods of change from one activity to another (includes lining up or quieting down for the next activity)
Management (M)	Time related to class business unrelated to instructional activity
Activity (A)	Students participating in skill practice, scrimmage, game, fitness, or other activities related to the lesson's objectives
Receiving Information (I)	Students attending to teacher directions or demonstrations or other class-related information

FIGURE 16.3 *Student time analysis using a time line*

tions could be further categorized to show the direction of the feedback (such as boy/girl, high/medium/low skilled students, and so forth).

4. *Student or class analysis using group time sampling.* When developing an observation format for student behavior, you must decide whether to observe one student, several students, or the entire class. The decision should be made on the basis of what kind of information will best serve the goal of the observation. On occasion, it is useful to get information relative to an entire class of students. The example in Figure 16.5 uses group time sampling to assess the degree students are behaving appropriately (for example, on-task regardless of whether the focus is managerial or instructional), engaged in subject-matter activity, or engaged in subject-matter activity at a high success rate, as is required for ALT-PE. When you review Box 2.1 you will see that the three measures of

Teacher: _Longlin_   Date: _3/9_   School: _Desert H.S._

Activity: _Track_   Time started: _9:05_   Time ended: _9:40_

Length of observation: _35_   Observer: _Cusimano_

Definitions:

1. _Providing exact commendatory information on performance. (motor)_
2. _Words supporting students' motor response._
3. _Providing commendatory statements on behavior, other than motor._
4. _Teacher comment to terminate a behavior._

Pos. Skill Fb. 1 (Specific)	Pos. Skill Fb. 2 (General)	Behavior 3 Praise	Desists 4
ЖЖ ЖЖ ЖЖ I	ЖЖ ЖЖ ЖЖ ЖЖ ЖЖ ЖЖ ЖЖ ЖЖ ЖЖ ЖЖ ЖЖ III	ЖЖ II	ЖЖ ЖЖ ЖЖ ЖЖ III

Totals: _16_   _58_   _1_   _23_

Data Summary:

Behaviors	Total frequency	Rate per minute
1 Pos. Skill Fb. (S)	16	.45
2 Pos. Skill Fb. (G)	58	1.65
3 Praise	1	.20
4 Desists	23	.65

Comments:

☆ You seem more specific toward male students.

☆ Let's work on behavior praise! (crucial this time of year)

☆ Be firm when you desist!!

FIGURE 16.4 *Teacher reaction analysis using event recording (Source: "Basic Recording Tactics" by H. van der Mars, in* Analyzing Physical Education and Sport Instruction, *2nd ed., pgs. 19–51, P. W. Darst, D. B. Zakrajsek, V. H. Mancini, eds., 1989, Champaign, IL: Human Kinetics. © 1989 Paul W. Darst, Dorothy B. Zakrajsek, Victor Mancini. Reprinted by permission)*

involvement used in this system provide very important information for the teacher. The observation strategy is group time sampling, where periodically the class is scanned and the number of students involved according to the three category definitions is recorded. In Figure 16.5, the time sampling is done once every 4 minutes. The data in this example show a class that is well behaved (98 percent appropriate), engaged

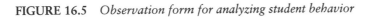

Student Behavior Analysis											
Class: *5Th PERIOD/VOLLEYBALL*		Teacher: *BROWN*					No. in Class: *30*				
Start Time: *1:30*		End Time: *2.10*			Length of Observation: *40 MINUTES*						
Student Behavior	Appropriate	*20*	*30*	*28*	*26*	*20*	*30*	*30*	*30*	*30*	*20*
	Engaged	*4*	*26*	*16*	*18*	*20*	*30*	*28*	*26*	*24*	*16*
	ALT-PE	*0*	*0*	*14*	*18*	*0*	*24*	*26*	*22*	*0*	*10*

Appropriate = *78%*   Engaged = *69%*   ALT-PE = *38%*

FIGURE 16.5 *Observation form for analyzing student behavior*

in the subject-matter activities at a high rate (69 percent), but not always successfully (38 percent).

5. *Analysis of managerial episodes.* Managerial episodes are important "teaching units" (see Chapter 1). The total time spent in management is crucial, as is the effective direction of each managerial episode. The observation system illustrated in Figure 16.6 was developed to focus exclusively on managerial episodes; thus, the structure of the observation format is by episode. Figure 16.6 uses event recording for the number of positive and negative teacher interactions within each episode, duration recording for the length of each episode, event recording for the number of managerial behaviors in each episode (such as, prompting, directing), and GTS for a measure of the appropriate behavior of the class during the episode. This example is from baseline measurement, so it is prior to an attempt to change, which is good because the teacher is clearly too negative and the episodes are too long.

6. *Analysis of managerial skills.* Figure 16.7 shows an observation system that can be used to assess and improve managerial skills. It has some of the features shown in 16.6, such as the length of each managerial episode and a group time sampling of appropriate student behavior by episode. It also includes a much more detailed analysis of behavioral interactions with four main categories (general, specific, general-value, specific-value), with recording further categorized by the direction of the feedback (to individuals, small groups, and group as a whole) and including separate coding of nonverbal interactions (facial, gesturing, contacting). There are specific spaces for the observer to rate modeling, use of extinction, appropriate targeting of reactions, and timing of reactions, as well as a space to comment on the teacher's use of voice and variety of interactions. The system requires use of event recording (done in this case in 5 minute intervals for 20 minutes), duration recording, and group time sampling.

7. *Analysis of ALT-PE.* ALT-PE is one of the criterion process variables most often used to judge teaching effectiveness in physical education. The most

Behavioral Interactions												
3- or 5-Minute Event-Recording Periods	+	−	+	−	+	−	+	−	+	−	+	−
	‖	⊬⊦⊦ I	I	‖‖		‖‖‖	⊬⊦⊦ ‖‖	I	‖‖‖	‖	⊬⊦⊦	
Managerial Episodes — Length	2:41		0:58		3:16		1:42		1:36		2:30	
Managerial Episodes — Number of Managerial Behaviors per Episode	⊬⊦⊦		‖‖		⊬⊦⊦ ‖		‖‖		⊬⊦⊦		‖‖‖	
GTS for Appropriate Behavior per Episode	22/28		25/28		24/28		21/28		26/28		22/28	

Class: _JONES 8th GRADE_   Date: _11/7_   Starting time: _9:30_   Ending time: _10:10_

Data Summary

Rate of + reactions per minute = _0.21_   Total time in management = _12:49_

Rate of − reactions per minute = _1.61_   Average time per episode = _6⟌769 = 128 sec. = 2:08_

Ratio +/− reactions = _4/15 = 1/4_   Average number of managerial behaviors per episode = _4.5_

Percentage of appropriate behavior = _184/224 = 82%_

Comments: _BASELINE - 2ND OBSERVATION_
BEGINNING AND ENDING MANAGEMENT MUCH TOO LONG
FOCUS ALMOST TOTALLY ON NEGATIVE INTERACTION
IT APPEARS THAT LONG MANAGEMENT EPISODES CONTRIBUTE
TO INAPPROPRIATE BEHAVIOR

FIGURE 16.6   *Analysis of managerial episodes*

common observation format for it is the interval recording system shown in Figure 16.8. The coding format is divided into intervals, with each interval "box" having an upper and lower level. The top level is used to describe the context of the interval, and the ten choices are from general content, subject-matter knowledge content, and subject-matter motor content. This decision is made on the basis of what the class as a whole is doing; for example, are they involved in warm-up, a lecture on strategy, or skill practice? The lower level of the interval box is used to describe the involvement of one student, with choices from the categories described as not motor engaged and those described as motor engaged. The letter code for the appropriate category is placed in the appropriate part of the interval box. This system provides a total picture of what the class does throughout a lesson and a finely grained picture of the involvement of several students. Typically, the suggestion is to observe three students of differing skill levels and to alternate observing them every interval. Those interval boxes marked as motor appropriate (MA) are ALT-PE intervals, and their total reveals the total ALT-PE for that student during the class.

8. *Analysis of OTR.* Opportunity to respond is another criterion process variable that is related to effective teaching. In OTR analyses, student

Behavioral Interactions

Length of Event- FOUR 5-MINUTE INTERVALS* Recording Time = 20 MINUTES	Positive (+)						Initiated by + Behavior	Negative (–)						Comments
	Direction			Nonverbal				Direction			Nonverbal			
	I	S	G	F	G	C		I	S	G	F	G	C	
General	///	HHH HHH		//	/	///	HHL /	/		////	IIk +			Staring down
Specific	HHH HHH/					///	/// NOT ENOUGH HERE	////	HHH/					
General-value	/	/	///				NOT ENOUGH HERE							
Specific-value	///	///	HHH/				//	//		///			//	

Voice and Variety	GOOD JOB- HHH // TOO MANY VOICE GOOD ON GROUP DIRECTED

Managerial Episodes	Length	0:32	0:41	0:16	1:02	0:18			
	Number of management behaviors	//	///	//	///	//			

GTS for Appropriate Behavior	22/24	24/24	21/24	22/24	20/24	23/24	24/24

Use of modeling: HHH	MUCH BETTER-USE OF JOHN TO MODEL FOLLOWING INSTRUCTIONS WELL-DONE- MOST GROUP FEED-BACK HAS INFO AND VALUE CONTENT	Rating of targeting:	MORE POSITIVE SPECIFIC FOR GETTING ORGANIZED QUICKLY-MORE POSITIVE FOR BILLY AND WALTER
Use of extinction: ///	STILL HAVE TROUBLE IGNORING NANCY	Rating of timing:	MUCH BETTER - WATCH "STARING DOWN" REACTION- GOOD DECISION ON CLASS DURING DRILL CHANGE

Class: CHAPMAN 4th   Date: 3/16 3rd OBSERVATION AFTER BASELINE   Starting time: 1:10   Ending time: 1:52

Data Summary

+ interaction/minute = 2.4
– interaction/minute = 1.3
Ratio of +/– = 48/26 = 2/1
% of interactions initiated by + = 23%

% of interactions nonverbal = 15/74 = 20%
Contact nonverbal/noncontact = 8/15 = 50%
% of interactions-specific = 43/74 = 58%
% of interactions-value = 26/74 = 35%

Total time in management = 2:55
Average time per episode = 0:35
Management behavior per episode = 2.4
% of appropriate behavior = 156/168 = 93%

FIGURE 16.7   *Analysis of managerial skills*

responses are evaluated as they occur using an event recording format. In the example in Figure 16.9, the topographical form of the response is evaluated as acceptable (A) or unacceptable (UA), and the success of the response within its context is evaluated as successful (S) or unsuccessful (US). This example shows skill codes for soccer and volleyball, so that a record can be made that is specific to the skill attempted by the student. The example also shows the time during the lesson that the response

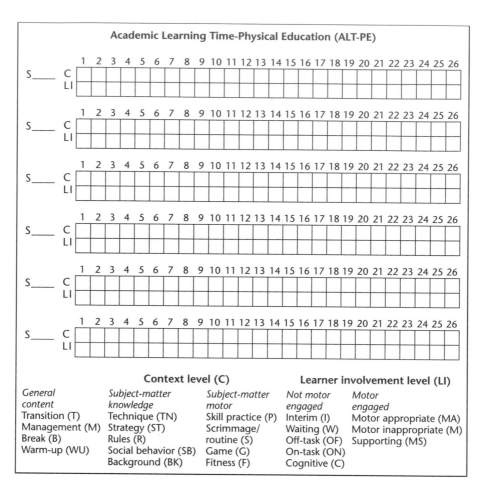

FIGURE 16.8 *Analysis of ALT-PE using internal recording (Source: Siedentop, Tousignant, & Parker, 1982)*

was made. Obviously, this kind of observation cannot be done for an entire class. The typical procedure is to observe two or three students of varying levels of skillfulness. The coding sheet in Figure 16.9 shows observations for two students in a volleyball class.

9. *A general supervision instrument.* During field experiences and student teaching, it is often useful for a program to adopt a general supervision observation system that will be used for all interns. Such a system serves several functions: It provides needed emphasis for achieving the major goals of the program, a means for evaluating program-level progress toward those goals, a means for evaluating individual interns, and a means for comparing the relative performance of different interns. The

Soccer		Volleyball		
Trap–T	Throw–C	Serve–S	Spike–I	Counter start <u>0268</u>
Kick–K	Goalkeep–G	Pass–P	Block–C	Counter stop <u>1396</u>
Dribble–D	No response–N	Bump–B	Dink–K	Timer stop <u>16:41</u>
	Uncodable–X	Dig–D	No response–N	Timer start <u>1:25</u>
				Total time <u>15:15</u>

Volleyball/Soccer Class # <u>1</u> of 20   Date of lesson <u>4/26</u> Modification <u>4</u>

Observer: <u>Brown</u>   Date of observation <u>2/17</u>

Subject: <u>James</u>   Subject: <u>Sally</u>

Response sequence		Skill code	Topography		Results		Response sequence		Skill code	Topography		Results	
			A	UA	S	US				A	UA	S	US
1	1:29	P	1		1		1	1:35	P		1	1	
2	2:13	P		1	1		2	1:46	B		1		1
3	2:25	N					3	1:54	N				
4	2:33	N					4	2:08	N				
5	4:20	P		1	1		5	2:12	P		1	1	
6	6:59	P		1		1	6	2:14	P		1		1
7	8:24	P		1		1	7	2:25	N				
8	8:42	P		1		1	8	3:47	S		1	1	
9	9:23	P		1		1	9	4:02	S		1	1	
10	9:45	P	1		1		10	4:06	P		1	1	
11	12:12	P		1		1	11	5:37	P		1		1
12	14:14	S	1			1	12	5:52	P		1	1	
13	15:01	P		1		1	13	6:43	S		1		1
14							14	8:21	S		1	1	
15							15	9:20	S		1	1	
16							16	9:45	P		1	1	
17							17	10:42	S	1			1
18							18	11:12	P		1		1
19							19	11:58	S		1		1
20							20	14:11	N				
21							21	15:20	P		1	1	
Totals			3	8	4	7	Totals			1	16	10	7

FIGURE 16.9 *Analysis of OTR using event recording (Source: "Systematic Observation of Student Opportunities to Respond (SOSOR)" by Will Brown, in* Analyzing Physical Education and Sport Instruction, *2nd ed., pp. 189–193, P. W. Darst, D. B. Zakrajsek, V. H. Mancini, eds., 1989, Champaign, IL: Human Kinetics. © 1989 by Paul W. Darst, Dorothy B. Zakrajsek, Victor H. Mancini. Reprinted by permission)*

observation system shown in Figure 16.10 uses event recording for teacher reactions (skill feedback and behavior interactions), a time line for duration recording of the important aspects of how class time is used (instruction, management, and activity), and group time sampling once every 3 minutes to assess two important features of class behavior

Record of Student Time Allotment in Class, Behavioral Interactions, and Skill Feedback Statements

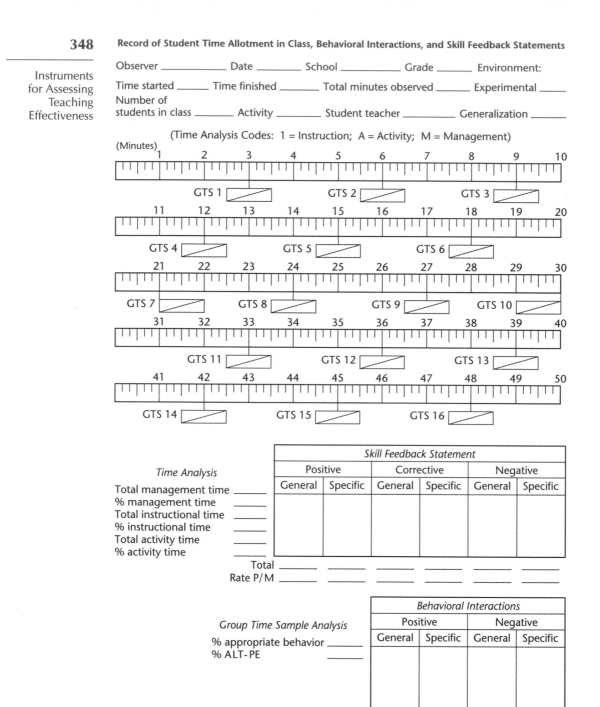

FIGURE 16.10 *A general supervision instrument*

(the number of students behaving appropriately and the number of students in ALT-PE). The appropriate summary statistics are presented toward the bottom of the coding sheet. This supervision coding system can be used by one observer—the university supervisor, the school cooperating teacher, or a peer intern. The data developed are important indicators of effectiveness, yet can be coded reliably and summarized quickly for conferencing with the intern who was observed.

10. *A supervision instrument based on lesson tasks.* An alternative to the time-based instrument shown in Figure 16.10 is an instrument based on the progression of tasks during a lesson. Because teachers often plan by tasks, this observation protocol is closest to how lessons are actually planned and delivered. Figure 16.11 shows the coding format, which is organized by tasks (management, transition, instruction, practice). The start time for each task is recorded, so the total time in that task is easily determined in reference to the starting time for the next task. The task type (informing, refining, extending, applying) is recorded. A different student is chosen to be observed for each task, typically rotating among gender and skill level. A decision is then made as to whether the student was performing on the stated task, modified the task, or went off task. Each student response is coded for appropriateness and success. This instrument provides a clear record of the tasks in any lesson, how much time each took, and what students did during tasks.

Record of Lesson Tasks and Student Performance

Date: 2/6   School: McVey

Lesson 2 of 18 Class size: Page 1 of 4

Time: 10:02

Task episode: M

Task type:

Student observed: MH

Task involvement: ST

entry routine -
well done !

Time: 10:03

Task episode: T

Task type:

Student observed: FH

Task involvement: ST

gather routine
quick !

Time: 10:04

Task episode: I

Task type: I

Student observed: ML

Task involvement: ST

explain and demonstrate
forearm pass
clear and accurate!

Time: 10:09

Task episode: P

Task type: I

Student observed: FL

Task involvement: ST

partners forearm pass

IU	AS	AS
IU	AS	
AU	AS	
AU	AS	

Episode: (M) management, (T) transition, (I) instruction, (P) practice
Type: (I) inform, (R) refine, (E) extend, (A) apply
Student observed: (M) male, (F) female, (H) higher skilled, (L) lower skilled
Involvement: (ST) on stated task, (M+) modified up, (M−) modified down, (OT) off task
Responses: (A) appropriate, (I) inappropriate, (S) successful, (U) unsuccessful

FIGURE 16.11   *Instrument based on task progression*

1. For teaching to improve, specific goals must be defined, appropriate practice provided, and relevant, accurate feedback given.

2. Data are reliable when two independent observers using the same definitions and observing the same teacher at the same time produce similar records.

3. Traditional methods for observing teaching have been intuitive judgments, eyeballing, anecdotal records, and checklists or rating scales. Each of these has problems of observer bias and tends to lack reliability.

4. Systematic observation techniques include event recording, duration recording, interval recording, and group time sampling.

5. Teachers can self-record their own teaching behavior and important learning-related behaviors of their students.

6. Observation techniques can be combined to produce a multidimensional observation system that focuses on both teacher and student behavior.

7. Decisions in developing an observation system include what goals are being sought in the teaching episodes, what teacher and student behaviors are valid indicators of those goals, what observation techniques are best suited to measure those indicators, and how much can be observed reliably.

8. Observation systems are built by matching the observation technique to the variable observed and integrating the various observation techniques in a workable system.

9. Observers need to have all materials needed to complete the observations as well as technological aids to cue their observations. They should be as unobtrusive as possible.

10. Observers need to be trained carefully and systematically, moving from understanding the category definitions, to video practice, to live practice in the field, and finally to establishing reliability with a trained observer.

11. The reliability of various observation techniques is calculated by comparing the observation records of the independent observers and calculating a percentage agreement score.

REFERENCES

Alexander, K. (1982). *Behavior analysis of tasks and accountability.* Unpublished doctoral dissertation, Ohio State University, Columbus.

Allen, V. (1996). A cultural look at integration. *Teaching Elementary Physical Education, 7,* 12–14.

Anderson, W., & Barrette, G. (Eds.). (1978). *What's going on in the gym. Motor Skills: Theory Into Practice.* Monograph 1.

Arbogast, G., & Misner, J. (1990). Guidelines for developing out-of-class assignments that are challenging and fun! *Strategies, 4*(1), 12, 15.

ASCD (1998a). Playing hardball with curriculum. *Education Update, 40*(8), 1.

ASCD (1998b). Six steps to school improvement. *Education Update, 40*(8), 3.

Asher, J. (1977). *Learning another language through actions: The complete teachers' guidebook.* Los Gatos, CA: Sky Oak Productions.

Aufderheide, S. (1983). ALT-PE in mainstreamed physical education classes. *Journal of Teaching in Physical Education, 1*(3), 22–26.

Barrett, K., Allison, P., & Bell, R. (1987). What preservice physical education teachers see in an unguided field experience: A follow-up study. *Journal of Teaching in Physical Education, 7,* 12–21.

Barrett, K., & Collie, S. (1996). Children learning lacrosse from teachers learning to teach it: The discovery of pedagogical content knowledge by observing children's movement. *Research Quarterly for Exercise and Sport, 67,* 297–309.

Behets, D. (1997). Comparison of more and less effective teaching behaviors in secondary physical education. *Teaching and Teacher Education, 13,* 215–224.

Bell, C. (1994). Elementary gymnastics. In D. Siedentop (Ed.), *Sport education: Quality PE through positive sport experiences.* Champaign, IL: Human Kinetics, pp. 47–60.

Bell, C., & Darnell, J. (1994). Elementary soccer. In D. Siedentop (Ed.), *Sport education: Quality PE through positive sport experiences.* Champaign, IL: Human Kinetics, pp. 37–46.

Berliner, D. (1986). In pursuit of the expert pedagogue. *Educational Researcher, 15*(7), 5–13.

Birdwell, D. (1980). *The effects of modification of teacher behavior on the academic learning time of selected students in physical education.* Unpublished doctoral dissertation, Ohio State University, Columbus.

Block, M. (1994). *A teacher's guide to including students with disabilities in regular physical education.* Baltimore, MD: Brookes.

Block, M., & Krebs, P. (1992). An alternative to least restrictive environments: A continuum of support to regular physical education. *Adapted Physical Education Quarterly, 9,* 104.

Bloom, B. (1980). The new direction in educational research: Alterable variables. *Phi Delta Kappan, 61*(6).

Bloom, B. (1984). The 2 sigma problem: The search for methods of group instructions as effective as one-to-one tutoring. *Educational Researcher, 13*(5).

Bloom, B. (1986). Automaticity. *Educational Leadership, 43*(5), 70–77.

Bosworth, K. (1995). Caring for others and being cared for: Students talk caring in school. *Phi Delta Kappan, 76*(9), 686–693.

Boyce, B. A., & Markos, N. (1995). Make the most of your grassroots network to promote your physical education program. *Strategies, 9*(2), 22–25.

Bradford-Krok, B. (1994). Citrus County fitness break: Funding and developing fitness videotapes. In R. Pate & R. Hohn (Eds.), *Health and fitness through physical education* (pp. 205–209). Champaign, IL: Human Kinetics.

Brophy, J. (1981). Teacher praise: A functional analysis. *Review of Educational Research, 51,* 5–32.

Brophy, J., & Good, T. (1974). *Teacher-student relationships: Causes and consequences.* New York: Holt, Rinehart & Winston.

Brophy, J., & Good, T. (1986). Teacher behavior and student achievement. In M. Wittrock (Ed.), *Handbook of research on teaching.* New York: Macmillan, pp. 328–375.

Brown, W. (1986). *The effects of game modifications on children's opportunity to respond in soccer and volleyball.* Unpublished doctoral dissertation, Ohio State University, Columbus.

Brown, W. (1989). Systematic observation of student opportunities to respond. In P. Darst, D. Zakrajsek, & V. Mancini (Eds.), *Analyzing physical education and sport instruction.* Champaign, IL: Human Kinetics, pp. 189–193.

Bryant, J., & Claxton, D. (1996). Physical education and the four-by-four schedule. *The Physical Educator, 53,* 203–209.

Bunker, D., & Thorpe, R. (1982). A model for the teaching of games in secondary schools. *Bulletin of Physical Education, 18,* 11.

Byra, M., & Jenkins, J. (1998). Thoughts and behaviors of learners in the inclusion style of teaching. *Journal of Teaching in Physical Education, 18*(1), 26–42.

CAPS. (1997). Principles of supervision. *CAPS Matters, 1*(4), 5.

Carlson, T. (1995). "Now I can think": The reaction of year eight low-skilled students to sport education. *ACHPER Healthy Lifestyles Journal, 42*(4), 6–8.

Carpenter, A. (1994). Fitness—the Ravenel way. In R. Pate & R. Hohn (Eds.), *Health and fitness through physical education* (pp. 211–214). Champaign, IL: Human Kinetics.

Centers for Disease Control and Prevention. (1997). Guidelines for school and community programs to promote lifelong physical activity among young people. *Morbidity and Mortality Weekly Report, 46*(RR-6), 1–36.

Chaskin, R., & Mendley-Rauner, D. (1995). Toward a field of caring: An epilogue. *Phi Delta Kappan, 76*(9), 718–719.

Chepyator-Thomson, J., & Ennis, C. (1997). Reproduction and resistance to the culture of femininity and masculinity in secondary school physical education. *Research Quarterly for Exercise and Sport, 68,* 89–99.

Chestnutt, C. B. (1997). *Personal sport and technology . . . Now more than a course!* Paper presented at the National Conference on Technology in Physical Education and Sport. Ball State University, Muncie, IN.

Clark, C., & Yinger, R. (1979). Teachers' thinking. In P. Peterson & H. Walberg (Eds.), *Research on teaching: Concepts, findings, and applications.* Berkeley, CA: McCutchan, pp. 231–263.

Cohen, E. (1994a). Designing groupwork: Strategies for the heterogeneous classroom (2nd ed.). New York: Teachers College Press.

Cohen, E. (1994b). Restructuring the classroom: Conditions for productive small groups. *Review of Educational Research, 64*(1), 1–35.

Cohen, S. (1987). Instructional alignment: Searching for a magic bullet. *Educational Researcher,* November, 16–20.

Colvin, A. (1995). Dyadic interactions between physical education teachers and kindergarten children based on gender. *Dissertation Abstracts International, 56*(3500) (University Microfilms No. 9600432).

Cone, S. L., & Cone, T. P. (1999). The interdisciplinary puzzle: Putting the pieces together. *Teaching Elementary Physical Education, 10*(1), 8–11.

Cone, T., Werner, P., Cone, S., & Woods, S. (1998). *Interdisciplinary teaching through physical education.* Champaign, IL: Human Kinetics.

Cooke, N. L., Heron, T. E., & Heward, W. L. (1983). *Implementing classwide peer tutoring programs in the primary grades.* Columbus, OH: Special Press.

Corbin, C., & Lindsey, M. (1993). *Concepts of fitness* (8th ed.). Dubuque, IA: Wm. C. Brown.

Corbin, C., & Lindsey, M. (1997). *Fitness for life* (4th ed.). Glenview, IL: Scott, Foresman-Addison-Wesley.

Cothran, D., & Ennis, C. (1998). Curricula of mutual worth: Comparisons of students' and teachers' curricular goals. *Journal of Teaching in Physical Education, 17*(3), 307–326.

Council on Physical Education for Children. (1992). *Developmentally appropriate physical education practices for children.* Reston, VA: NASPE/AAHPERD.

Cramer, C. (1977). *The effects of a cooperating teacher training program in applied behavior analysis on teacher behaviors of physical education student teachers.* Unpublished doctoral dissertation, Ohio State University, Columbus.

Cutforth, N., & Parker, M. (1996). Journal writing in physical education. *Journal of Physical Education, Recreation and Dance, 67*(7), 19–23.

Darst, P., Zakrajsek, D., & Mancini, V. (Eds.). (1989). *Analyzing physical education and sport instruction* (2nd ed.). Champaign, IL: Human Kinetics.

Davis, K. (1994). North Carolina children and youth fitness study. *Journal of Physical Education, Recreation and Dance, 65*(8), 65–72.

Davis, K. (1998). Integrating children with disabilities into gross motor activities. *Teaching Elementary Physical Education, 9*(5), 11.

DeKnop, P. (1986). Relationships of specified instructional teacher behaviors to student gain on tennis. *Journal of Teaching in Physical Education, 5*(2), 71–78.

Docheff, D. (1990). Well-designed homework assignments can not only enhance student learning, but increase motivation as well. *Strategies, 4*(1), 10–11, 13.

Dodds, P. (1994). Cognitive and behavioral components of expertise in teaching physical education. *Quest, 46,* 153–163.

Dodds, P., & Rife, F. (Eds.). (1983). Time to learn in physical education. *Journal of Teaching in Physical Education. Monograph* 1, Summer.

Doutis, P. (1997). Teachers' pedagogical content knowledge and pedagogical theories of content. *Dissertation Abstracts International, 58*(3872). (University Microfilms No. 9813254)

Doyle, W. (1979). Classroom tasks and students' abilities. In P. Peterson & H. Walberg (Eds.), *Research on teaching: Concepts, findings, and implications.* Berkeley, CA: McCutchan, pp. 183–209.

Doyle, W. (1980). *Student mediating responses in teaching effectiveness.* Denton, TX: North Texas State University. (ERIC No. ED 187 698)

Doyle, W. (1981). Research on classroom contexts. *Journal of Teacher Education, 32*(6), 3–6.

Doyle, W. (1983). Academic work. *Review of Educational Research, 53,* 159–199.

Doyle, W. (1986). Classroom organization and management. In M. C. Wittrock (Ed.), *Handbook of research on teaching* (3rd ed., pp. 392–431). New York: Macmillan.

Drowatzky, J. (1978). Liability: You could be sued! *Journal of Physical Education, Recreation and Dance, 49,* 17–18.

Dyson, B., & Harper, M. (1997). Cooperative learning in an elementary physical education program. *Research Quarterly for Exercise and Sport, 68* (Suppl. 1), A-68.

Eichner, M. (1996). Personal communication.

Eisenhower National Clearinghouse for Science and Mathematics Education. (n.d.). *Common bonds: Anti-bias teaching in a diverse society.* Columbus, Ohio: Author.

Eldar, E., Siedentop, D., & Jones, D. (1989). The seven elementary specialists. *Journal of Teaching in Physical Education, 8*(3), 189–197.

Emmer, E., & Evertson, C. (1981). Synthesis of research on classroom management. *Educational Leadership, 38*(4) 342–347.

Ennis, C. (1994a). Knowledge and beliefs underlying curricular expertise. *Quest, 46,* 164–175.

Ennis, C. (1994b). Urban secondary teachers' value orientations: Social goals for teaching. *Teaching and Teacher Education, 10,* 109–120.

Ennis, C. (1996). A model describing the influence of values and context on student learning. In S. Silverman & C. Ennis (Eds.), *Student learning in physical education: Applying research to enhance instruction* (pp. 127–147). Champaign, IL: Human Kinetics.

Ernst, M., & Pangrazi, R. (1996). Two by two: The benefits of peer teaching. *Strategies, 2*(6), 21–22.

Ernst, M., Pangrazi, R., & Corbin, C. (1998). Physical education: Making a transition toward activity. *Journal of Physical Education, Recreation and Dance, 69*(9), 29–32.

Evans, F. (1998, summer). *Zip Lines: The Voice for Adventure Education.*

Evans, J. (1986). A look at the team selection process. *Canadian Association of Health, Physical Education and Recreation Journal, 52*(5), 4–9.

Evertson, C. (1989). Classroom organization and management. In M. Reynolds (Ed.), *Knowledge base for the beginning teacher.* Washington, DC: American Association of Colleges for Teacher Education, pp. 59–70.

Ewert, A. (1986). The therapeutic modification of fear through outdoor recreation activities. *Bradford Papers Annual, 1,* 1–10.

Felshin, J., & Oglesby, C. (1986). Transcending tradition: Females and males in open competition. *Journal of Physical Education, Recreation and Dance, 57*(3), 44–47, 64.

Fink, J., & Siedentop, D. (1989). The development of routines, rules, and expectations at the start of the school year. *Journal of Teaching in Physical Education, 8*(3), 198–212.

Finnicum, P. (1997). Developing discipline policies to prevent problem behaviors. *Teaching Secondary Physical Education, 3*(4), 25–26.

Fogarty, R. (1991). *The mindful school: How to integrate the curriculum.* Palatine, IL: IRI/Skylight.

Freiberg, H. J. (1996). *From tourist to citizen: The influences of socially constructed classroom management on teacher and student roles.* Paper presented at the American Educational Research Association Conference, New York.

Gallahue, D. (1998). *Developmental physical education for today's children* (3rd ed.). Dubuque, IA: Brown & Benchmark.

Galloway, C. (1971). Teaching is more than words. *Quest, 15,* 67–71.

Gangstead, S., & Beveridge, S. (1984). The implementation and evaluation of a methodological approach to qualitative sport skill analysis instruction. *Journal of Teaching in Physical Education, 3,* 60–70.

Garcia, R., & Krouscas, J. (1995). Build class community. *Strategies, 9*(2), 14–18.

Gentile, A. (1972). A working model for skill acquisition with application to teaching. *Quest, 27,* 923.

Giebink, M., & McKenzie, T. (1985). Teaching sportsmanship in physical education and recreation: An analysis of interventions and generalization effects on moral development of children in physical education. *Journal of Teaching in Physical Education, 4,* 167–177.

Goodman, J., Sutton, V., & Harkavy, I. (1995). The effectiveness of family workshops in a middle school setting: Respect and caring make the difference. *Phi Delta Kappan, 76*(9), 694–700.

Graham, G. (1995). Physical education through students' eyes and in students' voices. *Journal of Teaching in Physical Education, 14*(4).

Graham, G., Holt/Hale, S., & Parker, M. (1998). *Children moving: A reflective approach to teaching physical education.* Mountain View, CA: Mayfield.

Grant, B. (1992). Integrating sport into the physical education curriculum in New Zealand secondary schools. *Quest, 44,* 304–316.

Grant, B. (1994). High school touch rugby and tennis. In D. Siedentop (Ed.), *Sport education: Quality PE through positive sport experiences.* (pp. 83–92). Champaign, IL: Human Kinetics.

Griffey, D., & Housner, L. (1991). Differences between experienced and inexperienced teachers' planning decisions, interactions, student engagement, and instructional climate. *Research Quarterly for Exercise and Sport, 62,* 196–204.

Griffin, P. (1981). Observations and suggestions for sex equity in coeducational physical education classes. *Journal of Teaching in Physical Education, 1*(1), 12–17.

Griffin, P. (1984). Girls' participation styles in a middle school physical education team sports unit. *Journal of Teaching in Physical Education, 4*(1), 30–38.

Griffin, L., Mitchell, S., & Oslin, J. (1997). *Teaching sport concepts and skills: A tactical games approach.* Champaign, IL: Human Kinetics.

Griffin, P., & Placek, J. (1983). *Fair play in the gym: Race and sex equity in physical education.* Amherst, MA: University of Massachusetts.

Gubacs, K. (1997). "They (teacher educators) told me how to teach forward rolls; they never told me how to handle a scared student:" The role of caring in physical education [Abstract]. *Research Quarterly for Exercise and Sport, 68*(1), A79–A80.

Gym Shorts. (1995). Walking: A natural physical activity. *Teaching Middle School Physical Education, 1*(5), 14–15.

Hall, V. (1971). *The measurement of behavior.* Lawrence, KS: H & H Enterprises.

Harari, I., & Siedentop, D. (1990). Relationships among knowledge, experience, and skill analysis ability. In D. Eldar & U. Simri (Eds.), *Integration or diversification of physical education and sport studies.* Wingate, Israel: Wingate Publishing.

Hastie, P. (1998). The participation and perceptions of girls during a unit of sport education. *Journal of Teaching in Physical Education, 18,* 157–171.

Hastie, P., & Siedentop, D. (1999). An ecological perspective on physical education. *European Physical Education Review, 5*(1), 9–29.

Hellison, D. (1978). *Beyond balls and bats: Alienated (and other) youth in the gym.* Washington, DC: AAHPERD.

Hellison, D. (1983). Teaching self-responsibility (and more). *Journal of Physical Education, Recreation and Dance, 54,* 23, 28.

Hellison, D. (1985). *Goals and strategies for teaching physical education.* Champaign, IL: Human Kinetics.

Hellison, D. (1995). *Teaching responsibility through physical activity.* Champaign, IL: Human Kinetics.

Hellison, D. (1996). Teaching personal and social responsibility in physical education. In S. Silverman & C. Ennis (Eds.), *Student learning in physical education: Applying research to enhance instruction* (pp. 269–286). Champaign, IL: Human Kinetics.

Herman, J., Aschbacher, P., & Winters, L. (1992). *A practical guide to alternative assessment.* Alexandria, VA: ASCD.

Hetherington, C. (1910). Fundamentals education. *American Physical Education Review, 15,* 629–635.

Housner, L. (1990). Selecting master teachers: Evidence from process-product research. *Journal of Teaching in Physical Education, 9*(3), 201–226.

Houston-Wilson, C., Lieberman, L., Horton, M., & Kasser, S. (1997). Peer tutoring: A plan for instructing students of all abilities. *Journal of Physical Education, Recreation and Dance, 68*(6), 39–44.

Huber, J. (1973). *The effects of a token economy program on appropriate behavior and motor task performance of educable mentally retarded children in adapted physical education.* Unpublished doctoral dissertation, Ohio State University, Columbus.

Hughley, C. (1973). *Modification of teacher behaviors in physical education.* Unpublished doctoral dissertation, Ohio State University, Columbus.

Hutslar, S. (1977). *The effects of training cooperating teachers in applied behavior analysis on student teacher behavior in physical education.* Unpublished doctoral dissertation, Ohio State University, Columbus.

Jambor, E., & Weeks, E. (1995). Videotape feedback: Make it more effective. *Journal of Physical Education, Recreation and Dance, 66*(2), 48–50.

Jansma, P., & French, R. (1994). *Special physical education: Physical activity, sports and recreation.* Englewood Cliffs, NJ: Prentice Hall.

Jensen, E. (1988). *Super-teaching.* Del Mar, CA: Turning Point.

Johnston, J., & Pennypacker, H. (1980). *Strategies and tactics of human behavioral research.* Hillsdale, NJ: L. Erlbaum Associates.

Jones, D. (1989). *Analysis of task structures in elementary physical education classes.* Unpublished doctoral dissertation, Ohio State University, Columbus.

Kagan, S. (1990). The structural approach to cooperative learning. *Educational Leadership, 47*(4), 12–16.

Kellum, S., Dixon, S., O'Sullivan, M., Kinchin, G., & Roberts, M. (1992). *High school physical education comes alive at your school: A unit on the culture of sport for you students.* Paper presented at the American Alliance for Health, Physical Education, Recreation and Dance, Atlanta, GA.

Kirk, D. (1993). Curriculum work in physical education: Beyond the objectives approach. *Journal of Teaching in Physical Education, 12*(3), 244–265.

Koczor, M. (1984). *Effects of varying degrees of instructional alignment in post-treatment tests of mastery learning tasks for fourth grade children.* Unpublished doctoral dissertation, Ohio State University, Columbus.

Kounin, J. (1970). *Discipline and group management in classrooms.* New York: Holt, Rinehart & Winston.

Kovalik, S., & Olsen, K. (1994). *ITI: The model: Integrated Thematic Instruction* (3rd ed.). Kent, WA: S. Kovalik and Associates.

Kovar, S., & Ermler, K. (1991). Grading: Do you have a hidden agenda? *Strategies, 4*(5), 12–14, 24.

Kutame, M. (1997). Teacher knowledge and its relationship to student success in learning a gymnastics skill (Doctoral dissertation, Ohio State University, 1997). *Dissertation Abstracts International, 58*(1637). (University Microfilms No. 9731661)

LaMaster, K., Gall, K., Kinchin, G., & Siedentop, D. (1998). Inclusion practices of effective elementary specialists. *Adapted Physical Activity Quarterly, 15,* 64–81.

Lambert, L. (1996). Goals and outcomes. In S. Silverman & C. Ennis (Eds.), *Student learning in physical education: Applying research to enhance instruction* (pp. 149–169). Champaign, IL: Human Kinetics.

Langendorfer, S. (1986). Label motor patterns, not kids: The developmental perspective for adapted physical education. *The Physical Educator, 42*(4), 175–179.

Lawson, H., & Placek, J. (1981). *Physical education in the secondary schools: Curricular alternatives.* Boston: Allyn & Bacon.

Lee, A. (1996). How and why we do research. In S. Silverman & C. Ennis (Eds.), *Student learning in physical education: Applying research to enhance instruction* (pp. 9–33). Champaign, IL: Human Kinetics.

Lewis, C., Schaps, E., & Watson, M. (1995). Beyond the pendulum: Creating challenging and caring schools. *Phi Delta Kappan, 76*(7), 547–554.

Lipsitz, J. (1995). Prologue: Why we should care about caring. *Phi Delta Kappan, 76*(9), 665–666.

Locke, L. (1975). *The ecology of the gymnasium: What the tourists never see.* Proceedings of Southern Association for Physical Education of College Women. (ERIC Document Reproduction Service No. ED 104823)

Locke, L. (1999). Retrieval and review. *Journal of Teaching in Physical Education, 18*(3), 357–371.

Luke, M. (1989). Research on class management and organization: Review with implications for current practice. *Quest, 41,* 55–67.

Lund, J. (1990). The effects of accountability on response rates in physical education. Unpublished doctoral dissertation, Ohio State University, Columbus.

Marks, M. (1988). *Development of a system for the observation of task structures in physical education.* Unpublished doctoral dissertation, Ohio State University, Columbus.

Marzano, R., Pickerington, D., & McTighe, J. (1993). *Assessing school outcomes: Performance assessment using the dimensions of learning.* Alexandria, VA: ASCD.

Matanin, M. (1993). Effects of performance principle training on correct analysis and diagnosis of motor skills. *Dissertation Abstracts International, 54*(1724A). (University Microfilms No. 9325550)

McBride, R. (1989). You, too can be a task master—using task sheets in the physical education program. *Journal of Physical Education, Recreation and Dance, 60*(2), 62–66.

McBride, R. (1991). Critical thinking: An overview with implications for physical education. *Journal of Teaching in Physical Education, 11,* 112–125.

McBride, R. (1995). Critical thinking in physical education . . . an idea whose time has come! *Journal of Physical Education, Recreation and Dance, 66*(6), 22–23.

McBride, R. (1997). Critical thinking: What do we know about it? Part 1. *Teaching Secondary Physical Education, 3*(1), 10–11, 13.

McGee-Banks, C., & Banks, J. (1995). Equity pedagogy: An essential component of multicultural education. *Theory into Practice, 34*(3), 152–158.

McKenzie, T. (1976). *Development and evaluation of a behaviorally-based teacher center for physical education.* Unpublished doctoral dissertation, Ohio State University, Columbus.

McKenzie, T., Nader, P., Strikmiller, P., Yang, M., Stone, E., Perry, C., Taylor, W., Epping, J., Feldman, H., Luepker, R., & Kelder, S. (1996). School physical education: Effect of the child and adolescent trial for cardiovascular health. *Preventive Medicine, 25*(4), 423–431.

McKenzie, T., & Sallis, J. (1996). Physical activity, fitness and health-related physical education. In S. J Silverman & C. D. Ennis (Eds.), *Student learning in physical education: Applying research to enhance instruction* (pp. 223–246). Champaign, IL: Human Kinetics.

McLeish, J. (1981). *Effective teaching in physical education.* Unpublished manuscript, Department of Physical Education, University of Victoria, British Columbia.

Metzler, M. (1979). *The measurement of academic learning time in physical education.* Unpublished doctoral dissertation, Ohio State University, Columbus.

Metzler, M. (1980). The measurement of academic learning time in physical education (Doctoral dissertation, Ohio State University, 1980). *Dissertation Abstracts International, 40,* 5365A.

Metzler, M. (1989). A review of research on time in sport pedagogy. *Journal of Teaching in Physical Education, 8*(2), 87–103.

Metzler, M. (1990). *Instructional supervision for physical education.* Champaign, IL: Human Kinetics.

Mize, M. (1990). Marketing elementary physical education. *Strategies, 3*(6), 15–18.

Mohnsen, B. (1995). *Using technology in physical education.* Champaign, IL: Human Kinetics.

Mosher, R., & Purpel, D. (1972). *Supervision: The reluctant profession.* Boston: Houghton Mifflin.

Mosston, M. (1966). *Teaching physical education.* Columbus, OH: Merrill.

Mosston, M., & Ashworth, S. (1986). *Teaching physical education.* Columbus, OH: Merrill.

Mosston, M., & Ashworth, S. (1994). *Teaching physical education* (4th ed.). New York: Macmillan.

National Association for Sport and Physical Education. (1992). *Outcomes of quality physical education.* Reston, VA: AAHPERD.

National Association for Sport and Physical Education. (1995). *Moving into the future: National standards for physical education.* St. Louis, MO: Mosby.

National Board for Professional Teaching Standards. (1989). *What teachers should know and be able to do.* Washington, DC: Author.

National Commission on Teaching and America's Future. (1996). *What matters most: Teaching for America's Future.* New York: Author.

Nilges, L. (1995). I thought only fairy tales had supernatural forces: Toward a radical feminist amendment to Title IX in physical education. *Dissertation Abstracts International, 56*(2607). (University Microfilms No. 9537678)

Noddings, N. (1992). *The challenge to care in schools.* New York: Teachers College Press.

Ohio Schools. (1996). Education today: Educating all children in the least restrictive environment.

Ormond, T. (1988). *An analysis of teaching and coaching behavior in invasion game activities.* Unpublished doctoral dissertation, Ohio State University, Columbus.

Oslin, J., Mitchell, M., & Griffin, L. (1998). Game performance assessment instrument (GPAI): Development and preliminary validation. *Journal of Teaching in Physical Education 17*(2), 231–243.

Oslin, J., Stroot, S., & Siedentop, D. (1997). Use of component analysis to promote development of the overarm throw. *Journal of Teaching in Physical Education, 16*(3), 340–356.

O'Sullivan, M. (1989). Failing gym is like failing lunch or recess: Two beginning teachers' struggle for legitimacy. *Journal of Teaching in Physical Education, 8*(3), 227–242.

O'Sullivan, M. (1996). What do we know about the professional preparation of teachers? In S. Silverman & C. Ennis (Eds.), *Student learning in physical education: Applying research to enhance instruction* (pp. 315–337). Champaign, IL: Human Kinetics.

O'Sullivan, M., Siedentop, D., & Tannehill, D. (1994). Breaking out: Codependency of high school physical education. *Journal of Teaching in Physical Education, 13,* 421–428.

Palmer, P. (1993). *To know as we are known: Education as a spiritual journey.* New York: HarperCollins.

Parker, M. (1984). *The effects of game modifications on the nature and extent of skill involvement in volleyball and softball.* Unpublished doctoral dissertation, Ohio State University, Columbus.

Parker, M. (1997). Cooperative learning: A strategy for teaching social skills. *Teaching Secondary Physical Education, 3*(5), 7–9.

Patrick, C., Ward, P., & Crouch, D. (1998). Effects of holding students accountable for social behaviors during volleyball games in elementary physical education. *Journal of Teaching in Physical Education, 17*(2), 143–156.

Phillips, A., & Carlisle, C. (1983). A comparison of physical education teachers categorized as most and least effective. *Journal of Teaching in Physical Education, 2*(3), 62–76.

Pieron, M. (1983). Teacher and pupil behavior and the interaction process in P.E. classes. In R. Telema et al. (Eds.), *Research in school physical education.* Jyvaskyla, Finland: Foundation for Promotion of Physical Culture and Health, pp. 13–30.

Placek, J. (1996). Integration as a curriculum model in physical education: Possibilities and problems. In S. Silverman & C. Ennis (Eds.), *Student learning in physical education: Applying research to enhance instruction* (pp. 287–311). Champaign, IL: Human Kinetics.

Pope, C., & Grant, B. (1996). Student experiences in Sport Education. *Waikoto Journal of Education, 2,* 103–118.

Pratt, D. (1994). *Curriculum planning: A handbook for professionals.* Fort Worth, TX: Harcourt Brace.

Price, P. (n.d.). Cedarwood project adventure school. Columbus, OH. Project Adventure [On-line]. 09/04/99 from the World Wide Web http://www.pa.org

Randall, L. (1992). *Systematic supervision for physical education.* Champaign, IL: Human Kinetics.

Randall, L., & Imwold, C. (1989). The effect of an intervention on academic learning time provided by preservice physical education teachers. *Journal of Teaching in Physical Education, 8*(4), 271–279.

Rate, R. (1980). *A descriptive analysis of academic learning time and coaching behavior in interscholastic athletic practices.* Unpublished doctoral dissertation, Ohio State University, Columbus.

Resnick, L., & Williams-Hall, M. (1998). Learning organizations for sustainable education reform. *Daedalus, 127*(4), 89–118.

Rink, J. (1985). *Teaching for learning in physical education.* St. Louis: C.V. Mosby.

Rink, J. (1993a). Teacher education: A focus on action. *Quest, 45,* 308–320.

Rink, J. (1993b). *Teaching physical education for learning.* St. Louis: Mosby.

Rink, J. (1996). Effective instruction in physical education. In S. Silverman & C. Ennis (Eds.), *Student learning in physical education: Applying research to enhance instruction* (pp. 171–198). Champaign, IL: Human Kinetics.

Rink, J. (1998). *Teaching physical education for learning.* Boston: W. C. Brown-McGraw-Hill.

Robbins, K. (1998). Devonshire project adventure, challenge by choice handout, Devonshire Elementary School, Columbus, OH.

Roefs, W. (1998). Better together. *Teaching Tolerance, 7*(2), 34–41.

Rohnke, K., & Butler, S. (1995). *Quicksilver.* Dubuque, IA: Kendall/Hunt.

Rolider, A., Siedentop, D., & Van Houten, R. (1984). Effects of enthusiasm training on subsequent teacher enthusiasm. *Journal of Teaching in Physical Education, 3*(2), 47–59.

Romar, J. E. (1995). *Case studies of Finnish physical education teachers: Espoused and enacted theories of action.* Abo, Finland: Abo Akademic University Press.

Rosenshine, B. (1979). Content, time, and direct instruction. In P. Peterson & H. Walberg (Eds.), *Research on teaching: Concepts, findings, and implications.* Berkeley, CA: McCutchan, pp. 28–56.

Rosenshine, B., & Meister, C. (1994). Reciprocal teaching: A review of the research. *Review of Educational Research, 64*(4), 479–530.

Rosenshine, B., & Stevens, R. (1986). Teaching functions. In M. Wittrock (Ed.), *Handbook of research on teaching* (3rd ed., pp. 376–391). New York: Macmillan.

Rovegno, I. (1993). Content knowledge acquisition during undergraduate teacher education: Overcoming cultural templates and learning through practice. *American Educational Research Journal, 30,* 611–642.

Samman, P. (1998). *Active youth: Ideas for implementing the CDC physical activity promotion guidelines.* Champaign, IL: Human Kinetics.

Sander, A. (1989). Class management skills. *Strategies 2*(3), 14–18.

Sarkin, J., McKenzie, T., & Sallis, J. (1997). Gender differences in physical activity during fifth-grade physical education and recess. *Journal of Teaching in Physical Education, 17*(1), 99–106.

Schaps, E., & Lewis, C. (1998). Breeding citizenship through community in school. *The School Administrator, 55*(5), 22–26.

Schempp, P., Manross, D., Tan, K. S., & Fincher, M. (1998). Subject expertise and teachers' knowledge. *Journal of Teaching in Physical Education, 17*(3), 342–356.

Schmid, S. (1994). Community asset. *Athletic Business, 18*(3), 20.

Schwager, S. (1992). Relay races: Are they appropriate for elementary physical education? *Journal of Physical Education, Recreation and Dance, 63*(6), 54–56.

Sharpe, T., Brown, M., & Crider, K. (1995). The effects of sportsmanship curriculum intervention on generalized positive social behavior of urban elementary school students. *Journal of Applied Behavior Analysis, 28,* 401–416.

Shortt, T., & Thayer, Y. (1998–99). Block scheduling can enhance school climate. *Educational Leadership, 56*(4), 76–81.

Shulman, L. (1987). Knowledge and teaching: Foundations of the new reform. *Harvard Educational Review, 57*(1), 1–21.

Siedentop, B. (1998). Personal communication.

Siedentop, D. (1980). *Physical education: Introductory analysis* (3rd ed.). Dubuque, IA: Wm. C. Brown.

Siedentop, D. (1981, Spring). The Ohio State supervision research program: Summary report. *Journal of Teaching in Physical Education*, pp. 30–38.

Siedentop, D. (1986). The modification of teacher behavior. In M. Pieron & G. Graham (Eds.), *Sport pedagogy*. Champaign, IL: Human Kinetics, pp. 3–18.

Siedentop, D. (1987). High school physical education: Still an endangered species. *Journal of Health, Physical Education, Recreation and Dance, 58*(2), 24–25.

Siedentop, D. (Ed.). (1991). The effective elementary specialist study [Monograph]. *Journal of Teaching in Physical Education, 8*(3).

Siedentop, D. (1994). *Sport Education: Quality PE through positive sport experiences*. Champaign, IL: Human Kinetics.

Siedentop, D. (1996). Physical education and educational reform. In S. Silverman & C. Ennis (Eds.), *Student learning in physical education: Applying research to enhance instruction* (pp. 247–267). Champaign, IL: Human Kinetics.

Siedentop, D. (1998). Introduction to physical education, fitness and sport. Mountain View, CA: Mayfield.

Siedentop, D., Birdwell, D., & Metzler, M. (1979). *Academic learning time—physical education coding manual*. Columbus, OH: School of Health, Physical Education and Recreation, Ohio State University.

Siedentop, D., Doutis, P., Tsangaridou, N., Ward, P., & Rauschenbach, J. (1994). Don't sweat gym: An analysis of curriculum and instruction. *Journal on Teaching in Physical Education, 13*, 375–394.

Siedentop, D., & Eldar, E. (1989). Expertise, experience, and effectiveness. *Journal of Teaching in Physical Education, 8*(3), 254–260.

Siedentop, D., Rife, F., & Boehm, J. (1974). *Modifying the managerial efficiency of student teachers in physical education*. Unpublished manuscript, School of Health, Physical Education and Recreation, Ohio State University, Columbus.

Siedentop, D., Tousignant, M., & Parker, M. (1982). *Academic learning time physical education coding manual*. Columbus, OH: School of Health, Physical Education and Recreation, Ohio State University.

Silverman, S. (1985). Relationship of engagement and practice trials to student achievement. *Journal of Teaching in Physical Education, 5*, 13–21.

Silverman, S. (1996). How and why we do research. In S. Silverman & C. Ennis (Eds.), *Student learning in physical education: Applying research to enhance instruction* (pp. 35–51). Champaign, IL: Human Kinetics.

Silverman, S., Devillier, R., & Ramirez, T. (1991). The validity of academic learning time–physical education (ALT-PE) as a process measure of student achievement. *Research Quarterly for Exercise and Sport, 62*, 319–325.

Silverman, S., Kulinna, P., & Crull, G. (1995). Skill-related task structures, explicitness, and accountability: Relationships with student achievement. *Research Quarterly for Exercise and Sport, 66*, 32–40.

Silverman, S., Subramaniam, P., & Woods, A. (1998). Task structures, student practice and student skill level in physical education. *Journal of Educational Research, 91,* 298–306.

Sizer, T. (1992). *Horace's school: Redesigning the American high school.* New York: Houghton Mifflin.

Slavin, R. (1980). Cooperative learning. *Review of Educational Research, 50,* 317–343.

Slavin, R. (1983). *Cooperative learning.* New York: Longman.

Slavin, R. (1990). Research on cooperative learning: Consensus and controversy. *Educational Leadership, 47*(4), 52–55.

Smith, B. (1983). Closing: Teacher education in transition. In D. Smith (Ed.), *Essential knowledge for beginning educators.* Washington, DC: American Association of Colleges for Teacher Education.

Smith, B., Markley, R., & Goc-Karp, G. (1997). The effect of a cooperative learning intervention on the social skill enhancement of a third grade physical education class. *Research Quarterly for Exercise and Sport, 68* (Suppl. 1), A-68.

Son, C-T. (1989). *Descriptive analysis of task congruence in Korean middle school physical education classes.* Unpublished doctoral dissertation, Ohio State University, Columbus.

Steller, J. (1994). The physical education performance troupe: A skill and fitness approach. In R. Pate & R. Hohn (Eds.), *Health and fitness through physical education* (pp. 191–195). Champaign, IL: Human Kinetics.

Strachan, K., & MacCauley, M. (1997). Cooperative learning in a high school physical education program. *Research Quarterly for Exercise and Sport, 68* (Suppl. 1), A-69.

Stroot, S. (1996). Organizational socialization: Factors impacting beginning teachers. In S. Silverman & C. Ennis (Eds.), *Student learning in physical education: Applying research to enhance instruction* (pp. 338–365). Champaign, IL: Human Kinetics.

Stroot, S., & Morton, P. (1989). Blueprints for learning. *Journal of Teaching in Physical Education, 8*(3), 213–222.

Taylor, J., & Chiogioji, E. (1987). Implications of educational reform on high school programs. *Journal of Physical Education, Recreation and Dance, 58*(2), 22–23.

Tinning, R. (1992, July). *Teacher education and the development of content knowledge for physical education teaching.* Keynote address presented at the Conference on Teaching Methods for Physical Education Teaching, Santiago de Compestela, Spain.

Tinning, R., & Siedentop, D. (1985). The characteristics of tasks and accountability in student teaching. *Journal of Teaching in Physical Education, 4*(4), 286–299.

Tousignant, M. (1981). *A qualitative analysis of task structures in required physical education.* Unpublished doctoral dissertation, Ohio State University, Columbus.

Tousignant, M. (1983). PSI in PE—it works! *Journal of Physical Education, Recreation and Dance, 54*(7), 33–34.

Tousignant, M., & Siedentop, D. (1983). A qualitative analysis of task structures in required secondary physical education classes. *Journal of Teaching in Physical Education, 3,* 47–57.

Turner, B. (1995). No more ifs, ands, or buts. *Teaching High School Physical Education, 1*(4), 11.

Turvey, J., & Laws, C. (1988). Are girls losing out? The effects of mixed sex grouping on girls' performance in physical education. *British Journal of Physical Education, 19,* 253–255.

U.S. Department of Health and Human Services. (1991). Healthy people 2000: National health promotion and disease prevention objectives. (DHHS Pub. No. [PHS] 91-50213). Washington, DC: U.S. Government Printing Office.

U.S. Department of Health and Human Services. (1996). *Physical activity and health: A report of the surgeon general.* Atlanta, GA: U.S. Department of Health and Human Services, Centers for Disease Control and Prevention, National Center for Chronic Disease Prevention and Health Promotion.

van der Mars, H. (1989). Basic recording tactics. In P. Darst, D. Zakrajsec, & V. Mancini (Eds.), *Analyzing physical education & sport instruction.* Champaign, IL: Human Kinetics, pp. 19–51.

Vickers, J. (1992). While Rome burns: Meeting the challenge of the second wave of the reform movement in education. *Journal of Physical Education, Recreation and Dance, 63*(7), 80–87.

Virgilio, S. (1996). A home, school, and community model for promoting healthy lifestyles. *Teaching Elementary Physical Education, 7*(5), 4–7.

Wang, M., & Palinscar, P. (1989). Teaching students to assume an active role in their learning. In M. Reynolds (Ed.), *Knowledge base for beginning teachers.* Washington, DC: American Association of Colleges for Teacher Education, pp. 71–84.

Ward, P. (1993). *An experimental analysis of skill responding in high school physical education.* Unpublished doctoral dissertation, Ohio State University, Columbus.

Wentzel, K. (1997). Student motivation in middle school: The role of perceived pedagogical caring. *Journal of Educational Psychology, 49*(3), 411–419.

Wiggins, G. (1987, Winter). Creating a thought-provoking curriculum. *American Educator,* pp. 10–17.

Wiggins, G. (1989, April). Teaching to the (authentic) test. *Educational Leadership,* pp. 41–47.

Wiggins, G. (1993a). Assessing student performance. San Francisco, CA: Jossey-Bass.

Wiggins, G. (1993b). Assessment: Authenticity, context and validity. *Phi Delta Kappan, 75*(3), 200–214.

Wilkerson, C., & Werner, P. (1994). The Springdale running program. In R. Pate & R. Hohn (Eds.), *Health and fitness through physical education* (pp. 187–189). Champaign, IL: Human Kinetics.

Wilkinson, S. (1991). A training program for improving undergraduates' analytic skill in volleyball. *Journal of Teaching in Physical Education, 11,* 177–194.

Williamson, K. (1996). Gender issues. In S. Silverman & C. Ennis (Eds.), *Student learning in physical education: Applying research to enhance instruction* (pp. 81–100). Champaign, IL: Human Kinetics.

Wuest, D., & Bucher, K. (1995). Why students should use multimedia. *Technology Connection, 2*(3), 19, 21.

Wurzer, D., & McKenzie, T. (1987). Constructive alternatives to punishment. *Strategies, 1*(1), 7–9.

Wynne, E., & Ryan, K. (1997). *Reclaiming our schools: Teaching character, academics and discipline* (2nd ed.). Upper Saddle River, NJ: Prentice Hall.

Young, L. (1998). Care, community, and context in a teacher education classroom. *Theory into Practice, 37*(2) 105–113.

Young, R. (1973). *The effects of various reinforcing contingencies on a second-grade physical education class.* Unpublished doctoral dissertation, Ohio State University, Columbus.

Zakrajsek, D., & Carnes, L. (1986). *Individualizing physical education* (2nd ed.). Champaign, IL: Human Kinetics.

Zeichner, K. (1998). This issue: Preparing teachers for cultural diversity. *Theory into Practice, 37*(2), 86–87.

Zimpher, N., & Asburn, E. (1992). Countering parochialism in teacher candidates. In M. Dilworth (Ed.), *Diversity in teacher education* (pp. 40–62). San Francisco: Jossey-Bass.

INDEX